CANNIBALS
AND
CHRISTIANS

BOOKS BY NORMAN MAILER

The Naked and The Dead

Barbary Shore

The Deer Park

Advertisements for Myself

Deaths for the Ladies and Other Disasters

The Presidential Papers

An American Dream

Cannibals and Christians

—*Simeon C. Marshall*

This photograph is of a construction seven feet tall, built of twenty thousand pieces, on a scale of one inch to forty feet (the U.N. Secretariat Building at the lower left is to the same scale), all representing a possible if vertical city of the future more than a half mile high, near to three-quarters of a mile in length, with 15,000 apartments for 50,000 people. It was constructed over a fair period by the writer and Eldred Mowery, Jr., with the assistance of Charlie Brown of "Charlie Brown's Generation."

Its relevance to this book may be found most directly on pages 233–40 but also in many of the pages of Part One and Part Four.

CANNIBALS
AND
CHRISTIANS

BY

NORMAN
MAILER

1966
THE DIAL PRESS *NEW YORK*

to Lyndon B. Johnson
whose name inspired young men to cheer for me in public

ACKNOWLEDGMENT

Acknowledgment is made to the following magazines and publishers in whose pages these essays first appeared.

Architectural Forum: "Mailer vs. Scully" excerpts from April 1964 issue. By permission of *Architectural Forum.* © 1964 by Urban America, Inc.

Commentary: August 1963, for "Responses and Reactions."

Dissent: For "Introducing Our Argument."

Esquire: for "In the Red Light: A History of the Republican Convention in 1964," "Some Children of the Goddess," "A Television Show with Nelson Algren," "The Last Night" and "Ballad of the Sad Saint."

Evergreen Review: for "The Killing."

Fuck You: for "The Executioners."

New York Herald Tribune: for "My Hope for America: A Review of a book by Lyndon B. Johnson" and "The Leading Man: A Review of JFK: MAN OR MYTH by Victor Lasky."

New York Review of Books: for "The Case Against McCarthy: A Review of THE GROUP" and "Punching Papa: A Review of THAT SUMMER IN PARIS."

The New York Times: for "Cities Higher than Mountains."

Paris Review: for "The First Days Interview" and "The Art of Fiction" originally published in a somewhat different form.

Partisan Review: for "Ministers of Taste" and excerpts from "A Partisan Review Symposium on Vietnam."

Playboy: portions of "Petty Notes on Some Sex in America" appeared originally in PLAYBOY Magazine, © 1961, 1962 by HMH Publishing Co.

G. P. Putnam's Sons: "The Metaphysics of the Belly" reprinted by permission of G. P. Putnam's Sons from THE PRESIDENTIAL PAPERS by Norman Mailer. Copyright © 1960, 1961, 1962, 1963 by Norman Mailer.

The Realist: for "A Speech at Berkeley on Vietnam Day" (originally published as "Norman Mailer on LBJ").

The Queen: for "Ode to A Lady" reprinted by permission of The Queen Magazine.

The Viking Press, Inc.: for "The Art of Fiction" to be published in its original form in WRITERS AT WORK, III, 1967.

Village Voice: for "A Vote for Bobby K" and "Lindsay and the City." Reprinted with permission of The Village Voice.

INTRODUCTION

This book is a collection of writings from 1960 to the present. As may be noticed, the political pieces were done after the writing of *An American Dream*, whereas the more literary subjects precede that novel. Their order of appearance is, however, somewhat reversed; the earlier pieces went into a few extreme situations—so the intellectual progression of the book is from the present forward to the past.

It may also be noticed that these separate pieces are assumed to have relations with one another; to underline this impression, a continuing presentation—titled here an *Argument*—runs along in italics. Argument is a curious word; it has odd attachments to the past—I would not certify its flavor to be necessarily eighteenth century, or scholastic, or 180 A.D., but since we deal here often with America, with all us electronic descendants of Rome, let the word give a taste of the Latin. Even if it does not, nothing is more acceptable to America than an excess of baroque. So: *Cannibals and Christians*, a book with an Argument.

Two sorts of writers make bold to present a collection. The first kind writes sufficiently well to induce his publisher to put together his very separate pieces, and they are printed as a convenience for his readers. In such collections there is a tendency for the attitude to belong to the subject more than to the author—professional football is seen as professional football and ladies' fashion as ladies' fashion. The other kind of writer can be better or worse, but the writings always have a touch of the grandiose, even the megalomaniacal: the reason may be that the writings are parts of a continuing and more or less comprehensive vision of existence into which everything must fit. Of course, if the vision is interesting, the fit can be startling, dramatic, illuminating, nourishing, or arouse a desire for more, but good or poor, the unspoken urge is to find secret relations between professional football and ladies' fashion and bring them in alive as partners to the vision. Such writers are of course rare, and occasionally they are important as D. H. Lawrence was important and Henry Miller and Ernest Hemingway were important, and everything they wrote was part of one continuing book—the book of their life and the vision of their existence.

Well, one enters the lists here on a more modest stage, modest enough to leave the question open whether the work is of surpassing value at all, but still the writer presumes: *Cannibals and Christians* is a book, not a collection, he will state: the art of putting it together was to cozen the reader into beginning at page 1 and hoping he would go on to finish at six in the morning on page 399; the clues and the connections are scattered therefore profusely. May they have a touch of the resonance we call aesthetic.

For seasoning, very short pieces of prose called short hairs are scattered at random—no, not altogether at random—but usually without Argument or introduction or title or listing. For to establish them in the Table of Contents, while a desirable precision, would have made the Table unwieldy if not over impressive in the number of pieces listed. Those few readers therefore who develop an outsize regard on first reading any of the unlisted short hairs are thus encouraged to go searching for them through the pages a second time. Here and there, however, sprigs, garlands, and clusters of poems are arranged under family titles like *Witches and Warlocks, Breadlines,* or *Boites and Bruisers.* Finally, a few longer poems appearing altogether by themselves are either listed if the author thinks it appropriate, or are left without record at all, lonely as orphans or waifs. In fact, let us start the book with such a stray.

You're not large enough
      for a whale
and much too fat
      to be a shark
said I to my love.
            Porpoise
was her reply

Sleek pig
  thought the mind
  of my eye

  Sleek pigs
    are porpoises
    said she
  and began to cry.

CONTENTS

PART ONE: LAMBS

1 · INTRODUCING OUR ARGUMENT

In Provincetown, a friend brought a gift. She brought a big round metal GULF *sign seven feet in diameter which another friend had discovered in the town dump and rescued. The hair of fashion came alert: we might make a coffee table. While we drank, we could look at the shading in the orange and blue letters. Poets in the room could contemplate the value of—*GULF*—even as a novitiate in Yoga will fix on the resonance of* OM. *Musicians could explore the tick of the cocktail glass against the metal. Intellectuals could . . .*

What a deal intellectuals could do. There would be those to claim Pop art is the line where culture meets mass civilization, and so Pop art is the vehicle for bringing taste to the masses; others to argue the debauch of Capitalism has come to the point where it crosses the doorstep and inhabits the place where you set your drink. And those to say fun; *fun is the salvation of society.*

It would go on: some might decide that putting a huge gasoline company's totem into one's private space helped to mock civilization and its hired man, the corporation; others would be certain the final victory of the corporation was near when we felt affection for the device by which a corporation advertised itself.

At last, nothing was done with the sign. I did not want to go through dialogue and the same dialogue about why it was there and whether it was good it was there, or bad it was there, and in truth I did not want the work of disposing of it when the fashion had passed. So I left the sign to rust on the beach, a mile from its burial ground on the dump.

1

List the symptoms. We live in a time which has created the art of the absurd. It is our art. It contains happenings, Pop art, camp, a theater of the absurd, a homosexual genius who spent thirty years as a thief; black humor is its wit; the dances are livid and solitary—they are also orgiastic: orgy or masturbation?—the first question posed by the art of the absurd. So the second: is the art rational or absurd? Do we have the art because the absurd is the patina of waste, and we are waiting in the pot for the big roar of waters when the world goes down the pipe? Or are we face to face with a desperate but most rational effort from the deepest resources of the unconscious of us all to rescue civilization from the pit and plague of its bedding, that gutted swinish foul old bedding on which two centuries of imperialism, high finance, moral hypocrisy and horror have lain. The skulls of black men and the bowels of the yellow race are in that bed, the death of the Bride of the Sabbath is in that bed with the ashes of the concentration camp and the ashes of the Kabbala, moonshots fly like flares across black dreams, and the Beatles—demons or saints?—give shape to a haircut which looks from the rear like nothing so much as an atomic cloud. Apocalypse or debauch is upon us. And we are close to dead. There are faces and bodies like gorged maggots on the dance floor, on the highway, in the city, in the stadium; they are a host of chemical machines who swallow the product of chemical factories, aspirin, preservatives, stimulant, relaxant, and breathe out their chemical wastes into a polluted air. The sense of a long last night over civilization is back again; it has perhaps not been here so intensely in thirty years, not since the Nazis were prospering, but it is coming back.

Well, it has been the continuing obsession of this writer that the world is entering a time of plague. And the continuing metaphor for the obsession —a most disagreeable metaphor—has been cancer. The argument is old by now: its first assumption is that cancer is a disease different from other diseases, an ultimate disease against which all other diseases are in design to protect us.

The difficulty—for one can always convince the literary world to accept a metaphor if one remains loyal to it—is that my obsession is not merely an obsession, I fear, but insight into the nature of things, perhaps the deepest insight I have, and this said with no innocence of the knowledge that the plague can have its home within, and these condemnations come to no more than the grapplings of a man with a curse on his flesh, or even the probability that society partakes of the plague and its critic partakes, and

*each wars against the other, the man and the society each grappling with
his own piece of the plague, as if, indeed, we are each of us born not only
with our life but with our death, with our variety of death, good death and
bad, and it is the act of each separate man to look to free himself from that
part of his existence which was born with the plague. Some succeed, some
fail, and some of us succeed nobly for we clear our own plague and help
to clear the plague upon the world, and others succeed, others—are we
those?—you don't know—who clear their plague by visiting it upon friends,
passing their disease into the flesh and mind of near bodies, and into the
circuits of the world. And they poison the wells and get away free, some
of them—they get away free if there is a devil and he has power, and that
is something else we do not know. But the plague remains, that mysterious
force which erects huge, ugly, and aesthetically emaciated buildings as the
world ostensibly grows richer, and proliferates new diseases as medicine
presumably grows wiser, nonspecific diseases, families of viruses, with new
names and no particular location. And products deteriorate in workman-
ship as corporations improve their advertising, wars shift from carnage and
patriotism to carnage and surrealism, sex shifts from whiskey to drugs.
And all the food is poisoned. And the waters of the sea we are told. And
there is always the sound of some electric motor in the ear.*

*In a modern world which produces mediocrities at an accelerating rate,
and keeps them alive by surgical gymnastics which go beyond anyone's
patience but the victim, the doctor, and the people who expect soon to be
on the operating tables themselves; in a civilization where compassion is of
political use and is stratified in welfare programs which do not build a better
society but shore up a worse; in a world whose ultimate logic is war, be-
cause in a world of war all overproduction and overpopulation is possible
since peoples and commodities may be destroyed wholesale—in a breath,
a world of such hypercivilization is a world not of adventurers, entrepre-
neurs, settlers, social arbiters, proletarians, agriculturists, and other ego-
centric types of a dynamic society, but is instead a world of whirlpools and
formlessness where two huge types begin to reemerge, types there at the
beginning of it all: Cannibals and Christians.*

*We are martyrs all these days. All that Right Wing which believes there
is too much on earth and too much of it is second-rate, all of that Right
Wing which runs from staunch Republicanism to the extreme Right Wing,
and then half around the world through the ghosts of the Nazis, all of that
persecuted Right Wing which sees itself as martyr, knows that it knows how*

to save the world: one can save the world by killing off what is second-rate. So they are the Cannibals—they believe that survival and health of the species comes from consuming one's own, not one's near-own, but one's own species. So the pure cannibal has only one taboo on food—he will not eat the meat of his own family. Other men he will of course consume. Their virtues he will conserve in his own flesh, their vices he will excrete, but to kill and to eliminate is his sense of human continuation.

Then come our Christians. They are the commercial. The commercial is the invention of a profoundly Christian nation—it proceeds to sell something in which it does not altogether believe, and it interrupts the mood. We are all of us Christians: Jews, liberals, Bolsheviks, anarchists, Socialists, Communists, Keynesians, Democrats, Civil Righters, beatniks, ministers, moderate Republicans, pacifists, Teach-inners, doctors, scientists, professors, Latin Americans, new African nations, Common Marketers, even Mao Tse-tung. Doubtless. From Lyndon Johnson to Mao Tse-tung, we are all Christians. We believe man is good if given a chance, we believe man is open to discussion, we believe science is the salvation of ill, we believe death is the end of discussion; ergo we believe nothing is so worthwhile as human life. We think no one should go hungry. So forth. What characterizes Christians is that most of them are not Christian and have no interest left in Christ. What characterizes the Cannibals is that most of them are born Christian, think of Jesus as Love, and get an erection from the thought of whippings, blood, burning crosses, burning bodies, and screams in mass graves. Whereas their counterpart, the Christians—the ones who are not Christian but whom we choose to call Christian—are utterly opposed to the destruction of human life and succeed within themselves in starting all the wars of our own time, since every war since the Second World War has been initiated by liberals or Communists; these Christians also succeed by their faith in science to poison the nourishment we eat and the waters of the sea, to alter the genetics of our beasts, and to break the food chains of nature.

Yet every year the girls are more beautiful, the athletes are better. So the dilemma remains. Is the curse on the world or on oneself? Does the world get better, no matter how, getting better and worse as part of the same process, or does the world get better in spite of the fact it is getting worse, and we are approaching the time when an apocalypse will pass through the night? We live after all in a time which interrupts the mood of everything alive.

Well, this is a book of writings on these themes. I will not pretend it is a book written with the clear cold intent to be always on one precise aim or another. I will not even pretend that all the targets are even necessarily on the same range or amenable to literary pieces. No, I would submit that everything here has been written in the years of the plague, and so I must see myself sometimes as physician more than rifleman, a physician half blind, not so far from drunk, his nerve to be recommended not at every occasion, nor his hand to hold at each last bed, but a noble physician none- theless, noble at least in his ideal, for he is certain that there is a strange disease before him, an unknown illness, a phenomenon which partakes of mystery, nausea, and horror; if the nausea gives him pause and the horror fear, still the mystery summons, he is a physician, he must try to explore the mystery. So, he does, and by different methods too many a time. We will not go on to speak of the medicines and the treatment, of surgeon, bonesetter, lab analyst—no, the metaphor has come to the end of its way. These writings are then attempts in a dozen different forms to deal with mysteries which offer the presumption that there is an answer to be found, or a clue. So I proceed, even as a writer when everything goes well, and per- haps a few matters are uncovered and more I know are left to chase.

There are times when I think it is a meaningless endeavor—that the only way to hunt these intimations is in the pages of a novel, that that is the only way this sort of mystery can ever be detected. Such a time is on me again, so it is possible this collection will be the last for a period. The wish to go back to that long novel, announced six years ago, and changed in the mind by all of seven years, may be here again, and if that is so, I will have yet to submit to the prescription laid down by the great physician Dr. James Joyce—"silence, exile, and cunning," he said. Well, one hopes not; the patient is too gregarious for the prescription. What follows, at any rate, are some explorations of the theme stated here, some talk of Cannibals and Christians, some writings on politics, on literary matters, on philosophy —save us all—on philosophy.

IN THE RED LIGHT: *A History of the Republican*

Convention in 1964

. . . He had drawn the burning city, a great bonfire of architectural styles, ranging from Egyptian to Cape Cod colonial. Through the center, winding from left to right, was a long hill street and down it, spilling into the middle foreground, came the mob carrying baseball bats and torches. For the faces of its members, he was using the innumerable sketches he had made of the people who come to California to die; the cultists of all sorts, economic as well as religious, the wave, airplane, funeral and preview watchers —all those poor devils who can only be stirred by the promise of miracles and then only to violence. A super "Dr. Know-All Pierce-All" had made the necessary promise of miracles and they were marching behind his banner in a great united front of screwballs and screwboxes to purify the land. No longer bored, they sang and danced joyously in the red light of the flames.

—NATHANAEL WEST, *The Day of the Locust*

Now, the city was beautiful, it was still the most beautiful city in the United States, but like all American cities it was a casualty of the undeclared war. There had been an undisclosed full-scale struggle going on in America for twenty years—it was whether the country would go mad or not. And the battle line of that war (which showed that yes slowly the country was losing the war, we were indeed going mad) was of course the progress of the new roads, buildings, and supermarkets which popped out all over the cities of the nation. San Francisco was losing her beauty. Monstrous corporations in combine with monstrous realtors had erected monstrous boxes of Kleenex ten, twenty, thirty stories high through the downtown section, and the new view from Telegraph Hill had shards of glass the size of a mountain wall stuck into the soft Italian landscape of St. Francis' City. The San Francisco Hilton, for an example, while close to twenty stories high was near to a square block in size and looked from the street to have the proportions and form of a cube of sugar. It was a dirty sugar-white in color and its windows were set in an odd elongated checkerboard, a harlequin pattern in which each window was offset from the one above and beneath like the vents in a portable radio.

The Hilton was only six weeks old, but already it was one of the architectural wonders of the world, for its insides were composed in large part of an automobile ramp on which it was possible to drive all the way up to the eleventh floor, open a door and lo! you were in your hotel corridor, twenty feet from your own room door. It was a startling way to exhaust the internal space of a hotel, but it had one huge American advantage: any guest at the Hilton could drive all the way to his room without ever having to steer a lady through the lobby. Of course, after all those automobile ramps, there was not much volume left, so the rooms were small, the rooms were very small for seventeen dollars a day, and the windows were placed to the extreme left or right of the wall and ran from ceiling to floor, in order to allow the building to appear to the outside eye like a radio being carried by a model who worked in the high nude. The carpets and wallpapers, the drapes and the table tops were plastic, the bathroom had the odor of burning insecticide. It developed that the plastic cement used to finish the tiling gave off this odor during the months it took to dry. Molecules were being tortured everywhere.

Well, that was American capitalism gainfully employed. It had won the war. It had won it in so many places you could picture your accommodations before you arrived. Such is the nature of the promiscuous. Flying out, way out on the jet, on the way West, not yet at the Hilton but knowing it would be there, I got into a conversation with the man who sat at the window, an Australian journalist named Moffitt, a short fellow with a bushwhacker's moustache; and he scolded me for reading Buchanan's book, *Who Killed Kennedy?* He wanted to know why a man of my intelligence bothered with trash. Well, the country had never been the same since Kennedy was assassinated, courtesy was ready to reply; some process of derailment, begun with Hemingway's death and the death of Marilyn Monroe, had been racing on now through the months, through the heavens, faster than the contrails of our jet across the late afternoon mind of America; so one looked for clues where they could be found. It would be easier to know that Oswald had done it all by himself, or as an accomplice to ten other men, or was innocent, or twice damned; anything was superior to that sense of the ship of state battering its way down swells of sea, while in the hold cargo was loose and ready to slide.

This conversation did not of course take place—an Astrojet is not the vehicle for metaphorical transactions, it is after all still another of the extermination chambers of the century—slowly the breath gives up some microcosmic portion of itself, green plastic and silver-gray plastic, the nostrils breathe no odor of materials which existed once as elements of nature, no wood, no stone, no ore, time molders like a sponge in the sink.

But Moffitt was Australian and fascinated with America, and had his quick comments to make, some provincial, some pure shrewd; finally he poked his finger on something I had never put together for myself, not quite: "Why is it," he asked, "that all the new stuff you build here, including the interior furnishings of this airplane, looks like a child's nursery?"

And that is what it was. The inside of our airplane was like a child's plastic nursery, a dayroom in the children's ward, and if I had been Quentin Compson, I might have answered, "Because we want to go back, because the nerves grew in all the wrong ways. Because we developed habits which are suffocating us to death. I tell you, man, we do it because we're sick, we're a sick nation, we're sick to the edge of vomit and so we build our lives with materials which smell like vomit, polyethylene and bakelite and fiberglas and styrene. Yes, our schools look like nurseries, and our factories and our temples, our kitchens and our johns, our airports and our libraries and our offices, we are one great big bloody nursery attached to a doctor's waiting room, and we are sick, we're very sick, maybe we always were sick, maybe the Puritans carried the virus and were so odious the British were right to drive them out, maybe we're a nation of culls and weeds and half-crazy from the start."

Nobody of course was Quentin Compson, nobody spoke that way any more, but the question was posed by a ghost and so had to linger: was there indeed a death in the seed which brought us here? was the country extraordinary or accursed, a junkyard where even the minnows gave caviar in the filthy pond in the fierce electric American night?

I

I must see the things; I must see the men.
                    —BURKE, *Reflections on the Revolution in France*

At the Mark Hopkins on Saturday morning two days before the convention would begin, the atmosphere had the same agreeable clean rather healthy excitement (that particular American excitement) one picks up on the morning of a big football game. The kids were out, the children who were for Goldwater and those who were for Scranton, and they milled about in the small open courtyard of the hotel, and in the small hopelessly congested lobby where lines one hundred long were waiting for each of the three overworked elevators beating up to the twelfth and fourteenth floors, Scranton and Goldwater Headquarters respectively. It was a clear day outside, one of those cool sunny days in July when San Francisco is as nice as New York on a beautiful day in October, and the city fell away from Nob Hill in a perfect throw. There were apples in the air. It was a perfect football day. There was even wistfulness to be eighteen and have a date for lunch before the game. So the teams lined up first this way in one's mind, the children, adolescents, and young men and women for Goldwater to one side, the Scrantons to the other, and you could tell a lot about the colleges and the teams by looking at the faces. The Goldwater girls and boys were for the most part innocent, and they tended to have large slightly protruded jaws, not unlike Big Barry himself, and blue eyes—an astonishing number had blue eyes (was the world finally coming to the war of the blue-eyed versus the brown-eyed?)— and they were simple, they were small-town, they were hicky, the boys tended to have a little acne, an introspective pimple or two by the corner of the mouth or the side of the chin, a lot of the boys looked solemn and serious, dedicated but slightly blank—they could fix a transistor radio, but a word like "Renaissance" would lay a soft wound of silence, stupefaction in their brain. They were idealists, nearly every last one of them, but they did not speak of the happier varieties of idealism; one thought of Lutherans from North Dakota, 4-H from Minnesota, and Eagle Scouts from Maine. Many of them wore eyeglasses. They were thrifty young men, hardworking young men, polite, slightly paralyzed before the variety of life, but ready to die for a cause. It was obvious they thought Goldwater was one of the finest men ever to be born into American life. And they were stingy, they wore store-bought ready-mades, skinny kids in twenty-dollar suits and that pinch of the jaw, that recidivism of the gums which speaks of false teeth before you are fifty.

The Goldwater girls ran to two varieties. There were the models who had been hired for the purpose, and they were attractive but not very imaginative, they looked like hookers on horses, and then there were the true followers, the daughters of delegates, the California children who belonged to one Goldwater club or another. They were younger than the models of course, they were most of them fifteen, sixteen, not even seventeen, wearing cowboy hats and white vests and shirts with fringes, white riding boots; nearly all of them were blonde and they had simple rather sweet faces, the sort of faces which television commercials used to use for such product fodder as biscuit batter before the commercials turned witty; these Goldwater girls had the faces of young ladies who listened to their parents, particularly to their fathers, they were full of character, but it was the character of tidiness, industry, subservience—unlike the Goldwater boys who looked on the whole not unintelligent though slightly maniacal in the singularity of their vision (the way young physicists look slightly maniacal) the girls seemed to be just about all quite dumb. There was one blonde little girl who was lovely, pretty enough to be a starlet, but she left a pang because her eyes when open were irremediably dim. Taken altogether, boys and girls, they were like

the graduating class of a high school in Nebraska. The valedictorian
would write his speech on the following theme: Why is the United States
the Greatest Nation on Earth?

Whereas the kids who were for Scranton were prep-school or country-
day. Some of the boys were plump and merry, some were mildly execu-
tive, but they shared in common that slightly complacent air of success
which is the only curse of the fraternity president or leader of the student
council. They were keen, they tended to be smooth, they had a penchant
for bow ties and they were the kind to drive Triumphs or Pontiac con-
vertibles, while the Goldwater boys would be borrowing their father's
Dodge Dart (except for the one in a hundred who was automotive in his
genius and so had built a dragster to top out at one-six-five). Then there
were the Scranton boys who were still the descendants of Holden Caul-
field. Faces like theirs had been seen for Stevenson in '60 in L.A. against
J.F.K., and faces like theirs might appear (one would hope) in '68 for
still another, but for now they were for the nearest candidate with wit,
class, and the born foreknowledge of defeat. Slim, slightly mournful, cer-
tainly acerb, and dubious of the fraternity presidents with whom they had
made cause, the Holden Caulfields were out for Scranton, and looked a
size overmatched by the girls who were for Scranton, good-looking most
of them, slightly spoiled, saucy, full of peeves, junior debs doing their
best to be cool and so wearing their hair long with a part down the center
in such a way that the face, sexy, stripped of makeup (except for some
sort of white libidinous wax on the lips) was half-concealed by a Gothic
arch of falling tresses. Such were Scranton's parts, such were Goldwater's,
as the children shaped up for the game.

*In this state of . . . warfare between the noble ancient landed interest
and the new monied interest, the . . . monied interest is in its nature more
ready for any adventure; and its possessors more disposed to new enterprises
of any kind. Being of a recent acquisition, it falls in more naturally with any
novelties. It is therefore the kind of wealth which will be resorted to by all
who wish for change.*

—BURKE, *Reflections on the Revolution in France*

*Among the young industrial and financial monopolies of the West and
Southwest that want a "bigger slice of the capitalist profit pie," Mr. Vasilyev
listed H.L. Hunt, the Texas multimillionaire, the Lockheed Aircraft Corpora-
tion, the Douglas Aircraft Company, the Boeing Company and the Northrup
Corporation and the Giannini "financial empire" headed by the Bank of
America.*

*These are the forces, Mr. Vasilyev said, that overcame the last-minute
effort by "Wall Street, the Boston financial group and the Pennsylvania
industrial complex" to promote the candidacy of Govenor William W.
Scranton of Pennsylvania at the Republican convention last month.*

*"But the 'new money' of the West proved to be stronger than the old
money of the Northeast," the Soviet commentator said.*

—New York Times, August 13, 1964

For a time it had been interesting history. You will remember that
Scranton decided to run for nomination after a talk in Gettysburg on
June 6 with President Eisenhower. He left with the solid assumption he
would receive Eisenhower's support, solid enough for Governor Scranton's
public-relations machine to announce this fact to the nation. That night
or early next morning President Eisenhower received a phone call from
George Humphrey. Eisenhower had been planning to visit Humphrey in
Cleveland during the week of the Governor's Conference. But it devel-
oped Barry Goldwater had already been invited to be at Humphrey's
home as well. A social difficulty thus presented itself. Humphrey resolved
it in this fashion: Eisenhower would understand if, under the circum-
stances, Goldwater having been invited first . . .

Ike knew what that meant. If his old friend, crony, subordinate and
private brain trust George Humphrey was willing to let the old gander-
in-chief come out second on a collision of invitations, then Ike had picked
a loser, Ike was in danger of being a loser himself. Well, Ike hadn't come
out of Abilene, Kansas, all those years ago *ever* to end on the losing side.
So he waddled back to the middle. He phoned Bill Scranton you will
remember but an hour before Scranton was ready to announce his
candidacy at the Governor's Conference on June 7, and told Scranton he
could not be party to a "cabal." It was obvious to everybody in America
that the old man had not labored through the night and through the day
to make the truth of his first conversation with the young man stand out
loud and clear in the high sun of ten a.m.

Still, one could not feel too sorry for the young man. It is never easy
to grieve for a candidate of the Establishment, particularly the Republi-
can Establishment of the East, which runs a spectrum from the Duke of
Windsor to Jerome Zerbe, from Thomas E. Dewey to Lowell Thomas,
from Drue Heinz to Tex and Jinx, from Maine to Nassau, New York to
South of France, from Allen Dulles to Henry Luce, Igor Cassini to Joe
Alsop, from Sullivan & Cromwell to Cartier's, and from Arthur Krock
to Tuxedo Park.

Well, the last two years, all the way from Arthur Krock to Tuxedo
Park, you could hear that Bill Scranton was going to be the Republican

candidate in '64. Attempts might be made to argue: Goldwater looks strong, somebody could say at a dinner table; hasn't got a chance, the Establishment would give back—it's going to be Scranton. What was most impressive is that the Establishment did not bother to photograph their man, immerse him in publicity, or seek to etch his image. It was taken for granted that when the time came, doors would open, doors would shut, figures would be inserted, heads would be removed, a whiff of incense, a whisk of wickedness—Scranton would be the candidate.

Of course, Goldwater, or the Goldwater organization, or *some* organization, kept picking up delegates for Goldwater, and from a year away there was a bit of sentiment that it might be easier to make a deal with Goldwater, it might be easier to *moderate* him than to excise him. Once upon a time, J.P. Morgan would doubtless have sent some bright young man out on the Southern Pacific with a bag full of hundred-dollar bills. Now, however, possessing a mass media, the buy-off could take place in public. Last November, three weeks before J.F.K. was assassinated, *Life* Magazine put Goldwater on their cover wearing a pearl-gray Stetson and clean, pressed, faded blue work shirt and Levi's while his companion, a Palomino named Sunny, stood with one of the Senator's hands on his bridle, the other laid over the vein of his nose. It was Hopalong Cassidy all baby fat removed, it gave promise of the campaign to come: the image of Kennedy was now to be combated by Sheriff B. Morris Goldwater, the Silver Gun of the West. It was one of those pictures worth ten thousand speeches—it gave promise of delivering a million votes. It was also a way of stating that the Establishment was not yet unalterably opposed to Goldwater, and could yet help him, as it had with this cover. But inside the magazine across the heads of seven million readers, another message was delivered to the Senator.

> *Financial interests in Ohio, Illinois, Texas, Los Angeles and San Francisco—all centers of wealth independent of eastern ties—have been lining up money and intense local pressure for Goldwater. But . . . people fail to realize there's a difference in kinds of money. . . . Old money has political power but new money has only purchasing power. . . . When you get to a convention, you don't buy delegates. But you do put the pressure on people who control the delegates—the people who owe the old money for their stake.*

Which was a way to remind Goldwater there were concessions to make. It was in foreign affairs that Goldwater had the most to explain about his policies.

Barry Goldwater [went Life's *conclusion] represents a valuable impulse in the American politics of '64. He does not yet clearly represent all that a serious contender for the Presidency should. "Guts without depth" and "a man of one-sentence solutions" are the epithets of his critics. The time has come for him to rebut them if he can.*

Two months later Goldwater announced his formal candidacy for the Republican nomination, and issued a pamphlet called "Senator Goldwater Speaks Out on the Issues." Written in that milk-of-magnesia style which is characteristic of such tracts, one could no longer be certain what he thought—he had moved from being a man of "one-sentence solutions" to a man who showed a preference for many imprecise sentences. Barry was treading water. As he did, his people, his organization, kept picking up delegates. It was not until he voted against the Civil Rights Bill that the open battle between old money and new was at last engaged. Too late on the side of the East. To anyone who knew a bit about the workings of the Establishment, a mystery was present. For unless the Establishment had become most suddenly inept, there was a buried motive in the delay, a fear, as if the Eastern money were afraid of some force in the American mind racing to power in defiance of them, some mystique from out the pure accelerating delirium of a crusade which would make cinder of the opposition. So they had waited, all candidates but Rockefeller had waited, none willing to draw the fires of the Right until Scranton was flushed by the ebb and flow, the mystery or murmur, in an old man's throat.

Somewhat later that morning, one saw Scranton in a press conference at the San Francisco Hilton. The Corinthian Room on the ballroom floor (Press Headquarters) was a white room, perhaps forty-five feet by forty feet with a low ceiling and a huge puff of a modern chandelier made up of pieces of plastic which looked like orange candy. The carpet was an electric plastic green, the bridge seats (some two hundred of them) were covered in a plastic the color of wet aspirin, and the walls were white, a hospital-sink white. The practical effect was to leave you feeling like a cold cut set in the white tray of a refrigerator.

The speaker, however, was like a fly annealed on the electric-light bulb of the refrigerator. The banks of lights were turned on him, movie lights, TV lights, four thousand watts in the eye must be the average price a politician pays for his press conference. It gives them all a high instant patina, their skin responding to the call of the wild; there is danger, because the press conference creates the moment when the actor must walk into the gears of the machine. While it is a hundred-to-one or a thousand-to-one he will make no mistake, his career can be extinguished by a blunder. Unless one is making news on a given day—which is to say an important announcement is to be made—the press conference is thus a virtuoso price to be paid for remaining in the game, since there are all too many days when it is to the interest of the speaker, or of his party, or his wing of the party, to make no particular news, but rather to repress news. Still, the speaker must not be too dull, or he will hurt his own position, his remarks will be printed too far back in the paper. So he must be interesting without being revealing. Whereas it is to the interest of the press to make him revealing. A delicate game of balance therefore goes on. Nixon used to play well until the day of his breakdown. Eisenhower was once good at it. Goldwater was considered bad at this game, sufficiently bad that at the convention he held but one press conference before his nomination, and in the six preceding weeks had given but two.

An opportunity to observe the game in operation came with Melvin Laird who tried to convince the Press Corps that the Republican platform was liberal, strong on civil rights, critical of extremists, and yet true to Goldwater. Laird, a smooth vigorous man with a bald domelike head, held the breech for half an hour, ducking questions with grace the way Negroes used once to duck baseballs in a carnival. When he got into trouble (it was after all a most untenable position), he called on one of the most necessary rules of the game, which is that you don't insult the good character of the speaker. So Laird would finally say, "We worked hard on this platform, it's a good platform, I'm proud of it." That made the questioners retreat and regroup for a new attack.

Now Scranton's press conferences were of course different—because no one could be certain if Scranton was part of the game or a wild hare diverting the chase from every true scent. The result was a choppiness to the questioning, a sense of irritation, a hint of vast contempt from the Press Corps; a reporter despises a politician who is not professional, for the game then becomes surrealistic, and it is the function of games to keep dreams, dread and surrealism out in the night where they belong. They would dog at Scranton, they would try to close: *Governor, Governor, could you give the name of any delegate who has moved over from Goldwater to you?* No, we are not prepared to say at this time, would come the answer. *Are there any?* (Titter from the audience.) Certainly. *But you do not care to say?* Not at this time. *Governor* (a new man now) *is there any truth to the rumor you are going to concede before the convention begins?* None whatsoever. *Governor, is it not true that you may be willing to run for vice-president?* For the eighty-eighth time, it is certainly not true. *Unqualifiedly?* Yes (said Scranton sadly) unqualifiedly.

He stood there like a saint, a most curious kind of saint. If he had been an actor he would have played the Dauphin to Ingrid Bergman's Joan of

Arc. He was obviously, on superficial study, a weak and stubborn man. One felt he had been spoiled when he was young by a lack of testing. It was not that he lacked bravery, it was that he had lacked all opportunity to be brave for much too long, and now he was not so much engaged in a serious political struggle as in a puberty rite. It was incredible that this pleasant urbane man, so self-satisfied, so civilized, so reasonable, so innocent of butchers' tubs and spleens and guts (that knowledge which radiates with full ceremony off Khrushchev's halo), should be now in fact the man the Eastern Establishment had picked as their candidate for President. He had a fatal flaw to his style, he was just very slightly delicate the way, let us say, a young Madison Avenue executive will seem petulant next to the surly vigor of a president of a steel corporation. Scranton had none of the heft of a political jockstrapper like Goldwater; no, rather he had the big wide thin-lipped mouth of a clown—hopeless! If the roles had been reversed, if it had been Scranton with six hundred delegates and Goldwater who led a rush in the last four weeks to steal the land, why Goldwater might still have won. Scranton was decent but some part of his soul seemed to live in the void. Doubtless he had been more formidable when he began, but he had been losing for four weeks, one loss after another, delegates, delegations, caucuses, he had been losing with Eisenhower, he had lost with Dirksen, he had lost Illinois, he was losing Ohio, his wheeler-dealers stood by idle wheels; you cannot deal when you are losing delegates, there is nothing to offer the delegate but the salvation of his soul, and the delegate has put salvation in hock a long time ago. So Scranton had begun with the most resistant of missions—there are few works in life so difficult as to pry delegates loose from a man who has a nomination virtually won. To be a delegate and stick with the loser is a kind of life, but no delegate can face the possibility of going from a winner to a loser; the losses are not measurable. People are in politics to win. In these circumstances, consider the political weight lifting required of Scranton. He announces his candidacy four weeks before the convention, Goldwater within fifty votes of the nomination. Is Scranton to pull delegates loose from such a scene by an unhappy faculty for getting pictures taken with his legs in the air doing polkas, R.C.A.F. exercises, and backhands in tennis? One knows Scranton's the product of a good many evenings when Eastern gentry circled around cigars and brandy and decided on poor Bill because he was finally not offensive to any. But it would have taken Paul Bunyan to claw into Goldwater's strength from four weeks out. His two hundred plus of Southern delegates were firm as marble, firm as their hatred of Civil Rights. And there was much other strength for Barry from the Midwest and the West, a hard core of delegates filled with hot scalding hatred for the

Eastern Establishment. They were (unlike the children who were for Goldwater) this hard core of delegates, composed in large part of the kind of tourists who had been poisoning the air of hotel lobbies for twenty years. You could see them now with their Goldwater buttons, ensconced in every lobby, a Wasp Mafia where the grapes of wrath were stored. Not for nothing did the White Anglo-Saxon Protestant have a five-year subscription to *Reader's Digest* and *National Geographic*, high colonics and arthritis, silver-rimmed spectacles, punched-out bellies, and that air of controlled schizophrenia which is the merit badge for having spent one's life on Main Street. Indeed there was general agreement that the basic war was between Main Street and Wall Street. What was not seen so completely is that this war is the Wagnerian drama of the Wasp. For a century now the best of the White Protestants have been going from the farm to the town, leaving the small city for the larger one, transferring from Shaker Heights High to Lawrenceville, from Missouri State Teacher's to Smith, from Roast Turkey to Cordon Rouge, off rectitude onto wickedness, out of monogamy into *Les Liaisons Dangereuses*, from *Jane Eyre* to *Candy*; it's a long trip from the American Legion's Annual Ball to the bust-outs of Southampton. There's the unheard cry of a wounded coyote in all the minor leagues of the Junior League, in all the tacky doings of each small town, the grinding rasp of envy rubs the liver of each big frog in his small pond, no hatred like hatred for the East in the hearts of those who were left behind: the horror in the heart of social life in America is that one never knows whether one is snubbed for too much or too little, whether one was too fine or not fine enough, too graceless or too possessed of special grace, too hungry for power or not ambitious enough—the questions are burning and never answered because the Establishment of the East rarely rejects, it merely yields or ignores, it promises and forgets, it offers to attend your daughter's party and somehow does not quite show up, or comes that fraction too late which is designed to spoil the high anticipation of the night. (Or worse, leaves a fraction too early.) The Wasps who were for Goldwater were the social culls of that Eastern Society which ran the land, yes, the Goldwater Wasps were the old doctors of Pasadena with their millions in stock and their grip on the A.M.A., the small-town newspaper editors, the president of the second most important bank, the wives of Texas oil, yes the wives and family of all the prominent and prosperous who had a fatal touch of the hick, all the Western ladies who did the Merengue at El Morocco on a trip to New York, and did it not quite well enough, you could just hear the giggles in the throat of Archie or Lightning Dick or Sad One-Eye, the Haitian and/or Jamaican who had taught them how. Yes the memory of those social failures is the saliva of intellectual violence.

The old Goldwater Wasps, the ones who had been sitting in the hotel lobbies, had an insane sting to their ideas—they were for birching America's bare bottom where Come-you-nisms collected: white and Negro equality; sexual excess; Jew ideas; dirty linen, muddled thinking, lack of respect for the Constitution. The Right in America had an impacted consistency of constipation to their metaphor. Small wonder they dreamed of a Republican purge. The Wasps were full of psychic wastes they could not quit—they had moved into the Middle West and settled the West, they had won the country, and now they were losing it to the immigrants who had come after and the descendants of slaves. They had watched as their culture was adulterated, transported, converted into some surrealist mélange of public piety *cum* rock and roll, product of the movies and television, of the mass media where sons of immigrants were so often king, yes the Wasps did not understand what was going on, they were not so ready after all to listen to those of their ministers who would argue that America had a heritage of sin and greed vis-à-vis the Negro, and those sins of the blood must be paid; they were not at all ready to listen to the argument that America's industry had been built out of the hardworking hard-used flesh of five generations of immigrants, no, they were Christian but they did not want to hear any more about the rights of others, they suffered from the private fear they were not as good, not as tough, not as brave as their great-grandfathers, they suffered from the intolerable fear that they were not nearly so good nor so tough as those other Christians close to two thousand years ago who faced Romans, so they were now afraid of the East which had dominated the fashion and style of their life, they were ready to murder the East, the promiscuous adulterous East—in a good fast nuclear war they might allow the Russians a fair crack at New York—yes they were loaded with one hatred: the Eastern Establishment was not going to win again, this time Main Street was going to take Wall Street. So Barry had his brothers, three or four hundred of the hardest delegates in the land, and they were ready to become the lifelong enemy of any delegate who might waver to Scranton.

That was the mood. That was the inner condition of the Goldwater delegates about the time Scranton announced he was going all out for the nomination and would pry these people loose from Barry. Henry Cabot Lodge came in from Vietnam. He was, you remember, going to help. Cynics in the Establishment were quick to inform you that Lodge was actually getting the hell out before the roof fell in, but Lodge gave this message to reporters:

> *. . . One of the things that always used to please me about being in Vietnam was the thought that I might as an older man be able to do something to help our soldiers who were out risking their lives.*

Well, a couple of weeks ago I ran into this captain who was one of the battalion advisors and he said, "Are you going back to help Governor Scranton?" And I said, "No." Well, he said, "You're not?" He said, "I think you ought to."

Well, that gave me quite a—that startled me, rather, because his attitude was: "I'm doing my duty out here, you'd better get back and do your duty pretty fast."

Obviously, no one had ever told Henry Cabot Lodge he might not necessarily be superb. So he came in, kingpin, boy, and symbol of the Establishment, and for two weeks he worked for Scranton (although most curiously—for Lodge was back in America a week before he even made arrangements to meet with Scranton). Still, Lodge announced his readiness to be first target of the Wasp Mafia. At the end of two weeks of picking up the telephone to call old friends only to have the telephone come back in the negative, Lodge looked like a man who had been handsome once. His color was a dirty wax yellow, his smile went up over the gums at the corner of his mouth and gave a hint of the skull the way ninety-year-old men look when their smile goes past the teeth. He looked like they had been beating him in the kidneys with his own liver. It was possible something had been beaten out of him forever.

Of course this was Sunday night—the first session of the convention was not ten hours off on Monday morning—and Scranton and Lodge had had a ferocious bad Sunday; the particular letter inviting Goldwater to debate Scranton before the convention had gone out earlier that day above the Governor's signature and it had gone so far as this:

Your managers say in effect that the delegates are little more than a flock of chickens whose necks will be wrung at will. . . . Goldwaterism has come to stand for a whole crazy-quilt collection of absurd and dangerous positions that would be soundly repudiated by the American people in November.

Denison Kitchel, Goldwater's General Director of the National Goldwater for President Committee, issued a statement:

Governor Scranton's letter has been read here with amazement. It has been returned to him.

Perhaps, upon consideration, the Governor will recognize the intemperate nature of his remarks. As it stands, they tragically reflect upon the Republican Party and upon every delegate to the convention.

Then Kitchel sent out mimeographed copies of Scranton's letter and his own reply to every Republican delegate. The Scranton mine caved in. Flooding at one end of the shaft, it was now burning at the other. Delegates do not like to be told they are a flock of chickens. It is one of those metaphors which fit like a sliver of bone up the nostril. Scranton was to repudiate his letter the following day; he accepted responsibility but disowned the letter—the language was not his—which is to say he admitted he could not run a competent organization. Nor, it developed, could he protect his own people: the name of the assistant who had actually written the letter slipped out quick enough.

Thus, one night before the convention, the letter public, Scranton may just conceivably have moved from deep depression to outright agony. The Republicans were having a Gala that night, five hundred dollars a plate for funds, the press not admitted, although many, some from the front, some from the rear, found a way in, and all the Republican luminaries were there, Eisenhower, and the Luces, Mrs. Eisenhower, Henry Cabot Lodge, Thruston Morton, George Murphy, Ray Bliss, Mrs. Goldwater, Scranton. All but Barry. In a much-announced rage about the letter, Goldwater was boycotting the Gala. Of course, it was essentially an Establishment Gala, that slowly came clear, and therefore was in degree a wake—news of the letter was passing around. The dance floor was not to be crowded this night.

Scranton came in. He walked down the center aisle between the tables looking like one of the walking wounded. People came up to greet him and he smiled wanly and sadly and a little stiffly as if he were very weary indeed, as if he had just committed hara-kiri but was still walking. When introduced, he said with wan humor, "I've read your books"—something finally splendid about Scranton.

A minute later, Scranton and Eisenhower came together. It was their first meeting in San Francisco; the General had just arrived that day, come into the Santa Fe depot after crossing the country by train. He was Scranton's last hope; he might still give momentum to the bogged-down tanks of Scranton's attack—what, after all, was the measure of magic? So Scranton must have looked for every clue in Eisenhower's greeting. There were clues running all over. Ike stood up from his table, he pumped Scranton's hand, he held his elbow, he wheeled about with him, he grinned, he smiled widely, he grinned again, his face flushed red, red as a two-week-old infant's face, his eyes twinkled, he never stopped talking, he never took his hands off Scranton, he never looked him in the eye. It was the greeting of a man who is not going to help another man.

Next day, Eisenhower dropped William Warren Scranton. He had a press conference at the Hilton in which he succeeded in saying nothing. It was obvious now he would not come out for anyone, it was also obvious he would not join the Moderates' call for a stronger civil-rights plank. "Well," he said, "he [Melvin Laird] came to see me, and the way he explained it to me, it sounded all right." Asked about an amendment the Moderates wished to put in the plank, "The authority to use America's

nuclear weapons belongs to the President of the United States," Eisen-
hower thought "this statement was perfectly all right with me because
it reaffirms what the Constitution means." Still he would not fight for it.
Asked how he reacted to the idea of a debate before the entire con-
vention between Senator Goldwater and Governor Scranton, a reference
directed to Scranton's now famous letter of the day before, Eisenhower
said, "This, of course, would be a precedent, and I am not against prec-
edents. I am not particularly for them." A little earlier he had said, "I
really have no feeling of my own." He didn't. He was in a private pond.
He had been in one for years. Something had been dying in him for
years, the proportions and magnitude of his own death no doubt, and he
was going down into the cruelest of fates for an old man, he was hooked
on love like an addict, not large love, but the kind of mild tolerant love
which shields an old man from hatred. It was obvious that Eisenhower
had a deep fear of the forces which were for Goldwater. He did not mind
with full pride any longer if people felt contempt for him, but he did not
want to be hated hard by anyone. So he could not declare himself, not
for anything, and as he made his lapses in syntax, in word orders, in
pronunciations, they took on more prominence than ever they had. At
times, they were as rhythmic as a tic, or a dog scratching at a bite. He
would say, "We must be objec*tive*, I mean ob*jec*tive, we must be objective
. . ." and on he would go as if he were sinking very slowly and quietly
into the waters of his future death which might be a year away or ten
years away but was receiving him nonetheless like a marsh into which
he disappeared twitch by twitch, some beating of wet wings against his
fate.

"*. . . Looke, Lord, and finde both Adams met in me.*"

—JOHN DONNE

Now, as for Goldwater, he had dimensions. Perhaps they were no more
than contradictions, but he was not an easy man to comprehend in a
hurry. His wife, for example, had been at the Gala, sitting with some
family and friends, but at one of the less agreeable tables on the floor, off
to the side and sufficiently back of the stage so that you could not see
the entertainer. It seemed a curious way for the Establishment to treat
the wife of the leading contender, but I was assured by the young lady
who brought me over for the introduction that Mrs. Goldwater preferred
it that way. "She hates being the center of attention," I was told. Well,
she turned out to be a shy attractive woman with a gentle not altogether
happy but sensual face. There was something nice about her and very

vulnerable. Her eyes were moist, they were luminous. It was impossible not to like her. Whereas her daughters were attractive in a different fashion. "I want the best ring in this joint, buster," I could hear them say.

Goldwater's headquarters, however, were at a remove from the ladies. Occupying the fourteenth and fifteenth floors of the Mark Hopkins, they were not easy to enter. The main elevators required a wait of forty-five minutes to go up. The alternate route was off the mezzanine through a pantry onto a service car. A half-filled twenty-gallon garbage can stood by the service-elevator door. You went squeezed up tight with high and low honchos for Goldwater, plus waiters with rolling carts working room service. Once there, the fourteenth and fifteenth floors were filthy. A political headquarters is never clean—stacks of paper, squeezed-out paper cups, typewriter carbons on the floor, jackets on wire hangers all angles on a rack—a political headquarters is like the City Room of a newspaper. But Goldwater's headquarters were filthier than most. There was a general detritus like the high-water mark on a beach. The armchairs were dusty and the sofas looked like hundred-dollar newlywed sofas dirty in a day. The air had the beat-out cigar smell of the waiting room in a large railroad station. It had nothing to do with the personnel. No one on the fourteenth or fifteenth floor had anything to do with his surroundings. You could have dropped them in Nymphenburg or a fleabag off Eighth Avenue—the rooms would come to look the same. A room was a place with a desk where the work got out.

They had something in common—professional workers for Goldwater—something not easy to define. They were not like the kids out in the street, nor did they have much in common with the old cancer-guns in the lobby; no, the worst of these workers looked like divinity students who had been expelled from the seminary for embezzling class funds and still felt they were nearest to J.C.—there was a dark blank fanaticism in their eyes. And the best of the Goldwater professionals were formidable, big rangy men, some lean, some flabby, with the hard distasteful look of topflight investigators for fire-insurance companies, field men for the F.B.I., or like bright young district attorneys, that lean flat look of the hunter, full of moral indignation and moral vacuity. But the total of all the professional Goldwater people one saw on the fourteenth and fifteenth floors was directly reminiscent of a guided tour through the F.B.I. in the Department of Justice Building in Washington, that same succession of handsome dull faces for guide, hair combed straight back or combed straight from a part, eyes lead shot, noses which offered nothing, mouths which were functional, good chins, deft moves. A succession of these men took the tourists through the halls of the F.B.I. and read aloud the signs on the exhibits for us and gave short lectures about the function of the F.B.I. (guard us from the enemy without, the enemy within, Communism and Crime—the statements offered in simple organizational prose of the sort used in pamphlets which welcome new workers to large corporations, soldiers to new commands, freshmen to high school, and magazine readers to editorials). The tourists were mainly fathers and sons. The wives were rugged, the kind who are built for dungarees and a green plaid hunting jacket, the sisters and daughters plain and skinny, no expression. They all had lead shot for eyes, the lecturers and the tourists. Most of the boys were near twelve and almost without exception had the blank private faces which belong to kids who kill their old man with a blast, old lady with a butcher knife, tie sister with telephone cord and hide out in the woods for three days. The climax of the tour was a demonstration by the F.B.I. agent how to use a tommy gun. For ten minutes he stitched targets, using one shot at a time, bursts of three, full magazine, he did it with the mild grace of a body-worker hitting small rivets, there was solemn applause after each burst of shots.

That was a part of the Republic, and here it was at Headquarters for Goldwater. The faces in these rooms were the cream of the tourists and the run of the F.B.I.; there was a mood like the inside of a prison: enclosed air, buried urgency. But that was not altogether fair. The sense of a prison could come from the number of guards and the quality of their style. They were tough dull Pinkertons with a tendency to lean on a new visitor. One desire came off them. They would not be happy if there were no orders to follow. With orders, they were ready to put the arm on Bill Scranton, Nelson Rockefeller, or General Eisenhower (if told to). Probably they would put the arm on Johnson if he appeared and was ordered out. Naturally they were not there for that, they were there to defend Headquarters from mobs (read: niggers) and the Senator from black assassination. It made sense up to a point: Goldwater was in more danger than Scranton, at least so long as Scranton showed no sign of winning; just that day, Sunday, there had been a civil-rights anti-Goldwater march down Market Street. The heavy protection was nonetheless a fraud. No mob was getting to the fourteenth floor, nor to Goldwater's fort on the fifteenth (a separate barricade of Pinkertons guarded the twenty-odd steps), no mob was going to get all the way up with just those three elevators and a wait of forty-five units of sixty seconds each, no assassin was likely to try Headquarters when there were opportunities on the street; no, the atmosphere was created to create atmosphere, the aura at Headquarters was solemnity, debris underfoot, and grave decisions, powers put to the service of order, some conspiracy of the vault, a dedication to the necessity of taking power. That was Headquarters. One never got to see Goldwater in the place.

There was opportunity, however, to come within three feet of him later that day, once at the caucus of the Florida delegation in the Beverly Plaza, once on the street moving from hotel to hotel (Pinkertons no longer in evidence now—just cops) and again at the Clift, where he talked to the Washington delegation. There was excitement watching Barry go to work with a group, an intensity in the air, a religious devotion, as if one of the most urbane priests of America was talking at a Communion breakfast, or as if the Principal-of-the-Year was having a heart-to-heart with honor students. The Florida delegation, meeting in a dingy little downstairs banquet room, was jammed. The afternoon had turned hot for San Francisco. Eighty degrees outside, it may have been ninety in the room. Everybody was perspiring. Barry sat in the front, a spotlight on him, a silver film of perspiration adding to his patina, and the glasses, those black-framed glasses, took on that odd life of their own, that pinched severity, that uncompromising idealism which made Goldwater kin to the tight-mouthed and the lonely. Talking in a soft modest voice, he radiated at this moment the skinny boyish sincerity of a fellow who wears glasses but is determined nonetheless to have a good time. Against all odds. It was not unreminiscent of Arthur Miller: that same mixture of vast solemnity and unspoiled boyhood, a sort of shucks and aw shit in the voice. "Well, you see," said Goldwater, talking to the Florida delegation, "if I was to trust the polls right now, I'd have to say I didn't have a chance. But why should I trust the polls? Why should any of us trust the polls? They've been wrong before. They'll be wrong again. Man is superior to the machine. The thing to remember is that America is a spiritual country, we're founded on belief in God, we may wander a little as a country, but we never get too far away. I'm ready to say the election is going to give the Democrats a heck of a surprise. Why, I'll tell you this," Goldwater said, sweating mildly, telling the folks from Florida just as keen as if he was alone with each one of them, each one of these elderly gents and real-estate dealers and plain women with silver-rimmed eyeglasses, "tell you this, I'm doing my best not to keep this idea a secret, but I think we're not only going to give the Democrats a heck of a surprise, I think we're going to win. [Applause, cheers.] In fact I wouldn't be in this if I didn't think we were going to win. [Applause.] Why, as I sometimes tell my wife, I'm too young to retire and too old to go back to work." [Laughter, loud cheers.] Goldwater was done. He smiled shyly, his glasses saying: I am a modest man, and I am severe on myself. As he made his route to the door, the delegates were touching him enthusiastically.

Back on the street—he was walking the blocks to the Hotel Clift where the Washington State delegation was having a Goldwater reception—his tail consisted of fifty or sixty excited people, some Florida delegates who didn't wish to lose sight of the man, plus a couple of cops glad to have the duty. Cars slowed down to look at him; one stopped. A good-looking woman got out and cheered. There was something in the way she did it. Just as strange Negroes scattered at random through a white audience may act in awareness of one another, so the Goldwater supporters in their thirties and forties gave off a similar confidence of holding the secret. This very good-looking woman yelled, "You go, Barry, you go, go." But there was anger and elation in her voice, as if she were declaring, "We're going to get the country back." And Goldwater smiled modestly and went on. He looked a little in fever. Small wonder. He could be President of the United States in less than half a year, he could stop a sniper's bullet he never knew when, he was more loved and hated than any man in America, and inside all this was just *him*, the man who adjusted radio knobs in the early morning in order to transmit a little better, and now conceivably adjusted a few knobs. . . .

At the Hotel Clift he talked to the Washington delegates. We were definitely back in high school. That was part of Goldwater's deal—he brought you back to the bright minted certitudes of early patriotism when you knew the U.S. was the best country on earth and there was no other. Yes, his appeal would go out to all the millions who were now starved and a little sour because some part of their life had ended in high school, and the university they had never seen. But then Barry had had but one year of college—he had indeed the mind of a powerful freshman. "I want to thank you folks from Washington for giving me this warm greeting. Of course, Washington is the name of a place I often like to get the heck out of, but I'm sure I won't confuse the two right here." [Laughter.] He was off, a short political speech. In the middle, extremism. "I don't see how anybody can be an extremist who believes in the Constitution. And for those misguided few who pretend to believe in the Constitution, but in secret don't, well they may be extremists, but I don't see any necessity to legislate against them. I just feel sorry for them." [Cheers. Applause. Happiness at the way Barry delivered anathemas.] At a certain point in the speech, he saw a woman in the audience whom he recognized, and stopped in the middle of a phrase. "Hi, honey," he sang out like a traveling salesman, which brought a titter from the delegation, for his voice had shifted too quickly, the codpiece was coming off, Rain and the Reverend Davidson. Something skinny, itchy, hard as a horselaugh, showed—he was a cannoneer with a hairy ear. Goldwater went on, the good mood continued; then at the end, speech done, he turned down a drink but said in his best gee-whizzer, "I'm sorry I have to leave because gosh I'd like to break a few with you." Laughter, and he took off head down, a little modest in the exit, a little red in the neck.

There was entertainment at the Republican Gala on Sunday night. The climax was a full marching band of bagpipers. They must have been hired for the week since one kept hearing them on the following days, and at all odd times, heard them even in my hotel room at four a.m., for a few were marching in the streets of San Francisco, sounding through the night, giving off the barbaric evocation of the Scots, all valor, wrath, firmitude, and treachery—the wild complete treachery of the Scots finding its way into the sound of the pipes. They were a warning of the fever in the heart of the Wasp. There are sounds which seem to pass through all the protective gates in the ear and reach into some nerve where the eschatology is stored. Few parents have failed to hear it in the cry of their infant through the morning hours of a bad night—stubbornness, fury, waste, and the promise of revenge come out of a flesh half-created by one's own flesh; the knowledge is suddenly there that seed is existential, no paradise resides in seed, seed can be ill-inspired and go to a foul gloomy end. Some find their part of the truth in listening to jazz—it is moot if any white who had no ear for jazz can know the passion with which some whites become attached to the Negro's cause. So, too, listening to the bagpipes, you knew this was the true music of the Wasps. There was something wild and martial and bottomless in the passion, a pride which would not be exhausted, a determination which might never end, perhaps should never end, the Faustian rage of a white civilization was in those Highland wails, the cry of a race which was born to dominate and might never learn to share, and never learning, might be willing to end the game, the end of the world was in the sound of the pipes. Or at very least the danger one would come closer to the world's end. So there was a vast if all-private appeal in listening to the pipes shrill out the herald of a new crusade, something jagged, Viking, of the North in the air, a sense of breaking ice and barbaric shields, hunters loose in the land again. And this had an appeal which burrowed deep, there was excitement at the thought of Goldwater getting the nomination, as if now finally all one's personal suicides, all the deaths of the soul accumulated by the past, all the failures, all the terrors, could find purge in a national situation where a national murder was being planned (the Third World War) and one's own suicide might be lost in a national suicide. There was that excitement, that the burden of one's soul (always equal to the burden of one's personal responsibility) might finally be lifted—what a release was there! Beauty was inspired by the prospect. For if Goldwater won, and the iron power of the iron people who had pushed him forth—as echoed in the iron of the Pinkertons on the fourteenth and fifteenth floor—now pushed forth over the nation an iron regime with totalitarianism seizing the TV in every frozen dinner, well then at last a true underground might form; and liberty at the thought of any catalyst which could bring it on. Yes, the Goldwater movement excited the depths because the apocalypse was brought more near, and like millions of other whites, I had been leading a life which was a trifle too pointless and a trifle too full of guilt and my gullet was close to nausea with the endless compromises of an empty liberal center. So I followed the four days of the convention with something more than simple apprehension. The country was taking a turn, the colors were deepening, the knives of the afternoon were out, something of the best in American life might now be going forever; or was it altogether to the opposite? and was the country starting at last to take the knots of its contradictions up from a premature midnight of nightmare into the surgical terrains of the open skin? Were we in the beginning, or turning the middle, of our worst disease? One did not know any longer, you simply did not know any longer, but something was certain: the country was now part of the daily concern. One worried about it for the first time, the way you worried about family or work, a good friend or the future, and that was the most exceptional of emotions.

II

". . . When men are too much confined to professional and faculty habits, and as it were inveterate in the recurrent employment of that narrow circle, they are rather disabled than qualified for whatever depends on the knowledge of mankind, on experience in mixed affairs, on a comprehensive, connected view of the various, complicated, external and internal interests, which go to the formation of that multifarious thing called a state."
            —BURKE, *Reflections on the Revolution in France*

If the details of the Republican convention of 1964 were steeped in concern, it was nonetheless not very exciting, not technically. As a big football game, the score might have been 76 to 0, or 76 to 3. (There were sentimentalists who would claim that Rockefeller kicked a field goal.) Compared however to the Republican Convention of 1940 when Wendell Willkie came from behind to sweep the nomination on the sixth ballot, or the 1952 convention when Eisenhower defeated Taft on the second roll call of the states, compared even to the Democratic Convention of 1960, there were few moments in this affair, and nothing even remotely comparable in excitement to the demonstration for Adlai Stevenson four years ago when Eugene McCarthy put him in nomination. Yet this convention of 1964 would remain as one of the most important in our history; it took place with religious exaltation for some, with dread for others, and in sheer trauma for the majority of the press and television who were present on the scene. For them it offered four days of anxiety as pure and deep as a child left alone in a house. The purpose of the press in America has been to tinker with the machine, to adjust, to prepare a seat for new valves and values, to lubricate, to excuse, to justify, to serve in the maintenance of the Establishment. From I. F. Stone on the left, going far to the right of Joseph Alsop, over almost so far as David Lawrence, the essential understanding of the mass media is that the machine of the nation is a muddle which is endlessly grateful for ministrations of the intellect; so a game is played in which the Establishment always forgives the mass media for its excesses, and the mass media brings its sense of civilization (adjustment, psychoanalysis, responsibility, and the milder shores of love) to the service of the family Establishment. Virtually everything is forgiven by both sides. The contradictory remarks of politicians are forgotten, the more asinine predictions of pundits are buried with mercy. The Establishment for example would not remind Joe Alsop that in March 1964 he had written, "No serious Republican politician, even of the most Neanderthal type, any longer takes Goldwater seriously." No, the Press was not to be twitted for the limits of their technique because half their comprehension of the nation derived after all from material supplied by the Establishment; the other half came from conversations with each other. All too often the Press lives in the investigative condition of a lover who performs the act for two minutes a day and talks about it for twenty hours of the twenty-four. So a daisy chain like the *National Review* proves to be right about Goldwater's strength and the intellectual Establishment with its corporate resources is deep in error.

An explanation? Those who hold power think the devil is best contained by not mentioning his name. This procedure offers a formidable shell in which to live, but its cost is high; the housing is too ready to collapse when the devil decides to show. There has been no opportunity to study him. Just as a generation of the Left, stifled and ignored through the McCarthyism of the Fifties and the Eisenhowerism of the Fifties, caused panic everywhere when they emerged as the Beat Generation, so another generation, a generation of the Right, has been stifled, their actions reported inaccurately, their remarks distorted, their ideals (such as they are) ignored, and their personal power underestimated. The difference however is that the Beat Generation was a new flock of early Christians gathered prematurely before the bomb, an open-air asylum for the gentle and the mad, where in contrast the underground generation of the Right is a frustrated posse, a convention of hangmen who subscribe to the principle that the executioner has his rights as well. The liberal mind collapses before this notion but half of nature may be contained in the idea that the weak are happiest when death is quick. It is a notion which since the Nazis has been altogether detestable, but then the greatest intellectual damage the Nazis may have done was to take a few principles from nature and pervert them root and nerve. In the name of barbarism and a return to primitive health they accelerated the most total and surrealistic aspects of civilization. The gas chamber was a full albino descendant of the industrial revolution.

But that is a digression. To return to the as yet milder political currents of the Left and the Right in America, one could say the Beat Generation was a modest revolution, suicidal in the center of its passion. At its most militant it wished for immolation rather than power, it desired only to be left free enough to consume itself. Yet in the mid-Fifties liberals reacted with a profound terror, contumely, and ridicule to its manifestations as if their own collective suicide (the private terror of the liberal spirit is invariably suicide, not murder) was to be found in the gesture of the Beat. What then the panic of the liberal Establishment before a revolution of the Right whose personal nightmare might well be their inability to contain their most murderous impulse, a movement of the Right whose ghost is that unlaid blood and breath of Nazism which has hovered these twenty years like a succubus over the washed-out tissues of civilization. Consider but one evidence of the fear: that part of the Press called Periodicals sat in a section of the gallery to the left of the speakers in the Cow Palace. There were one hundred writers in this Periodical section of the gallery and six passes to get down to the floor where one could talk to delegates and in turn be looked at by them. Of those six passes, one or two were always available. Which meant that the majority of writers did not try to get down to the floor very often. Sitting next to one another the writers were content to observe—there were killers on the floor.

There were. It was a convention murderous in mood. The mood of this convention spoke of a new kind of society. Chimeras of fascism hung like fogbank. And high enthusiasm. Some of the delegates were very happy. "*Viva*," would shout a part of the gallery. "*Olé*," would come the answer. There was an éclat, a bull roar, a mystical communion in the sound even as *Sieg Heil* used to offer its mystical communion. *Viva-Olé*. Live-Yay! Live-Yay! It was the new chic of the mindless. The American mind had gone from Hawthorne and Emerson to the Frug, the Bounce, and Walking the Dog, from *The Flowering of New England* to the cerebrality of professional football in which a quarterback must have not only heart, courage, strength and grace but a mind like an I.B.M. computer. It marks the turn we have taken from the Renaissance. There too was the ideal of a hero with heart, courage, strength, and grace, but he was expected to possess the mind of a passionate artist. Now the best heroes were—in the sense of the Renaissance—mindless: Y. A. Tittle, John Glenn, Tracy, Smiling Jack; the passionate artists were out on the hot rods, the twist band was whipping the lovers, patriotism was a football game, a fascism would come in (if it came) on Live-Yay! Let's live-yay! The hype had made fifty million musical-comedy minds; now the hype could do anything; it could set high-school students to roar *Viva-Olé*, and they would roar it while victims of a new totalitarianism would be whisked away to a new kind of camp—hey, honey, do you twist, they would yell into the buses.

"When men of rank sacrifice all ideas of dignity to an ambition without a distinct object, and work with low instruments and for low ends, the whole composition becomes low and base."
    —BURKE, *Reflections on the Revolution in France*

First major event of the convention was Eisenhower's appearance at the Cow Palace to give a speech on Tuesday afternoon. The arena was well-chosen for a convention. Built in the Thirties when indoor sports stadiums did not yet look like children's nurseries, the Cow Palace offered echoes—good welterweights and middleweights had fought here, there was iron in the air. And the Republicans had installed the speaker's platform at one end of the oval; the delegates sat therefore in a file which was considerably longer than it was wide, the speaker was thus installed at the handle of the sword. (Whereas the Democrats in 1960 had put the speaker in the middle of the oval.) But this was the party after all of Republican fathers rather than Democratic mothers. If there were any delegates to miss the psychic effect of this decision, a huge banner raised behind the speaker confronted them with the legend: Of the people, By the people, For the people. "Of the people" was almost invisible; "By the people" was somewhat more clear; "For the people" was loud and strong. This was a party not much "of the people" but very much "for the people," it presumed to know what was good for them.

And for fact, that had always been Ike's poor lone strength as a speaker, he knew what was good for you. He dipped into his speech, "here with great pride because I am a Republican," " my deep dedication to Republicanism"—he had not been outward bound for five minutes before the gallery was yawning. Ike had always been a bore, but there had been fascination in the boredom when he was President—this, after all, was *the* man. Now he was just another hog wrassler of rhetoric; he pinned a few phrases in his neat determined little voice, and a few phrases pinned him back. Ike usually fought a speech to a draw. It was hard to listen. All suspense had ended at Monday morning's press conference. Ike would not come out in support of Scranton. So the mind of the Press drifted out with the mind of the gallery. If Ike said a few strong words about the Civil Rights Bill—"Republicans in Congress to their great credit voted far more overwhelmingly than did our opponents to pass the Civil Rights Bill"—it meant nothing. The Moderates tried to whoop it up, the Goldwater delegations looked on in ranked masses of silence. Ike went on. He gave the sort of speech which takes four or five columns in the New York *Times* and serves to clot the aisles of history. He was still, as he had been when he was President, a cross between a boy and an old retainer. The boy talked, earnest, innocent, a high-school valedictorian debating the affirmative of, Resolved: Capitalism is the Most Democratic System on Earth; and the old retainer quavered into the voice, the old retainer could no longer live without love.

Ike had bored many a crowd in his time. He had never bored one completely—he had always known how to get some token from a mob. Ever since 1952, he had been giving little pieces of his soul to draw demonstrations from the mob. You could always tell the moment. His voice shifted. Whenever he was ready to please the crowd, he would warn them by beginning to speak with a brisk little anger. Now it came, now he said it. ". . . Let us particularly scorn the *divisive* efforts of those outside our family, including sensation-seeking columnists and commentators [beginning of a wild demonstration] because," said Ike, his voice showing a glint of full spite, "I assure you that these are people who couldn't care less about the good of our party." He was right, of course. That was not why he said it, however; he said it to repay the Press for what they had said about him these last three weeks; the sensation they had been seeking was—so far as he was concerned—to arouse needles of fury in an old man's body—he said what he said for revenge. Mainly he said it to please the Goldwater crowd, there was the hint of that in his voice. The Goldwater delegations and the gallery went into the first large demonstration of the convention. Trumpets sounded, heralds of a new crusade: cockroaches, columnists, and Communists to be exterminated. There were reports in the papers next day that delegates shook their fists at newspapermen on the floor, and at the television men with their microphones. The mass media is of course equipped for no such war. Some of the men from the mass media looked like moon men: they wore red helmets and staggered under the load of a portable camera which must have weighed fifty pounds and was packed on their back; others of the commentators had portable mikes and hats with antennae. To the delegates they must have looked like insects grown to the size of a man. Word whipped in to the delegations from the all-call telephone in the office trailer of the Goldwater command post back of the Cow Palace. Cut the demonstration, was the word from F. Clifton White. The demonstration subsided. But the Press did not, the rest of the mass media did not. They remain in a state of agitation: if Ike was ready to accuse, anyone could serve as hangman. Anyone would. Anyone they knew.

Much later that Tuesday, after the full reading of the full platform, came a debate between the Moderates and the Conservatives. Success in politics comes from putting one's seat to a chair and sitting through dull wrangles in order to be present after midnight when the clubhouse vote is cast. Playboys do not go far in these circumstances, nor adventurers; the mediocre recognized early that a society was evolving which would enable them to employ the very vice which hitherto had made life intolerable— mediocrity itself. So the cowardly took their place in power. They had the superior ability to breathe in hours of boredom.

Politics was now open however to the disease of the bored—magic. Magic can sweep you away. Once a decade, once every two decades, like a big wind which eludes the weather charts and seems to arise from the caverns of the ocean itself, so does a hurricane sweep a convention. It happened with Wendell Willkie in 1940; it flickered on the horizon with Stevenson in '60; it was Scranton's hope to work a real debate on the last session before the balloting. If he could win even once on some small point, rumors of magic could arise. The Moderates had forced therefore a floor fight to propose a few amendments to the Republican platform of '64. One: that only the President have the authority to use America's nuclear weapons. Two: repudiate the John Birch Society. Three: introduce a language of approval for the Civil Rights Act. The chances of success were small at best: only an extraordinary assault on the emotions of the Goldwater delegations could sway them to vote yes for the amendments.

The Moderates however went to battle moderately. Their speakers were impressive (as such a quality is measured in the *Times*). They were Christian Herter, Hugh Scott, Clifford Case, George Romney, Lindsay, Javits, Rockefeller. They were not, however, lively speakers, not this night. Lindsay and Javits were presentable in professional groups; devoted to detailed matters, they spoke with reason; Case spoke like a shy high-school teacher; Christian Herter was reminiscent of Mr. Chips; Hugh Scott owned no fire. Carlino (Majority Leader in the New York Assembly) sounded like a successful restaurant owner. And Governor Romney of Michigan had his own special amendments, he was a moderation of the moderates. As he spoke, he looked like a handsome version of Boris Karloff, all honesty, big-jawed, soft-eyed, eighty days at sea on a cockeyed passion.

He spoke in a loud strong voice yet one sensed a yaw at the center of his brain which left his cerebrations as lost as Karloff's lost little voice. No, the only excitement had come at the beginning. Rockefeller was not a man who would normally inspire warmth. He had a strong decent face and something tough as the rubber in a handball to his makeup, but his eyes had been punched out a long time ago—they had the distant lunar glow of the small sad eyes you see in a caged chimpanzee or gorilla. Even when hearty he gave an impression the private man was remote as an astronaut on a lost orbit. But Rockefeller had his ten minutes at the podium and as he talked of suffering "at first-hand" in the California primary from the methods of "extremist elements," threatening letters unsigned, bomb threats, "threats of personal violence," telephone calls, "smear and hate literature," "strong-arm and goon tactics," the gallery erupted, and the boos and jeers came down. Rockefeller could have been Leo Durocher walking out to the plate at Ebbets Field to protest an umpire's decision after Leo had moved from the Dodgers to the Giants. Again the all-call in the Goldwater trailer outside the Cow Palace was busy, again the delegations were told to be silent, and obeyed. But the gallery would not stop, and Thruston Morton, the Chairman, came forward like one of the sweepers in *Camino Real* to tell Kilroy his time was up. Rockefeller had his moment. "You quiet them," he said to Morton. "That's your job. I want my time to speak." And there was a conception of Rockefeller finally—he had few ideas and none of them were his own, he had a personality which was never in high focus (in the sense that Bobby Kennedy and Jimmy Hoffa are always in high focus) but he had an odd courage which was profound—he could take strength from defying a mob. Three hundred thousand years ago, a million years ago, some gorilla must have stood up to an enraged tribe and bellowed back and got away alive and human society was begun. So Rocky finally had his political moment which was precisely right for him.

But the other Moderates did not. There was in their collective voice a suggestion of apology: let-us-at-least-be-heard. Speakers who were opposed to the amendments sounded as effective, sometimes more. Ford from Michigan spoke after Rockefeller, and had better arguments. It was not, he suggested, the purpose of a party which believed in free speech to look for formulas to repress opinion. He was right, even if he might not be so ready to protect Communists as Reactionaries. And Senator Dominick of Colorado made a bright speech employing an editorial from *The New York Times* of 1765 which rebuked Patrick Henry for extreme ideas. Delegates and gallery whooped it up. Next day Dominick confessed. He was only "spoofing." He had known: there was no *New York Times* in 1765. Nor was there any editorial. An old debater's trick. If there are no good facts, make them up. Be quick to write your own statistics. There was some umbilical tie between the Right Wing and the psychopathic liar.

More speakers came on. After four or five speakers for each side, a vote would come. Each time the amendment was voted down. Eight hundred and ninety-so-many to four hundred-and-a-few, went the votes. Hours went by, three hours of debate. After a while, the Moderates came collectively to seem like a club fighter in still another loser. A vacuum hung over empty cries for civil rights. One wondered why a Negro delegate loyal to the Party for thirty years had not been asked by the Moderates to make a speech where he could say: *You are sending me home to my people a mockery and a shame. My people have been saying for thirty years that the Republican Party has no love for the colored man, and I have argued back. Tonight you will tell me I was wrong. You are denying me the meaning of my life.*

Such a speech (and there were Negro delegates to give it) might not have turned the vote, doubtless it would not have turned the vote, but it was the Moderates' sole chance for an explosion which could loose some petrified emotion, some magic. They did not take it. Probably they did not take it because they did not care that much if they lost. By now, it might be better to lose decisively than come nearer to winning and divide the party more. So they accepted their loser's share of the purse, which is that they could go back East and say: I campaigned at the convention for civil rights. Tomorrow was nominating day. The last chance in a hundred had been lost.

. . . The Bleat, the Bark, Bellow & Roar—
*   Are Waves that Beat on Heaven's Shore. . . .*

                    —WILLIAM BLAKE, *Auguries of Innocence*

Everett Dirksen gave the nominating speech for Goldwater, Dirksen from Illinois, the Silver Fox of the Senate, the Minority Leader, the man who had done the most, many would claim, to pass the Civil Rights Bill, for it was his coalition with Hubert Humphrey on cloture which had carried the day. "I guess Dirksen finally got religion," Humphrey said, and Dirksen, making his final speech for the bill, declared, "There is no force so powerful as an idea whose time has come." It was said that when Goldwater voted against the bill, Dirksen would not speak to him. Two weeks later, Dirksen agreed to nominate Goldwater. "He's got it won, that's all," Dirksen said of Goldwater, "this thing has gone too far."

This day, nominating day, any orator could have set fire to the Cow Palace. The gallery and Goldwater delegations were as tense and impatient as a platoon of Marines going down to Tijuana after three weeks in the field. But this day Dirksen had no silver voice. He made a speech which contained such nuggets as, "In an age of do-gooders, he was a good doer." Dirksen was an old organist who would play all the squeaks in all the stops, rustle over all the dead bones of all the dead mice in all the pipes. He naturally made a large point that Barry Goldwater was "the grandson of the peddler." This brought no pleasure to the crowd. Main Street was taking Wall Street; Newport Beach, California, would replace Newport; and General Goldwater, Air Force Reserve, possessed sufficient cachet to negotiate the move; but not the grandson of the peddler. Dirksen however went on and on, making a sound like the whir of the air conditioning in a two-mile tunnel.

When he was done, they blew Dirksen down, the high screams of New Year's Eve went off, a din of screamers, rattles, and toots, a clash of bands, a dazzle of posters in phosphorescent yellow and orange and gold, the mad prance of the state standards, wild triumphant pokes and jiggles, war spears, crusader's lances, an animal growl of joy, rebel cries, eyes burning, a mad nut in each square jaw, *Viva-Olé, Viva-Olé,* bugle blasts and rallying cries, the call of heralds, and a fall from the rafters of a long golden rain, pieces of gold foil one inch square, hundreds of thousands of such pieces in an endless gentle shimmer of descent. They had put a spot on the fall—it was as if sunlight had entered every drop of a fine sweet rain. I ran into Mike Wallace on the floor. "The guy who thought of this was a genius," said Mike. And the sounds of the band went up to meet the rain. There was an unmistakable air of beauty, as if a rainbow had come to a field of war, or Goths around a fire saw visions in a cave. The heart of the beast had loosed a primitive call. Civilization was worn thin in the center and to the Left the black man raised his primitive cry; now to the far Right were the maniacal blue eyes of the other primitive. The jungles and the forests were readying for war. For a moment, beauty was there— it is always there as tribes meet and clans gather for war. It was certain beyond certainty now that America was off on a ride which would end— was it God or the Devil knew where.

But the ride did not begin for another seven hours and seven nominations. Knowland seconded Goldwater's nomination; and Clare Boothe Luce, Charlie Halleck, Senator Tower. Then Keating nominated Rockefeller, a twenty-two-minute demonstration, decent in size but predictably hollow. More seconding speeches. Next came Scranton's turn. Dr. Milton Eisenhower, Ike's younger brother, did the nominating. It was good, it was clear, but there was not much excitement any more. One knew why the older Eisenhower had wanted the younger Eisenhower to be President. One also knew why he had not come very near—he gave a hint of Woodrow Wilson. Then the demonstration for Scranton. It was respectable, it let loose a half hour of music, it had fervor, the Scranton supporters died pure, an enjoyable demonstration. But the music was softer. Instead of *Viva-Olé* and the bugle blasts and rallying cries of the crusaders, one now heard *Boys and Girls Together*, or *Hail, Hail, the Gang's All Here*. And the Scranton posters did not have the deep yellow and deep orange of the phalanxes who had jammed the gorge for Goldwater; no, they bore blue and red letters on white, or even black on white, a gray photograph of Scranton on a white background with letters in black— the sign had been designed by Brooks Brothers, you may bet. Even some of the lapel buttons for Scranton revealed a camp of understatement, since they were five inches in diameter, yet Scranton's name was in letters one-eighth of an inch high. It made one think of *The New Yorker* and the blank ordered harmoniums of her aisles and text.

Now went the nominations hour after hour like the time between four in the morning and breakfast at a marathon dance. Here came the nominating speeches and the pumped-up state demonstrations on the floor which spoke of plump elderly tourists doing the hula in Hawaii. Then would come a team of seconding speeches, the weepers and the wringers, the proud of nose and the knotty of nose, the kickers and the thumpers, the ministerial bores and the rabbinical drones, the self-satisfied, the glad-to-be-there, the self-anointed, the unctuous, the tooth suckers, the quaverers.

Fong was nominated, and Margaret Chase Smith, first woman ever to be nominated for President. Now she had a lock on the footnotes in the history books. Romney was nominated, and Judd, defeated Congressman Walter H. Judd of Minnesota, given a grand-old-man-of-the-party nominating speech. The band played *Glory, Glory, Hallelujah*. Just after World War II, early in 1946, Judd had been one of the first to talk of war with Russia. Last came Lodge who scratched himself. The nominations were done. The balloting could begin. They cleared the floor of the Press.

We had been there off and on for seven hours, circling the delegations, talking where we could, a secondary sea of locusts. All through the seven hours of this afternoon and evening, there was the California delegation. They could not be ignored. They sat in the front rows off the center aisle just beneath the speaker on the podium. They wore yellow luminescent Goldwater shirts, the sort of sleeveless high-colored shirts which highway workers wear to be phosphorescent at night. On the floor there were a thousand sights and fifty conversations those seven hours, but there was nothing like the California delegation. In California Rockefeller had lost to Goldwater by less than three percent of the vote, and, losing, had lost all the delegates. California had eighty-six delegates—all eighty-six by the rules of the victory were for Goldwater. So there were eighty-six yellow shirts right down front. Winning California, the Right had also won the plums of the convention, the distribution of tickets in the gallery, central placement on the floor, the allegiance of the Cow Palace cops. They had won the right to have their eighty-six faces at the center of the convention.

Most of the California delegation looked like fat state troopers or prison guards or well-established ranchers. A few were thin and looked like Robert Mitchum playing the mad reverend in *Night of the Hunter*. One or two were skinny as Okies, and looked like the kind of skinny wild-eyed gas-station attendant who works in a small town, and gets his picture in the paper because he has just committed murder with a jack handle. Yes, the skinny men in the California delegation leered out wildly. They looked like they were sitting on a body—the corpse of Jew Eastern Negritudes— and when the show was over, they were gonna eat it. That was it—half the faces in the California delegation looked like geeks. They had had it and now they were ready to put fire to the big tent.

There was one man who stood out as their leader—he had the face to be a leader of such men. Of course he looked not at all like a robber baron, the pride of Pinkerton, and a political boss all in one, no, nor was he in the least like an amalgam of Wallace Beery and fat Hermann Goering, no he was just Bill Knowland, ex-Senator William F. Knowland, Lord of the China Lobby, and honcho number one for Barry in Northern and Southern Cal.

So began the balloting. In twenty minutes there was another demonstration. The California standard, a white silk flag with a beast, some mongrel of bear and wild boar, danced in the air as if carried by a knight on a horse. The chairman for South Carolina intoned, "We are humbly grateful that we can do this for America. South Carolina casts sixteen votes for Senator Barry Goldwater." Barry was in. Four years of work was over. Final score: 883 for Goldwater. Scranton, 214. Rockefeller had 114, Romney 41. Smith received 27, Judd 22, Lodge 2, and Fong had 5.

When the voting was done, when the deliriums were down, an ooh of pleasure came up from the crowd, like the ooh for an acrobat. For Scranton accompanied by his wife was walking down the ramp to the podium, down the high ramp which led from the end-arena exits to the speaker's stand. It was a walk of a hundred feet or more, and Scranton came down this ramp with a slow measured deferential step, like a boy carrying a ceremonial bowl.

He made a clear speech in a young rather vibrant voice. He was doing the thing he was best at. He was making a gesture his elders would approve. He called on Republicans "not to desert our party but to strengthen it."

They cheered him modestly and many may have thought of his comments about Goldwater. On different days through June and July he had said: "dangerously impulsive," "spreading havoc across the national landscape," "a cruel misunderstanding of how the American economy works," "injurious to innumerable candidates," "chaos and uproar," "talking off the top of his head." "Hypocrisy . . ." says our friend Burke, "delights in the most sublime speculations; for never intending to go beyond speculation, it costs nothing to have it magnificent." "I ask . . ." Scranton said. He asked his delegates to make Goldwater's nomination unanimous.

Anywhere but in politics the speed with which the position had been shifted would be sign of a monumental instability. But politics was the place where finally nobody meant what they said—it was a world of nightmare; psychopaths roved. The profound and searing conflicts of politicians were like the quarrels between the girls in a brothel—they would tear each other's hair one night, do a trick together the next. They had no memory. They had no principles but for one—you do not quit the house. You may kill each other but you do not quit the house.

One could imagine the end of an imaginary nightmare: some time in the future, the Iron Ham (for such had become the fond nickname attached to President Barry Goldwater) would be told, thinking back on it all, that Billy-boy Scranton should be removed for some of the things he had said, and old Eisenhower, our General Emeritus, would find it in himself to say at a press conference on TV that while removal could not in itself be condoned, that is for high political figures, still it was bad, of course, policy, for people to have gotten away with insulting the President even if it was in the past and in the guise of free speech which as we all know can be abused. They would shave Scranton's head. Like a monk would he take the walk. And Old Ike would walk with him, and tell Willy S. a joke at the end, and have his picture taken shaking hands. Then, back to the White House for a two-shot drinking beer with Barry, the Iron Ham. After it was over, Barry would go back to the people who had put the ring in his nose.

. . . They should not think it amongst their rights to cut off the entail, or commit waste on the inheritance, by destroying at their pleasure the whole original fabric of their society; hazarding to leave to those who come after them a ruin instead of a habitation.

—**BURKE,** *Reflections on the Revolution in France*

Goldwater: "There have been several suggestions made. I don't think we would use any of them. But defoliation of the forests by low-yield atomic weapons could well be done. When you remove the foliage, you remove the cover."

—New York Post, May 27, 1964

Driving away from the Cow Palace after the nomination, I could hear Goldwater on the car radio. He was celebrating. He was considerably more agreeable than Dick Nixon celebrating—no all-I-am-I-owe-to-my-mother-and-father-my-country-and-church; no, Goldwater was off instead on one of his mild rather tangy excursions, "I feel very humble," he said, and you could feel the itch in the long johns and the hair in the nose, a traveling salesman in an upper berth, belt of bourbon down the hatch—as Mrs. Goldwater entered the room, he cried out, "Hi, honey," and added just a touch mean and small-town, "You didn't cry very much tonight."

"No," said Mrs. Goldwater, "wait till tomorrow."

The questioning went back and forth. He was all voice and very little mind, you could tell he had once been so bright as to invent and market a novelty item called Antsy Pants, men's white shorts with red ants embroidered all over them. But he had a voice! It made up for the mind. Lyndon Johnson's hambone-grits-and-turnip-greens was going to play heavy to this; Goldwater on radio was sweet and manly, clean as Dad in the show of new shows, One Man's Dad. They asked him, *Senator, you said that you would not wage a personal campaign against the President.* Yes, said Goldwater. *Well, sir,* said the interviewer now, *today you called President Johnson the biggest faker in the U.S.* Butters of ecstasy in the interviewer's mouth. *It's going to be a hard-hitting campaign, I assume then?* "Oh," said Goldwater, "I think you'll find some brickbats flying around."

The dialogue went on: *Could you tick off just a few of the major issues you think will be in the campaign against the Democrats?* "I think," said Goldwater, "law and dis—the abuse of law and order in this country, the total disregard for it, the mounting crime rate is going to be another issue —at least I'm going to make it one, because I think the responsibility for this has to start someplace and it should start at the Federal level with the Federal courts enforcing the law.

"I noticed one tonight in the evening paper, for example—a young girl in New York who used a knife to attack a rapist is now getting the worst of the deal and the rapist is probably going to get the Congressional Medal of Honor and sent off scot-free," said Goldwater, neglecting to tell us that the girl had had her indictment dismissed, and the alleged rapist was already up on a charge of attempted rape. Goldwater now said in the sort of voice Daddy employs when he is ready to use the strap, "That kind of business has to stop in this country and, as the President, I'm going to do all I can to see that women can go out in the streets of this country without being scared stiff." Yes, he would. He was a Conservative and he was for States' Rights. It was just that he wasn't for *local* rights.

"By this wise prejudice we are taught to look with horror on those children of their country, who are prompt rashly to hack that aged parent in pieces, and put him into the kettle of magicians, in hopes that by their poisonous weeds, and wild incantations, they may regenerate the paternal constitution, and renovate their father's life."
—BURKE, *Reflections on the Revolution in France*

Next day was the last day of the convention. Bill Miller was nominated for Vice-President. He was not a very handsome man nor did his manner seem particularly agreeable, but then the thought obtruded itself that the President of the United States was now in a more dramatic statistical relation to violent death than a matador. So a candidate would not necessarily look for too appealing a Vice-President—it might encourage notions of succession in the mind of an assassin. One would look instead for deterrents. William Miller was a deterrent.

III

A little later on the last day, Nixon made the speech of introduction for Goldwater. In the months ahead, when the bull in Barry swelled too wild and he gave promise of talking again of Negro assailants getting Medals of Honor, they would send in Nixon to calm him down. The Eastern Establishment, hydra head, was not dead after all; they still had Nixon. He was the steer to soothe the bull. Poor Barry. He had tried to lose Nixon in Cleveland, he had said, "He's sounding more like Harold Stassen every day." Nixon however was as easy to lose as a plain wife without prospects is easy to divorce.

"My good friend and great Republican, Dick Nixon . . ." was how Goldwater began his historic acceptance speech. It had come after a rich demonstration of happiness from the delegates. A boxcar of small balloons was opened in the rafters as Goldwater came down the ramp with his wife, his sons, his daughters. The balloons tumbled in thousands to the floor where (fifty balloons being put out each second by lighted cigarettes) a sound like machine-gun fire popped its way through the cheers. Fourth of July was here once more. He looked good, did Gold-water. Looking up at him from a position just beneath the speaker's stand, not twenty feet away, it was undeniable that Barry looked as handsome as a man who had just won the five-hundred-mile race in Indianapolis, had gone home to dress, and was now attending a party in his honor. He was even, protect the mark, elegant.

Then he began his speech. Today, the voice for large public gatherings had dignity. It was not a great voice, as Churchill's voice was great; there were no majesties nor storms of complexity, no war of style between man-ner and the obligation to say truth; but it was a balanced manly voice which would get votes. His speech was good in its beginning.

> *Now my fellow Americans, the tide has been running against freedom. Our people have followed false prophets. . . . We must, and we shall, set the tide running again in the cause of freedom. . . . Every breath and every heartbeat has but a single resolve, and that is freedom. . . . Tonight there is violence in our streets, corruption in our highest offices, aimlessness among our youth, anxiety among our elderly . . . despair among the many who look beyond material success toward the inner meaning of their lives.*

As the speech went on, the mind went out again on a calculation that this candidate could win. He was humbug—H. L. Hunt's idea of freedom would not be very close to the idea of freedom in the minds of the children who were for Barry, no, nor William Knowland's idea either, no, nor the Pinkertons, the hawkshaw *geist* of the F.B.I., nor the fourteenth and fifteenth floor. Goldwater was a demagogue—he permitted his sup-porters to sell a drink called Gold Water, twenty-five cents a can for orange concentrate and warm soda—let no one say it went down like piss—he was a demagogue. He was also sincere. That was the damnable diffi-culty. Half-Jew and blue-eyed—if you belonged in the breed, you knew it was manic-depressive for sure: a man who designed his own electronic flagpole to raise Old Glory at dawn, pull her down at dusk—he had an instinct for the heart of the disease—he knew how to bring balm to the mad, or at least to half the mad; Goldwater would have much to learn about Negroes. But one thing was certain: he could win. He would be breadwinner, husband and rogue to the underprivileged of the psyche, he would strike a spark in many dry souls for he offered release to frustra-tions deeper than politics. Therefore, he could beat Lyndon Johnson, he could beat him out of a variety of cause, out of natural flood or hurricane, in an epidemic of backlash, or by an epidemic of guilt—how many union workers fed to the nose with exhortations that Johnson was good for take-home pay might rise and say to themselves, "I've been happy with less." Indeed I knew Goldwater could win because something in me leaped at the thought; a part of me, a devil, wished to take that choice. For if Goldwater were President, a new opposition would form, an underground —the time for secret armies might be near again. And when in sanity I thought, Lord, give us twenty more years of Lyndon Johnson, nausea rose in some cellar of the throat, my stomach was not strong enough to bear such security; and if true for me, true for others, true perhaps for half or more of a nation's vote. Yet what of totalitarianism? What of war? But what of war? And the answer came back that one might be better a little nearer to death than the soul dying each night in the plastic en-circlements of the new architecture and the new city, yes better, if death had dimension and one could know the face of the enemy and leave a curse. What blessing to know the face of the enemy by the end of the second third of the twentieth century.

And what of the Negro if Goldwater won? What of all the small-town Southern sheriffs who wished to wipe their hands in the black man's hair? And a fury, a white fury, burst out of the mind and said, "No white sheriff is necessarily so very much worse than the worst Negro," no, the mad light of the black hoodlum might be getting equal geek to geek to the worst of the California delegation. Then came a memory of James Baldwin and Diana Sands on a show called *Night Line* where television viewers could make a telephone call to the guests. Baldwin had received a call from a liberal which went, "I'd like to help, and I'm asking you how." "Don't ask me, baby," said Baldwin, "ask yourself." "You don't understand," said the liberal, "I know something about these matters, but it's getting confusing for me. I'm asking you in all sincerity where you think my help could be best offered." "Well, baby," said Baldwin, "that's *your* problem." And Diana Sands, pinky extended in total delicate black-lady disgust, put the receiver back in the cradle. "You see," said Baldwin, talking to Les Crane, the master of ceremonies, "I remember what an old Negro woman told me once down South. She said, 'What the white man will someday learn is that there is no remission of sin.' That I never forgot," said Jimmy, "because you see it's perfectly possible the white will not be forgiven, not for a single cut or whipping or lynch mob or rape of a black woman," his voice now as soft and reminiscent of the wind as some African man of witchcraft. And I had to throttle an impulse to pick up the phone and call Baldwin, and say, "You get *this*, baby. There's a shit storm coming like nothing you ever knew. So ask yourself if what you desire is for the white to kill every black so that there be total remission of guilt in your black soul." And the mind went out still again.

The country was in disease, it was conceivably so ill that a butcher could operate with dirty hands and have magic sufficient to do less harm than the hospital with its wonder drugs and the new pestilence. (As the oil goes out, the earth turns cold, an arid used-up space, a ground for jumping off Texas to the used-up pits of the moon.) Still, you could not keep Americans from madness; our poetry was there, our symbolic logic: $AuH_2O + GOP + 64 =$ Victory! color of orange juice, Go, Go, Goldwater. Mrs. Goldwater's maiden name was Johnson, a portent of triumph to Barry? *Viva-Olé*. Eager to slay.

The country was in disease. It had been in disease for a long time. There was nothing in our growth which was organic. We had never solved our depression, we had merely gone to war, and going to war had never won it, not in our own minds, not as men, no, we had won it but as mothers, sources of supply; we did not know that we were equal to the Russians. We had won a war but we had not really won it, not in the secret of our sleep. So we had not really had a prosperity, we had had fever. *Viva-Olé*. We had grown rich because of one fact with two opposite interpretations: there had been a cold war. It was a cold war which had come because Communism was indeed a real threat to freedom, or it had come because capitalism would never survive without an economy geared to war; or was it both—who could know? who could really know? The center of our motive was the riddle wrapped in the enigma—was the country extraordinary or accursed? No, we had not even found our Communist threat. We had had a secret police organization and an invisible government large enough by now to occupy the moon, we had hunted Communists from the top of the Time-Life Building to the bottom of the Collier mine; we had not found that many, not that many, and had looked like Keystone cops. We had even had a Negro Revolution in which we did not believe. We had had it, yes we had had it, because (in the penury of our motive) we could not afford to lose votes in Africa and India, South America and Japan, Vietnam, the Philippines, name any impoverished place: we were running in a world election against the collective image of the Russ, and so we had to give the black man his civil rights or Africa was so much nearer to Marx. But there had not been much like love in the civil rights. Just Dirksen. So we were never too authentic. No.

We had had a hero. He was a young good-looking man with a beautiful wife, and he had won the biggest poker game we ever played, the only real one—we had lived for a week ready to die in a nuclear war. Whether we liked it or not. But he had won. It was our one true victory in all these years, our moment; so the young man began to inspire a subtle kind of love. His strength had proved stronger than we knew. Suddenly he was dead, and we were in grief. But then came a trial which was worse. For the assassin, or the man who had been arrested but was not the assassin— we would never know, not really—was killed before our sight. In the middle of the funeral came an explosion on the porch. Now, we were going mad. It took more to make a nation go mad than any separate man, but we had taken miles too much. Certainties had shattered. Now the voice of our national nerves (our arts, our events) was in a new state. Morality had wed itself to surrealism, there were cockroaches in all the purple transistors, we were distractable. We had an art of the absurd; we had moral surrealism. Our best art was *Dr. Strangelove* and *Naked Lunch, Catch-22; Candy* was our heroine; Jack Ruby our aging juvenile; Andy Warhol, Rembrandt; our national love was a corpse in Arlington; and heavyweight champion turned out to be Cassius Clay; New York was the World's Fair plus the Harlem bomb—it would take a genius to explain they were the same—and Jimmy Baldwin said, "That's *your* problem," on the Les Crane show at one a.m. Even the reverends were salty as the sea.

Yes, our country was fearful, half mad, inauthentic. It needed a purge. It had a liberal Establishment obeisant to committees, foundations, and science—the liberal did not understand that the center of science was as nihilistic as a psychopath's sense of God. We were a liberal Establishment, a prosperous land—we had a Roman consul among us—the much underrated and much disliked Lyndon Johnson was become a power in the land and doubtless a power upon the land; civilization had found its newest helmsman in the restraints, wisdom, and corruption of a major politician, of an organization boss to whom all Mafias, legit and illegit, all syndicates, unions, guilds, corporations and institutions, cadres of conspiracy and agents for health, Medicare, welfare, the preservation of antibiotics, and the proliferation of the Pentagon could bend their knee. The Establishment (the Democratic Establishment and the reeling columns of the Republican Establishment, falling back upon the center in the thundering confusion of Barry Goldwater's breakthrough) had a new leader, a mighty Caesar had arisen, Lyndon Johnson was his name, all hail, Caesar. Caesar gave promise to unify the land. But at what a cost. For if the ideology were liberal, the methodology was total—to this political church would come Adlai Stevenson and Frank Sinatra, the President of U.S. Steel and the President of the Steel Worker's Union, there would be photographs of Johnson forty feet high in Atlantic City— Big Bubber Lyndon—and parties in which minority groups in native costume would have their folk dance: could one see the ghost of Joe Stalin smiling on his pipe?

Yes, if we all worked to beat Barry, and got behind Lyndon and pushed, radicals and moderate Republicans, Negroes and Southern liberals, college professors and Cosa Nostra, café society and Beatniks-for-Johnson, were we all then going down a liberal superhighway into the deepest swamp of them all? For Johnson was intelligent enough to run a total land, he had vast competence, no vision, and the heart to hold huge power, he had the vanity of a Renaissance prince or a modern dictator, whereas Barry might secretly be happier with his own show daily on radio. If Goldwater were elected, he could not control the country without moving to the center; moving to the center he would lose a part of the Right, satisfy no one, and be obliged to drift still further Left, or moving back to the Right would open schisms across the land which could not be closed. Goldwater elected, America would stand revealed, its latent treacheries would pop forth like boils; Johnson elected, the drift would go on, the San Francisco Hiltons would deploy among us. Under Goldwater, the odds were certainly greater that nuclear war would come, but under Johnson we could move from the threat of total war to war itself with nothing to prevent it; the anti-Goldwater forces which might keep the country too divided to go to war would now be contained within Johnson. Goldwater promised to lead the nation across the edge of a precipice, Johnson would walk us through the woods, perchance to quicksand itself. Goldwater would open us to the perils of our madness, Johnson would continue our trip into the plague. Goldwater could accelerate the Negro Revolution to violence and disaster—Johnson might yet be obliged to betray it from within. And what a job could be done! Who in such a pass should receive the blessing of a vote—the man who inspired the deepest fear, or the man who encouraged us to live in a lard of guilt cold as the most mediocre of our satisfied needs?

Still, the more Goldwater talked, the less impressive became his voice. When he went on too long, his voice grew barren. One could never vote for him, one could not vote for a man who made a career by crying Communist—that was too easy: half the pigs, bullies, and cowards of the twentieth century had made their fortune on that fear. I had a moment of rage at the swindle. I was tired of hearing about Barry Goldwater's high fine courage. Yesterday, on the floor, talking to a young delegate from Indiana, I had said, "Did it ever occur to you that Fidel Castro might have more courage than Barry Goldwater?"

"Yes, but Castro is a criminal mentality," said the boy.

I had cut off the argument. I was too close to losing my temper. Would the best of the young in every hick town, washed by the brainwater of the high school and the Legion, come to join this conservative crusade because Goldwater made an appeal to freedom, to courage, to change? What a swindle was in the making, what an extinction of the best in Conservative thought. They were so righteous, these Republicans. Goldwater might end with more warfare, security, and statism than any Democrat had ever dared; as a conservative, he would fail altogether (doubtless!) but certain he was to do one thing: he would march into Cuba. That was too much. One could live with a country which was mad, one could even come to love her (for there was agony beneath the madness), but you could not share your life with a nation which was powerful, a coward, and righteously pleased because a foe one-hundredth our size had been destroyed. So one got up to leave at this—we would certainly be strong enough to march into Cuba.

Then Goldwater uttered his most historic words: "Extremism in the defense of liberty is no vice. . . . Moderation in the pursuit of justice is no virtue," and I sat down and took out my notebook and wrote in his words, since I did not know how famous they would become. And thought: Dad, you're too much. You're really too much. You're too hip, baby. I have spent my life seeking to get four-letter words into U.S. magazines, and now you are ready to help me.

And as I left the arena, there was a fire engine and the cry of a siren and the police with a gaunt grim look for the end of the week. There had been a fire burning, some small fire.

On the way out, outside the Cow Palace, a wet fog was drifting, and out beyond the exits, demonstrators from CORE were making a march. They had been out there every day of the convention: Monday, Tuesday, Wednesday, and Thursday now, each day had demonstrated, carrying their placards, marching in a circle two abreast, singing *We Shall Overcome*, shouting, "Goldwater Must Go," marching round and round like early Christians in the corrals waiting to be sent to the arena, while about them, five, six, ten deep, was a crowd of the Republican curious, some with troubled faces, some with faces troubled by no more than appetite, hounds staring at the meat, these white girls and Negro boys walking side by side, the girls pale, no lipstick, nunlike, disdainful, wearing denim shirts and dungarees; the Negroes tall and sometimes handsome, not without dignity, bearded almost all, the wild Negro girl in the center screaming savage taunts at the watching crowd, rude as Cassius Clay with a high-yaller mouth, and the crowd dreaming of an arena where lions could be set on these cohabiting blacks and whites, and the blacks and whites in the marching circle with their disdainful faces. Yes, kill us, says the expression on the face of the nunlike girl with no lipstick, you will kill us but you will never digest us: I despise you all. And some of the old Wasps are troubled in their Christian heart, for the girl is one of theirs, no fat plain Jewess with a poor nose is this one, she is part of the West, and so their sense of crisis opens and they know like me that America has come to a point from which she will never return. The wars are coming and the deep revolutions of the soul.

2 · OUR ARGUMENT PICTURESQUELY
CONTINUED

One extraordinary error in the last piece. It assumed Goldwater
would do well. He proved too dogged, however, to be a dema-
gogue, and his campaign was singularly inept—the real possibility of what
he had to offer America would not appear until Vietnam. In the meantime,
one had been to the Democratic Convention. It took place in Atlantic City,
which is perhaps the filthiest city in America, its window sills as greasy as its
alleys, over a stretch of sultry days which spoke of future hurricane, and
Hubert Humphrey was the symbol, appearing everywhere, smiling, smiling
with the used-up, spirit-sucked face of an actor who has been smiling for
twenty years.

The Mafia was there on the fringe, minor-league Mafia, with beehive
head-dresses on the hustlers from Newark, and small-beer hoods, and the
Democratic Establishment everywhere, blank, blank as the smile in a dull
woman's eye. And Lyndon Johnson's two pictures flank and flank to the
podium, two pictures going forty feet up. On the floor were factions. They
had little to do with one another. They were too far apart in their beginnings,
C.I.O. and Southern manse, but they were gotten together for the convention,
and between speeches there was as much enthusiasm on the floor of Con-
vention Hall as can be found in a large railroad station on a summer after-
noon.

The next piece and the piece which follows about Bobby Kennedy were
written with this drear convention in mind.

MY HOPE FOR AMERICA: A *Review of a Book by*

Lyndon B. Johnson

In 20 years it may be taken for granted that 1964 was the year in which a major party nominated a major pretender to conservatism. It was a loss, and it was conceivably a horror, for 1964 was also a year in which a real conservative still had a great deal to say to the nation. He could have demonstrated with no vast difficulty that America was under the yoke of a monstrous building boom whose architecture gave promise of being the ugliest in the history of man, that our labor unions had watered the value of labor until physical work had become as parasitical as white-collar work, and that our medicine had been overburdened beyond repair by a proliferation of wonder drugs whose side effects (with the notable exception of thalidomide) were still largely unknown—hence a delayed mass poisoning might yet be the fruit of this research. Our fruits, our vegetables, our cattle, had lost the opportunity to feed on native soil and organic food; the balance of nature, the fisheries, the economy of marine life, and the insect economies were being disrupted to the root by marinas and insecticides; our old neighborhoods and old homes were being— one could swear it—systematically demolished, and our educational system was glutted by a host of intellectual canapés: art appreciation, domestic economy, sexual efficiency, the modern novel, and so forth.

A real conservative could also have pointed out that the Civil Rights Act, no matter how imperfect and conceivably unconstitutional, was an act to be voted for, since finally there was a matter more important than the protection of property rights—it was spiritual rights: the Negro was entitled to his spiritual rights even if there were hard niggling costs to the rights of the Constitution. Finally, a great conservative could have noted that the health of Communism was its misery, that like all top-heavy structures its greatest danger was in its growth. Prosperity was Communism's poison, but attack from capitalism was its tranfusion of blood. So the time was open for a great debate. Should we go back to isolationism? Did we not already possess enough nuclear Doomsdays to protect ourselves, was it not perhaps time to recognize that the industrialization of the backward nations was a thankless venture which wise men would avoid? Might it not be best to let the Communists have Asia and Africa after all? Would they not strangle on the meal? Yes, America was perhaps ready to listen to the sophistications of a conservative, if such a man was there to appear in 1964.

But what a conservative came down the pike! Marooned in a hopeless traffic with hate groups and bigots, Southern bullies and oil pirates, offering a program of sinister hints that a Federal police force would protect the young ladies of our land on their walk through our streets at night; reasoning with all the homely assurance of a filthy sock that he would protect the past by destroying the present (as in those remarks about scorching the foliage in Vietnam in order to keep the guerrillas from concealing themselves); wasting the substance of his campaign in pointless technical arguments with the Pentagon; and boring reconciliations and new feuds with the stricken Moderates of his party—the alleged conservative candidate was perhaps no more than a demagogue of the Right with a manly Christian air, a sweet voice, eyeglasses, and total innocence of a sense of contradiction, a spirit so naturally conservative that on the grounds of his home he raised the American flag with an electronic flagpole. Up at dawn, down at dusk, commanded the photoelectric cells in the mast. Well, one couldn't vote for such a man. He pressed the wrong buttons.

The mandate would go therefore to Lyndon Johnson. So most of America had seemed to decide by the eve of election. But it was nonetheless a vote heavy with gloom, and stricken with a sense of possible bad consequence, for there was much about Johnson which appealed not at all, and some of the evidence was intimate. He had written a book. That is intimate evidence. *My Hope for America,* he had called it. Now, of course, a book written by a high official must not be judged by average standards, or one would be forced to say, for example, that Jack Kennedy was not a very good writer and that Bobby Kennedy, at last reading, wrote a dead stick's prose—his style almost as bad as J. Edgar Hoover's. But even at its worst, the prose style of Jack Kennedy (and his ghost writers) is to the prose style of L.B.J. (and *his* ghost writers) as de Tocqueville is to Ayn Rand. It is even not impossible that *My Hope for America* is the worst book ever written by any political leader anywhere.

The private personality of L.B.J., as reported by the authority of the best gossip, is different from his public presence. He is, one is told, not too unlike Broderick Crawford in *All the King's Men,* roaring, smarting, bellowing, stabbing fingers on advisers' chests, hugging his daughters, enjoying his food, mean and unforgiving, vindictive, generous, ebullient, vain, suddenly depressed, then roguish, then overbearing, suddenly modest again only to bellow once more. It is somewhat like the description of an early Renaissance prince, and if one looks hard at the photograph of the President on the cover of *My Hope for America,* a leader of *condottieri* stands forth—hard, greedy, exceptionally intelligent eyes whose cynicism is spiked by a fierce pride, big fleshy inquisitive (and acquisitive) nose, thin curved mouth (a boss mouth) and a slab of round hard jaw, deep dimple on the upper lip, deep dimple on the chin. It is not a bad face altogether, it is sufficiently worldly to inspire a kind of confidence that while no age of high ideals is close at hand, yet no martyrs are to be tortured, for there is small profit in that.

It is a face and a concealed personality which could even, considering the Republican alternative, inspire a touch of happiness, if it were not for the public image—that boundless sea of overweening piety which collects here in this slim volume, this cove of Presidential prose whose waters are so brackish that a spoonful is enough to sicken the mind for hours. *My Hope for America* is an abominable, damnable book, and what makes it doubly awful is that nearly all of its ideas are blessed. It is in fact difficult to disagree with almost any one of them.

Who can argue on the side of poverty, or against justice, or against the idea of a Great Society? Let Barry Goldwater argue, not I. No, the ideals in this book are double-barreled, double-ringed, a double end of the cornucopia. More for the poor, more for the rich; more for peace, more for war; dedicatedly opposed to Communism, cautiously conciliatory; out to raise the income of poor nations, out to squash the economy of Cuba; all out for the Negro, all violence to be checked in city streets; all for the Democratic party, all for a party which includes Democrats *and* Republicans. There is even, and it is the achievement of this book, a curious sense of happiness running through its paragraphs. It is that happiness which is found at the end of the vision. It is as if the dream of Rousseau and Condorcet and Bakunin and Herzen and Marx and Lenin and Trotsky and John Dewey and the Webbs and Keynes and Roosevelt, Dreiser, and Darrow—name any of a hundred, any of that long stream of political engineers who dreamed of changing a material world by material means to make all men free and equal—had come down at the end to Little Ol' Lyndon, and hot damn, he had said, discovering Progressive religion in 1964, that's the ticket, that's the liver-eating ticket! And he was off to bring it off. And happy as a clam. That's the happiness which comes off this book. It is like a dream of heaven in a terminal ward.

For beneath this odd disembodied happiness is a prose more sinister than the most pious of Lyndon Johnson's misrepresentations of his own personality; it is a prose which stirs half-heard cries of the death by suffocation of Western Civilization, it is a prose almost so bad and so deadening as the Georgian catechisms Josef Stalin used to hammer out: "Why is the Communist Party the party of the Soviet people? The Communist Party is the party of the Soviet people because . . ." It was enough at the time, reading Stalin, to keep from becoming a Communist.

Now, reading Lyndon!—the horror is that one must still vote for him. But what a book is *My Hope for America*.

Examine it: 127 pages, a little more than 200 words to a page, most of the pages half pages or blank pages so that in bulk there are 17,000 words collected in 13 short chapters; they have titles like this—*President of All the People, A President's Faith and Vision, Building the Atlantic Partnership, This Developing World, Creative Federalism*. Each page of each chapter is divided into paragraphs. Page 8 has 12 paragraphs; the average page has four or five with a generous space between each paragraph. This is not because the remarks have the resonant echo of Pascal's *Pensées*, rather— one idea does not lead to another. So the space must be there. It is useful for burying whichever infinitesimal part of the brain died in the gas of the preceding phrase.

Yet every altruistic idea and every well-tuned moderation which Lyndon Johnson's political experience has put together over the years is somehow worked into the organum of his credo. It is impossible to disagree with a single of its humanistic desires ("We know that we can learn from the culture, the arts, and the traditions of other countries"); it is equally impossible to feel the least pleasure at the thought these goods may yet come to be—just so bad and disheartening is the style of this book:

> *Reality rarely matches dream. But only dreams give nobility to purpose. This is the star I hope to follow—which I know most of you have seen, and which I first glimpsed many years ago in the Texas night.*

> *When the helpless call for help—the hearing must hear, the seeing must see, and the able must act.*

> *It is an America where every man has an equal chance for the well-being that is essential to the enjoyment of the freedom that we brag about.*

> *The Gulf of Tonkin may be distant Asian waters, but none can be detached about what happened there.*

High-school students will be writing essays on these paragraphs. One's stomach turns over. It is certain that if Barry Goldwater had written the same book, everyone would be agreed his style was a menace. Still, what is quoted up to here is still English, English more or less. It is in the depth of the real prose articulated by Johnson and his corps of ghost writers that the heart of the darkness resides. For Johnson is not a writer and has no wish to be. He is a communications engineer. He uses words in interlocking aggregates which fence in thoughts like cattle. At bottom, the style consists of nothing but connectives and aggregate words—that is, political phrases five words long which are one aggregate word and so should be hyphenated. Example:

> *And it is one-of-the-great-tasks-of-Presidential-leadership to make our people aware that they share-a-fundamental-unity-of-interest-and-purpose-and-belief.*

The essence of totalitarian prose is that it does not define, it does not deliver. It oppresses. It obstructs from above. It is profoundly contemptuous of the minds who will receive the message. So it does its best to dull this consciousness with sentences which are nothing but bricked-in power structures. Or alternately a totalitarian prose slobbers upon an audience a sentimentality so debauched that admiration for shamelessness is inspired. But then, sentimentality is the emotional promiscuity of those who have no sentiment:

> *When I was a child, one of my first memories was hearing the powder go off on an anvil on Armistice Day. I remember the terror that flowed from the* Lusitania. *I remember seeing boys come marching home, and the welcome we gave them at our little schoolhouse. When Pearl Harbor was attacked* . . .

There is one expanding horror in American life. It is that our long odyssey toward liberty, democracy and freedom-for-all may be achieved in such a way that utopia remains forever closed, and we live in freedom and hell, debased of style, not individual from one another, void of courage, our fear rationalized away. We will all have enough money and we will all have a vote. The money will buy appliances made of plastic, and the money will buy books just as bad as *My Hope for America* or *The Conscience of a Conservative*.

The dream of democracy—that the average man possesses riches within himself worthy of a lord—will evolve into some anomalous electronic shape of human, half genius, half lout, and the liberation of existence will not take place. Only the buildings will continue to be built—bigger housing for all, slum clearance, urban renewal, Edward Durrell Stone, until we will look as if indeed we lost a war, as if we had been bombed to the ground, and built ourselves up again just so quickly and cheaply as the barracks could be slapped together.

"In the next forty years," writes Johnson, "we must rebuild the entire urban United States." But who will do it? Whose vision will prevail? Which head of horror may condemn generations not yet born to look at faceless buildings and roofless roofs, the totalitarianism stealing in from without, from the formless forms and imprisoned air of a new society which had lost the clue that a democracy could become equable only if it became great, that finally the world would continue to exist only by an act of courage and a search for style. Democracy flowers with style; without it, there is a rot of wet weeds. Which is why we love the memory so of F.D.R. and J.F.K. For they offered high style to the poor. And that is worth more than a housing project. That is the war against poverty.

Still, Lyndon Johnson must be given a vote. Because *My Hope for America* contains one good sentence, one more than Barry Goldwater could claim. This sentence reads: ". . . the wall between rich and poor is a wall of glass through which all can see." It inspires a corollary which is almost as good—the space between hypocrisy and honest manner may not forever insulate the powerful from the poor.

God's got the liver
in him
said Texas
Kill all taxes
Piss
clear water
on the clay
Naught but mud
at break of day
in Texas,
our Texas.

EROSIONS

      Money
        is a
        river
         flowing
         downhill
           over
           hills
            of
            character
               in the
                 rich

Mafia
    ran all
    the joints
until the people
    looked like spaghetti
    and only the witches
    could say
      pasta fazool

3 · THE ARGUMENT MOST SOBERLY

CONTINUED

The next two pieces are written by an occasional voter. If he
stood in line on Election Day for Henry Wallace in 1948, and
John F. Kennedy in 1960, he did not vote at all in the years between. The
act of giving assent to people whose politics were essentially similar seemed
to him part of a tremendous swindle.

Perhaps it was. One reason the plague may have set its roots so deep
was that all extremes in American politics decamped or absconded
after the Second World War. The liberal Left fell into the Center with a
whimper, the Right discovered itself to be respectable so long as it left
anti-Semitism and/or rabid Jim Crow to its own fringe and contented itself
with hunting Communists in exchange for accepting the foreign policy of
the Center. In truth, there seemed little to vote about between 1948 and
1960. Adlai Stevenson may have been somewhat more agreeable than
Dwight D. Eisenhower, but in those days I had a formula—it is still, I
think, accurate—that the Republicans plotted war, but the Democrats were
the only ones who could go to war; if it was the Democrats who looked
generally to make peace, it was, in fact, the Republicans who were able to
arrange the peace. The cause was not mysterious. The Republicans put
forth war policies for their millions of patriots which only the Democrats
could carry out, since only the Democrats could bring the liberals and the
labor unions along. On the other hand, one had to be Republican to make
peace without being seriously accused of Communist sympathy. Thus,
Truman undertook the Korean War, and Eisenhower ended it.

The other part of the formula read: do not, however, vote for a man or
a party who is uncongenial, even if an objective superiority is obvious—as,
for example, the Republicans' superior ability to make peace. There was
obviously an ambiguity present in the hard Marxist front of one's ideas,
some notion that the personality of the candidate was not separate from
the history he would make. That soft idea arrived at its climax with Ken-
nedy. For it was obvious something odd had occurred in American politics:
for once, the image and the politics diverged critically. Jack Kennedy was
a moderate liberal in program but a romantic figure in image—so all variety

of ferment grew out of his image. Jack Kennedy may not have been as skillful a politician as Lyndon Johnson, but he had one hundred times as much effect on the styles and modes of American life, on the desires of Americans, on what they finally demanded from life; so Jack Kennedy had a revolutionary effect on American life. A new political principle was at loose—where a difference in issues was not simple to measure, then the candidate whose personality was least predictable and platitudinous, or ideally most brilliant, complex and intriguing, was the man who was going to bring the most political good to the voting populace, because he was going to enrich the emotional complexity of their lives. It was a way of saying that in a time of no real political differences, a real contrast of personality was going to make a political difference.

That this new principle is still but one principle among others may be demonstrated by the next two pieces. The first, about the senatorial campaign between Bobby Kennedy and Kenneth Keating, is a pure application of the principle; but the second, about the New York Mayoralty campaign, engages the idea in more complex fashion. John Lindsay was running against Abe Beame—it was obviously going to be more interesting to live with Lindsay every day than Beame—about equal to the difference between Kennedy and Johnson. But William F. Buckley was also in the race, and it is possible no one in political life had a personality so glittering as Buckley's. If he had been elected, New York would have had a robber bridegroom for mayor.

But there was no question of voting for him, not even temptation. For his local politics were absurd—he was not serious about the city, or at least there was no suggestion for a moment that he understood New York or cared to—he was more eager to go to war with China. So politics came before image. And that left one with the job of writing about John Lindsay, a difficult matter, for it is hard to convince New Yorkers to vote for a man you admire—it is necessary to get into the bedrock of the admiration, and this, here, in this case, meant that you had to write about New York and what it might be like to campaign for six months in its junkyards and canyons.

A VOTE FOR BOBBY K.

When there first began to be talk, back last winter, of Bobby Kennedy going in against Kenneth Keating, I had the reaction of a prize-fight manager who has seen better days: Put down no bets, they're a couple of bums. Keating never did a thing to me. He had a face like the plastic dough children play with. Smells like a bottle of moistened saccharine, sticks to the fingers, fails to hold its shape. I disliked the rhetoric with which he strutted into discussions of Cuba; the righteousness was enough to make you throw up. For righteous politicians, like bullies, have their greatest test of character when they've got you on the ground—can they keep from kicking you in the ear? At his best, Keating seemed a passable if unctuous assistant to a hard worker like Javits—at his worst he was errand boy for Rockefeller plus every special interest there to be discovered. So Keating lit the kind of fire in my political heart which a turkey gobbler would light on the table if you developed the suspicion he was still alive. If one had to vote for Keating, there was no vote. The choice was left with Bobby. Bobby!—whom everybody I know called Raul Castro. Bobby!—the Irish equivalent of Roy Cohn on the good old McCarthy team; Bobby!—with the face of a Widmark gunsel, that prep-school arrogance which makes good manual laborers think of smashing a fist through a wall; Bobby! who wrote books called *The Enemy Within*, about Come-You-Nism and crooked unions, Bobby who wrote in a style so bad that (to repeat from something just written) he had a dead stick's prose; Bobby, who had always had it break the right way for him; Bobby, who played the game down the center, so had no sense at all of how it felt to be outside, try to get in. Who could vote for Bobby?

But we've had a couple of months of the campaign, and a liberal hogshead of much ado about almost no difference. Since each of the candidates was considerably farther to the right even a few years ago, their protestations of liberalism now, about which Hentoff, I. F. Stone, and Arthur Schlesinger have given us copious documentation back and forth, are not finally convincing, or even important to the vote. If Keating and Kennedy were both cons up before a parole board and were debating who had prayed his way back closer to Jesus, and each was buttressed in his arguments by impossible-to-follow allegations, and by disputes over microscopic facts delivered by lawyers altogether skillful at working the grit from a detail, one would have a natural suspicion that when a con claims he is close to Jesus it is to get parole—

which con is actually the closest would have little to do with allegations, facts, or details. Or, in this case, issues. It would take a constitutional lawyer to decide on the issues whether Keating or Kennedy is now more liberal. When it comes to being more liberal in this hour, in this election, you could not get a short curled hair between them. They're so liberal you don't have to vote, not for liberalism—you got a liberal either way. Of course, if the country turns right, you got a conservative either way. Have you? Well, you know you have with Ken Keating. He doesn't have a face like plastic dough for nothing. But we are with Bobby. Here the difference begins to appear. I don't know. I wouldn't pretend to say Bobby Kennedy is not capable of marching at the front of a Right Wing movement. But the Right is not likely to suffer from a lack of leaders. Goldwater may be no more than the cork out of the bottle. The appeal of the Right, since it is emotional, will attract demagogues. I think Bobby Kennedy may be the only liberal about, early or late, who could be a popular general in a defense against the future powers of the Right Wing. For there's no one else around. The Democratic Party is bankrupt, bankrupt of charisma; the Right Wing has just begun. Anyone who was at the Democratic Convention in Atlantic City must confess—if they can afford to—that the mood was equal to a yellow jaundice ward on the banks of a swamp.

By this logic, it comes to this: we are in the absence of real and immediate political issues. So we must vote for one candidate because he is a neutron, or must vote for the other because he is an active principle who will grow and change and become—odds are—a powerful leader of the Left or the Right. Posed that way, I take the second alternative. I vote for the active principle. To vote for a man who is neuter is to vote for the plague. I would rather vote for a man on the assumption he is a hero and have him turn into a monster than vote for a man who can never be a hero. For follow it through: a hero, even a failed-hero, or a hero-as-monster, is more likely to create other heroes, by his example or by opposition to him, than a man who gains power and has never been anything at all. A forceful political structure with a great number of particular heroes is a way to describe the Renaissance; a powerful political structure governed by faceless men is a way to describe the Mafia. The vote goes then to Bobby Kennedy. He has finally a face.

Say one thing more. Few vote by logic alone. Sentiment enters. I have affection for Bobby Kennedy. I think something came into him with the death of his brother. I think Bobby Kennedy has come a pilgrim's distance from that punk who used to play Junior D. A. for Joe McCarthy and grabbed headlines by riding Jimmy Hoffa's back. Something compassionate, something witty, has come into the face. Something of sinew.

So I think. I could be wrong, but I'd rather go this way and be wrong, than vote the other way trying to stop a possibility with a nonentity. When the issues at stake are small, it is natural to vote for the man who has the more arresting personality, as once before, when issues were small, America elected Jack Kennedy. Of course, if you remember, Jack Kennedy was not then enormously popular in New York. He had a dubious liberal record and seemed unpredictable. New York voted for him but did not like him. In New York we prefer to vote to stop things. So New Yorkers know nonentity. They know durance sufficiently vile to have endured for twelve years a nonentity for Mayor and a nonentity, these last six years, for Senator. My vote goes therefore to establishing a new face in the Senate. Is that not half the welfare of a liberal society —to have something new to discuss at the dinner table? Consider: six more years of Ken Keating with Brussels sprouts or six with Bobby K. and some red snapper.

DIAMONDS

They are
  not
  poetry
they
  never
  are
  depressing

I think
  they are
  bad
  for
  the weak,
  the spoiled,
    the rich

They are
  good
  for rocks
    who
    are
  waiting
  for a
    gleam
    to open
  their crack

LINDSAY AND THE CITY

I was talking to a woman at a party the other night, and she said Abe
Beame was an old machine politician and so she was going to vote for
him because he would know how to run the machine. And I said New
York is not a machine but a malignancy.

Well, I repeat the story not only to take a bow for having the last word
with a lady, but because I've brooded on the remark and think it has
something to do with why John Lindsay may not be our next Mayor. He
has been running day in, day out, about as hard as a man can run these
last six months and yet there seems a quicksand beneath the effort—as
votes are won, others slip away—I know whenever I say I am going to
vote for him, I hear the same bad news: he has been a disappointment,
say some, his personality has failed to come alive, so has his campaign.
The campaign and the man are long and dull, I am told, and ill-tempered;
there have been no real issues, or at least no ability to find and dramatize
the real issues, Lindsay has somehow allowed a fine beginning to dissi-
pate itself. And I think then of that campaign he has run and the extraor-
dinary difficulty of it, for Lindsay has been running against the malig-
nancy and how do you dramatize that? You cannot dramatize a condition
which is concealed by the organism itself because it is too terrifying to
contemplate: the separate organs accommodate one another no longer
but must grow each of them at their own best speed. Cooperation impos-
sible, only separate growth remains. That is malignancy.

New York is ill beyond belief. There are forces in the city, Left, Right
and Center, which are out of control. They cannot collaborate with other
forces, they cannot, in fact, *exist* with other forces—their only logic is to
grow by themselves. There is a Right Wing in New York whose only
ultimate satisfaction will come from deporting every Negro to Jersey
unless he has been taught to say Yessir all over again; there is a militant
black Left who swear Whitey must eat the turd before peace is here, and
there is the Mob and the machine in the center, all the highways and
housing projects gutting the city of its last purchase on beauty in order to
manufacture new money for themselves. The action in the center is the
worst of all for it is mined into the vaults of all the banks in town and all
the concrete blocks and the cement mixers, into the cops (Bill Buckley's
noble hard-working much-abused cops) and it is the secret sweat in the
pores of every bureaucrat in this thicket-ridden legalistically-swindled city,
this jungle of ordinances and metastatic deals which has polluted the air,

leaked away the water, defaced the architecture, and made our subways as famous in Asia as the Georgia chain gangs.

There is something else to make it worse. For each malignancy begins with an intolerable and just need which cannot be satisfied and cannot be forgotten. The paranoia of the Right develops because they want—or believe they want—quiet houses on quiet streets, and healthy food, and decent air, and a life lived by principle; since everything in the scheme of things works to deny them, so everything in the scheme of things seems to point to a conspiracy which springs violence loose at random, and puts poisons in food, and looks to rebuild and so destroy old neighborhoods, and shatters every principle into chaos and active contradiction. Whereas the need of the Center is for power, but its power came originally out of loyalties. Every mob guy and machine politician was gutting the city with one hand and feeding a lot of particular families with the other. So there are still memories of favors and good nights of drinking in bars and the old days in the old neighborhood and legends of men who were real men. The machine is a method which used to be able to work, for it was the closest thing to a culture for the poor, and the poor still need it, they need a personal touch in the big anonymous void of the city, a sense of myth and connection, a league of the hot guys and the hard guys, a hope to satisfy some greed. Many of the poor need the machine with a passion, for if they lose it, they are lost in the city, they are adrift in the void; so they have to keep coming out for the machine. But the machine can't take care of them properly any more, for the machine knows it has nothing to offer to the Left and to the Right but placation, and that is equal to just letting the malignancies grow—so the machine sees that the city is not going to go on forever. It starts to grow too, it accelerates the rate at which it devours, it starts to bulldoze wholesale and to squeeze money from the juice of concrete, and from union jurisdictions and courts and clubs and covenants and realtors on the fix until the entire city gives promise it soon will look like a convention of prisons.

And on the Left, in that Harlem where the blood of eight generations has come to a boil, there are men who live their life for a cause—they are trying to save their people from going mad, and they have a sense at times that the pursuit of their life is in itself mad, for eight generations boil in the blood, and the blood goes over, it is kept on the boil by events which take place eight hundred miles and a thousand south of here, and so more and more of the kids in Harlem want not justice but revenge and threaten to become implacable and grow not on liberty but power and so must demand more and more and more before they have yet anything at all.

That is another aspect of the horror—violence, sickness, greed and rage,

Right, Center and Left, and all of it with origins in passion and loyalty, in idealism, principle, all the ingredients for building the new world and the great city.

But of course there is no great city. Just the malignancy and Lindsay in a situation where he must get his money from the Republican machine and his votes from the Right and the Left. On the Right is Bill Buckley, all bless, and on the Left is Adam Clayton Powell, an undisputed genius. Any man who can still run Harlem in any way at all is an undisputed genius, but it is part of Powell's peculiarly private luck to tie himself up always with the worst candidate in town, now known lately as Honest Abe D. (D. for Dog–I'm no Dog) Beame.

That's a pretty combination for any candidate. And Buckley accuses Lindsay of being in league with Adam Clayton Powell, in a debate, no-where else, and Lindsay answers, Why, no, Mr. Powell has given his support to Mr. Beame, and Buckley is silent on that. Bill is not one of the major debaters in America for nothing–a week later he is making the same accusation and they are cheering his words in Queens. Debating, you see, is a highly difficult but very low art since it depends upon being scru-pulously dishonest. You fix facts with fancy and throw the suspicion of fancy on the other man's facts. Nobody in America is better at this than William B., just as no one I suspect is more majestically unsuited for here becoming Mayor since it is possible Old Bill has never been in a subway in his life. To be fair it must also be said that no one could have been more majestically suited for spoiling Lindsay's campaign. Buckey's per-sonality is the highest Camp we are ever going to find in a Mayoralty. No other actor on earth can project simultaneous hints that he is in the act of playing Commodore of the Yacht Club, Joseph Goebbels, Robert Mitchum, Maverick, Savonarola, the nice prep-school kid next door, and the snows of yesteryear. If he didn't talk about politics–if he was just the most Camp gun ever to walk into Gunsmoke I'd give up Saturday nights to watch him. But he does talk about politics time to time, and his pro-gram for New York is to drop an atom bomb posthaste on the atom bomb of the Chinese.

A man like that cannot be kept from getting an enormous minority vote. The aged put rouge on their cheeks, and in a dying city, theatre is life, Camp is all. Camp is going to defeat John Lindsay, for Camp is the iridescence of the malignant and cancer cells are bizarre but beautiful under a microscope–they look like a shopping center in the night. Of course Buckley's votes will not come from people who even know the word "Camp," no, his sort of votes come from the kind of girls who want to work at Bell Telephone; but if Lindsay loses, Camp will still have defeated him—a secret admiration for Buckley's high Camp has been cutting into the righteous wrath of all us Wagner-aged citizens—we are finally apathetic about the great dump in which we live, we laugh at Buckley, we laugh with him, we say let the city burn, let it burn, and Lindsay goes wrong, a little solemn, a little empty, too earnest much.

Well, fellow voters, call on the Lord, Jack Kennedy was that way in '60, swear it. Tall, slightly blank, slightly dull as a speaker, full of facts, no fire, and a bemused slightly out-of-it look. Which comes I think from the schizophrenic recognition that one is a man trying to contend with the relations between miracles (for how else can politics appear at the top?) and that the means of acquiring the power to go out and save the world (for that is the secret glory and ambition of a major politician) can be obtained only by talking about all the things which have nothing to do with miracles, or society, or even with people, but are instead statistics and programs and situation papers and debater's tricks and well-timed name-calling and allegations and shaking hands so slimy a clam would throw up, and worst of all saying the same thing day in, day out, week, week, month after month until your soul begins to die, because repetition, kids, kills the soul, and even as it is dying and the manner gets empty and the rhetoric more flat, one is grappling out there in those great celestial regions at the empty back of the brain, wrestling with the wonder of how do you create a miracle, how do you give Harlem what it begins to need, and keep your own Republicans from going mad, and get the money to do it, and clean the slime and the concrete, and get the water back and get the fire out of the air and the fumes and clear out the sense of the city dying in its own corruption like a monster eating himself to death in a dungeon, and with it all, being out every day, out to capture the same votes and having to make the same speeches.

The last time I saw Lindsay was in June. He was in great form, his color was great, vitality came off him—huge enthusiasm. He looked like a man of twenty-eight. He won every vote in the house. That was in June. Now he's empty, people say. He looks much older in photographs. I do not wonder. The wonder is that he is not half dead.

But just as he was leaving that afternoon in June, he said with a big grin like a sailor in a boxing ring, "Mailer, you know you have to be a little insane to run for Mayor of this town." Yes, you do, I think, and yes John Lindsay may be a little insane to have tried, but by God I write this to say I hope he wins, John Lindsay, because I think he's okay, in fact I think he's a great guy, and it would be a miracle if this town had a man for mayor who was okay. Ill-tempered the campaign may have been, empty and dull to some, and with no real issue but malignancy, but cheers to you, John Lindsay, and honors to your run.

LICENSES

We live in a world filled with all the wonderful things

    which did not happen
    all the passion which was never born
    because the sperm sailed into the sheet
    and left a quiver of empty arrows

    (did your little womb go pity pat pat
    when midnight passed and I wasn't there?)

We walk about in cities filled with second choice
you and me planned by calculation of the budget

    those neon signs cold compromise
    to cheat the savage dream of fire
    you do not control the flame say the mediocre
    until you put it under glass

    (all those lovely modern shacks
    fifty stories steel and mass
    second choice in a new idea)

It is better far, you hear, when prisons look like public schools
and airports shake their hips in plastic luxury
like hotels and housing projects rich and poor all alike

all of them clean in mind like hospitals
what a world of second choice besets the eye
no wonder I am going blind says the Lord
and oh that static in my ear

(must everyone speak in an accent
borrowed from another and all
food die a second death?—freeze my juices
seal my flesh—and all materials?)

Devil torture me no longer I confess
cries the molecule joining the giant
carbon chain where one does not choose
one's qualities but bows one's head to trend

that oscillation in the vacuum tube
second choice of the wind when
the spirits of the dead failed, you
hear, to make us feel their hurt

4 · OUR ARGUMENT IS ABRUPTLY

ADVANCED

Lyndon Johnson is a triumph of spirit, wholly scientific. He carries polls on his hip, takes a look at society with the worries of a big-time contractor, constructs jobs, and with his pal McNamara is off to war as a statistician. He can tell you that yesterday we knocked off ninety-four gooks. Science is, of course, the only true religion Americans still have left: like all religions it is worshiped abjectly by those who know it least. Beautiful women, literary people, social planners, editorial writers, presidents, politicians, and a sprinkling of illiterates do not know that science is most exact in those regions where it has progressed into the secrets of the universe about as far as the precision and exactitude of English spelling has advanced us into the secret lore of meaning. Which is to say: a distance. But not a great distance. Where science is exact, it is vastly insignificant; where it is significant, it is open-ended, not certain, prey to reasoning by analogy, torn by debate, sustained by darkest mystery, and when all is said about as scientific as literary criticism. Be it understood between us that science possesses no secure idea of what is electricity, time, space, and the structure of the atom. Yet science has come together with love-of-America to form the latest amalgam in the guaranteed most awful religion of them all: love-of-America plugged in to some intellectual supermachine.

For one hundred years, love-of-America (as a secret primitive religion—a shy girl whose still waters run damnably Fatherland deep) has been running around with one stout dull thunder or another. The beaux have names like capitalism, conformity, medicine, corporate spirit, mass communication, Red-hunting or science. Science is the latest and comes in as the word made flesh, as the Sacred Name which punishes and preserves all us people, the brave lad who lifts rockets off their base, and even tomorrow will take out your old used liver and replace it with a new eight-year-old's liver. The new liver is available because the boy died of some mysterious new disease they can name but cannot cure. However, the research assistants who researched this operation have declared authoritatively that this specific mysterious disease does not affect the liver. Of course these are the research assistants who did the work on possible side effects of thalidomide before there were side effects and declared the drug harmless. Of course research assistants are like Hollywood producers. The more failures, the more jobs. But on to Vietnam.

Two pieces follow about this most scientific war. The first was a speech written for Vietnam Day, May 25, 1965, in Berkeley, California, and printed later in The Realist *(with a prefatory note to explain that four or five paragraphs in the speech had been taken, in slightly altered form, from the book review of* My Hope *for America, and from the piece on the Republican Convention of 1964). The second article on Vietnam is a reply to a symposium in* Partisan Review *and is furnished with the editor's statement from which it departed.*

Both pieces say the same thing, yet emphases are different, tone is very different, and the second goes further than the first. Its last sentence is not uncertain to damage a general welcome for this book.

A SPEECH AT BERKELEY ON VIETNAM DAY

Years ago in Austin, Texas, not far from the L.B.J. Ranch, even less far from the radio station owned by Lady Bird Johnson, at a time when our President was still Vice-President, I read a few lines I had written about Lyndon Johnson to an audience at the University of Texas:

> *Johnson had compromised too many contradictions, and now the contradictions were in his face: when he smiled, the corners of his mouth squeezed gloom; when he was pious, his eyes twinkled irony; when he spoke in a righteous tone, he looked corrupt; when he jested, the ham in his jowls looked to quiver. He was not convincing.*

That Texas audience laughed as if I were William Faulkner talking about the Snopes family.

Years later, getting ready to write about Johnson again, I endeavored to come closer:

> *The private personality of L.B.J., as reported by the authority of the best gossip, is different from his public presence. In private, one is told,*

he is not too unlike Broderick Crawford in All the King's Men, *roaring, smarting, bellowing, stabbing fingers on advisers' chests, hugging his daughters, enjoying his food, belching, burping, mean and unforgiving, vindictive, generous, ebullient, vain, suddenly depressed, then roguish, then overbearing, suddenly modest again only to bellow and fart once more.*

I was trying to convince myself to vote for him. I had already decided Goldwater had all the homely assurance of a filthy sock. My vote nonetheless was heavy with gloom, stricken with a sense of bad consequence. There was much about Johnson which appealed not at all, and some of the evidence was intimate.

He had written a book. *My Hope for America,* he called it. Now, a book written by a high official must not be judged by average standards or one would be forced to say, for example, that Jack Kennedy was not a very good writer and Bobby Kennedy, at last reading, wrote a dead stick's prose. But even at its worst, the prose style of Jack Kennedy (and his ghost writers) is to the prose style of L.B.J. (and *his* ghost writers) as de Tocqueville is to Ayn Rand. Reviewing Johnson's book for the *Herald Tribune,* I said:

> *Is is even not impossible that* My Hope *for* America *is the worst book ever written by any political leader anywhere . . . a boundless sea of overweening piety . . . an abominable damnable book . . . a prose which stirs half-heard cries of death by suffocation.*

I went on to say that Johnson was not a writer but a communications engineer.

> *The essence of totalitarian prose is that it does not define, it does not deliver. It oppresses. It obstructs from above. It is profoundly contemptuous of the minds who will receive the message. So it does its best to dull this consciousness with sentences which are nothing but bricked-in power structures.*

It was obvious *My Hope for America* was part of the expanding horror of American life. It would be used to brain-wash high-school kids. Like all horror, it stayed in the memory. For it offered a surrealistic clue to Lyndon Johnson's real secret vision of a Great Society: jobs for all, everybody with an interesting job, the farmers taken care of—their subsidy checks written by computers—every industrial worker with his own psychoanalyst, every student who was able to pass the aptitude tests able to stay in school forever, Medicare, antibiotics in every glass of drinking water, tranquilizers added to the television dinners, birth-control pills in the booze.

The President was willing to go even further. One could conceive of him making a speech: "Let us reason together. Freedom is indivisible. Marijuana might be just such a freedom. But there are those who argue with justice that marijuana is passed from mouth to mouth. That is, by common consent, unsanitary. Therefore I propose Congress draw up a law requiring marijuana to be marketed solely in suppositories."

There would be a recreation program for all American children—mass calisthenics in air-conditioned stadiums with a glassed-over dome. The majors would have eighty-two baseball teams in each league and the additional teams would take their names from the new housing complexes built around shopping centers—the teams would be called Bypass 60, Ramp 6, Belt 1, Lower Alternate Freeway 4, the Coral Gate Arms.

The colleges would look like factories, the housing projects would keep looking like prisons, the corporation office buildings would be indistinguishable from the colleges, and not even an airline hostess would know where the airport ended and the motel bedroom began.

The sexual revolution would push on. Ladies' magazines would wonder whether the orgy had become a vital solution to suburban life. If there would be statisticians to point out that the modern orgy grouping showed an average of eight people and one erection, still State Department intellectuals could point out on their orientation tours through the universities of America that the Sexual Revolution was just begun, and ways would be found to increase vitality.

Camp would have moved on to the Happy Hunting Ground of old art movement. A new art movement would be in. It would be called Shit. Its test would be: is this object, happening, work, event or production more resonant than it was yesterday? Movies about the Strategic Air Command with Jimmy Stewart, Hubert Humphrey speeches, old Lawrence Welk records, news photographs of Mayor Wagner, Senate testimony by Robert McNamara, interviews with J. Edgar Hoover—these would be the artifacts of the new art movement—Camp was out and Shit was in.

Well, the President contemplating this perspective could not be altogether happy. "The Great Society is a dud," was his lament. "I don't even have an issue with which to slow down the Nigras and their Rights."

The President believed very much in image. He believed the history which made the headlines each day was more real to the people than the events themselves. It was not the Negro movement that possessed the real importance, it was the Movement's ability to get space in the papers. That ability was equaled only by the President's ability to attach himself to the image of civil rights. But his ability to control the image, even put it down when necessary, was hampered by one fact. In the Great Society there was no movement, program, plan or ideal which was even remotely as dramatic as the Civil-Rights movement. So the Civil-Rights movement was going to crowd everything else out of the newspapers. There was going to be no way to control the Negro Movement, and no way to convince the Negro Movement that their victory was due to his particular attentions. You can never convince a movement of your power unless you can send them back after you have called them forth. So the President needed another issue. Then it came to the President.

Hot damn. Vietnam.

Vietnam, that little old country which had been under his nose all these years. Things were getting too quiet in Vietnam. If there was one thing hotter than Harlem in the summer, it was air raids on rice paddies and napalm on red gooks. Now he had a game. When the war got too good, and everybody was giving too much space to that, he could always tell the Nigras it was good time to be marching on the White House; when they got a little too serious he could bring back Vietnam. He could even make all those Barry Goldwater rednecks and state troopers happy—that was a happy nation, when everybody had something going for them. The Nigras had their Civil Rights and the rednecks could be killing gooks. Yes, thought the President, his friends and associates were correct in their estimate of him as a genius. Hot damn. Vietnam. The President felt like the only stud in a whorehouse on a houseboat.

Ladies and gentlemen, you will notice that up to this point, I have offered little in the way of closely reasoned quiet argument. I did observe for myself that in the discussions about Vietnam which took place last Saturday in Washington, and were seen by many of us on television, there was an abundance of rational arguments advanced for our escalation in Vietnam and an equal abundance of equally rational arguments against our involvement there.

Well, so far you have received no rational arguments from me today and you are not likely to receive many more as we go on. I believe our present situation in Vietnam is so irrational that any attempt to deal with it logically is illogical in the way surrealism is illogical, and rational political discussion of Adolf Hitler's motives was illogical and then obscene. Bombing a country at the same time you are offering it aid is as morally repulsive as beating up a kid in an alley and stopping to ask for a kiss. Reading the papers these days is a nightmare of unrequited love. If one's country lives like a woman in some part of the unconscious dream life of each of us, if beneath all our criticisms and detestations of America's vulgarity, misuse of power, and sheer pompous stupidity there has been still some optimistic love affair with the secret potentialities of this nation, some buried unvoiced faith that the nature of America was finally good, and not evil, well, that faith has taken a pistol whipping in the last months. The romance seems not even tragic or doomed, but dirty and misplaced.

Still, let me assume there is some point in trying to be reasonable about Vietnam even if it is only to discover that there is no logic in the situation. But let me at least make one straightforward attempt to understand what transpires there. I will, however, insist that the logic we employ runs close to the vein of theological argument, for we must try to speak rationally about a mystery.

Since any interpretation which seeks to justify our role in Vietnam on legal grounds is criminal—since we have no legal justification to be in the country; we are in fact there (as many of you doubtless know already) in violation of the Treaty of the Geneva Conference of 1954 which we were pledged not to obstruct—the only positive argument for our presence is that while we are illegally in Vietnam we are there at least to fight communism.

Well, that is a large question. It is part of a large mystery. We may leave the largest parts of it for last. What may properly concern us first are the arguments and complexes of argument which revolve around the domino theory. Vietnam, says this much discussed theory, is a domino, supporting all the other dominoes of Southeast Asia. This is, of course, argument with the aid of metaphor, argument by image. But metaphors have curious mechanics. There is much dispute about their properties. Edgar Snow, for example, would argue that the dominoes of Southeast Asia are already falling. Insofar as they are dominoes, Indonesia has fallen, and Cambodia. Both nations recognize the Viet Cong as the legitimate government of South Vietnam. Burma gives guarantees to China not to give bases to any U.S. forces. India and Pakistan oppose a U.S. invasion of North Vietnam. Japan makes known its desire not to fight, de Gaulle excludes French aid, no NATO power promises support for a wider war.

The suspicion must begin that we are not protecting a position of connected bastions so much as we are trying to conceal the fact that the bastions are just about gone—they are not dominoes, but sand castles, and a tide of nationalism is on the way in. It is curious foreign policy to use metaphors in defense of a war; when the metaphors are critically imprecise, it is a swindle.

It is worse than that. The escalation in February began immediately after the Viet Cong attacked our air base near Pleiku, and killed seven American soldiers. In retaliation for this attack, or using the attack as our pretext for an offensive we had already planned, the Air Force proceeded—for the first time—to bomb areas over the Seventeenth Parallel in North Vietnam. It is, if we are to use metaphors, it is as if you and I have a small street fight on a city block. You catch me by surprise, you win, and I choose to come back with my gang and stick a plastic bomb on your house. Your maid loses a hand in the explosion; your friend, paying a visit, is blown to bits. I send flowers to the funeral, and a card offering my services as a fire-insurance adjuster. Is it possible the ideology of the Communists is being opposed by the spirit of the Cosa Nostra?

Let me list another difficulty to fighting communism in Vietnam. It is that the communism of the Viet Cong is attached to the local nationalism. With the exception of a few dedicated career soldiers, however, the average American in Vietnam is not much interested in the future of Asia. The freedom-loving spirit of our experts in Saigon has about as much real comprehension of the life of the Asian peasant as the President of the Hilton Hotels Incorporated is on talking terms with his dishwashers at the Hilton Istanbul.

For those of us here, for close to 200,000,000 Americans, Vietnam is faceless. How many Americans have ever visited that country? Who can say which language is spoken there, or what industries might exist, or even what the country looks like? We do not care. We are not interested in the Vietnamese. If we were to fight a war with the inhabitants of the planet of Mars there would be more emotional participation by the people of America than there is even now for our share of the war in Vietnam. Until recently, until February of this year, South Vietnam could have fallen and most of us would not have known nor cared particularly if the territory acquired by the Viet Cong were as big as Brooklyn or as big as the state of Texas. Never in our history has so portentous a war been accelerated in a place which means so little to Americans. Therefore we must admit that we confront a mystery. Which is: why are we already thus involved in a combat which is potentially huge, yet empty of emotional meaning?

The only answer which makes sense is that we are in this war to drive matters to a military climax, we are escalating the war in Vietnam, we are bombing North Vietnam, as the first steps in a sequence which is aimed to destroy the nuclear plant of China. But, if escalation carries up to the summits and abysses of such a moment, then the odds are large that an atomic war will also be upon us. Civilization as we know it would be gone. It is possible all life as we know it would be gone. So we are back to the mystery. Only now it is worse. It asks us to explain why all life would be destroyed for a war in a country we do not care about.

The ill of civilization is that it is removed from nature—disproportions thrive everywhere. The war in Vietnam is just such a monstrous disproportion. We are present at a mystery. All monstrous disproportion conceals a mystery or an insanity. If a man suffering from a fever decides to cure it by walking through fire, we must say he has either a secret motive or is insane.

Perhaps President Johnson has a secret motive.

I do not speak of the desire to bomb the atomic works of China as his secret motive. That desire is, for one thing, public—William Buckley was writing in *National Review* about his desire for such an act a month before the first big February air raids on North Vietnam were begun. Indeed, a large part of the Pentagon has been obsessed with similar desires since 1946. For twenty years Congressmen have been standing up in Congress to read speeches written by War Department officials which exhort America to destroy the Soviet Union by atom bomb before the Soviet Union becomes too strong. That desire has never ceased. *We are a conservative property-loving nation obsessed with the passion to destroy other nations' property.*

So one would not speak of the impulse to bomb the nuclear industry of China as a secret motive. That is a public motive. It is merely not overpublicized. Not yet. If President Johnson has a secret motive, it would have to be then of another sort. Most strong motives are finally psychological—money or power is required to satisfy some imbalance in ourselves.

So President Johnson's motive in escalating the war in Vietnam may be psychic in its nature. This assumes of course that the prime mover in the new war in Vietnam is precisely the President, it assumes that Vietnam is not the unhappy expression of vast inevitable historic forces too large for any man; no, to the contrary this premise supposes flat-out that there was a choice in Vietnam, and one man, balanced at the fulcrum of power between the Pentagon on one side and his liberal support on the other, decided to accelerate the war.

So it is a thesis which would say that the mystery of Vietnam revolves around the mystery of Lyndon Johnson's personality.

To ferret one's way into the recesses of that mysterious and explosive personality is an activity which would give pause to many. It gives pause to me. He is after all a very intelligent man. He is doubtless more intelligent than you or me. He is certainly most intelligent about getting his way. He is also a complex man, and his sides are many. The only side of him which is evident to all is that he is famished for popularity.

At the Democratic Convention in Atlantic City in 1964, not one picture of the President was hung behind the speaker's rostrum, but two. They were each forty feet high. So said his public relations. These photographs, however, looked like they were eighty feet high, high as an eight-story motel. They dominated every moment of the Convention. They spoke of an ego which had the voracity of a beast.

At that convention, there were other clues to the mystery of the President's personality. It was apparent he had vast affection for the powers of television, an affection so huge it shrank from any pretext that he might have equally large affection for his delegates. They were left marooned for the most part behind two huge television towers.

Perhaps a fifth of the delegates were seated in front of those towers. The rest were installed behind. From nearly every position behind the television towers, it was not possible to have a direct view of the speaker on the rostrum. One had to watch him on television. Delegates began to fight for a seat which gave them a good view rather than a poor view of the television set.

The Republican Convention in San Francisco which nominated Barry Goldwater had been not quite so orderly as a rodeo. The Democratic Convention was cancerous—the electronic machines were more crucial than the men.

It was evident that the Establishment was in the service of a most subtle and modern tyrant, an Emperor, to whom all Mafias, legit and illegit, all syndicates, unions, guilds, corporations and institutions . . . could bend their knee. The Establishment had a new leader, a mighty Caesar had arisen, Lyndon Johnson was his name, all hail, Caesar.

Caesar gave promise to unify the land. But at what a cost. For if the ideology were liberal, the methodology was total—to this political church would come Adlai Stevenson and Frank Sinatra, the President of U.S. Steel and the President of the Steel Worker's Union, the C.I.O. and the C.I.A., Martin Luther King and the Pentagon.

Even before the election, a question was there. If we all worked to beat Barry, and got behind Lyndon and pushed, radicals and moderate Republicans, Negroes and Southern liberals, college professors and Cosa Nostra, café society and Beatniks-for-Johnson, were we all then going down a liberal superhighway into the deepest swamp of them all?

For Johnson was intelligent enough to run a total land, he had vast competence, no vision, and the heart to hold huge power, he had the vanity of a modern dictator. Under Johnson we could move from the threat of total war to war itself with nothing to prevent it; the anti-Goldwater forces which might keep the country too divided to go to war would now be contained within Johnson.

That was a final description of the Democratic Convention, and still it missed the point. Because the final unhappy point was that Barry Goldwater had established Johnson's power with such total perfection that the man elected had come closer to total control of America than any President before him. What could increase the fear is that Johnson might not be a whole man so much as he was alienated, a modern man, a member in a most curious sense of a minority group.

Lyndon Baines Johnson a member of a minority group? It is an extraordinary forcing of category. It is obvious some other notion is intended than a description of a Negro, a Jew, a Mexican, a Nisei, or a Puerto Rican. Will it make sense if we say Lyndon Johnson is alienated? Alienated from what, you may ask.

But one must speak first of alienation, that intellectual category which would take you through many a turn of the mind in its attempt to explain that particular corrosive sensation so many of us feel in the chest and the gut so much of the time, that sense of the body growing empty within, of the psyche pierced by a wound whose dimensions keep opening, that unendurable conviction that one is hollow, displaced, without a single identity at one's center. I quote Eric Josephson:

> It [alienation] has been used to refer to an extraordinary variety of psychosocial disorders, including loss of self, anxiety states, anomie, despair, depersonalization, rootlessness, apathy, social disorganization, loneliness, atomization, powerlessness, meaninglessness, isolation, pessimism and the loss of belief or values. Among the groups . . . described as alienated . . . are women, industrial workers, white-collar workers, migrant workers, artists, suicides, mentally disturbed, addicts, the aged, the young generation as a whole, juvenile delinquents in particular, voters, nonvoters, consumers, audiences of mass media, sex deviates, victims of prejudice and discrimination, the prejudiced, bureaucrats, political radicals, the physically handicapped, immigrants, exiles, vagabonds and recluses.

What a huge and comprehensive list. Is anything to be gained by adding to it the name of Lyndon Johnson? You may still ask—what is he alienated from? The Asian peasant? The dishwasher at the Istanbul Hilton? Of course not. You cannot be alienated unless you wish to participate. Lyndon Johnson does not wish to share a bowl of rice with an Asian peasant.

How then is he alienated, and from what? And I say to you in no disrespect and much uneasiness that it is possible he is alienated from his own clear sanity, that his mind has become a consortium of monstrous disproportions, of pictures of himself in duplicate forty feet high, eighty feet high. Lyndon Johnson is not alienated from power, he is the most powerful man in the United States, but he is alienated from judgment, he is close to an imbalance which at worst could tip the world from orbit.

The legitimate fear we can feel is vast. Because there was a time when

Lyndon Johnson could have gotten out of Vietnam very quietly—the image had been prepared for our departure—we heard of nothing but the corruption of the South Vietnam government and the professional cowardice of the South Vietnamese generals. We read how a Viet Cong army of 40,000 soldiers was whipping a government army of 400,000. We were told in our own newspapers how the Viet Cong armed themselves with American weapons brought to them by deserters or captured in battle with government troops; we knew it was an empty war for our side, Lyndon Johnson made no attempt to hide that from us. He may even have encouraged the press in this direction for a time. Abruptly, he dropped escalation into our daily life.

There is fear we must feel. It was not the action of a rational man, but a man driven by need, a gambler who fears that once he stops, once he pulls out of the game, his heart will rupture from tension. You see, Lyndon Johnson is a member of a minority group and so he must have action. But now let me explain. A member of a minority group is—if we are to speak existentially—not a man who is a member of a category, a Negro or a Jew, but rather a man who feels his existence in a particular way. It is in the very form or context of his existence to live with two opposed notions of himself.

What characterizes a member of a minority group is that he is forced to see himself as both exceptional and insignificant, marvelous and awful, good and evil. So far as he listens to the world outside he is in danger of going insane. The only way he may relieve the unendurable tension which surrounds any sense of his own identity is to define his nature by his own acts; discover his courage or cowardice by actions which engage his courage; discover his judgment by judging; his loyalty by being tested; his originality by creating. A Negro or a Texan, a President or a housewife, is by this definition a member of a minority group if he contains two opposed notions of himself at the same time. What characterizes the sensation of being a member of a minority group is that one's emotions are forever locked in the chains of ambivalence—the expression of an emotion forever releasing its opposite—the ego in perpetual transit from the tower to the dungeon and back again. By this definition nearly everyone in America is a member of a minority group, alienated from the self by a double sense of identity and so at the mercy of a self which demands action and more action to define the most rudimentary borders of identity. It is a demand which will either kill a brave man or force him to grow, but when a coward is put in need of such action he tears the wings off flies.

The great fear that lies upon America is not that Lyndon Johnson is privately close to insanity so much as that he is the expression of the near insanity of most of us, and his need for action is America's need for action; not brave action, but action; any kind of action; any move to get the motors going. A future death of the spirit lies close and heavy upon American life, a cancerous emptiness at the center which calls for a circus.

The country is in disease. It has been in disease for a long time. There has been nothing in our growth which was organic. We never solved our depression, we merely went to war back in 1941, and going to war never won it, not in our own minds, not as men, no, we won it but as sources of supply; we still do not know that we are equal to the Russians. We won a war but we did not really win it, not in the secret of our sleep.

So we have not really had a prosperity, we have had fever. We have grown rich because of one fact with two opposite interpretations: There has been a cold war. It has been a cold war which came because Communism was indeed a real threat to our freedom, or a cold war which came because capitalism could not survive without an economy geared to war; or is it both—who can know? Who can really know?

The center of our motive is an enigma—is this country extraordinary or accursed? And when we think of Communism, we have to wonder if we are accursed. For we have not even found our Communist threat. We have had a secret police organization and an invisible government large enough by now to occupy the moon, we have hunted Communists from the top of the Time-Life Building to the bottom of the Collier mine, we have not found that many, not that many, and we have looked like Keystone Cops.

We have even had a Negro Revolution in which we did not believe. We have had it, yes we have had it, because (in the true penury of our motive) we could not afford to lose votes in Africa and India, South America and Japan, Vietnam, the Phillippines, name any impoverished place: we have been running in a world election against the collective image of the Russ, and so we have had to give the black man his civil rights or Africa was so much nearer to Marx. But there has not been much like love in the civil rights. We have never been too authentic. No.

We have had a hero. He was a young good-looking man with a beautiful wife, and he won the biggest poker game we ever played, the only real one—we lived for a week ready to die in a nuclear war. Whether we liked it or not. But he won. It was our one true victory in all these years, our moment; so the young man began to inspire a subtle kind of love. His strength proved stronger than we knew. Suddenly he was dead, and we were in grief.

But then came a trial which was worse. For the assassin, or the man who had been arrested but was not the assassin—we will never know, not really—was killed before our sight. In the middle of the funeral came an explosion on the porch. Now, we were going mad. It took more to make a nation go mad than any separate man, but we had taken miles too much. Certainties had shattered.

Our country was fearful, half-mad, inauthentic—it needed a war or it needed a purge. Bile was stirring in the pits of the national conscience and little to oppose it but a lard of guilt cold as the most mediocre of our needs. We took formal public steps toward a great society, that great society of computers and pills, of job aptitudes and bad architecture, of psychoanalysis, superhighways, astronauts, vaccinations, and a Peace Corps, that great society where nothing but frozen corn would be sold in the smallest towns of Iowa, where censorship would disappear but every image would be manipulated from birth to death.

Something in the buried animal of modern life grew bestial at the thought of this Great Society—the most advanced technological nation of the civilized world was the one now closest to blood, to shedding the blood and burning the flesh of Asian peasants it had never seen. The Pentagon had been kept on a leash for close to twenty years. Presidents so mediocre in their talents as Truman and Eisenhower had kept the military from dominating the nation.

But Johnson did not.

Out of the pusilanimities or the madnesses of his secret sleep he came to a decision to listen to the advice of his military machine, that congeries of Joint Forces, War Department and C.I.A. which had among other noteworthy achievements planned the Bay of Pigs. It was now planning its escalation in Vietnam. And Johnson was in accord. The body of a consummate politician took recognition as it slept that the nation was in disease and its only cure—out where the drums were beating and the fires would not cease—was to introduce us to the first anxieties of a war whose end might be limitless. Miserable nation cursed with a computer for its commander-in-chief, a computer with an ego so vain it could not bear the memory of his predecessor and the power he had had for a week when the world was on the edge of nuclear war.

Yet, there still remains the largest question of them all. It is the question of fighting Communism. Look, you may say, is it not possible that with all our diseases admitted, we are still less malignant than the Communists, we are the defense of civilization and they, not us, are the barbarians who would destroy it? If that is true, then—as some of you may argue—the logic must be faced, the Chinese must be stopped, we must bomb their bomb. And I would argue in return that neither capitalism nor Communism is the defense of civilization but that they are rather each—in their own way—malignancies upon the spirit of honest adventure and open inquiry which developed across the centuries from primitive man to the Renaissance, and that therefore there is no man alive who can say at this point which system will perpetrate the greater harm upon mankind.

But this I do know: existence alters the nature of essence. An unjust war, an unnatural war, an obscene war brutalizes what is best in a nation and encourages every horror to rise from its sewer.

The Communists could capture every nation on earth but our own and we would still be safe if our intention were clean. Yes. For in the vertiginous terrors of nuclear warfare rests one rock ledge of safety—in future no great power can ever be destroyed without destroying every other power which would attack it. As a corollary no philosophy of government can occupy nine-tenths of the globe without being altered to its roots. The health of Communism, its secret necessity, is an enemy external to itself; war is indeed the health of the totalitarian state, and peace is its disease. Communism would split and rupture and war upon itself if ever it occupied most of the world, for then it would have to solve the problems of most of the world and those problems are not soluble in the rigidity of a system. Like all top-heavy structures the greatest danger to Communism lies in its growth. Prosperity is its poison, for without a sense of crisis, Communism cannot discipline its future generations. Attack from capitalism is Communism's transfusion of blood. So our war against Communism, most particularly our war against Communism in Asia, is the death of our future. I am going to quote Senator Wayne Morse:

> *We shall win one military victory after another; we shall destroy cities, industrial installations, and nuclear installations; we shall kill by the millions. . . . That course of action will lay a foundation of hatred on the part of the colored races of the world against the American people. In due time, those installations will be rebuilt . . . on the foundation of intense hatred by Asians for the people of the United States. That hatred will even be inherited by generations of American boys and girls fifty, seventy-five, one hundred, yes, two hundred years from now.*

I say: end the cold war. Pull back our boundaries to what we can defend and to what wishes to be defended. Let Communism come to those countries it will come to. Let us not use up our substance trying to hold onto nations which are poor, underdeveloped, and bound to us only by the depths of their hatred for us. We cannot equal the effort the Communists make in such places. We are not dedicated in that direction. We were not born to do that. We have had our frontier already. We cannot be excited to our core, our historic core, by the efforts of new underdeveloped nations to expand their frontiers.

Let the Communists flounder in the countries they acquire. The more countries they hold, the less supportable will become the contradictions of their ideology, the more bitter will grow the divisions in their internal interest, and the more enormous their desire to avoid a war which could only destroy the economies they will have developed at such vast labor and such vast waste. Let it be their waste, not ours. Our mission may be not to raise the level of minimum subsistence in the world so much as it may be to show the first features and promise of that incalculable renaissance men may someday enter.

I have one set of remarks more to make. They concern practical suggestions. I have been visionary in my demands. For it is visionary in 1965 to ask of America that it return to isolationism. No, this country wishes to have an empire. The grimmest truth may be that half of America at least must be not unwilling to have a war in Vietnam. Otherwise Lyndon Johnson could not have made his move, since Lyndon Johnson never in his life has dreamed of moving against a majority.

Let us then insist on this—it is equally visionary, but it is at least visionary in a military way and we are talking to militarists—let us say that if we are going to have a war with the Viet Cong, let it be a war of foot soldier against foot soldier. If we wish to take a strange country away from strangers, let us at least be strong enough and brave enough to defeat them on the ground. Our Marines, some would say, are the best soldiers in the world. The counter-argument is that native guerrillas can defeat any force of a major power man to man.

Let us, then, fight on fair grounds. Let us say to Lyndon Johnson, to Monstrous McNamara, and to the generals on the scene—fight like men, go in man to man against the Viet Cong. But first, call off the Air Force. They prove nothing except that America is coterminous with the Mafia. Let us win man to man or lose man to man, but let us cease pulverizing people whose faces we have never seen.

But of course we will not cease. Nor will we ever fight man to man against poor peasants. Their vision of existence might be more ferocious and more determined than our own. No, we would rather go on as the most advanced monsters of civilization pulverizing instinct with our detonations, our State Department experts in their little bow ties, and our bombs.

Only, listen, Lyndon Johnson, you have gone too far this time. You are a bully with an Air Force, and since you will not call off your Air Force, there are young people who will persecute you back. It is a little thing, but it will hound you into nightmares and endless corridors of nights without sleep, it will hound you. For listen—this is only one of the thousand things they will do. They will print up little pictures of you,

Lyndon Johnson, the size of post cards, the size of stamps, and some will glue these pictures to walls and posters and telephone booths and billboards—I do not advise it, I would tell these students not to do it to you, but they will. They will find places to put these pictures. They will want to paste your picture, Lyndon Johnson, on a post card, and send it to you. Some will send it to your advisers. Some will send these pictures to men and women at other schools. These pictures will be sent everywhere. These pictures will be pasted up everywhere, upside down.

Silently, without a word, the photograph of you, Lyndon Johnson, will start appearing everywhere, upside down. Your head will speak out—even to the peasant in Asia—it will say that not all Americans are unaware of your monstrous vanity, overweening piety, and doubtful motive. It will tell them that we trust our President so little, and think so little of him, that we see his picture everywhere upside down.

You, Lyndon Johnson, will see those pictures up everywhere upside down, four inches high and forty feet high; you, Lyndon Baines Johnson, will be coming up for air everywhere upside down. Everywhere, upside down. Everywhere. Everywhere.

And those little pictures will tell the world what we think of you and your war in Vietnam. Everywhere, upside down. Everywhere, everywhere.

A HAPPY SOLUTION TO VIETNAM:

From a Partisan Review *Symposium*

Statement by the EDITORS of *Partisan Review*

We do not think that the present or past policies of the United States in Vietnam are good ones, and we lament the increasing and often self-defeating military involvements which those policies require. We have not heard of any alternative policy, however, which would actually lead to a negotiated peace in Vietnam or promote the interests of the people of Southeast Asia. This is not to say that the critics of American actions in Vietnam are therefore required to propose a specific policy. But it is not unfair to ask that their criticism be based on more than the apolitical assumption that power politics, the Cold War, and Communists are merely American inventions. Most of the criticism of Administration policy at the teach-ins and in the various petitions we have been asked to sign has simply taken for granted that everything would be fine if only the Yanks would go home. It is not clear whether these critics think Asia will not go Communist if American troops are withdrawn or whether they don't care. Nor is it clear whether they really care what happens to the people of Southeast Asia so long as America gets out.

The creation of a world in which free societies can exist should be the goal of any international policy. Our policies in Vietnam do not promote that end, even though it is claimed that they are justified because the United States is preventing a Communist take-over. Nor do the policies of North Vietnam, Communist China or the Viet Cong, however they are explained. As for our policies in the Dominican Republic, they cannot be justified even on the grounds that the United States is preventing a Communist coup. They are a disastrous violation of any democratic principle, a violation likely to alienate the people of South America, especially the youth, or even drive them into an alliance with precisely those Communist forces our government claims to be combatting.

The fiasco in the Dominican Republic illustrates, we think, what is basically wrong with our policies. So long as we are not able to understand the political and economic problems of rapidly changing countries, and to support democratic revolutionary groups, we are bound to find ourselves in a false dilemma, always having to decide at the last minute whether to intervene, as though that were the only solution. Military action can be a substitute for political foresight only if we propose to police the whole world, and to imagine that we can do that is to lack even hindsight.

Obviously, the time has come for some new thinking. And some of it has to be about what's happening in different parts of the world, regardless of what the United States does or fails to do.

ELEANOR CLARK		WILLIAM PHILIPS
MARTIN DUBERMAN	BERNARD MALAMUD	NORMAN PODHORETZ
IRVING HOWE	STEVEN MARCUS	RICHARD POIRIER
ALFRED KAZIN		RICHARD SCHLATTER

Three cheers, lads. Your words read like they were written in milk and milk of magnesia. Still, your committee didn't close shop until close after this extraordinary remark: "The time has come for new thinking." Cha cha cha.

We will do our best to serve. First let it be established—as is done nowhere in the statement—that the editors support the war in Vietnam. For after all somber dubiety, and every reservation, we are left back at the beginning—"we have not heard of any alternative policy which would actually lead to a negotiated peace in Vietnam . . ." But to provide alternative policy, people's front must remind you how the war in Vietnam goes on. The following statistics are furnished by Ho Chi Minh. No, indeed they are not. They are from a statement by Robert McNamara before the Senate Subcommittee on Department of Defense Appropriations and appeared August 5 in the *Times*.

We now estimate the hard core of Viet Cong strength at some 70,000 men. . . . In addition, they have some 90,000 to 100,000 irregulars and some 30,000 in their political cadres, i.e., tax collectors, propagandists, etc. We have also identified at least three battalions of the regular North Vietnamese Army, and there are probably considerably more.

At least three battalions! That is to say, at most, 3,000 North Vietnamese. If the battalions are understrength the figure may be half the size. But, continue with McNamara:

At the same time the government of South Vietnam has found it increasingly difficult to make a commensurate increase in the size of its own forces, which now stand at about 545,000 men, including the regional and local defense forces but excluding the national police.

Clearly, the time has come when the people of South Vietnam need more help from us and other nations if they are to retain their freedom and independence.

We have already responded to that need with some 75,000 United States military personnel, including some combat units. This number will be raised to 125,000 almost immediately. . . . But, more help will be needed in the months ahead . . . to back up the hard-pressed army of South Vietnam.

"Responded to that need." McNamara is the best thing to come along since Elmer Gantry. Let me give a little more. From a news conference, two months earlier, June 16. "In 1964 alone . . . about 10,000 men were brought from North Vietnam to fight in South Vietnam." Whereas in 1965 we will only bring in 100,000 Americans.

Well, McNamara is on record (again June 5) about ratios:

The South Vietnamese regular and paramilitary forces facing the Viet Cong total something in excess of 500,000 men. And they're facing, as I mentioned, about 165,000 guerrillas, a ratio something on the order of 4 to 1 [sic]. That's considerably less than is recognized as required to effectively deal with guerrillas.

The Pentagon's argument is that a government army must outnumber guerrillas in the ratio of ten to one if they are to hold the countryside and administer it well. But in South Vietnam, it happens to be the Viet Cong which holds most of the countryside and proceeds each year with its 30,000 political troops, its "tax collectors," to occupy and *govern* more land than the year before, against an army—depending on how you count—from three to eight times its own size. Only an army fighting a war in which the agricultural population is near to unanimous behind them (or near to unanimous *against* the South Vietnamese) can do thus well. Can you conceive of another explanation?

Now, our entrance in force will shift this imbalance. It will certainly prolong the war. It will also shift the moral center of America. I quote a piece by Charles Mohr, *New York Times*, August 9.

The attempts by public information officers to de-emphasize the importance of civilian deaths and the burning of village huts at the hands of United States marines have not been duplicated by senior Marine Corps officers here. . . .

General Walt quickly conceded last week that on one military operation his troops had killed three children and a woman. He expressed deep regret. The marines have also conceded that at least 51 huts were burned on another operation.

A Vietnamese observer who discussed the incident shook his head and said, "The 10-year-old children who witnessed their village being burned are the ones who at 15 will take up rifles for the Viet Cong and fight to the death."

If World War II was like *Catch-22*, this war will be like *Naked Lunch*. Lazy Dogs, and bombing raids from Guam. Marines with flame throwers. Jungle gotch in the gonorrhea and South Vietnamese girls doing the Frug. South Vietnamese fighter pilots "dressed in black flying suits and lavender scarves" (*The New York Times*).

Add a little to this: let us recognize that we are in a war commanded by a President whose deepest and tenderest emotion seems to be directed toward his own boils and rash. Public life, he forever reminds us, is cruel to public figures. There is a catch in his voice as he makes such remarks. He is happier with the balm of paid prose. Remember Jack Valenti's words last June?

> . . . *The new President sat there, like a large gray stone mountain, untouched by fear or frenzy, from whom everyone began to draw strength. And suddenly, as though the darkness of the cave confided its fears to the trail of light growing larger as it banished the night, the nation's breath, held tightly in its breast, began to ease, and across the land the people began to move again. The President, thank the Good Lord, has extra glands . . .*

Well, we are literary politicians—we know what to deduce from such a style. It is of course possible that Johnson is no more Machiavellian than any major gent. But it is also possible there are disproportions to the man. Should one think of Macbeth or Uriah Heep? Valenti's prose opens the drawer to some fine horrors.

Besides, our present policy in Vietnam which the editors gloomily, glumly, *inevitably* (they are liberals after all) proceed to defend, is in fact a policy which is the antithesis of the previous policy. The previous policy, the policy in effect just before escalation, was the unstated policy to lose quietly in Vietnam, and get out. There were better countries to defend. It was a practical policy which might in practice have worked or not worked, but the new policy, the policy of escalation, is a radical policy; it is a policy of the radical right, right out of the naked-lunching heart of the Wasp in his fevers. For no one can know, not even Johnson himself, if escalation is our best defense against Communism, a burning of orphans to save future orphans, or if the war is the first open expression of a totalitarian Leviathan which will yet dominate everything still not nailed down in American life: art, civil rights, student rebellions, public criticism in mass media. We may be living in the shadow of the biggest hype of them all, our last con game: redneck dynamics; liberal rhetoric. There is the ineradicable suspicion that liberal rhetoric was conceived by Satan to kiss the behind of something unspeakable.

Recapitulate: we have an accelerating war whose justification by the Establishment is that there is final and historic honor in fighting an unpopular war if the cause is grave and just. That is one possibility. I cannot say with certainty that this cannot be so. But, in turn, who of you can say with greater certainty that the President is not insomniac in his vanities; and that the nation is not insane with Christ, Pop art, Fiberglass, moonshots, race riots, and Hilton Hotel architecture.

The editors ask for a counterpolicy. I offer it. It is to get out of Asia. A Communist bureaucrat is not likely to do any more harm or destroy any more spirit than a wheeler-dealer, a platoon sergeant, or a corporation executive overseas. We have our malignancies, Communism has theirs. Whether capitalism or Communism will finally prove more monstrous is out of my capacity, or yours, to guess, but it is perhaps evident to both of us that Communism cannot grow without exploding its own form. If Marx's vision conceivably left room for some minds to remain fertile, Stalin fixed a process of petrifying thought until post-Marxian thought is now an ideology which cannot change remotely so fast as reality and so must be insulated from reality by war. War is the health of Communist ideology, whereas peace and the abrupt *strifeless* acquisition of backward countries is a nightmare to ideology. For backward lands which are not used up by war have wealths of primitive lore with which to mine the foundations of ideology.

Consider: a quiet end to the war in Vietnam by the agency of a quiet victory of the Viet Cong might have given the world one more backward Red nation with still one more tenacious home-grown stubborn little Communist party at odds with China and in intrigue with Russia, thereby dividing world Communism somewhat further. Now, grace of escalation, we have the likelihood that any future alignment between Russia and China will be a little more on China's terms; and for China vis-à-vis North Vietnam (which countries formerly shared the distaste of England and Ireland for one another) we have accelerated a collaboration.

Of course all those Washington Pistols, all those keepers of the chalice, will talk about India falling if we "get out." And there will be tears in Joe Alsop's eyes. Of course. And I, of course, don't know. Maybe if Vietnam falls, so, too, falls India. So to what? Do we really want India? Do we desire it? Do we desire deeply to die of indigestion? Might it not be simpler if the Communists die of the same disease? But, in fact, might they not hesitate? For, the more Communism grows at a vertiginous rate, the more it must suffer from vertigo. It is like America. So, Communism might even come to recognize that Communism in possession of three-quarters of the world cannot have any world. The world is now balanced on too much. So Communism might even retreat before the terror of ideology being lost in the jungles and grasslands. What if Communism is not an unstoppable force—but is rather (since we can only approach comprehension of these matters by metaphor) a giant with a specific neurosis that it will awake one morning on the compulsion to eat its own limbs. I say: throw Asia open to Communism. The meal will not be taken. If it is, we will even live to see the Communists destroy themselves. It is certain we cannot destroy them. We, like them, can only eat upon ourselves—this is after all a century for perverts and Reds.

But, believe me not. Take the alternative: might against might. Our troops against theirs—no, of course we are not serious. Even Barry Goldwater knows that we can't defeat the Communists militarily, not even with atom bombs. How could we occupy what was left? The cost of rebuilding it. The boredom for America's young couples—obliged to live out their early married years in rebuilt cities in Siberia and Mongolia. All the ration stamps. All the ghosts of 900,000,000 atomized corpses. No, we don't really want to defeat Communism militarily. But we do want to stand up man to man, stick to stick. If we cannot stop Communism by the force of our armies, we could of course pitch in to help create a world society of military and bureaucratic behemoths who will nibble at one another forever in small dribbled-out land wars while totalitarian tissues fill up with the waters of political edema, yes, just as our good prophet and saint, George Orwell, was dying to remind us.

Look to the other side. To absolute isolation. If all the world were Communist but America, America would be militarily in no poor position. We could still fight the rest of the world if we chose to. That is the paradoxical nature of nuclear war. But it is doubtful if Communism would then have the impetus to fight anything. Can anyone—even Dwight —conceive of Communism remaining unruptured in its cast-concrete heart on a diet of English lords, French intellectuals, Italian lovers, African drums, Zen, Yoga, pot, the New Wave, Pop art, camp—the prospect invites occupation. "Come on in, honey, this hustler's got enough diseases to keep you dripping all your days."

That, of course, is not programmatic, I would assure you. The world will never go to the Communists because they will never get through Asia, Africa and South America. They will bog down in the cultural swamps of our imperial wastes; their minds will rupture in the new pressures on their cast-iron formulations. For Communism contends with an impossibility: one cannot bring a modern economy to a backward country in a hurry, bulldozing through a wealth of primitive lore, without manufacturing a horde of mass men. And mass man is equal to the plague. Nihilistic, he is addicted to modern communications. Shakespeare, comic books, motors, electronics, jazz, plastic, fucking, frozen food, are all equal grit to his Dispose-all. He consumes whatever culture is before him and is the secret enemy of any government which presumes to rule him. His secret allegiance is always to the enemy. So let the Communists rather than the Americans do the manufacturing of mass men in backward lands, in order that the secret allegiance of those new mass men be exactly to us.

For there is one way in which the West is superior to the Communists, and without that superiority, mass man cannot live. Mass man is an insatiable man, a malignancy of directionless greed at the mercy of his secret addiction—which is art. No population ever on earth has loved art so much as mass man, for that is the only hope of his deliverance: that he may encounter some great art before he is dead. Only great art can penetrate into the tomb of the modern soul and bring a moment of cease to the backed-up murders of the modern heart. Here, on this violent spit, friends, is the place we are ahead in the Cold War. For our artists are better, our writers are better, our jazz musicians are better, our painters go further, our vision is more fierce, it explores more. It is relentless we almost dare to think. It may even prevail if we do not burn too many women and children fighting for Christ. Oh, Christ, what assholes be Americans.

Yet it may be too easy to end on this fine proud and strenuous moral note. For the sweet bloody truth is not so neat. If the Lord of the Snopes went to war in Vietnam because finally he didn't have the moral courage to try to solve an impossible mix of Camp, redneck, civil rights, street violence, playboy pornography and all the glut which bugs our works, if Lyndon Johnson finally decided in his fine brain that only a war was going to get America off the pot (we were that mercilessly screwed to the john by fifty years of smelling our national armpit every time the truth rose up to kiss us) well, what he didn't realize was that the war in Vietnam was not going to serve as cloaca for our worst emotions but instead was going to up the ante and give us more Camp, more redneck, more violence in the streets, more teen-age junkies, more polite society gone ape, more of everything else Lyndon was trying to ship overseas.

Still, with it all, confess it, Mailer, the country is now in good humor. A wild good humor—it has been the wildest summer in years from Watts to Easthampton; it has been wild. The truth is, maybe we need a war. It may be the last of the tonics. From Lydia Pinkham to Vietnam in sixty years, or bust. We're the greatest country ever lived for speeding up the time. So, let's do it right. Let's cease all serious war, kids. Let's leave Asia to the Asians. Let us, instead, have wars which are like happenings. Let us have them every summer. Let us buy a tract of land in the Amazon, two hundred million acres will do, and throw in Marines and Seabees and Air Force, Scuba divers for the river bottom, motorcyclists for the mud-races, carrier pilots landing on bounce-all decks in typhoons, invite them all, the Chinks and the Aussies, the Frogs and the

Gooks and the Wogs, the Wops and the Russkies, the Yugos, the Israelis, the Hindoos, the Pakistanis. We'll have war games with real bullets and real flame throwers, real hot-wire correspondents on the spot, TV with phone-in audience participation, amateur war movie film contests for the soldiers, discotheques, Playboy Clubs, pictures of the corpses for pay TV, you know what I mean—let's get the hair on the toast for breakfast. So a write-in campaign (all of us) to King Corporation Exec Mr. Pres; let us tell him to get the boys back home by Christmas, back from Vietnam and up the Amazon for summer. Yours—readers—till the next happening.

Unless Vietnam is the happening. Could that be? Could that really be? Little old Vietnam just a happening? Cause if it is, Daddy Warbucks, couldn't we have the happening just with the Marines and skip all that indiscriminate roast tit and naked lunch, all those bombed-out civilian ovaries, Mr. J., Mr. L.B.J., Boss Man of Show Biz—I salute you in your White House Oval; I mean America will shoot all over the shithouse wall if this jazz goes on, Jim.

5 · THE ARGUMENT NOW MILDLY

ILLUMINED

As is evident by now, the only explanation I can find for the war in Vietnam is that we are sinking into the swamps of a plague and the massacre of strange people seems to relieve this plague. If one were to take the patients in a hospital, give them guns and let them shoot on pedestrians down from hospital windows you may be sure you would find a few miraculous cures. So the national mood is bound to prosper from the war in Vietnam. For a time. Let us go back to our hospital patients. Some of them we see stripped to the waist, crying with joy as they fire off their machine-gun blast. All the light of the Lord is in their eye again. But not all can fire at once, and some on the sidelines throw up in sheer excitement, others are forced to eat from nervousness, others diddle in the slop, and zap! there went the first—the nice old man about to die has just bit the jugular of the nice old lady, and some are beginning to slide in the blood. And some are beginning to slide like snakes. Sellah, sellah—is it better to be a foul old Cannibal or a Christian dying of nausea?

I wonder which is worse
 the solitary East
 or the West
 chewing on
 Momma's
 lover's
 lesbian
 breast.

STATIC

Dah dit dit dah dit dit dah
dah dah dit dit dah dah
dah dit dit dah dit dit dah
dah dah dit dit dah dah

Mentally cool and bright
Arms fly is the war song
Father of strong in your nave
Bold slave of a fierce light

Dum ditty, dum ditty, dum
  dah dah dit dah dit dit

Bold old gold is the grave
  of those
  who want to bleed
    for United
      Sexual
      Appeal
against the oncoming night
  which does not slay
  but reduces
  the best and worst
  to mediocre

  dit dit dah
  dah dah dit

The Mediocre.

Do not
   ask
   for
   whom
   the
   television
   tolls

PART TWO: LIONS

6 · *THE ARGUMENT REINVIGORATED*

Reader, a telegram: SHIFT MCNAMARA LAMBS FROM WARS OF
JELLIED FIRE TO LIONS IN BURNING BUSH.

*Everything in this book is attached to everything else. Trust me for a
time. Indulge me:*

*Assume I am a lecturer in the fields of Fellowship surrounding Literature
(American) and am trying to draw some grand design in twenty minutes on
a talk devoted to "The Dynamic of American Letters." Knowing attention is
iron for the blood of a Fellow, I will not be so foolish as to perish without a
look at the topical and the interesting. No, I will use "The Dynamic of
American Letters" as preparation for a lightning discussion of Herzog and
Terry Southern, with a coda on the art of the absurd. Let me then have my
first sentence as lecturer: "There has been a war at the center of American
letters for a long time." That is not so poor. The look of absolute com-
prehension on the face of the audience encourages the lecturer to go on.*

*The war began as a class war; an upper-middle class looked for a develop-
ment of its taste, a definition of its manners, a refinement of itself to prepare
a shift to the aristocratic; that was its private demand upon culture. That
demand is still being made by a magazine called* The New Yorker. *This
upper-class development of literature was invaded a long time ago, however,
back at the cusp of the century, by a counter-literature whose roots were
found in poverty, industrial society, and the emergence of new class. It was
a literature which grappled with a peculiarly American phenomenon—a
tendency of American society to alter more rapidly than the ability of its
artists to record that change. Now, of course, one might go back two*

*thousand years into China to find a society which did not alter more rapidly
than its culture, but the American phenomenon had to do with the very
rate of acceleration. The order of magnitude in this rate had shifted. It was
as if everything changed ten times as fast in America, and this made for
extraordinary difficulty in creating a literature. The sound, sensible, morally
stout delineation of society which one found in Tolstoy and Balzac and Zola,
in Thackeray and in Trollope, had become impossible. The American
novelist of manners had to content himself with manners—he could not put
a convincing servant into his work, and certainly not a workingman, because
they were moving themselves in one generation out from the pantry into the
morning dress of the lady in the parlor and up from the foundry to the master
of the factory. The novelist of manners could not go near these matters—
they promised to take over all of his book. So the job was left to Howells,
Stephen Crane, to Dreiser, and in lesser degree to such writers as Norris,
Jack London, Upton Sinclair—let us say it was left to Dreiser. A funda-
mental irony of American letters had now presented itself. For in opposition
to Dreiser was the imperfectly developed countertradition of the genteel.
The class which wielded the power which ran America, and the class which
most admired that class, banded instinctively together to approve a genteel
literature which had little to do with power or the secrets of power. They
encouraged a literature about courtship and marriage and love and play
and devotion and piety and style, a literature which had to do finally with
the excellence of belonging to their own genteel tradition. Thus it was a
literature which borrowed the forms of its conduct from European models.
The people who were most American by birth, and who had the most to
do with managing America, gave themselves a literature which had the least
to say about the real phenomena of American life, most particularly the
accelerated rate, the awful rate, of growth and anomaly through all of
society. That sort of literature and that kind of attempt to explain America
was left to the sons of immigrants who, if they were vigorous enough,
and fortunate enough to be educated, now had the opportunity to see that
America was a phenomenon never before described, indeed never before
visible in the record of history. There was something going on in American
life which was either grand or horrible or both, but it was going on—at a
dizzy rate—and the future glory or doom of the world was not necessarily
divorced from it. Dreiser labored like a titan to capture the phenomenon;
he became a titan; Thomas Wolfe, his only peer as giant (as the novelist-
as-giant), labored also like a titan, but for half as long and died in terror
of the gargantuan proportions of the task. Yet each failed in one part of*

the job. They were able to describe society—Wolfe like the greatest five-year-old who ever lived,* an invaluable achievement, and Dreiser like some heroic tragic entrepreneur who has reasoned out through his own fatigue and travail very much how everything works in the iron mills of life, but is damned because he cannot pass on the knowledge to his children. Dreiser and Wolfe were up from the people, and Dreiser particularly came closer to understanding the social machine than any American writer who ever lived, but he paid an unendurable price—he was forced to alienate himself from manner in order to learn the vast amount he learned. Manner insists one learn at a modest rate, that one learn each step with grace before going on to the next. Dreiser was in a huge hurry, he had to learn everything—that was the way he must have felt his mission, so there is nothing of manner in his work; which is to say, nothing of tactics.

If the upper-class quite naturally likes a literature which is good for them, a literature at the surface perhaps trivial, but underneath amusing, elucidative, fortifying, *it is because this kind of literature elaborates and clarifies the details of their life, and thus adjusts their sense of power, their upper-class sense of power, which is invariably lubricated by a sense of detail. So too does that other class of readers in American literature, that huge, loose, all but unassociated congregation of readers—immigrant, proletarian, entrepreneur—wish in turn for a literature which is equally good for them. That is where Dreiser had to fail. He was only half-good for such readers. He taught them strategy as Americans had never gotten it before in a novel. If they were adventurers, he was almost as useful to them as Stendhal was exceptionally useful to a century of French intellectuals who had come to Paris from the provinces. But not quite. Dreiser, finally, is not quite as useful, and the difference is crucial. Because a young adventurer reads a great novel in the unvoiced hope it is a grindstone which sharpens his axe sufficiently to smash down doors now locked to him. Dreiser merely located the doors and gave warnings about the secret padlocks and the traps. But he had no grindstone, no manner, no eye for the deadly important manners of the rich, he was obliged to call a rich girl "charming"; he could not make her charming when she spoke, as Fitzgerald could, and so he did not really prepare the army of his readers for what was ahead. His task was doubly difficult—it was required of him to*

---

* This Argument was delivered, originally, as a talk to The American Studies Association and the M.L.A. This remark brought laughter from the audience. Since I did not wish to insult the memory of Wolfe, it would have been happier and perhaps more accurate to have said: like the greatest fifteen-year-old alive.

give every upstart fresh strategy and tactics. No less than the secret sociology of society is what is needed by the upstart and that strategy Dreiser gave him. But tactics—the manners of the drawing room, the deaths and lifes of the drawing room, the cocktail party, the glorious tactics of the individual kill—that was all beyond him. Dreiser went blind climbing the mountains of society, so he could not help anyone to see what was directly before him—only what had happened and what was likely to come next.

That was the initial shape of the war, Naturalism versus the Genteel Tradition it has been called, and one might pose Henry James against Dreiser, but James is sufficiently great a writer to violate the generalizations one must make about the novel of manners which must always—precisely because it deals with manners—eschew the overambitious, plus extremes of plot—which James of course did not. So let us say the war was between Dreiser and Edith Wharton, Dreiser all strategy, no tactics; and Wharton all tactics. Marvelous tactics they were—a jewel of a writer and stingy as a parson—she needed no strategy. The upper-class writer had all strategy provided him by the logic of his class. Maybe that is why the war never came to decision, or even to conclusion. No upper-class writer went down into the pits to bring back the manner alive of the change going on down *there, certainly not Edith Wharton, not James Branch Cabell, of course not, nor Hergesheimer nor even Cather or Glasgow, not Elinor Wylie, no, nor Carl Van Vechten, and no diamond in the rough was ever reshaped by the cutters of Newport. The gap in American letters continued. Upper-class writers like John Dos Passos made brave efforts to go down and get the stuff and never quite got it, mainly in Dos Passos's case because they lacked strategy for the depths—manners may be sufficient to delineate the rich but one needs a vision of society to comprehend the poor, and Dos Passos had only revulsion at injustice, which is ultimately a manner. Some upper-class writers like Fitzgerald turned delicately upon the suppositions of their class, lost all borrowed strategy and were rudderless, were forced therefore to become superb in tactics, but for this reason perhaps a kind of hysteria lived at the center of their work; lower-class writers like Farrell and Steinbeck described whole seas of the uncharted ocean but their characters did not push from one milieu into another, and so the results were more taxonomic than apocalyptic.*

Since then the war has shifted. No writer succeeded in doing the single great work which would clarify a nation's vision of itself as Tolstoy had done perhaps with War and Peace *or* Anna Karenina, *and Stendhal with* The Red and the Black, *no one novel came along which was grand and daring and comprehensive and detailed, able to give sustenance to the adventurer and merriment to the rich, leave compassion in the icechambers of the upper class and energy as alms for the poor.* (*Not unless it was* Tropic of Cancer.) *Dreiser came as close as any, and never got close at all, for he could not capture the moment, and no country in history has lived perhaps so much for the moment as America. After his heroic failure, American literature was isolated—it was necessary to give courses in American literature to Americans, either because they would not otherwise read it, or because reading it, they could not understand it. It was not quite vital to them. It did not save their lives, make them more ambitious, more moral, more tormented, more audacious, more ready for love, more ready for war, for charity and for invention. No, it tended to puzzle them. The realistic literature had never caught up with the rate of change in American life, indeed it had fallen further and further behind, and the novel gave up any desire to be a creation equal to the phenomenon of the country itself; it settled for being a metaphor. Which is to say that each separate author made a separate peace. He would no longer try to capture America, he would merely try to give life to some microcosm in American life, some metaphor —in the sense that a drop of water is a metaphor of the seas, or a hair of the beast is for some a metaphor of the beast—and in that metaphor he might— if he were very lucky—have it all, rich and poor, strategy and tactics, insight and manner, detail, authority, the works. He would have it all for a particular few. It was just that he was no longer writing about the beast but, as in the case of Hemingway (if we are to take the best of this), about the paw of the beast, or in Faulkner about the dreams of the beast. What a paw and what dreams! Perhaps they are the two greatest writers America ever had, but they had given up on trying to do it all. Their vision was partial, determinedly so, they saw that as the first condition for trying to be great—that one must not try to save. Not souls, and not the nation. The desire for majesty was the bitch which licked at the literary loins of Hemingway and Faulkner: the country could be damned. Let it take care of itself.*

And of course the country did. Just that. It grew by itself. Like a weed and a monster and a beauty and a pig. And the task of explaining America was taken over by Luce magazines. Those few aristocratic novelistic sensibilities which had never seen the task of defining the country as one for them—it was finally most unamusing as a task—grew smaller and smaller and more and more superb. Edith Wharton reappeared as Truman

Capote, even more of a jewel, even stingier. Of writers up from the bottom there were numbers: Dreiser's nephews were as far apart as Saul Bellow and James Jones. But the difference between the two kinds of writers had shifted. It had begun to shift somewhere after the Second World War, and the shift had gone a distance. One could not speak at all now of aristocratic writers and novelists whose work was itself the protagonist to carry the writer and his readers through the locks of society; no, the work had long since retreated, the great ambition was gone, and then it was worse, even the metaphor was gone, the paw of the beast and the dreams of the beast, no, literature was down to the earnest novel and the perfect novel, to moral seriousness and Camp. Herzog and Candy had become the pro-tagonists.

Frank Cowperwood once amassed an empire. Herzog, his bastard great-nephew, diddled in the ruins of an intellectual warehouse. Where once the realistic novel cut a swath across the face of society, now its reality was concentrated into moral seriousness. Where the original heroes of naturalism had been active, bold, self-centered, close to tragic, and up to their nostrils in their exertions to advance their own life and force the webs of society, so the hero of moral earnestness, the hero Herzog and the hero Levin in Malamud's A New Life, *are men who represent the contrary—passive, timid, other-directed, pathetic, up to the nostrils in anguish: the world is stronger than they are; suicide calls.*

Malamud's hero is more active than Herzog, he is also more likeable, but these positive qualities keep the case from being so pure. There is a mystery about the reception of Herzog. *For beneath its richness of texture and its wealth of detail, the fact remains: never has a novel been so successful when its hero was so dim. Not one of the critics who adored the book would ever have permitted Herzog to remain an hour in his house. For Herzog was defeated, Herzog was an unoriginal man, Herzog was a fool—not an attractive God-anointed fool like Gimpel the Fool, his direct progenitor, but a sodden fool, over-educated and inept, unable to fight, able to love only when love presented itself as a gift. Herzog was intellectual but not bright, his ideas not original, his style as it appeared in his letters unendurable—it had exactly the leaden-footed sense of phrase which men laden with anxiety and near to going mad put into their com-munications. Herzog was hopeless. We learned nothing about society from him, not even anything about his life. And he is the only figure in the book. His wives, his mistress, his family, his children, his friends, even the man who cuckolds him are seen on the periphery of a dimming vision. Like all men near to being mad, his attention is within, but the inner attention is without genius. Herzog is dull, he is unendurably dull—he is like all those bright pedagogical types who have a cavity at the center of their brain.*

Yet the novel succeeds. There is its mystery. One reads it with compassion. With rare compassion. Bored by Herzog, still there is a secret burning of the heart. One's heart turns over and produces a sorrow. Hardly any books are left to do that.

Of course, Herzog is alive on sufferance. He is a beggar, an extraordinary beggar who fixes you with his eye, his breath, his clothing, his dank near-corrupt presence; he haunts. Something goes on in Herzog's eye. It says: I am debased, I am failed, I am near to rotten, and yet something just as good and loving resides in me as the tenderest part of your childhood. If the prophet Elijah sent me, it is not to make you feel guilt but to weep. Suddenly, Herzog inspires sorrow—touch of alchemy to the book —Herzog is at the center of the modern dilemma. If we do not feel compassion for him, a forceful compassion which sends blood to warm the limbs and the heart, then we are going to be forced to shoot him. Because if Herzog does not arouse your compassion there is no other choice—he is too intolerable a luxury to keep alive in his mediocrity unless he arouses your love. The literary world chose to love him. We were not ready to shoot Herzog. It all seemed too final if we did. Because then there would be nothing left but Camp, and Camp is the art of the cannibal, Camp is the art which evolved out of the bankruptcy of the novel of manners. It is the partial thesis of these twenty minutes that the pure novel of manners had watered down from The House of Mirth *to the maudlin middle reaches of* The Rector of Justin; *had in fact gone all the way down the pike from* The Ambassadors *to* By Love Possessed. *So, one does not speak of the novel of manners any longer—one is obliged to look at the documentary,* In Cold Blood—*or one is obliged to look at satire. The aristocratic impulse turned upon itself produced one classic—Terry Southern's* The Magic Christian. *Never had distaste for the habits of a mass mob reached such precision, never did wit falter in its natural assumption that the idiocies of the mass were attached breath and kiss to the hypocrisies, the weltering grandeurs, and the low stupidities of the rich, the American rich. The aristocratic impulse to define society by evocations of manner now survived only in the grace of any cannibal sufficiently aristocratic to sup upon his own family.* The Magic Christian *was a classic of Camp.*

Note then: The two impulses in American letters had failed, the realistic impulse never delivered the novel which would ignite a nation's conscious-

ness of itself, and the aristocratic impulse clawed at the remaining fabric of a wealthy society it despised and no longer wished to sustain. Like a Tinguely machine which destroys itself, Camp amused by the very act of its destruction. Since it was also sentimental, the artifacts were necrophiliac.

Literature then had failed. The work was done by the movies, by television. The consciousness of the masses and the culture of the land trudged through endless mud.

The American consciousness in the absence of a great tradition in the novel ended by being developed by the bootlicking pieties of small-town newspaper editors and small-town educators, by the worst of organized religion, a formless force filled with the terrors of all the Christians left to fill the spaces left by the initial bravery of the frontiersman, and these latterday Christians were simply not as brave. That was one component of the mud. The other was the sons of the immigrants. Many of them hated America, hated it for what it offered and did not provide, what it revealed of opportunity and what it excluded from real opportunity. The sons of these immigrants and the sons' sons took over the cities and began to run them, high up in the air and right down into the ground, they plucked and they plundered and there was not an American city which did not grow more hideous in the last fifty years. Then they spread out—they put suburbs like blight on the land—and piped mass communications into every home. They were cannibals selling Christianity to Christians, and because they despised the message and mocked at it in their own heart, they succeeded in selling something else, a virus perhaps, an electronic nihilism went through the mass media of America and entered the Christians and they were like to being cannibals, they were a tense and livid people, swallowing their own hate with the tranquilizers and the sex in the commercials, whereas all the early cannibals at the knobs of the mass-media made the mistake of passing on their bleak disease and were left now too gentle, too liberal, too programmatic, filled with plans for social welfare, and they looked and talked in Show Biz styles which possessed no style and were generally as unhealthy as Christians who lived in cellars and caves.

Yes, the cannibal sons of the immigrants had become Christians, and the formless form they had evolved for their mass-media, the hypocritical empty and tasteless taste of the television arts they beamed across the land encountered the formless form and the all but tasteless taste of the small-town tit-eating cannibal mind at its worst, and the collision produced schizophrenia in the land. Half of America went insane with head colds and medicaments and asthmas and allergies, hospitals and famous surgeons with knives to cut into the plague, welfares and plans and committees and cooperations and boredom, boredom plague deep upon the land; and the other part of America went ape, and the motorcycles began to roar like lions across the land and all the beasts of all the buried history of America turned in their circuit and prepared to slink toward the market place, there to burn the mother's hair and bite the baby to the heart. One thought of America and one thought of aspirin, kitchen-commercials, and blood. One thought of Vietnam. And the important art in America became the art of the absurd.

There will be talk before this book is done of the nature of the art of the absurd, there will be perhaps even an attempt to explain it, but for now we have come to another explanation. For a good deal follows about the writing of contemporaries; there is criticism, some of it very critical. But then, good writing is not an act to excite tolerance because it is good, but anguish because it is not better. Who can swear there has not been something catastrophic to America in the failure of her novelists? Maybe we are the last liberators in the land, and if we continue to thrive on much less than our best, then the being of all of us may be deadened before we are done.

That is a statement which sups on the essence of extravagance, and yet it is the distance of the bridge to be built. It may be necessary that a communication of human experience, of the deepest and most unrecoverable human experience, must yet take place if we are to survive. Such at least is the covert opinion beneath the criticism which now follows.

SOME CHILDREN OF THE GODDESS

The last time I remember talking about the novel was a year ago, last June or July, and it was in a conversation with Gore Vidal. We were reminiscing in mutually sour fashion over the various pirates, cutthroats, racketeers, assassins, pimps, rape artists, and general finks we had encountered on our separate travels through the literary world, and we went on at length, commenting—Gore with a certain bitter joy, I with some uneasiness—upon the decline of the novel in recent years. We were speaking as trade unionists. It was not that the American novel was necessarily less good than it had been immediately after the war, so much as that the people we knew seemed to care much less about novels. The working conditions were not as good. One rarely heard one's friends talking about a good new novel any more; it was always an essay in some magazine or a new play which seemed to occupy the five minutes in a dinner party when writers are discussed rather than politicians, friends, society or, elevate us, foreign affairs. One could not make one's living writing good novels any more. With an exception here and there, it had always been impossible, but not altogether—there had used to be the long chance of having a best seller. Now with paperback books, even a serious novel with extraordinarily good reviews was lucky to sell thirty thousand copies—most people preferred to wait a year and read the book later in its cheap edition.

So we went on about that, and the professional mediocrity of book reviewers and the indifference of publishers, the lack of community among novelists themselves, the backbiting, the glee with which most of us listened to unhappy news about other novelists, the general distaste of the occupation—its lonely hours, its jealous practitioners, its demands on one's character, its assaults on one's ego, its faithlessness as inspiration, its ambushes as fashion. Since we had both begun again to work on a novel after many years of working at every other kind of writing, there was a pleasant irony to all we said. We were not really as bitter as we sounded.

Finally, I laughed. "Gore, admit it. The novel is like the Great Bitch in one's life. We think we're rid of her, we go on to other women, we take our pulse and decide that finally we're enjoying ourselves, we're free of her power, we'll never suffer her depredations again, and then we turn a corner on a street, and there's the Bitch smiling at us, and we're trapped. We're still trapped. We know the Bitch has still got us."

Vidal gave that twisted grin of admiration which is extracted from him when someone else has coined an image which could fit his style. "Indeed," he said, sighing, "the novel *is* the Great Bitch."

We've all had a piece of her, Nelson Algren, Jack Kerouac, myself, Ross Lockridge, Thomas Heggen, Truman Capote, John Horne Burns, Calder Willingham, Gore Vidal, Chandler Brossard, Walter van Tilburg Clark, Vance Bourjaily, William Humphrey, Willard Motley, Wright Morris, William Gaddis, Alex Trocchi—as well as the writers I'm going to talk about here, specifically James Jones, William Styron, Joseph Heller, John Updike, Philip Roth, Jimmy Baldwin, William Burroughs, Saul Bellow, J. D. Salinger—and all the writers there's not been time to read or write about this trip: James Purdy, Walker Percy, J. F. Powers, Ken Kesey, John Hawkes, Mark Harris, Louis Auchincloss, John Hersey, Clancy Sigal, J. P. Donleavy, Bernard Malamud, and how many others I've missed, and all the women, all the lady writers, bless them. But one cannot speak of a woman having a piece of the Bitch.

Let me list the novels I wish to discuss. They are *The Thin Red Line; Set This House on Fire; Naked Lunch; Catch-22; Rabbit, Run; Letting Go; Another Country; Henderson the Rain King; Franny and Zooey;* and *Raise High the Roof Beam, Carpenters.* They are not necessarily the best novels to have been written in America in the last few years, although if one could pick the best ten books of fiction which have been done in this country for the period, four or five of the titles on my list might have to be included. I chose these particular volumes by a particular test which might as well be explained.

It is impossible to read each good novel as it comes out. If you're trying to do your own work, it's distracting. Generally you stay away from the work of contemporaries for a year or two at a time: it saves a good deal of reading. It is amazing how many much-touted novels disappear in eighteen months. The underlying force in book reviewing is journalism. The editor of a book review has a section which he hopes to make as interesting to the owner of the newspaper as any other department. If, for two or three days, a newspaper is filled with news about a murder, one can be certain it is treated implicitly as the most exciting murder in the last twenty years. So with war novels, first novels, novels about homosexuality, politics, novels by authors of the Establishment, and historical novels. If I had a chapter of a novel for each review I've read of a new war novel which was said to be as good as *The Naked and the Dead* or *From Here to Eternity,* I would have fifty chapters. One never knows, of course. Maybe a few of these books are as good as they're said to be, and even if they've since disappeared, they will emerge again in ten or twenty years or in a century, but it is easier and much more logical to ignore what is said about a book when it first appears. There is too much direct and personal interest in the initial opinions, and much too much logrolling. The editor of a large book review is of course not owned by the Book-of-the-Month Club, but on the other hand the editor would just as soon not give more than two or three bad reviews in a year to book-club choices. Nor is his attitude dissimilar when it comes to choosing a reviewer for the novel which a big publishing house has chosen for its big book of the season. Robert Ruark, James Michener, Allen Drury will pick up their occasional roasts and slams, but considering how bad their books can be, it's impressive what attention they get. The slack (since a book review, depending on local tradition, can have just a certain proportion of good reviews) is taken up by misassigning small, determined literary types onto most of the really good novels, which then receive snide treatment and/or dismissal. *Catch-22*, for example, was reviewed on page fifty of *The New York Times Book Review*. Since this causes a vague uneasiness afterward in the book-review editor, there are always good young writers like Updike and Roth who get on the approved list and get many too many good reviews from bad reviewers. The point is that any serious novelist knows enough to stay out of the flurry which hits a new book. Every year whether the books deserve it or not, four or five first novelists will be provided a brilliant debut and four or five respectable young novelists will receive the kind of review which "enhances their reputation as one of the most serious and dedicated voices in the vineyard of literature."

So you stay away. If your friends keep talking about certain books, and young writers, and girls at cocktail parties, if the talk is intriguing because as the months go by, you begin to have less and less of a clear impression of the books, then they come to install themselves on your reading list. And every year, or two years, or three, you go off on a binge for a month and gorge on the novels of your contemporaries and see how they made out on their night with the Bitch. But of course there are many books which you know are good and yet never get around to reading. For example, I had a lot of respect for *The Violated* by Vance Bourjaily. It gave me the feeling Bourjaily was capable of writing a major novel before he was through. His next book was *Confessions of a Spent Youth*. I dipped into it, and it seemed good to me, but it was good in the way of *The Violated*; it did not seem to go further. What I heard about it did not contradict my impression. So although Bourjaily was a friend, I never got around to reading *Confessions of a Spent Youth*. I still think that in ten years Bourjaily can be one of our four or five major novelists. He has great stamina and very decent insights which ride on a fine oil of humor, but the implicit logic of my method

directed me away from Vance's last novel. It was not that I didn't
think it would be good, but rather that I didn't think it would be
different from what I expected. And when you're a professional and a
gentleman gangster, your taste is for new weapons, not improvements
on the old ones.

Now this emphasis upon the personal method of the critic may have
justification. Trotsky once wrote that you can tell the truth by a com-
parison of the lies. Every novelist who has slept with the Bitch (only
poets and writers of short stories have a *Muse*) comes away bragging
afterward like a G.I. tumbling out of a whorehouse spree—"Man, I made
her moan," goes the cry of the young writer. But the Bitch laughs after-
ward in her empty bed. "He was so sweet in the beginning," she declares,
"but by the end he just went, 'Peep, peep, peep.'" A man lays his char-
acter on the line when he writes a novel. Anything in him which is lazy,
or meretricious, or unthought-out, or complacent, or fearful, or overambi-
tious, or terrified by the ultimate logic of his exploration, will be revealed
in his book. Some writers are skillful at concealing their weaknesses,
some have a genius for converting a weakness into an acceptable man-
nerism of style. (One can even go so far as to say that Hemingway could
never write a really good long sentence, and so cultivated the art of the
short, whereas Faulkner could never express the simple very simply, and
so flowered a great garden in the thicket of nonstop prose.)

The notion is that a writer, no matter how great, is never altogether
great; a small part of him remains a liar. Tolstoy evaded the depths
which Dostoevsky opened; in turn Dostoevsky, lacking Tolstoy's majestic
sense of the proportions of things, fled proportion and explored hysteria.
A writer is recognized as great when his work is done, but while he is
writing, he rarely feels so great. He is more likely to live with the anxiety
of "Can I do it? Should I let up here? Should I reconnoiter there? Will
dread overwhelm me if I explore too far? or depression deaden me if
I do not push on? Can I even do it?" As he writes, the writer is reshaping
his character. He is a better man and he is worse, once he has finished
a book. Potentialities in him have been developed, other talents have
been sacrificed. He has made choices on his route and the choices have
shaped him. By this understanding, a genius is a man of large talent
who has made many good choices and a few astounding ones. He has
had the wit to discipline his cowardice and he has had the courage to be
bold where others might cry insanity. Yet no matter how large his genius,
we can be certain of one thing—he could have been even greater. Dostoev-
sky was a very great writer, but if he had tried to be even greater he
would either have cracked up or found impetus to write the *Confessions
of a Great Sinner*. And if he had, the history of the world might have

been different for it. It is even possible that Dostoevsky died in anguish, complimenting himself not at all for *The Brothers Karamazov* but hating himself for having so wasted a part of his talent that the greatest novel of them all was not written and he went with terror into death believing he had failed his Christ.

The example is extreme. Just so. There is a kind of critic who writes only about the dead. He sees the great writers of the past as simple men. They are born with a great talent, they exercise it, and they die. Such critics see the mastery in the work; they neglect the subtle failures of the most courageous intent, and the dramatic hours when the man took the leap to become a great writer. They do not understand that for every great writer, there are a hundred who could have been equally great but lacked the courage. For that reason it may be better to think of writers as pole vaulters than as artists. Pole vaulting is an act. The man who wins is the man who jumps the highest without knocking off the bar. And a man who clears the stick with precise form but eighteen inches below the record commands less of our attention. The writer, particularly the American writer, is not usually—if he is interesting—the quiet master of his craft; he is rather a being who ventured into the jungle of his unconscious to bring back a sense of order or a sense of chaos, he passes through ambushes in his sleep and, if he is ambitious, he must be ready to engage the congealed hostility of the world. If a writer is really good enough and bold enough he will, by the logic of society, write himself out onto the end of a limb which the world will saw off. He does not go necessarily to his death, but he must dare it. And some of us do go into death: Ross Lockridge, Thomas Heggen, Thomas Wolfe most especially, firing the passions which rotted his brain on those long paranoid nights in Brooklyn when he wrote in exaltation and terror on the top of a refrigerator. And Hemingway who dared death ten times over and would have had to dare it a hundred more in order to find more art, because each time he passed through death the sweet of new creativity was offered.

Well, few of us dare death. With the trinity of booze, coffee and cig-arettes, most of us voyage out a part of the way into our jungle and come back filled with pride at what we dared, and shame at what we avoided, and because we are men of the middle and shame is an emotion no man of the middle can bear for too long without dying, we act like novelists, which is to say that we are full of spleen, small gossip, hatred for the success of our enemies, envy at the fortunes of our friends, ideologues of a style of fiction which is uniquely the best (and is invariably our own style), and so there is a tendency for us to approach the books of our contemporaries like a defense attorney walking up to a key witness for the prosecution. The average good novelist reads the work of his fellow racketeers with one underlying tension—find the flaw, find where the other guy cheated.

One cannot expect an objective performance therefore when one novelist criticizes the work of other novelists. It is better to realize that a group of men who are to a degree honest and to another extent deceitful (to the reader, or to themselves, or to both) are being judged by one of their peers who shares in the rough their proportions of integrity and pretense and is likely to have the most intense vested interest in advancing the reputation of certain writers while doing his best to diminish others. But the reader is at least given the opportunity to compare the lies, a gratuity he cannot always get from a good critic writing about a novelist, for critics implant into their style the fiction of disinterested passion when indeed *their* vested interest, while less obvious, is often more rabid, since they have usually fixed their aim into the direction they would like the novel to travel, whereas the novelist by the nature of his endeavor is more ready to change. One need not defend the procedure used here any further than to say it is preferable to warn a reader of one's prejudices than to believe the verdict of a review which is godly in its authority and psychologically unsigned.

I doubt if there is any book I read in the last few years which I approached with more unnatural passion than *Set This House on Fire.* Styron's first novel, *Lie Down in Darkness,* was published when he was twenty-six, and it was so good (one need today only compare it to *Rabbit, Run* to see how very good it was) that one felt a kind of awe about Styron. He gave promise of becoming a great writer, great not like Hemingway nor even like Faulkner, whom he resembled a bit, but great perhaps like Hawthorne. And there were minor echoes of Fitzgerald and Malcolm Lowry. Since his first novel had failed to make him a household word in America, he had a justifiable bitterness about the obscurity in which good young writers were kept. But it poisoned his reaction to everything. One of the traps for a writer of exceptional talent, recognized insufficiently, is the sort of excessive rage which washes out distinction. Styron was intensely competitive—all good young novelists are—but over the years envy began to eat into his character. Months before James Jones' *Some Came Running* was published (and it had the greatest advance publicity of any novel I remember—for publicity seemed to begin two years before publication), Styron obtained a copy of the galleys. There were long nights in Connecticut on "Styron's

Acres" when he would entertain a group of us by reading absurd passages from Jones' worst prose. I would laugh along with the rest, but I was a touch sick with myself. I had love for Jones, as well as an oversized fear for the breadth of his talent, and I had enough envy in me to enjoy how very bad were the worst parts of *Some Came Running*. But there were long powerful chapters as well; some of the best writing Jones has ever done is found in that book. So I would laugh in paroxysms along with the others, but I was also realizing that a part of me had wanted *Some Came Running* to be a major book. I was in the doldrums, I needed a charge of dynamite. If *Some Came Running* had turned out to be the best novel any of us had written since the war, I would have had to get to work. It would have meant the Bitch was in love with someone else, and I would have had to try to win her back. But the failure of *Some Came Running* left me holding onto a buttock of the lady—if she had many lovers, I was still one of them. And so everything in me which was slack and conservative could enjoy Styron's burlesque readings. Yet I also knew I had lost an opportunity.

A few months later, I ceased seeing Styron—it would take a chapter in a novel to tell you why. I liked the boy in Styron, disliked the man, and had vast admiration for his talent. I was hardly the one to read *Set This House on Fire* with a cool mind. Nine years had gone by since *Lie Down in Darkness* was published, and the anticipation of the second novel had taken on grandiloquent proportions among his friends and his closest enemies. One knew it would be close to unbearable if his book were extraordinary; yet a part of me felt again what I had known with *Some Came Running*—that it would be good for me and for my work if Styron's novel were better than anything any of us had done. So I read it with a hot sense of woe, delighted elation, and a fever of moral speculations. Because it was finally a bad novel. A bad maggoty novel. Four or five half-great short stories were buried like pullulating organs in a corpse of fecal matter, overblown unconceived philosophy, Technicolor melodramatics, and a staggering ignorance about the passions of murder, suicide and rape. It was the magnum opus of a fat spoiled rich boy who could write like an angel about landscape and like an adolescent about people. The minor characters were gargoyles, and badly drawn. Here and there quick portraits emerged, there was one excellent still life of an Italian police official who was Fascist, the set pieces were laid out nicely, but the vice of the talent insisted on dominating. Whenever Styron didn't know what to do with his men and women (which was often, for they repeated themselves as endlessly as a Southern belle) Styron went back to his landscape; more of the portentous Italian scenery blew up its midnight storm. But Styron was trying to write a book about good and evil, and his good was as vacuous as the spirit of an empty water bag:

> *I can only tell you this, that as for being and nothingness, the one thing I did know was that to choose between them was simply to choose being, not for the sake of being, or even the love of being, much less the desire to be forever—but in the hope of being what I could be for a time.*

Which is a great help to all of us.

His evil character took on the fatal sin of an evil character: he was not dangerous but pathetic. A fink. Styron was crawling with all ten thumbs toward that ogre of mystery who guards the secrets of why we choose to kill others and quiver in dread at the urge to kill ourselves. But like a bad general who surrounds himself with a staff which daren't say no, Styron spent his time digging trenches for miles to the left and miles to the right, and never launched an attack on the hill before him. It was the book of a man whose soul had gotten fat.

And yet, much as I could be superior to myself for having taken him thus seriously, for having written predictions in *Advertisements for Myself* that he would write a very good book which the mass media would call great, much as I would grin each day after reading a hundred pages of hothouse beauty and butter bilge, much as I would think, "You don't catch the Bitch that way, buster, you got to bring more than a trombone to her boudoir," much so much as I was pleased at the moral justice which forbids a novelist who envied too much the life of others to capture much life in his own pages, I was still not altogether happy, because I knew his failure was making me complacent again, and so delaying once more the day when I would have to pay my respects to the lady.

And indeed I lost something by the failure of *Some Came Running* and *Set This House on Fire*. I never did get going far on my novel. I wrote a four-hour play and essays and articles, two hundred thousand words accumulated over the years since *Advertisements for Myself*, and I showed a talent for getting into stunts, and worse, much worse. Years went by. Now once again, in this season, ready to start my novel about the mysteries of murder and suicide,* I found by taking stock of psychic credit and debit that I had lost some of my competitive iron. I knew a bit of sadness about work. I did not feel sure I could do what I had now settled for doing, and to my surprise I was curious what others were up to. If I couldn't bring off the work by myself, it might be just as well if someone else could give a sign of being ready to make

---

* This novel was a continuation thematically of the long novel announced in *Advertisements for Myself*. It was put aside six months later to go to work on *An American Dream*.

the attempt. In this sad dull mellow mood, feeling a little like a middle-aged mountaineer, I read at one stretch over three weeks the novels I want to write about here.

There was a time, I suspect, when James Jones wanted to be the greatest writer who ever lived. Now, if *The Thin Red Line* is evidence of his future, he has apparently decided to settle for being a very good writer among other good writers. The faults and barbarities of his style are gone. He is no longer the worst writer of prose ever to give intimations of greatness. The language has been filed down and the phrases no longer collide like trailer trucks at a hot intersection. Yet I found myself nostalgic for the old bad prose. I never used to think it was as bad as others did, it was eloquent and communicated Jones' force to the reader. It is not that *The Thin Red Line* is dishonest or narrow; on the contrary it is so broad and true a portrait of combat that it could be used as a textbook at the Infantry School if the Army is any less chicken than it used to be. But, sign of the times, there is now something almost too workmanlike about Jones. He gets almost everything in, horror, fear, fatigue, the sport of combat, the hang-ups, details, tactics; he takes an infantry company through its early days in combat on Guadalcanal and quits it a few weeks later as a veteran outfit, blooded, tough, up on morale despite the loss of half the original men, gone, dead, wounded, sick or transferred. So he performs the virtuoso feat of letting us know a little about a hundred men. One can even (while reading) remember their names. Jones' aim, after all, is not to create character but the feel of combat, the psychology of men. He is close to a master at this. Jones has a strong sense of a man's psychology and it carries quietly through his pages.

   The Thin Red Line was of course compared to *The Naked and the Dead*, but apart from the fact that I am the next-to-last man to judge the respective merits of the two books, I didn't see them as similar. *The Naked and the Dead* is concerned more with characters than military action. By comparison it's a leisurely performance. *The Thin Red Line* is as crammed as a movie treatment. No, I think the real comparison is to *The Red Badge of Courage*, and I suspect *The Red Badge of Courage* will outlive *The Thin Red Line*. Yet I don't quite know why. *The Thin Red Line* is a more detailed book; it tells much more of combat, studies the variations in courage and fear of not one man but twenty men and gets something good about each one of them. Its knowledge of life is superior to *The Red Badge of Courage*. *The Thin Red Line* is less sentimental, its humor is dry to the finest taste, and yet . . . it is too technical. One needs ten topographical maps to trace the action. With all its variety, scrupulosity, respect for craft, one doesn't remember *The Thin Red Line* with that same nostalgia, that same sense of a fire on the horizon which comes back always from *The Red Badge of Courage*.

No, Jones' book is better remembered as satisfying, as if one had studied geology for a semester and now knew more. I suppose what was felt lacking is the curious sensuousness of combat, the soft lift of awe and pleasure that one was moving out onto the rim of the dead. If one was not too tired, there were times when a blade of grass coming out of the ground before one's nose was as significant as the finger of Jehovah in the Sistine Chapel. And this was not because a blade of grass was necessarily in itself so beautiful, or because hitting the dirt was so sweet, but because the blade seemed to be a living part of the crack of small-arms fire and the palpable flotation of all the other souls in the platoon full of turd and glory. Now, it's not that Jones is altogether ignorant of this state. The description he uses is "sexy," and one of the nicest things about Jim as a writer is his ease in moving from mystical to practical reactions with his characters. Few novelists can do this, it's the hint of greatness, but I think he steered *The Thin Red Line* away from its chance of becoming an American classic of the first rank when he kept the mystical side of his talents on bread and water, and gave his usual thoroughgoing company man's exhibition of how much he knows technically about his product. I think that is the mistake. War is as full of handbooks as engineering, but it is more of a mystery, and the mystery is what separates the great war novels from the good ones. It is an American activity to cover the ground quickly, but I guess this is one time Jones should have written two thousand pages, not four hundred ninety-five. But then the underlying passion in this book is not to go for broke, but to promise the vested idiots of the book reviews that he can write as good as anyone who writes a book review.

When you discuss eight or ten books, there is a dilemma. The choice is to write eight separate book reviews, or work to find a thesis which ties the books together. There is something lickspittle about the second method: "Ten Authors in Search of a Viable Theme," or "The Sense of Alienation in Eight American Novelists." A bed of Procrustes is brought in from the wings to stretch and shorten the separate qualities of the books. I would rather pick up each book by itself and make my connections on the fly. The thesis of the Bitch is thesis enough for me. Its application to Jones would say that *The Thin Red Line* is a holding action, a long-distance call to the Goddess to declare that one still has one's hand in, expect red roses for sure, but for the time, you know, like there're contacts to make on the road, and a few Johns to impress.

Another Country, by James Baldwin, is as different from *The Thin Red Line* as two books by talented novelists published in the same year can turn out to be. It does not deal with a hundred characters, but eight, and they are very much related. In fact there is a chain of fornication which is all but complete. A Negro musician named Rufus Scott has an affair with a white Southern girl which ends in beatings, breakdown, and near-insanity. She goes to a mental hospital, he commits suicide. The connection is taken up by his sister who has an affair with a white writer, a friend of Rufus' named Vivaldo Moore, who in turn gets into bed with a friend named Eric who is homosexual but having an affair with a married woman named Cass Silenski, which affair wrecks her marriage with her husband, Richard, another writer, and leaves Eric waiting at the boat for his French lover Yves. A summary of this sort can do a book no good, but I make it to trace the links. With the exception of Rufus Scott, who does not go to bed with his sister, everybody else in the book is connected by their skin to another character who is connected to still another. So the principal in the book, the protagonist, is not an individual character, not society, not a milieu, not a social organism like an infantry company, but indeed is sex, sex very much in the act. And almost the only good writing in the book is about the act. And some of that is very good indeed. But *Another Country* is a shocker. For the most part it is an abominably written book. It is sluggish in its prose, lifeless for its first hundred pages, stilted to despair in its dialogue. There are roles in plays called actor-proof. They are so conceived that even the worst actor will do fairly well. So *Another Country* is writer-proof. Its peculiar virtue is that Baldwin commits every *gaffe* in the art of novel writing and yet has a powerful book. It gets better of course; after the first hundred pages it gets a lot better. Once Eric, the homosexual, enters, the work picks up considerably. But what saves the scene is that Baldwin has gotten his hands into the meat and won't let go. All the sex in the book is displaced, whites with blacks, men with men, women with homosexuals; the sex is funky to suffocation, rich but claustrophobic, sensual but airless. Baldwin understands the existential abyss of love. In a world of Negroes and whites, nuclear fallout, marijuana, bennies, inversion, insomnia, and tapering off with beer at four in the morning, one no longer just falls in love—one has to take a brave leap over the wall of one's impacted rage and cowardice. And nobody makes it, not quite. Each of the characters rides his sexual chariot, whip out, on a gallop over a solitary track, and each is smashed, more or less by his own hand. They cannot find the juice to break out of their hatred into the other country of love. Except for the homosexuals who can't break into heterosexual love. Of all the novels talked about here, *An-*

other Country is the one which is closest to the mood of New York in our time, a way of saying it is close to the air of the Western world, it is at least a novel about matters which are important, but one can't let up on Baldwin for the way he wrote it. Years ago I termed him "minor" as a writer; I thought he was too smooth and too small. Now on his essays alone, on the long continuing line of poetic fire in his essays, one knows he has become one of the few writers of our time. But as a Negro novelist he could take lessons from a good journeyman like John Killens. Because *Another Country* is almost a major novel and yet it is far and away the weakest and worst near-major novel one has finished. It goes like the first draft of a first novelist who has such obvious stuff that one is ready, if an editor, to spend years guiding him into how to write, even as one winces at the sloppy company which must be kept. Nobody has more elegance than Baldwin as an essayist, not one of us hasn't learned something about the art of the essay from him, and yet he can't even find a good prose for his novel. Maybe the form is not for him. He knows what he wants to say, and that is not the best condition for writing a novel. Novels go happiest when you discover something you did not know you knew. Baldwin's experience has shaped his tongue toward directness, for urgency—the honorable defense may be that he has not time nor patience to create characters, milieu, and mood for the revelation of important complexities he has already classified in his mind.

Baldwin's characters maim themselves trying to smash through the wall of their imprisonment. Willian Burroughs gives what may be the finest record in our century of the complete psychic convict. *Naked Lunch* is a book of pieces and fragments, notes and nightmarish anecdotes, which he wrote—according to his preface—in various states of delirium, going in and out of a heroin addiction. It is not a novel in any conventional sense, but then there's a question whether it's a novel by any set of standards other than the dictum that prose about imaginary people put between book covers is a novel. At any rate, the distinction is not important except for the fact that *Naked Lunch* is next to impossible to read in consecutive fashion. I saw excerpts of it years ago, and thought enough of them to go on record that Burroughs "may conceivably be possessed by genius." I still believe that, but it is one thing to be possessed by genius, it is another to be a genius, and *Naked Lunch* read from cover to cover is not as exciting as in its separate pieces. Quantity changes quality, as Karl Marx once put it, and fifty or sixty three-page bits about homosexual orgies, castration, surgeon-assassins, and junkie fuzz dissolving into a creeping green ooze leaves one feeling pretty tough. "Let's put some blue-purple blood in the next rape," says your jaded taste.

This is, however, quibbling. Some of the best prose in America is graffiti found on men's-room walls. It is prose written in bone, etched by acid, it is the prose of harsh truth, the virulence of the criminal who never found his stone walls and so settles down on the walls of the john, it is the language of hatred unencumbered by guilt, hesitation, scruple, or complexity. Burroughs must be the greatest writer of graffiti who ever lived. His style has the snap of a whip, and it never relents. Every paragraph is quotable. Here's a jewel among a thousand jewels:

> *Dr. Benway . . . looks around and picks up one of those rubber vacuum*
> *cups at the end of a stick they use to unstop toilets . . . "Make an incision,*
> *Doctor Limpf. . . . I'm going to massage the heart." . . . Dr. Benway*
> *washes the suction cup by swishing it around in the toilet-bowl. . . .*
> *Dr. Limpf: "The incision is ready, doctor."*
> *Dr. Benway forces the cup into the incision and works it up and down.*
> *Blood spurts all over the doctors, the nurse and the wall. . . .*
> *Nurse: "I think she's gone, doctor."*
> *Dr. Benway: "Well, it's all in the day's work."*

Punch and Judy. Mr. Interlocutor and Mr. Bones. One, two, three, bam! two, four, eight, bam! The drug addict lives with a charged wire so murderous he must hang his nervous system on a void. Burroughs' achievement, his great achievement, is that he has brought back snowflakes from this murderous void.

Once, years ago in Chicago, I was coming down with a bad cold. By accident, a friend took me to hear a jazz musician named Sun Ra who played "space music." The music was a little like the sound of Ornette Coleman, but further out, outer space music, close to the EEEE of an electric drill at the center of a harsh trumpet. My cold cleared up in five minutes. I swear it. The anger of the sound penetrated into some sprung-up rage which was burning fuel for the cold. Burroughs' pages have the same medicine. If a hundred patients on terminal cancer read *Naked Lunch,* one or two might find remission. Bet money on that. For Burroughs is the surgeon of the novel.

Yet he is something more. It is his last ability which entitles him to a purchase on genius. Through the fantasies runs a vision of a future world, a half demented welfare state, an abattoir of science fiction with surgeons, bureaucrats, perverts, diplomats, a world not describable short of getting into the book. The ideas have pushed into the frontier of an all-electronic universe. One holds onto a computer in some man-eating machine of the future which has learned to use language. The words come out in squeaks, spiced with static, sex coiled up with technology like a scream on the radar. Bombarded by his language, the sensation is like being in a room where three radios, two television sets, stereo hi-fi, a pornographic movie, and two automatic dishwashers are working at once while a mad scientist conducts the dials to squeeze out the maximum disturbance. If this is a true picture of the world to come, and it may be, then Burroughs is a great writer. Yet there is sadness in reading him, for one gets intimations of a mind which might have come within distance of Joyce, except that a catastrophe has been visited on it, a blow by a sledge hammer, a junkie's needle which left the crystalline brilliance crashed into bits.

Now beyond a doubt, of all the books discussed here, the one which most cheats evaluation is Joseph Heller's *Catch-22*. It was the book which took me longest to finish, and I almost gave it up. Yet I think that a year from now I may remember it more vividly than *The Thin Red Line*. Because it is an original. There's no book like it anyone has read. Yet it's maddening. It reminds one of a Jackson Pollock painting eight feet high, twenty feet long. Like yard goods, one could cut it anywhere. One could take out a hundred pages anywhere from the middle of *Catch-22*, and not even the author could be certain they were gone. Yet the length and similarity of one page to another gives a curious meat-and-potatoes to the madness; building upon itself the book becomes substantial until the last fifty pages grow suddenly and surprisingly powerful, only to be marred by an ending over the last five pages which is hysterical, sentimental and wall-eyed for Hollywood.

This is the skin of the reaction. If I were a major critic, it would be a virtuoso performance to write a definitive piece on *Catch-22*. It would take ten thousand words or more. Because Heller is carrying his reader on a more consistent voyage through Hell than any American writer before him (except Burroughs who has already made the trip and now sells choice seats in the auditorium), and so the analysis of Joseph H.'s Hell would require a discussion of other varieties of inferno and whether they do more than this author's tour.

Catch-22 is a nightmare about an American bomber squadron on a made-up island off Italy. Its hero is a bombardier named Yossarian who has flown fifty missions and wants out. On this premise is tattooed the events of the novel, fifty characters, two thousand frustrations (an average of four or five to the page), and one simple motif: more frustration. Yossarian's colonel wants to impress his general and so raises the number

of missions to fifty-five. When the pilots have fifty-four, the figure is
lifted to sixty. They are going for eighty by the time the book has been
done. On the way every character goes through a routine *on every page*
which is as formal as a little peasant figure in a folk dance. Back in school,
we had a joke we used to repeat. It went:

"Whom are you talking about?"

-"Herbert Hoover."

"Never heard of him."

"Never heard of whom?"

"Herbert Hoover."

"Who's he?"

"He's the man you mentioned."

"Never heard of Herbert Hoover."

So it went. So goes *Catch-22*. It's the rock and roll of novels. One finds
its ancestor in Basic Training. We were ordered to have clean sheets for
Saturday inspection. But one week we were given no clean sheets from
the Post laundry so we slept on our mattress covers, which got dirty.
After inspection, the platoon was restricted to quarters. "You didn't have
clean sheets," our sergeant said.

"How could we have clean sheets if the clean sheets didn't come?"

"How do I know?" said the sergeant. "The regulations say you gotta
have clean sheets."

"But we can't have clean sheets if there are no clean sheets."

"That," said the sergeant, "is tough shit."

Which is what *Catch-22* should have been called. The Army is a village
of colliding bureaucracies whose colliding orders cook up impossibilities.
Heller takes this one good joke and exploits it into two thousand varia-
tions of the same good joke, but in the act he somehow creates a rational
vision of the modern world. Yet the crisis of reason is that it can no longer
comprehend the modern world. Heller demonstrates that a rational man
devoted to reason must arrive at the conclusion that either the world is
mad and he is the only sane man in it, or (and this is the weakness of
Catch-22—it never explores this possibility) the sane man is not really
sane because his rational propositions are without existential reason.

On page 178, there is a discussion about God.

". . . *how much reverence can you have for a Supreme Being who finds
it necessary to include such phenomena as phlegm and tooth decay in His
divine system of creation. . . . Why in the world did He ever create pain?"*

*"Pain?" Lieutenant Scheisskopf's wife pounced upon the word victoriously.
"Pain is a useful symptom. Pain is a warning to us of bodily dangers."*

*. . . "Why couldn't he have used a doorbell instead to notify us, or one
of His celestial choirs?"*

Right there is planted the farthest advance of the flag of reason in his cosmology. Heller does not look for any answer, but there is an answer which might go that God gave us pain for the same reason the discovery of tranquilizers was undertaken by the Devil: if we have an immortal soul some of us come close to it only through pain. A season of sickness can be preferable to a flight from disease, for it discourages the onrush of a death which begins in the center of oneself.

Give talent its due. *Catch-22* is the debut of a writer with merry gifts. Heller may yet become Gogol. But what makes one hesitate to call his first novel great or even major is that he has only grasped the inferior aspect of Hell. What is most unendurable is not the military world of total frustration so much as the midnight frustration of the half world, Baldwin's other country, where a man may have time to hear his soul, and time to go deaf, even be forced to contemplate himself as he becomes deadened before his death. (Much as Hemingway may have been.) That is when one becomes aware of the anguish, the existential *angst*, which wars enable one to forget. It is that other death—without war—where one dies by a failure of nerve, which opens the bloodiest vents of Hell. And that is a novel none of us has yet come back alive to write.

With the exception of *Another Country*, the novels talked about up to now have been books written for men. *Catch-22* was liked, I believe, by almost every man who read it. Women were puzzled. The world of a man is a world of surface slick and rock knowledge. A man must live by daily acts where he goes to work and works on the world some incremental bit, using the tools, instruments, and the techniques of the world. Thus a man cannot afford to go too deeply into the underlying meaning of a single subject. He prefers to become interested in quick proportions and contradictions, in the practical surface of things. A book like *Catch-22* is written on the face of solemn events and their cockeyed contradictions. So it has a vast appeal: it relieves the frustration men feel at the idiocy of their work. *Naked Lunch* fries the surface in a witch's skillet; the joy in reading is equal to the kick of watching a television announcer go insane before your eyes and start to croon obscenely about the President, First Lady, Barry Goldwater, Cardinal Spellman, J. Edgar. Somewhere in America somebody would take out his pistol and shoot the set. Burroughs shatters the surface and blasts its shards into the madness beneath. He rips the reader free of suffocation. Jones wrote a book which a dedicated corporation executive or an ambitious foreman would read with professional avidity because they would learn a bit about the men who work for them. *The Thin Red Line* brings detail to the surprises on the toughest part of the skin. So these three books are, as I say, books for men.

Whereas *Another Country,* obsessed with that transcendental divide keeping sex from love, is a book more for women, or for men and women. So too is *Set This House on Fire.* And much the same can be said of *Rabbit, Run* and *Letting Go.*

On record are the opinions of a partisan. So it is necessary to admit that John Updike's novel was approached with animus. His reputation has traveled in convoy up the Avenue of the Establishment, *The New York Times Book Review* blowing sirens like a motorcycle caravan, the professional muse of *The New Yorker* sitting in the Cadillac, membership cards to the right Fellowships in his pocket. The sort of critics who are rarely right about a book—Arthur Mizener and Granville Hicks, for example—ride on his flanks, literary bodyguards. *Life* magazine blew its kiss of death into the confetti. To my surprise, *Rabbit, Run* was therefore a better book than I thought it would be. The Literary Establishment was improving its taste. Updike was not simply a junior edition of James Gould Cozzens. But of course the Establishment cannot nominate a candidate coherently. Updike's merits and vices were turned inside out. The good girlish gentlemen of letters were shocked by the explicitness of the sex in *Rabbit, Run,* and slapped him gently for that with their fan, but his style they applauded. It is Updike's misfortune that he is invariably honored for his style (which is atrocious—and smells like stale garlic) and is insufficiently recognized for his gifts. He could become the best of our literary novelists if he could forget about style and go deeper into the literature of sex. *Rabbit, Run* moves in well-modulated spurts at precisely those places where the style subsides to a ladylike murmur and the characters take over. The trouble is that young John, like many a good young writer before him, does not know exactly what to do when action lapses, and so he cultivates his private vice, he *writes.* And there are long over-fingered descriptions in exacerbated syntax, airless crypts of four or five pages, huge inner exertion reminiscent of weight lifters, a stale sweet sweat clings to his phrases.

Example: *Redbook, Cosmopolitan, McCall's.*

Boys are playing basketball around a telephone pole with a backboard bolted to it. Legs, shouts. The scrape and snap of Keds on loose alley pebbles seems to catapult their voices high into the moist March air blue above the wires. Rabbit Angstrom, coming up the alley in a business suit, stops and watches, though he's twenty-six and six-three. So tall, he seems an unlikely rabbit, but the breadth of white face, the pallor of his blue irises, and a nervous flutter under his brief nose as he stabs a cigarette into his mouth partially explain the nickname.

Example: *True Confessions.*
Outside in the air his fears condense. Globes of ether, pure nervousness, slide down his legs. The sense of outside space scoops at his chest.

Example: *Elements of Grammar.*
His hands lift of their own and he feels the wind on his ears even before, his heels hitting heavily on the pavement at first but with an effortless gathering out of a kind of sweet panic growing lighter and quicker and quieter, he runs. Ah: runs. Runs.

It's the rare writer who cannot have sentences lifted from his work, but the first quotation is taken from the first five sentences of the book, the second is on the next-to-last page, and the third is nothing less than the last three sentences of the novel. The beginning and end of a novel are usually worked over. They are the index to taste in the writer. Besides, trust your local gangster. In the run of Updike's pages are one thousand other imprecise, flatulent, wry-necked, precious, overpreened, self-indulgent, tortured sentences. It is the sort of prose which would be admired in a writing course overseen by a fussy old nance. And in Updike's new book, *The Centaur,* which was only sampled, the style has gotten worse. Pietisms are congregating, affirmations à la Archibald MacLeish.

The pity is that Updike has instincts for finding the heart of the conventional novel, that still-open no man's land between the surface and the deep, the soft machinery of the world and the subterranean rigors of the dream. His hero, Rabbit Angstrom, is sawed in two by the clear anguish of watching his private vision go at a gallop away from the dread real weight of his responsibility. A routine story of a man divided between a dull wife he cannot bear to live with and a blowsy tough tender whore he cannot make it with, the merit of the book is not in the simplicity of its problem, but in the dread Updike manages to convey, despite the literary commercials in the style, of a young man who is beginning to lose nothing less than his good American soul, and yet it is not quite his fault. The power of the novel comes from a sense, not absolutely unworthy of Thomas Hardy, that the universe hangs over our fates like a great sullen hopeless sky. There is real pain in the book, and a touch of awe. It is a novel which could have been important, it could have had a chance to stay alive despite its mud pies in prose, but at the very end the book drowns in slime. Updike does not know how to finish. Faced with the critical choice of picking one woman or another (and by the end, both women are in fearful need), his character bolts over a literal hill and runs away. Maybe he'll be back tomorrow, maybe he'll never be back, but a decision was necessary. The book ends as minor, a pop-out.

One is left with the expectation that Updike will never be great; there is something too fatally calculated about his inspiration. But very good he can be, a good writer of the first rank with occasional echoes from the profound. First he must make an enemy or two of the commissioners on the Literary Mafia. Of course a man spends his life trying to get up his guts for such a caper.

Letting Go, by Philip Roth, has precisely the opposite merits and faults. As a novel, its strategy is silly, tiresome, and weak. But its style, while not noteworthy, is decent and sometimes, in dialogue, halfway nice. It is good time spent to read any ten pages in the book. The details are observed, the mood is calm, the point is always made. It is like having an affair with a pleasant attentive woman—the hours go by neatly. It is only at the end of a year that one may realize the preoccupations of the mistress are hollow, and the seasons have been wasted.

Letting Go is a scrupulous account in upper Jewish New Yorker genre of a few years in the lives of two English department college instructors, one married to that most coveted of creatures, a fragile dreary hang-up of a heroine, the other a bachelor and lover of worried proportions. Very little happens. The wife goes on being herself, the husband remains naturally frozen and stingy, and the instructor-lover has a small literary breakdown. One can say, well isn't this life? didn't Chekhov and de Maupassant write about such things? And the answer is yes they did, in five pages they did, and caught that mood which reminds us that there is sadness in attrition and grinding sorrows for decency. But Roth is not writing a book with a vision of life; on the contrary, one could bet a grand he is working out an obsession. His concentration is appropriated by something in his life which has been using him up in the past. Virtually every writer, come soon or late, has a cramped-up love affair which is all but hopeless. *Of Human Bondage* could be the case study of half the writers who ever lived. But the obsession is opposed to art in the same way a compulsive talker is opposed to good conversation. The choice is either to break the obsession or enter it. The compulsive talker must go through the herculean transformation of learning to quit or must become a great monologuist. Roth tried to get into the obsession—he gave six hundred pages to wandering around in a ten-page story—but he did it without courage. He was too careful not to get hurt on his trip and so he does not reveal himself: he does not *dig.* The novel skitters like a water fly from pollen spread to pollen spread; a series of good short stories accumulate en route, but no novel. The iron law of the conventional novel, the garden novel, is that the meaning of the action must grow on every page or else the book will wither. It is Updike's respectable achievement in *Rabbit, Run* that he writes just such a book, or tries to until the last three pages when he vanishes like a sneak thief. Roth never gets into the game. One senses a determined fight to maintain *Letting Go* as a collection of intricately intercollected short stories.

But the short story has a tendency to look for climates of permanence —an event occurs, a man is hurt by it in some small way forever. The novel moves as naturally toward flux. An event occurs, a man is injured, and a month later is working on something else. The short story likes to be classic. It is most acceptable when one fatal point is made. Whereas the novel is dialectical. It is most alive when one can trace the disasters which follow victory or the subtle turns that sometimes come from a defeat. A novel can be created out of short stories only if the point in each story is consecutively more interesting and incisive than the point before it, when the author in effect is drilling for oil. But Roth's short stories in *Letting Go* just dig little holes in many suburban lawns until finally the work of reading it becomes almost as depressing as must have been the work of writing it. Roth has to make a forced march in his next book, or at least, like Updike, get around to putting his foot in the whorehouse door. If he doesn't, a special Hell awaits his ambition—he will be called the Rich Man's Paddy Chayefsky, and Paddy without his grasp of poverty is nothing much at all.

It is necessary to say that the four stories about the Glass family by J. D. Salinger, published in two books called *Franny and Zooey* and *Raise High the Roof Beam, Carpenters,* seem to have been written for high-school girls. The second piece in the second book, called *Seymour— An Introduction,* must be the most slovenly portion of prose ever put out by an important American writer. It is not even professional Salinger. Salinger at his customary worst, as here in the other three stories of the two books, is never bad—he is just disappointing. He stays too long on the light ice of his gift, writes exquisite dialogue and creates minor moods with sweetness and humor, and never gives the fish its hook. He disappoints because he is always practicing. But when he dips into Seymour, the Glass brother who committed suicide, when the cult comes to silence before the appearance of the star—the principal, to everyone's horror, has nausea on the stage. Salinger for the first time is engaged in run-off writing, free suffragette prose; his inhibitions (which once helped by their restraint to create his style) are now stripped. He is giving you himself as he is. No concealment. It feels like taking a bath in a grease trap.

Now, all of us have written as badly. There are nights when one comes home after a cancerously dull party, full of liquor but not drunk, leaden with boredom, somewhere out in Fitzgerald's long dark night. Writing at such a time is like making love at such a time. It is hopeless, it desecrates one's future, but one does it anyway because at least it is an act. Such writing is almost always unsprung. It is reminiscent of the wallflower who says, "To hell with inhibitions, I'm going to dance." The premise is that what comes out is valid because it is the record of a mood. So one records the mood. What a mood. Full of vomit, self-pity, panic, paranoia, megalomania, *merde,* whimpers, excuses, turns of the neck, flips of the wrist, transports. It is the bends of Hell. If you purge it, if you get sleep and tear it up in the morning, it can do no more harm than any other bad debauch. But Salinger went ahead and reread his stew, then sent it to *The New Yorker,* and they accepted it. Now, several years later, he reprints it in book covers.

There is social process at work here. Salinger was the most gifted minor writer in America. *The New Yorker's* ability is to produce such writers. The paradox comes from the social fact that *The New Yorker* is a major influence on American life. Hundreds of thousands, perhaps millions of people in the most established parts of the middle class kill their quickest impulses before they dare to act in such a way as to look ridiculous to the private eye of their taste whose style has been keyed by the eye of *The New Yorker.* Salinger was the finest writer *The New Yorker* ever produced, but profoundly minor. The major writer like James Jones, indeed James Jones, leads the kind of inner life which enables him to study victories as well as defeats; Salinger was catapulted by a study of excruciating small defeats into a position of major importance. The phenomenon in the nation was the same those years. Men of minor abilities engaged America in major brinkmanships.

But it is always dangerous when the Literary Mafia (*The New Yorker,* the *Saturday Review, The New York Times Book Review, Time* magazine's book reviews, and the genteel elements in publishing) promote a minor writer into a major writer. A vested interest attaches itself to keeping the corpse of the violated standards buried. Readers who might be average keen in their sense of literary value find their taste mucked up. The greatest damage in this case, however, seems to have been to Salinger himself. Because a writer, with aristocratic delicacy of intent and nerves so subtle that only isolation makes life bearable for him, has been allowed to let his talent fester in that corrupt isolation. Salinger has been the most important writer in America for a generation of adolescents and college students. He was their leader in exile. The least he owed them for his silence was a major performance.

But it's a rare man who can live like a hermit and produce a major performance unless he has critics who are near to him and hard on him.

No friend who worried about Salinger's future should have let him publish *Seymour—An Introduction* in *The New Yorker* without daring to lose his friendship first by telling him how awful it was. Yet there was too much depending on Salinger's interregnum—he was so *inoffensive*, finally. So a suspension of the critical faculty must have gone on in the institutional wheels of *The New Yorker* which was close to psychotic in its evasions.

As for the other three stories in the two books, they are not as good as the stories in *Nine Stories*. Affectations which were part once of Salinger's charm are now faults. An excessive desire to please runs through his pages. There is too much sweetness. He is too pleased with himself, too nice, he lingers too much over the happy facility of his details in a way Fitzgerald never would. He is no longer a writer so much as he is an entertainer, a slim much-beloved version of Al Jolson or Sophie Tucker; the music hall is in the root of his impulse as much as the dungeons and mansions of literature. Does one desire the real irony? There is nothing in *Franny and Zooey* which would hinder it from becoming first-rate television. It is genre with all the limitations of genre: catalogs of items in the medicine chest, long intimate family conversations with life, snap with mother, crackle and pop. If I were a television producer I'd put on *Franny and Zooey* tomorrow. And indeed in ten years they will. America will have moved from *One Man's Family* to the *Glass Family*. Which is progress. I'd rather have the Glass family on the air. But don't confuse the issue. The Glass stories are not literature, but television. And Salinger's work since *The Catcher in the Rye* is part of his long retreat from what is substantial, agonizing, uproarious, or close to awe and terror. *The Catcher in the Rye* was able to change people's lives. The new books are not even likely to improve the conversation in college dormitories. It is time Salinger came back to the city and got his hands dirty with a rough corruption or two, because the very items which composed the honor of his reputation, his resolute avoidance of the mass media and society, have now begun to back up on him. There is a taste of something self-absorptive, narcissistic, even putrefactive in his long contemplation of a lintless navel.

The value of past predictions by this critic may be judged by the following about Saul Bellow. It is taken from page 467 in *Advertisements for Myself*.

When and if I come to read Henderson the Rain King, *let me hope I do not feel the critic's vested interest to keep a banished writer in limbo, for I sense uneasily that without reading it, I have already the beginnings of a negative evaluation for it since I doubt that I would believe in Henderson as a hero.*

Well, one might as well eat the crow right here. Henderson is an exceptional character, almost worthy of Gulliver or Huckleberry Finn, and it is possible that of all the books mentioned in this piece, *Henderson the Rain King* comes the closest to being a great novel. Taken even by its smallest dimension, and its final failure, it will still become a classic, a fine curiosity of a book quite out of the main stream of American letters but a classic in the way *The Innocents Abroad*, or *The Ox-Bow Incident*, *The Informer*, or *A High Wind in Jamaica* is classic.

Bellow's main character, Henderson, is a legendary giant American, an eccentric millionaire, six-four in height, with a huge battered face, an enormous chest, a prodigious potbelly, a wild crank's gusto for life, and a childlike impulse to say what he thinks. He is a magical hybrid of Jim Thorpe and Dwight Macdonald. And he is tormented by an inner voice which gives him no rest and poisons his marriages and pushes him to go forth. So he chooses to go to Africa (after first contemplating a visit to the Eskimos) and finds a native guide to take him deep into the interior.

The style gallops like Henderson, full of excess, full of light, loaded with irritating effusions, but it is a style which moves along. *The Adventures of Augie March* was written in a way which could only be called *all writing*. That was one of the troubles with the book. Everything was mothered by the style. But Henderson talks in a free-swinging easy bang-away monologue which puts your eye in the center of the action. I don't know if Bellow ever visited Africa, I would guess he didn't, but his imaginative faculty—which has always been his loot—pulls off a few prodigies. I don't know if any other American writer has done Africa so well. As for instance:

> *I was in tremendous shape those first long days, hot as they were. At night, after Romilayu had prayed, and we lay on the ground, the face of the air breathed back on us, breath for breath. And then there were the calm stars, turning around and singing, and the birds of the night with heavy bodies, fanning by. I couldn't have asked for anything better. When I laid my ear to the ground, I thought I could hear hoofs. It was like lying on the skin of a drum.*

After a series of tragicomic adventures, Henderson reaches a royal almost Oriental tribe with a culture built upon magic and death. He is brought to the King, Dahfu, who lives in a wooden palace attended by a harem of beautiful Amazons. (One could be visiting the royalest pad in

Harlem.) Dahfu is a philosopher-king, large in size, noble, possessed of grace, complex, dignified, elegant, educated, living suspended between life and death. The King, delighted with his new friend, takes him into the secrets of his mind and his palace, and one begins to read the book with a vast absorption because Bellow is now inching more close to the Beast of mystery than any American novelist before him. Dahfu is an exceptional creation, a profoundly sophisticated man with a deep acceptance of magic, an intellectual who believes that civilization can be saved only by a voyage back into the primitive, an expedition which he is of course uniquely suited to lead.

As the action explores its way down into an underworld of plot and magical omens, one ceases to know any longer whether Dahfu is potentially an emperor who can save the world, or a noble man lost in a Faustian endeavor. The book is on the threshold of a stupendous climax —for the first time in years I had the feeling I was going to learn something large from a novel—and then like a slow leak the air goes out of the book in the last fifty pages. Dahfu is killed in a meaningless action, Henderson goes home to his wife, and the mystery that Bellow has begun to penetrate closes over his book, still intact.

He is a curious writer. He has the warmest imagination, I think, of any writer in my generation, and this gift leads him to marvelous places— it is possible that Bellow succeeds in telling us more about the depths of the black man's psyche than either Baldwin or Ellison. He has a widely cultivated mind which nourishes his gift. He has a facility for happy surprises, and in Henderson, unlike Augie March, he has developed a nose for where the treasure is buried. Yet I still wonder if he is not too timid to become a great writer. A novelist like Jones could never have conceived *Henderson the Rain King* (no more could I), but I know that Jones or myself would have been ready to urinate blood before we would have been ready to cash our profit and give up as Bellow did on the possibilities of a demonically vast ending. The clue to this capitulation may be detected in Bellow's one major weakness, which is that he creates individuals and not relations between them, at least not yet. Augie March travels alone, the hero of *Seize the Day* is alone, Henderson forms passionate friendships but they tend to get fixed and the most annoying aspect of the novel is the constant repetition of the same sentiments, as if Bellow is knocking on a door of meaning which will not open for him. It is possible that the faculty of imagination is opposed to the gift of grasping relationships—in the act of coming to know somebody else well, the point of the imagination may be dulled by the roughness of the other's concrete desires and the attrition of living not only in one's own boredom but someone else's. Bellow has a lonely gift, but it is a gift. I would guess he is more likely to write classics than major novels, which is a way of saying that he will give intense pleasure to particular readers over the years, but is not too likely to seize the temper of our time and turn it.

For those who like the results of a horse race, it should be clear that the novels I liked the most in this round of reading were *Henderson, Naked Lunch,* and *Catch-22. The Thin Red Line* if not inspired was still impressive. *Another Country* suffered from too little style but compensated by its force. *Rabbit, Run* was better than expected but cloyed by too much writing. *Set This House on Fire* was rich in separate parts, and obese for the whole. *Letting Go* gave a demonstration of brilliant tactics and no novelistic strategy at all. *Franny and Zooey* and *Raise High the Roof Beam, Carpenters* was a literary scandal which came in last.

It has been said more than once that Tolstoy and Dostoevsky divided the central terrain of the modern novel between them. Tolstoy's concern —even in the final pessimism of *The Kreutzer Sonata*—was with men-in-the-world, and indeed the panorama of his books carries to us an image of a huge landscape peopled with figures who changed that landscape, whereas the bulk of Dostoevsky's work could take place in ten closed rooms: it is not society but a series of individuals we remember, each illuminated by the terror of exploring the mystery of themselves. This distinction is not a final scheme for classifying the novel. If one can point to *Moby Dick* as a perfect example of a novel in the second category—a book whose action depends upon the voyage of Ahab into his obsession—and to *An American Tragedy* as a virile example of the first kind of novel, one must still come up short before the work of someone like Henry James, who straddles the categories, for he explores into society as if the world were a creature in a closed room and he could discover its heart. Yet the distinction is probably the most useful single guide we have to the novel and can even be given a modern application to Proust as a novelist of the developed, introspective, but still objective world, and Joyce as a royal, demented, most honorable traveler through the psyche. The serious novel begins from a fixed philosophical point— the desire to discover reality—and it goes to search for that reality in society, or else must embark on a trip up the upper Amazon of the inner eye.

It is this necessity to travel into one direction or the other up to the end which makes the writing of novels fatal for one's talent and finally for one's health, as the horns of a bull are final doom for the suit of lights. If one explores the world, one's talent must be blunted by punishment, one's artistic integrity by corruption: nobody can live in the world without shaking the hand of people he despises; so, an ultimate purity must be surrendered. Yet it is as dangerous to travel unguided into the mysteries of the Self, for insanity prepares an ambush. No man explores into his own nature without submitting to a curse from the root of biology since existence would cease if it were natural to turn upon oneself.

This difficulty has always existed for the novelist, but today it may demand more antithesis and more agony than before. The writer who would explore the world must encounter a society which is now conscious of itself, and so resistant (most secretly) to an objective eye. Detours exist everywhere. There was a time when a writer had to see just a little bit of a few different faces in the world and could know that the world was still essentially so simple and so phrased that he might use his imagination to fill in unknown colors in the landscape. Balzac could do that, and so could Zola. But the arts of the world suffered a curious inversion as man was turned by the twentieth century into mass man rather than democratic man. The heartland which was potential in everyone turned upon itself; people used their personal arts to conceal from themselves the nature of their work. They chose to become experts rather than artists. The working world was no longer a panorama of factories and banks so much as it was reminiscent of hospitals and plastic recreation centers. Society tended to collect in small stagnant pools. Now, any young man trying to explore that world is held up by pleasures which are not sufficiently intense to teach him and is dulled by injustices too elusive to fire his rage. The Tolstoyan novel begins to be impossible. Who can create a vast canvas when the imagination must submit itself to a plethora of detail in each joint of society? Who can travel to many places when the complexity of each pool sucks up one's attention like a carnivorous cess-fed flower? Of all the writers mentioned here, only Jones, Heller and Burroughs even try to give a picture of the world, and the last two have departed from conventional reality before financing the attempt. It may be that James Jones is indeed the single major American writer capable of returning with a realistic vision of the complex American reality. But by his method, because of the progressively increasing confusion and contradiction of each separate corner in American society, he will have to write twenty or thirty books before he will have sketched even a small design.

Yet a turn in the other direction, into the world of the Self, is not less difficult. An intellectual structure which is cancerous and debilitating to the instinct of the novelist inhabits the crossroads of the inner mind. Psychoanalysis. An artist must not explore into himself with language given by another. A vocabulary of experts is a vocabulary greased out and sweated in committee and so is inimical to a private eye. One loses what is new by confusing it with what may be common to others. The essential ideas of psychoanalysis are reductive and put a dead weight on the confidence of the venture. If guilt, for example, is neurotic, a clumsy part of the functioning in a graceful machine, then one does not feel like a hero studying his manacles, nor a tragic victim regarding his just sentence, but instead is a skilled mechanic trying to fix his tool. Brutally, simply, mass man cannot initiate an inner voyage unless it is conducted by an expert graduated by an institution.

Set This House on Fire, Another Country, Rabbit, Run, Letting Go, Henderson, and the Glass stories were all amateur expeditions into the privacy of the Self, but they are also a measure of the difficulty, because one could sense the exhaustion of talent in the fires on the way, as if a company of young untried men were charging a hill which was mined and laid across with fire lanes for automatic weapons.

Yet the difficulty goes beyond the country of psychoanalysis. There are hills beyond that hill. The highest faces an abyss. Man in the Middle Ages or the Renaissance, man even in the nineteenth century, explored deep into himself that he might come closer to a vision of a God or some dictate from eternity, but that exploration is suspect in itself today, and in the crucial climactic transcendental moments of one's life, there is re- vealed still another dilemma. God, is it God one finds, or madness?

The religious temper of these books is significant. Of them all, only *The Thin Red Line, Naked Lunch, Another Country,* and *Letting Go* have no overt religious preoccupation. Yet altogether one could make a kind of case that *Naked Lunch* and *Another Country* are not divorced from religious obsessions. The suggestion of still another frontier for the American novel is here. A war has been fought by some of us over the last fifteen years to open the sexual badlands to our writing, and that war is in the act of being won. Can one now begin to think of an attack on the stockade—those dead forts where the spirit of twentieth-century man, frozen in flop and panic before the montage of his annihilation, has collected, like castrated cattle behind the fence? Can the feet of those infantrymen of the arts, the novelists, take us through the mansions and the churches into the palace of the Bitch where the real secrets are stored? We are the last of the entrepreneurs, and one of us homeless guns had better make it, or the future will smell like the dead air of the men who captured our time during that huge collective cowardice which was the aftermath of the Second War.

THE EXECUTIONER'S SONG

I think if I had three good years to give
    in study at some occupation
    which was fierce and new
    and full of stimulation
I think I would become
            an executioner
    with time spent out in the field
    digging graves for bodies I had made
            the night before.
You see: I am bad at endings
My bowels move without honor
    and flatulence is an affliction
    my pride must welcome with gloom
It comes I know from preoccupation
    much too much with sex
Those who end well do not spend their time
    so badly on the throne

For this reason I expect the task
    of gravedigger welcomes me
I would like to kill well and bury well
Perhaps then my seed would not shoot
    so frantic a flare
If I could execute neatly
    (with respect for whatever romantic
                    imagination

gave passion to my subject's crime)
and if I buried well
(with tenderness, dispatch, gravity
and joy that the job was not jangled—
giving a last just touch of the spade
to the coffin

in order to leave it
quivering

like a leaf—for forget not
coffins quiver as the breath goes out
and the earth comes down)

Yes if I could kill cleanly
and learn not to turn my back
on the face of each victim
as he chooses

what is last to be seen
in his eye,

well, then perhaps,
then might I rise so high upon occasion
as to smite a fist of the Lord's creation
into the womb of that muse
which gives us poems
Yes, then I might
For one ends best when death is clean
to the mind

and calm in its proportions
fire in the orchard and flame at the root

THE CASE AGAINST McCARTHY: *A Review of*

The Group

It had to happen. It was in the command of all the ironies that there would come a day when our First Lady of Letters would write a book and lo! the lovers would stand. Arthur Mizener would stand to be counted, and Granville Hicks, Clifton Fadiman, W. G. Rogers, and Gilbert Highet, Edmund Fuller, all those Virgilia Petersons, Dennis Powers's and Glendy Culligans. The reviews came in on wings of gold, "Brilliant" "Sheer" "Superlative" "Highly" "Generous" "Wonderfully Worth" "Great Joy To." Not since Elizabeth Janeway wrote *The Walsh Girls* has any lady-book been given such praise by people such as these. Yet it has happened to Mary, our saint, our umpire, our lit arbiter, our broadsword, our Barrymore (Ethel), our Dame (dowager), our mistress (Head), our Joan of Arc, the only Joan of Arc to travel up and down our raddled literary world, our poor damp kingdom, her sword breathing fire while she looked for a Dauphin to save us, looked these twenty years, and brought back nought. Even the patience of Joan cannot endure. She found a Dauphin at last in the collective masculinity which is to be scraped together out of eight Vassar girls, class of '33. "Miss McCarthy has come through brilliantly," writes David Boroff. "It is sheer exhilaration to watch her nimble intelligence at work, great joy to read her rich and supple prose. *The Group* clearly is one of the best novels of the decade." What has Mary done that now she is guilty by association with the Boroffs and the Fullers and the Hicks? Is this true guilt or innocence in disarray? Can she be conspiring with the epigones? Is the witch plotting how *not* to give the goose away? What a case!

Barrister William Barrett, late of Heidegger Row, finds for the defendant:

The novel opens with a wedding and closes with a funeral. The two scenes, particularly the first, are beautifully composed tableaux, magnificent photographs of an occasion with all the details meticulously assembled, including those that give the picture its haunting period quality. Between these two scenes, in which all of the group are assembled, the tangled skeins of eight different lives unwind, and interweave. Yet the eight different stories have the unity of a novel, for they turn around the pivotal figure of the group, Kay Strong. . . . Kay is the bellwether of the group in their struggle for emancipation. Though the girls are all solidly middle-class, and six of them from the Social Register, they insist on meeting life free from parental protection or guidance. Kay's death at the end— whether by accident or suicide—is a symbol of a kind. It is now 1940, the time of the Battle of Britain, and she falls from the window of her room in the Vassar Club while doing some volunteer airplane spotting. "In a sense," somebody remarks at her funeral, "Kay is the first war casualty." This is Miss McCarthy's neat way of ringing out the old years of the New Deal and ushering in the new period of the war.

Mr. Norman Podhoretz is a villainous, impressive, and magnetically disdainful prosecutor. What demolishment in his summation!

Any Vassar girl of the Class of '33 who could so violate her true nature as to have a wedding like that was bound to jump out of a window sooner or later. The leopard ought to know better than to think he can change his spots.

It is this aspect of the Thirties that Miss McCarthy finally hates the most: the atmosphere of the period demanded of all the leopards that they work as hard as they could at doing something about their spots. Wilfully blind to the spirit of moral ambition and the dream of self-transcendence that animated this demand, she can see nothing in it but foolishness and insincerity—despite the fact that she herself was produced by that spirit and was beautified once by the dream. The Muses have rewarded her for the trahison she is now committing by presenting her with a flatly written and incoherently structured book, a trivial lady writer's novel that bears scarcely a trace of the wit, the sharpness and the vivacity which glowed so often in her earlier work. A well-deserved fiasco, if you ask me.

Well, what is one to do? It is a busy season and the aspect most annoying of this trial is the time it will take to render a fair verdict for the defendant. The case begs for a brief of ten or fifteen thousand words. Yet it is a matter of dispute whether it is worth anything like this at all. Still, it is annoying to pass judgment lightly, for the defendant has curious merits and odd charms, little glints of gold in a ton of clay.

It is as if one were panning a sample. The nuggets are few, but the ore washes oddly. Only a step away, a shovelful deeper, perhaps there is high rich count. *The Group* is thus a book which could be said to squat on the Grand Avenue of the Novel like a shabby little boutique, a place which offers treasure in the trash. One has even had to ignore rumors that the nice shabby saleslady—alias Joan of Arc—is a princess whose family lost its fortune in the revolution; one hears other reports that she is also a miser and the swag is buried in the cellar.

That is why a concentrated act of detection is necessary. For this little shop don't belong on the Avenue, and it's got to be improved or else ripped down. Yet the saleslady is a good worker considering she's a princess; even a literary commissar might regret an act of *inégalité* here.

Which last remark must of course reveal the bias of the judge and the true nature of this court. Miss McCarthy has been summoned to a Tribunal, and will be offered revolutionary justice. All stand. The defendant's Fellow-Worker's Court will now find:

Ergo: *The Group,* as all good literary workers keeping up the work must know by now, is a collective novel about a near (or let us say quasi-) revolutionary period in American life, the nineteen-thirties; its heroines are eight nice girls, all or conceivably all of them Episcopalian at some time or another (one needs a revolutionary statistician to set these matters straight), all of them Upper-Middle Class and all of them civilized to that point of Christless High Church rectitude whose communal odor is a cross between *Ma Griffe* and contraceptive jelly. So it is no easy task Miss McCarthy has set herself. She has eight well-to-do young ladies moving through the thirties on the very outer fringe of events, and none of them has an inner passion large enough to take over the book and make it run away. Indeed the only character one would not likely flee at a cocktail party, a rich arrogant green-eyed beauty named Eastlake, decides to separate from the book herself. She takes off for Europe after the first few chapters and does not get around to coming back until the book is almost done. She has in the interim become an open lesbian as opposed to—would it be a Closet King? Which encourages the single medical prescription one can elucidate from the book: It tacitly states that a mixture of passionless goodness and squashed mendacity, precisely the lot of average nice rich bright young Protestant girls, is so regurgitative a violation of their nature that cancer or psychosis are now house percentage against any decent woman. No wonder Miss Eastlake left—she would have been unconvincing if she had remained. Still, Lady McCarthy is an unhappy hostess. What if you were to give a party for Christine Keeler and invited all your friends. Then Christine didn't show. What a party!

So, here, let's refine Comrade Mary's problem a little further. A collective novel in which the most interesting character is missing, a collective novel in which none of the characters have sufficient passion to be interesting in themselves, yet none have the power or dedication to wish to force events. Nor does any one of the characters move critically out of her class by marrying drastically up, or savagely down. Not one of the girls even exhibits an engaging bitchery. (The nearest to this existential condition, Norine Schmittlapp, is more pig than tootsie.) Correlatively, no one of the girls falls deeply and tragically in love. The formal heroine,

Kay Strong Petersen, entered as evidence previously by Barrister Barrett, does indeed fall literally out of a twenty-story window in the Vassar Club; clearly, she is a suicide-by-accident before the failure of her love, but she is somehow too horsey, and all-but-dyke, to buy a single revolutionary tear—one receives instead the impression that she might smell like a locker room of dedicated handball players—gloom, determination, and the void ooze from her persona. The nicest of the heroines by sentimental measure is Polly, but she and her husband are too nice; one cannot even cash an allusion to the *Ladies' Home Journal*—some checks should not be spent. There is of course a second nice heroine named Dottie. She is clean, Boston clean; her conscience moves with the drilled but never unimpressive grace of a fine ballerina. Indeed she has the grace to come to orgasm on the night she gives her first flower to still another in the endless gallery of Mary McCarthy's feverish, loud-talking, drunken, neurotic, crippled, and jargon-compensated louts. Did our First Lady of Letters never meet a gentleman on the flying trapeze? No, McCarthy's lout smells like fertilizer and he ploughs Dottie under—there is a good novelistic harvest for the next twenty pages. We are given Dottie's purchase of a diaphragm at her lover's demand; her subsequent repudiation —he is not at home when she calls; her act of renunciation—she quits her purchase beneath a bench in Washington Square Park; and her moment of final suspense when chapters later she confesses to her mother (who has a first-rate sense of modest conscience) that she is still in love with the lout. Her mother's conscience takes the inner journey from Boston to a village garret and she begs her daughter not to marry the new man she has taken in compensation (a nice rancher who is never to appear in evidence), but instead advises Dottie to go back to her lover of one night and find out what is finally in her love. It is the voice of a most refined moral instinct, and Dottie says no. Dottie ducks. She is our second-best nice heroine, but one crack on the mouth and she's out.

Thus it goes. There's Helena with the finest mind in the book, a quiet girl who rides her considerable culture like a consummate horseman. But she is a eunuch for others, void of relation. There's Pokey Prothero, rich, society, dumb, sexy, potentially interesting, but never given attention; there's Priss, a young New Dealer who has no breasts but breast-feeds her baby—one can hardly remember more about her. Finally there's a real duncey broad who becomes a literary agent. One can't even recall her name.

Now, this sparse gallery offers a flaccid springboard from which to jump into a major novel of the thirties. But Mary McCarthy is too much of an old pro not to see the odds. Her characters will come from one class and make no heroic journeys to other classes, they will not look to participate in the center of the history which is being made, and they will be the victim of no outsize passion. Nor will they be made sufficiently eccentric to separate clearly from one another. They will be called Lakey and Kay, Pokey and Polly, Dottie, Helena, Norine, and Priss. (And Duncey.) Nor will there be an attempt to avoid the proportions which are consequent. She will take these women, nearly all finally dull, because they have neither the interest to break out of the cage of their character, nor even the necessity—the cage is not that cruel, the girls are merely premature suburbanites—and she will obey the logic of the intricately educated and dull, she will follow them through their furniture and their recipes, she will give us lists of categories that no sociologist would ever dare. This is the most dangerous hurdle of them all, this is the one any professional knows to avoid unless he is willing to dare a real fall. Because lists and categories in novels must be consummately perfect, each detail quivering with the illumination of a touch of true love, or a hint of the deep, or indeed you are dead. Lists and categories are always the predictable refuge of the passionless, the mediocre, the timid, and the bowel-bound who will not make another move until they have exhausted the last.

These are real odds, what! These piss-out characters with their cultivated banalities, their lack of variety or ambition, perversion, simple greed, or depth of feeling, their indifference to the bedrock of a collective novel—the large social events of the season or decade which gave impetus to conceiving the book in such a way. Yes, our Mary's a sneak. Like any First Lady she disapproves of unseemly ambition, and yet she is trying a novel which is all but impossible to bring off in a big way. No ordinary ambition here. Megalomania indeed. Her little boutique on the Avenue is going to open in competition to Proust's Tiffany.

Well the Court would not certify her as mad. The odds are a hundred to one or a thousand to one against bringing off the book, but it is possible. At least it is existentially possible. For until some great new realist arises, some modern Zola, we will not know. The work of realism was done for the nineteenth century, but whether it can be done for the middle of the twentieth century we shall indeed not know unless the attempt is made. So may have reasoned McCarthy. If one takes a little stillwater of society and captures it in its proportions, its style, its affairs, its moods, *its very relation to reality* (which is to say the mode by which it attempts to perceive reality) if one brings it to life in such a way as to transcend the journeyman novelist's little spill of life (his verisimilitude and occasional good moments) and instead creates a work which is true in its very relation to the perception of reality (one repeats the notion) then a magic is worked. The little book of realistic details has of a sudden its resonance, it has come to life, it is a

Being, a psychological reality which lives afterward in our brain, touches our motives, affects the history we in turn will make. Any book can do this if it is pure enough and true enough to create a turn of being in the mind of the reader. So goes the existential premise.

Say, then, did Lady M. bring it off? And the answer is that she came just far enough to irritate the life out of us, because it was just far enough to reinvigorate the premise—it is the grand premise of the novel— but she did not climb high enough nor cleanly enough in the deep councils of her sleep to get up over the first ridge and start a base camp from which one could decide if the mountain is to be negotiated from this direction. She got just so far symbolically as the episode in one of her scenes where the butler comes in to whisper to his mistress that the child of the visiting lady has had an unfortunate accident in his pants. Yes, Mary deposited a load on the premise, and it has to be washed all over again, this little long-lived existential premise.

All right, but why did she fail? Where did she fink the job? And this is how ten thousand more words are demanded and one thousand must suffice. But first let credit be given to her formal virtues. Because her sense of detail, while suffering from a fatal if tiny taint of the monotonous and overindulgent, is still her single most impressive achivement. Her book fails as a novel by being good but not nearly good enough, it fails for a variety of temperamental and characerological reasons soon to be listed, but it is enormously successful as sociology. It will continue to exist as a classic in sociology long after it is dim and dull as a novel, it will survive in Soc Sci I at every university and junior college: the specific details are to be mined by the next twenty-five classes of PhD's.

And at its best, *The Group* is far better than that. It is skillful, in-tricately knitted as a novel, its characters while not always distinguishable from one another are true in their reactions, or at least are true in the severe field of limitation she puts on their comings and goings, their paltry passions, their lack of grasp, their lack of a desire to grasp. It is all true what she does, it is just not true enough. Her eye sees with a knife's edge, but her hand, overwary of drama and surprise, blunts the stroke. The book like a person in depression is dull in its basic condition— it comes to life only by a stirring, a moment of inspiration, then it lapses into dullness again. And details sweep in and sweep away the possibilities for each little scene to become sufficiently alive to wake up the others. She is to be given respect for conceiving a novel such as this and laying out the ground plan, she is an engineer *manqué* in literature, but her failure diverts judgment away from her technique and over to her character. She is simply not a good enough woman to write a major novel;

not yet; she has failed, she has failed from the center out, she failed out of vanity, the accumulated vanity of being overpraised through the years for too little and so being pleased with herself for too little; she failed out of profound timidity—like any good Catholic-born she is afraid to unloose the demons; she failed out of snobbery—if compassion for her characters is beginning to stir at last in this book, she can still not approve of anyone who is incapable of performing the small act exquisitely well; she failed by an act of the imagination; she is, when all is said, a bit of a duncey broad herself, there is something cockeyed in her vision and self-satisfied in her demands and this contributes to the failure of her style. The long unbroken paragraphs settle in like bricks. They are all too equal to one another—it is the wrong book in which to lose one's place; there is even mild physical boredom in the act of reading as if one were watching a wall being stacked up rather than seeing the metamorphosis of a creature.

Finally she suffers from a lack of reach. She chooses to be not close enough to the horror in the closet. Her nice girls are refugees from the schisms, the wrinklings, and the crater mold of the Upper Middle Class, that radiation belt of well-to-do Protestants full of Church, rectitude, exclusion, guilt, and insanity. Is there a nice rich Episcopalian family or fine Presbyterian clan in our American world which does not have its important secret member raving mad? Nice girls live on the thin juiceless crust of the horror beneath, the screaming incest, the buried diabolisms of the grand and the would-be grand. One does not have to have that in one's novel, but one has to have a sense of that madness if the book is to be resonant. Yet Mary is too weak to push through the crust and so cannot achieve a view of the world which has root.

Ultimately, novelists must believe that the people who run the world are essentially good, are an expression of God's work (a conservative view), or in antithesis must decide that the Devil is at the shoulder of every ruler (which is where the Bolsheviks and the Black Muslims come together). One can presumably write a great novel from either point of view or some conciliation of the two (Proust, Henry James, James Joyce, André Malraux come to mind) but one cannot make a Being of a realistic novel if it has no root. Then there are merely sniffings, snippings and clippings, codicils of taste, and quick exits for bad taste. Mary's vice is her terror of being ridiculous, and so she is in danger of ending up absurd, an old-maid collector of Manx cats, no tails and six toes, an anomaly of God. It even invades her vision. One called her cockeyed for a cause. There is an atrocious anachronism in the book. Her characters while engaged in the activities of the thirties have a consciousness whose style derives directly from the fifties. One has to keep reminding oneself that these events did not take place ten years ago, but thirty years ago, and this is unforgivable. It is like wrapping a tuning fork in velvet. Her little book so full of promise and quiver ends up soggy and damp. What rings true does not please the ear, what pleases is not quite true. So the book seems stuffed with cotton and catalogues as Podhoretz was quick to accuse.

Yet when all is said, *The Group* has one fresh virtue. It has something new in it; it has a conception of the novel which is Mary's own, a tool by which to cut an ascent into some of the sheer ice faces of the social world. And that is her method. Her Method. For she has divined the first law of our social world, which is that we learn by what we can glean from a hundred alienations of context, from a thousand suffocations of our emotions. So we are deep in an affair, close to growing nearer or being spoiled for love another year, and then our context is ripped. A commercial is on the air. A recipe is to be discussed at dinner. Ten years later we hear of the beloved at a cocktail party. Was it this girl or that? The names have slid around into one another or have divided. Memory is in mitosis. Mary may be the first American to try this in a thoroughgoing way. Everything in the profound materiality of women is given its full stop until the Eggs Benedict and the dress with the white fichu, the pessary and the whatnot, sit on the line of the narrative like commas and periods, semicolons, italics, and accents. The real interplay of the novel exists between the characters and the objects which surround them until the faces are swimming in a cold lava of anality, which becomes the truest part of her group, her glop, her impacted mass.

If, at the highest level, she has failed and even failed miserably to do more than write the best novel the editors of the women's magazines ever conceived in *their* secret ambitions, it is nonetheless possible now to conceive that McCarthy may finally get tough enough to go with the boys. She has been a very bad girl these years, mean and silly, postured and overpetted, petty in the extreme, but now there's a hint she may be capable some day of taking a real step, a suggestion that the Saints will preserve our Mary-Joan and bless her with a book which can comprehend a man. Does anyone know where society will end if the heroine of *The Company She Keeps* should encounter Julien Sorel?

But that drama of conjecture is moot. For the present, a decision: Mary McCarthy is judged Guilty of Meretriciousness and equally: Guilty of conspiring not to give the goose away, which means thus, Guilty of refusing to reveal that the genteel lords and ladies who manage America are the psychic descendants of Conrad's Kurtz. "Ah, the horror, the horror," and she will not take a burning look.

WITCHES AND WARLOCKS: *Poems and Short Hairs*

Hallelujah!

Children
   who issue
      from
         a matrimony
         of the usual misery
         go forth
         into lives
   which are best spent
         in sin
         said the Lord

ODE TO A LADY

Cold and swinish are your crafts
Mean and nasty, foul your arts
The spirit of a lover you would never kill
'Tis tastier far to deaden him.
   Yes, maggots are your pets
     and garlic your bouquet

Cold and swinish are your crafts
   a pestilence on me
For I have primed my iron
   in your lore and now
your faults revealed
   my eyes are blinded still
     by the image of a woman
Child bitch of a dear Irish maid
   who is virgin to my touch
   and never smiles the lover's dirty grin
   of sweets we shared
     and share we will again

No, you are a work of art
   pristine, inviolate,
   shiver of midnight away
     from the touch of my tip all
     fingers stretched

You call to artists
   in other lands
   singing sweetly:

Create me
dear singing loin
of some manly harp
create me
for I stifle where I stand
and lady-like
must drown the moment
in the lake of much too many
    who leave me lazy
        like a snake

Create me,
    dear man,
    beyond my eye.

And I answer:
    snake and foulest bitch
    swine of a hundred feet
    I am the artist across the seas
        and love you, heart,
        because you are purer far
        than all your arts
            and all your swilling crafts,
        purer far because your heart
            dared to call
            when others—
            cats, grandes dames,
            fraises fatales,
            and all the avaricious humps
            could think of nothing
                but flight from me.

Come back,
　says piggy
　in your voice
Can it be, poor harp
　Can it really be
that you are the voice
　　　　　across the sea?

Yes, come back, says swine-song in your voice
Come back, come back, come back
For names you've called me
　　　　far and wide
Wine of a hundred feet
　　　Sweet lord you're kind
Yes come to me honey-bee
　　　and I will kill you.
Over here my lad,
　　　God, you're bad.

Coda

And they were married
and had a laugh to say goodbye
    for he wrote a poem
    and she liked it.
It went: Cha cha cha

MARRIAGE À LA MODE REMODELED
poem in 5 parts

1.

Cook for him?
Of course not.
We eat out
    all the time.
He's gotten fat
He's gotten
    very
    fat
    longing
    for good
        cooking
        said the Bitch
    in a voice
        of absolute
        tenderness for Mr. Bitch
        curious fellow
        her husband.

145

2.

He makes love
     like a little
         pig's tail
         thought she
     all tight
         kinky
         curly cue
     and full of squeal
         why can't he
             go
         dark and deep?

Cheep!
     beep beep a beep!
     went the tail
         of the pig
     roar! went the
                 boar
     and with a crash
         and a snore
     he went dark
         and deep
         into himself
         and sleep.

3.

Ladies
teach
one
leçon
seul
one
that the
essence
of perfume
is duty

4.

I'm fast
  becoming
  a goose
    said the witch
    blinking her eye
    to the beat
      of my
        intent
        light, deliberate and dry

I hate to have a ball
    which goes de trop said I

De trop, said the witch,
    or not de trop
    dare your
      deliberations
      go deeper
        ducks?
      for love
        which is light
        and dry
        makes me think of money
          and her dirty bucks
          so waltz me
    around again willie
    hard dark and deep
    the keys to the dungeon
        are buried
    in mummie's
    murderous
    keep.

5.

The Shortest Novel of Them All

At first she thought she could kill him in three days.

She did nearly. His heart proved nearly unequal to her compliments.

Then she thought it would take three weeks. But he survived.

So she revised her tables and calculated three months.

After three years, he was still alive. So they got married.

Now they've been married for thirty years. People speak warmly of them. They are known as the best marriage in town.

It's just that their children keep dying.

You bruise
  my
  catatonia
  said
    the saint
    to the
      white witch
  after he had
    fallen
    so far
  as to nod
    assent
    to a
    shitty suggestion

Is that all
  asked the witch
  accoutumé ma foi
    to eat the shit
    of the
    superior.

The saint forgave her
  and kissed a sore
  content with the
    notion
  it came from mort.

THE RIDE OF THE SAD SAINT

1.

The air was full of curses
   looking for no fight.
   The devils and the witches'
    were all alone tonight
   save for a saint
    who was sad.

Mad, mad, you're mad,
   cried a lad in the garb
    of a girl
Saints are not sad
    but sadistic

Cruelty is the kindest wound
   for dung, replied the saint.
   Go forth and sin
    in such a way
    you need not run
     at break of day

Not one said yea.
   Still the saint merely sighed
   he knew a saint
    must not aspire
   to the courage of a God
   nor try too long
   to bear His pain.

Besides, the saint was vain.
It was the drop life left
   in his humility
   in the couloirs of his humility
   in the catatonia of his senility
   in the crease of Carmen's ear
   in the crease of Carmen's ear.

I am brave by an act
  of will, said the saint
  my nature is to fear
O saint even you must fear
  the crease of Carmen's ear.

       2.

For Carmen is a cutthroat
  Carmen is a queen
  Carmen sings of passion
    and blows her breath at me.

Carmen is a royal whore
  Carmen is a slut
  Carmen has a mustache
    and smiles at flowing blood.

I knew Carmen when she was young
  Before her mustache bleached
  A colored flag around her neck
    she kissed the pirate's fleet
  and seduced herself to me
  and stole from me a steed

Her head upon the pillow
  she caught her flesh to mine
  And went off at a gallop
    some galley's keep to find
    presenting me her ear
    returning greed a fiend.

Oh, I was a young man
  Cold, evil and strong
  And few were the ladies
    I couldn't dog, dog—
    bitch, you're in my bed
    and cue them out half-dead.

Five children started in my land
    Six across the sea.
    None knew my hand upon
        their head. Royal bastards all.
        One swore my death was in
    his vow. Loyal bastards royal.

But Carmen was a crueler siege
    Than all my evil gathered
    And tore the heart right out the ram
        while all that's vain was shattered.
And now I am a saint. (O pity me.)
Now I am a saint. (O pity me.)

    I stare into the eyes
        of devils,
            devils dark and foul
    and look them down
    and steal their ground
while in me tolls a hollow
    by the heart
        of Carmen's ear
    near the heart of Carmen's ear
    that scar on horror's breast
        which fears no fire
for death to Carmen is Devil's dare
for Hell to Carmen is heaven's mare:

        a trot away from this flat world
        where saints and witches stale
        and war's too whored for open fight
        swears the heart of Carmen's ear
        swings the hooves of Carmen's steed:
            ride, ride, ride with me.

Come ride with me into my land
Down down along my crease
And we will live forever
   in the marrow of the beast
   and we will live forever
   in the sweetmeat of desire
Oh we will live forever
   In the sweetmeat of disease
   oh we will live forever
   by the steeps at Carmen's knees
   we will live forever
in the crease of Carmen's ear
in the crease
in the crease
in the crease of Carmen's ear.

The most
  eligible
  bachelor
  in London
  is a category
  conceived
  by presumptive
    witches
    weary
    of doing
    without
  their widow's weeds—
  whispered
    the epigram
  to the boutonniere.

Go fix the flowers fuck-face
    was the King's reply

PUNCHING PAPA: *A Review of*

That Summer in Paris

There is an irony which usually defeats the memoir and makes it an inferior art. The man who can tell a good story in company about his friends is usually not able to find a prose which can capture the nuances of his voice. Invariably, the language is leached out—the account tends to have a droning episodic quality as if some movie queen were recounting the separate toils of her lovers to a tape recorder.

Now the worst to be said for *That Summer in Paris* is that Morley Callaghan has not altogether avoided this blight. Using himself as a character of reasonable dimensions, an honest sensible hard-nosed ego-bastard, a talented short-story writer, a good husband, a good Irish Catholic, a good college boxer, and a good expatriate, his memoir is built on the premise that catgut is good for stringing pearls. So one is taken by Callaghan for a three-to-five-page description of each of his separate meetings with Maxwell Perkins, Sherwood Anderson, Ford Madox Ford, Josephine Herbst, Sinclair Lewis, Robert McAlmon, Sylvia Beach, James Joyce, Pauline Hemingway, Michael Arlen, Ludwig Lewisohn, Allen Tate, Edward Titus, Joan Miró, and Zelda Fitzgerald. It is dim writing. One has only to compare the chapter he gives to Sinclair Lewis (one of the more elaborate cameos) against some equivalent number of pages Wolfe devoted to a similar portrait, and the result is no contest. A deadness comes back from Callaghan's echo. His short portraits are written at the level of a conversation with somebody who might tell you he met Truman Capote.

"Well," you might respond, "what is he like?"

"Well," says your friend, "he's small, you know, and he's kind of bright."

If one knows some of the people mentioned, or is obsessed with the period, then Morley Callaghan's memoir will satisfy. But it is not a good book. It is in fact a modest bad dull book which contains a superb short story about Hemingway, Fitzgerald, and Callaghan. One can push so far as to say it is probably the most dramatic single story about Hemingway's relation to Fitzgerald in the literature. If Callaghan had been ready to stop at this, he could have had a long short story or a short memoir which might have become a classic. Instead he attenuated his material over a run of 255 pages, and so reminds one of a remark Fitzgerald once made to Callaghan. Talking about *The Great Gatsby*, he said the book had done reasonably well but was hardly a best seller. "It was too short a book," Fitzgerald said. "Remember this, Morley. Never write a book under sixty thousand words."

That's it. Callaghan has remembered, and has proceeded to stretch it out. As literature, it's a mistake. Financially, Fitzgerald's advice might still prove wise. The author now has a book instead of a story; the value of a movie sale is increased. The story about Hemingway, Fitzgerald, and Callaghan done by John Huston, produced by Sam Spiegel, could make a very good movie. For the first time one has the confidence that an eyewitness has been able to cut a bonafide trail through the charm, the mystery, and the curious perversity of Hemingway's personality. One gets a good intimation of what was very bad in the man, and the portrait is reinforced by the fact that Callaghan was not out to damage the reputation—on the contrary, he is nearly obsessed by the presence of taint in a man he considers great.

In turn, Fitzgerald is also admired. In fact he is even loved as a friend, loved perhaps more than Hemingway. Yet Callaghan fixes his character for our attention. Like many an American writer to come after him, Fitzgerald was one of those men who do not give up early on the search to acquire more manhood for themselves. His method was to admire men who were strong. In this sense he was a salesman. When the beloved object did not smile back, Fitzgerald, like Willy Loman, looked into an earthquake. We are offered Fitzgerald at just such a moment.

Talking to Callaghan one day, Fitzgerald referred to Hemingway's ability as a boxer, and remarked that while Hemingway was probably not good enough to be heavyweight champion of the world, he was undoubtedly as good as Young Stribling, the light-heavyweight champion. "Look, Scott," said Callaghan, "Ernest is an amateur. I'm an amateur. All this talk is ridiculous." Unconvinced, Fitzgerald asked to come along to the gym at the American Club and watch Hemingway and Callaghan box. But Callaghan has let the reader in earlier on one small point. Hemingway, four inches taller and forty pounds heavier than Callaghan, "may have thought about boxing, dreamed about it, consorted with old fighters and hung around gyms," but Callaghan "had done more actual boxing with men who could box a little and weren't just taking exercise or fooling around."

So on an historic afternoon in June in Paris in 1929, Hemingway and Callaghan boxed a few rounds with Fitzgerald serving as timekeeper.

The second round went on for a long time. Both men began to get tired, Hemingway got careless. Callaghan caught him a good punch and dropped Hemingway on his back. At the next instant Fitzgerald cried out, "Oh, my God! I let the round go four minutes."

"All right, Scott," Ernest said. "If you want to see me getting the shit knocked out of me, just say so. Only don't say you made a mistake."

According to Callaghan's estimate, Scott never recovered from that moment. One believes it. For months later, a cruel and wildly inaccurate story about this episode appeared in the *Herald Tribune* book section. It was followed by a cable sent collect by Fitzgerald at Hemingway's insistence. "HAVE SEEN STORY IN HERALD TRIBUNE. ERNEST AND I AWAIT YOUR CORRECTION. SCOTT FITZGERALD."

Since Callaghan had already written such a letter to the paper, none of the three men could ever forgive each other.

As the vignettes, the memoirs, and the biographies of Hemingway proliferate, Callaghan's summer in Paris may take on an importance beyond its literary merit, for it offers a fine clue to the logic of Hemingway's mind, and tempts one to make the prediction that there will be no definitive biography of Hemingway until the nature of his personal torture is better comprehended. It is possible Hemingway lived every day of his life in the style of the suicide. What a great dread is that. It is the dread which sits in the silences of his short declarative sentences. At any instant, by any failure in magic, by a mean defeat, or by a moment of cowardice, Hemingway could be thrust back again into the agonizing demands of his courage. For the life of his talent must have depended on living in a psychic terrain where one must either be brave beyond one's limit, or sicken closer into a bad illness, or, indeed, by the ultimate logic of the suicide, must advance the hour in which one would make another reconnaissance into one's death.

That may be why Hemingway turned in such fury on Fitzgerald. To be knocked down by a smaller man could only imprison him further into the dread he was forever trying to avoid. Each time his physical vanity suffered a defeat, he would be forced to embark on a new existential gamble with his life. So he would naturally think of Fitzgerald's little error as an act of treachery, for the result of that extra minute in the second round could only be a new bout of anxiety which would drive his instinct into ever more dangerous situations. Most men find their profoundest passion in looking for a way to escape their private and secret torture. It is not likely that Hemingway was a brave man who sought danger for the sake of the sensations it provided him. What is more likely the truth of his long odyssey is that he struggled with his cowardice and against a secret lust to suicide all of his life, that his inner landscape was a nightmare, and he spent his nights wrestling with the gods. It may even be that the final judgment on his work may come to the notion that what he failed to do was tragic, but what he accomplished was heroic, for it is possible he carried a weight of anxiety within him from day to day which would have suffocated any man smaller than himself. There are two kinds of brave men: those who are brave by the grace of nature, and those who are brave by an act of will. It is the merit of Callaghan's long anecdote that the second condition is suggested to be Hemingway's own.

WAKE: *Short Hairs*

The timid
  engage
  the
  profound
    through
    horror
said
    the crippled
    old
    spider

A Waltz

Paper covers rock
  rock breaks scissor
  scissor cuts paper

A woman can always
  take a man

A fag may always
  take a woman

A man may always
  take a fag

Circles bore me.

They obey
    too many laws

Epitaph for a man of parts

I do not think there was an occasion
in my life
which did not have
me
fatally
misquoted

Dr. Hu
speaks
twenty-three
  languages.

What loneliness.

the English are fey
   said the electronic ray
By God, sir,
   says Neptune
bring such
   phosphorescence
      to me.

THE LEADING MAN: *A Review of* J.F.K.:

The Man and the Myth

Co-author of *Seeds of Treason*, a book on the Hiss-Chambers case, Victor Lasky has now written a giant political biography of John Fitzgerald Kennedy. It is a thoroughgoing performance which begins with the career of Joseph Kennedy Sr., then moves from Jack Kennedy's first political musings in college on through the separate stations of his career all the way into the first years of the Presidency. A considerable number of vignettes are offered as well of other members of the Kennedy family and such figures in the New Frontier as Theodore Sorensen, Arthur Schlesinger Jr., and John Kenneth Galbraith. It is close to being a monumental study of Jack Kennedy's stops and starts, dips and swoops, turns to Right and Left as he advanced along his political life, and the work becomes an indispensable if not altogether trustworthy reference to anyone who would study the peculiar logic of political success, the practical details in the art of the possible.

Lasky has done an impressive amount of work. He has hunted down a thousand anecdotes in newspapers and magazines (half of them sufficiently apocryphal to be worthless, we can suspect), he has talked to everyone who knew Kennedy and would agree to talk to Lasky, he has come up with much of the goods and a hundred goodies. Did Jack Kennedy ever kiss a baby in the congressional campaign of 1946 and turn to a friend to say, "Kissing babies gives me asthma"? Well, you may be certain Lasky has found the item and put it in. *J. F. K.: The Man and the Myth* is a book which will give pleasure to every Kennedy-hater who reads it—they will feel as if they are dipping into a box of creamy chocolate. Indeed, at his best and worst, Lasky is reminiscent of Lait and Mortimer—he could have called his job *John F. Kennedy—Confidential*.

And there is value in such an undertaking: a man *is* responsible for his past. It is not fitting that Jack Kennedy should get away with all of it. The Republicans will employ these pages as a running handbook for the '64 campaign, and it will be of inestimable use to them, good use and dirty use, but ideally the book can be worth even more for liberal

Democrats, since their chronic disease is hero worship, and Lasky's pages are effective antitoxin. For example:

> *In 1950, John F. Kennedy made a personal contribution to Richard M. Nixon in his Senate campaign against the California Congresswoman [Helen Gahagan Douglas] . . . Like any other contribution it was turned over to the Nixon Senate Campaign Committee in California.*

On the preceding page is one of numerous references to the President's not unfavorable attitude toward McCarthy in the early Fifties: "he thought he 'knew Joe pretty well, and he [McCarthy] may have something.' "

But then the Kennedy of 1948 was making these sorts of headlines in the Boston *Herald:* "Kennedy says Roosevelt sold Poland to Reds." F.D.R. had done this "because he did not understand the Russian mind." So had gone a modest speech Congressman Kennedy had given to the *Polish*-American Citizens Club in Roxbury.

Lasky is unrelenting. A letter from the President to his father, written in 1937 when he was 20, goes in part (note the fence straddling):

> *. . . while I felt that perhaps it would be far better for Spain if Franco should win—as he would strengthen and unite (sic) Spain—yet at the beginning the government was in the right morally speaking as its program was similar to the New Deal.*

A little later, in his undergraduate thesis, "Appeasement at Munich," he was defending the Munich Pact: "The state of British opinion and the condition of Britain's armaments . . . made 'surrender' inevitable."

But these, after all, were the somewhat Right Wing views of a very young man. The embarrassment for liberals is that the attitude persisted almost up to his nomination. Calculated, in retrospect, seems J.F.K.'s courtship of President Eisenhower, his announcement in 1955 that he was only in "moderate opposition" to the White House, and Lasky's evidence that all through the late Fifties Jack Kennedy was doing his best to seduce the South. "Georgia loves him," reported the political editor of the Atlantic *Constitution.*

This catalogue of Right Wing sins and stances does, however, a violence to the balance. Kennedy's real political art—Lasky's documentation is more than adequate here—came from his ability to occupy the political Center yet move simultaneously to the Right and to the Left. He committed himself, for example, to the legislative programs of Walter Reuther and George Meany while engaging at the same time in an all-out attack on Dave Beck and Jimmy Hoffa. Thus he could nail down the support of the most powerful sectors of organized labor in the Democratic Party for his nomination while advancing himself in the public eye as a militant crusader against union rackets. At the junction of these two prongs is pure political sugar. The instrument of his attack on Hoffa had been the McClellan Labor Rackets Committee; Jack and Bobby Kennedy dominated the committee to the point where other senators would arrive for hearings to find witnesses called without their knowledge. Lasky's explanation is that the brothers were able to attain this exceptional power over a committee only because they possessed "the blessing of the Majority Leader of the Senate, Lyndon B. Johnson." It was Johnson's notion presumably to bind Jack Kennedy over to the idea of a Johnson-Kennedy ticket for President. The shade of Frankenstein falls dark on the shoulder of a politician.

Barry Goldwater once remarked bitterly that the Kennedys had nothing working for them but "money and gall," and when one thinks of the devoted work Bobby Kennedy gave to the McCarthy committee as a lawyer on McCarthy's staff, quitting finally only because he refused, according to Lasky, "to play second fiddle to Roy Cohn," there is either high comedy or the suspicion of horror in Bobby Kennedy's subsequent attack on Hubert Humphrey's tactics as McCarthyite during the West Virginia primaries seven years later.

The political point, of course, is that one can usually get away with it. For every man who would remember that Bobby Kennedy was once a McCarthyite, there would be a dozen others who would forget and call the first man a liar. A speech made in one city does not have the same magic when it is read about in another city. A promise made in private to a politician will not interfere with a contradictory promise made to another politician. When the time comes to fulfill the promise, one can reward the man who did the most for you, or is strongest, or indeed one can break both promises and make a deal with a third politician. One can promise the Negro his rights in the North while giving intimations to the South that one is secretly sympathetic to their fears. The art is to practice duplicity and double-dealing with a sense of moderation, taste, and personal style; the secret is to remain alert to the subtler shifting realities of mass communication: what sort of news in this season is likely to become national, which oratory will happily or unhappily remain local.

These are some of the lessons to be elucidated from the political career of John Fitzgerald Kennedy. If Lasky's work had been an objective study, if Kennedy had been considered merely the first among equals, if it had been understood that such men as Barry Goldwater, Hubert Humphrey, and Dick Nixon are all in their way equally adept as political operators—if Lasky's work had risen into an unbiased exploration of political mendacity in general and President Kennedy in particular, there might have been a hard remaining substance to the book. He could have left us with a classic in political biography. (A badly written classic, be it said—the prose is left without comment.) Instead, Lasky's pretense to be objective, which keeps the first half of his book interesting, begins even as pretense to disappear about the time Jack Kennedy begins to work for his nomination. Lasky's bias shows itself. He is, we discover, a Nixon man, an all-out Nixon man. The moral judgments slide over into propaganda. Nixon is invariably presented as honest, self-effacing, put upon, unjustly rejected; Kennedy grows into a villain of the first proportions. So a work which might have reminded us that we take the politician too seriously is replaced by Lasky's more specific objective—which is to stitch up a campaign flag for the return of Richard M. Nixon; so a work which could have reminded Jack Kennedy that there is still a public conscience becomes instead a campaign tract to be overpraised by Republicans and damned by Democrats. That is the crime of commission in *J. F. K.: The Man and the Myth.*

The void of omission is more grave. For, with all his documentation of Jack Kennedy's political life, the large disappointment in the book is that Lasky has no intimation of the curious depths in the President's nature. J.F.K. is a divided man, and only half his nature is political. Even through the lenses of his bias, Lasky understands that half very well—that half-man comes through the pages as one of the most consummate political animals in the history of America. But the half omitted is more crucial. For Jack Kennedy is a new kind of political leader, and a study of his past political sins will not help us to comprehend his future. The likelihood is that our President is a new kind of Commander-in-Chief. He is not a father, nor a god, nor a god-figure, nor an institution, nor a symbol. He is in fact—permit the literary conceit— a metaphor. Which is to say that Jack Kennedy is more like a hero of uncertain moral grandeur: is his ultimate nature tragic or epic? Is he a leading man or America's brother? A symbol is static. It exists eternally, immutably. It is the circle of the sun or the wave of the sea. But a metaphor is a relation. It changes as our experience changes. We say for example: the sun was burning with hate. A day later the meaning alters and we say to ourselves that it is only our own hatred we perceived in the sun; in a week the metaphor has come to mean something else again, something deeper perhaps—between the sun and ourselves is a celestial terrain of hatreds which alter our understanding of the sun at every moment.

These poetic mechanics are of course far indeed from Victor Lasky's prose, stance, and intention. But *J. F. K.: The Man and the Myth* is an irritating, frustrating, and finally disappointing book because it offered the promise of becoming a first-rate job, and was spoiled—this spoliation being a first-rate loss—by Lasky's incapacity to entertain a poetic concept of his subject. Jack Kennedy is somewhat more and considerably less after all than a hero or a villain—he is also an empty vessel, a man of many natures, not all of them necessarily rooted in granite. He is, it must be said, a Kierkegaardian hero. One can assume that in the private stricken moments of his life, those moments all of us know at rare and best-forgotten times, it is impossible for him to be certain of his moral bedrock. Kierkegaard was probably the first Western mind to have an intimation that either the nature of man was changing or had never been properly understood, that it was just as natural for man to be flooded with sensations of goodness when he was most evil as it was for him to taste his evil, and that a man in the act of being good could equally be depressed with an awareness of his profound evil. In this sense one did not have a nature which was formed already—on the contrary, one created one's nature by the depth or power of one's acts. Kierkegaard had divined that there was probably no anguish on heaven or earth so awful as the inability to create one's nature by daring, exceptional, forbidden, or socially impossible acts.

This impulse—to create and forever re-create his nature—has been the President's dominant passion. There is no other way to comprehend him. From the Hairbreadth Harry of his P. T. boat exploits through the political campaigns with their exceptional chances (who could beat Cabot Lodge in Massachusetts in 1952?) through the lively bachelordom, through the marriage to the impossibly beautiful and somewhat madcap wife, the decision to run for President, a decision worthy of Julien Sorel, the adventure in Cuba, the atomic poker game with Khrushchev last October when the biggest bluff in the history of the world was called—yes, each is a panel of scenes in the greatest movie ever made.

The President is not a great mind, and it may be that he will prove ultimately not to be a good man—those who are forever re-creating their personalities can end with a mediocre nature even more naturally than a great one—but he had genius in one respect. Jack Kennedy understood that the most important, probably the only dynamic culture in America, the only culture to enlist the imagination and change the character of Americans, was the one we had been given by the movies. Therefore a void existed at the center of American life. No movie star had the mind, courage or force to be national leader, and no national leader had the epic adventurous resonance of a movie star. So the President nominated himself. He would fill the void. He would be the movie star come to life as President. That took genius. For Jack Kennedy grew up in the kind of milieu which was so monumental with finance and penurious with emotion that everybody's breath smelled like they had been swallowing pennies and you were considered mentally disturbed if you did not bet on the New York Yanks. He had a character thus created of the most impossible ingredients for his venture: overweening ambition and profound political caution—he had been taught never to commit himself to a political idea since ideas often pass, weaken, and die long before the men who believed in them.

Yes, John F. Kennedy was without principles or political passions except for one. He knew the only way he could re-create the impoverished circuits which lay between himself and the depths of his emotions was to become President. *He* was his own idea, and he had the luck to have a powerful father who agreed entirely with his venture. So he combined the two halves of his nature, the Faustian adventurer and the political opportunist, and behind him left a record of deceits, evasions, broken promises, Congressional absenteeism, political pusillanimities, after-dinner clichés, amoral political negotiations and a complete absence on the record of a single piece of important legislation. Or the utterance of a single exciting political idea. He didn't have to. He was on the trail of something else and the people who gathered to his support were in quest of something else.

His impulse, that profound insight into the real sources of political power in America, came from a conscious or unconscious cognition that the nation could no longer use a father; it was Kennedy's genius to appreciate that we now required a leading man. The contradictions of our national character had become so acute that no symbol of authority could satisfy our national anxiety any longer. We had become a Kierkegaardian nation. In the deep mills of our crossed desires, in the darkening ambiguities of our historic role, we could know no longer whether we were good or evil as an historic force, whether we should prosper or decline, whether we were the seed of freedom or the elaboration of a new tyranny. We needed to discover ourselves by an exploration through our ambiguity. And that precise ambiguity is embodied in the man we chose for our President. His magnetism is that he offers us a mirror of ourselves, he is an existential hero, his end is unknown, it is even unpredictable, even as our end is unpredictable, and so in this time of crisis he is able to perform the indispensable psychic act of a leader, he takes our national anxiety so long buried and releases it to the surface—where it belongs.

Now we must live again as a frontier nation, out on a psychic frontier without the faith of children or the security of answers. So the country, for better or for worse, is now again on the move, and the President is the living metaphor of our change. It is this power in him to excite— whether he desires it or no—our change, our discord, and our revolt, which Victor Lasky has failed most resolutely to comprehend. He does not see that Kennedy is the agent of our ferment and that we now go forth into the future ignorant of whether the final face of the Presidency and Amer- ica shall prove to be Abraham Lincoln or Dorian Gray.

Tallyrand
said the grave
de Sade
has put
a curse on you

7 · THE LINE OF ARGUMENT NOTED

*The last phrase of the previous piece ended: we . . . go forth
. . . ignorant of whether the final face of the Presidency shall
prove to be Abraham Lincoln or Dorian Gray. That piece was written
about twelve weeks before Jack Kennedy took his visit to Dallas. Less
than eight weeks before the assassination, work was begun on* An American
Dream. *The name of the formal villain in that novel comes up on the first
page. It is Kelly—Barney* Oswald *Kelly. If psychic coincidences give
pleasure to some, I do not know if they give them to me.*

*The time has come to call intermission. We've had hard matters, buckets
of blood on the sand, lambs roaring, lions bleating, Cannibals and Chris-
tians—now time for a sideshow or two, for the sort of piece which need
not in the best name of literature be printed, or reprinted.*

*After the intermission, the audience of this book will be welcomed to the
last part: glum, near desperate, I assure you, in its importance. Arena, it is
called. The Argument will resume in the Arena.*

PART THREE: RESPITES

8 · *THE LINE OF ARGUMENT*

FURTHER NOTED

*Well, deprive not this section of a touch of import. Every piece
printed here is not only respite but confrontation. That is to say:
a meeting whose outcome is unknown. None of these meetings are excep-
tional and a number are as trivial as their outcome; still, some are sharp,
some are curious. Meetings which are sharp and curious give taste to face
the plague. Three cheers for existential pharmacology.*

First meeting is Nelson Algren and Norman Mailer.

A TELEVISION SHOW WITH NELSON ALGREN

A couple of months ago Nelson Algren brought out a book called *Who Lost an American?* (Macmillan—$5.95). It's a work which gets better as it goes along, but the worst to be said about the first chapter is that somebody might read it. It has a parody of James Baldwin and myself which hits at everything but the ring rope, and keeps missing altogether. I don't know about Baldwin, but it ought to be relatively easy to do a job on me. Only Algren was throwing too hard. The first chapter read like the prose of a girl who has broken into hysteria trying to beat up her big big boyfriend. Indeed it was so bad it sounded like a parody of what one's best friend on *Time* might write.

I went through these pages the night before I was scheduled to go on a television show with Algren. This act of reading startled me. What had I done to Nelson? We hardly knew each other. The only crime I could remember was that once some years ago in *Advertisements for Myself* I had shaded lukewarm praise for Algren's books with a few tart remarks, the worst of which maybe in Nelson's eyes was to call him "The Grand Odd-Ball" of American letters. Of course "odd-ball" was not an altogether unsympathetic word, and "grand" was fine, but then Algren's eye might see it in other focus. Still? The parody was frantic, I decided, too frantic to keep one awake. I went to bed pleased (about something else, naturally) and aroused myself at six-thirty with four hours of sleep, to make my way to the television studio. Our show was *Calendar*, Harry Reasoner's C.B.S. morning production; they tape early. To my surprise, I was not suffering. I had had a good night and a good four hours of sleep, and I was alert. Which put me in a most excellent mood. I hadn't felt this good with four hours of sleep in quite a while.

Algren, when I saw him, was not looking his best. He too obviously had had four hours of sleep, but he looked like he'd awakened with somebody else's liver in his windpipe. Nelson has an interesting face when you get a chance to study it, but at first sight he slides into your vision like an ex-con who's put twenty years in the can. Pallor for one thing, and a skinny flick in his eyes which promises nothing but angles.

"You're looking well, Norman," was his formal greeting.

"Fat and pretty." I was feeling genial and I was acting even more genial than I felt. I think he was feeling a classic embarrassment.

There's nothing exactly so dim as meeting somebody you've written about savagely if you no longer feel savage.

Perhaps the television promoters of this show had the idea we would offer a literary war for their camera—their introduction was calculated to nip the tail feathers of two fighting cocks, which is what novelists usually are not—but in any case Reasoner's questions cast Algren and me willy-nilly together. We expended most of our first ten minutes in defense of authors who write about the "seamy side of life." Since we were banded together against the common enemy—most of America out there in televisionland—we could hardly throw any roundhouses at each other. Occasionally I'd stick a jab at Algren, but he was on his bicycle. Nelson seemed to be looking for no fight. If it were going to be a personality contest, obviously I was going to win going away. One of the things I sometimes distrust about myself is that I'm fairly good on television. Nelson isn't. He's a gentle voice, and needs time and a coterie around him to be very funny. Then he can be so funny. This morning he was just doing his hangover best, a club fighter out of training who would like to go the distance, pick up his paycheck and not get hurt.

But he dropped a bomb on me. The show was a half-hour offering, with two stops for commercials. Just before the second half Algren was asked who he considered the best American writer around, and he said William Styron was far and away the best because Styron'd written two major novels which nobody else in the generation had done. Yes, said Algren, queried by Harry Reasoner, Styron was better than say a writer like Scott Fitzgerald. Came the commercial. Silence.

My feud with Styron was not exactly a young widow's secret. During the break for the product, I realized Algren had done it. I had the choice of keeping my mouth shut, or shoving into a back-and-forth. (I don't think he's that good—I say he is.) I took the first option. Nobody up at that hour would be able to remember Styron's name anyway. Best to drop the matter cold. Only I was mad. Algren had gotten into me. That tired hungover club fighter had studied me enough to know where my guard was cute, and he dropped a big one in. I was as mad as a lazybitch boxer (a cassiusclay so to speak) who has been winning every round by a fraction and gets decked in the ninth with a manager's punch. That is to say, a punch which was conceived in training camp before the fight. I was mad enough to ignore my own decision and talk about Styron, but the questions went to another direction and we rode out the rest of the show with nothing further for a happening.

I told myself to hold my temper, but succeeded merely by half. "Listen," I said, coming on Algren the moment the cameras were done, "you're twice the writer Styron is, and you aren't even that good."

"Well, I was impressed with him," Algren said.

"Come on." We were talking with the quick intricacy of cellmates. "You know that second novel is as full of shit as a Yuletide turkey."

"But the first is good," said Algren. "I just read *Lie Down in Darkness* last summer. It's a most remarkable book."

"It is," I said, "but the second . . ."

"Well . . ." said Algren. I had the feeling he didn't necessarily disagree with me. Nelson put on his twenty-years-in-the-pen look again. "Tell you," he said, "you know what I admire about Styron. He gets a picture taken of Mr. and Mrs. William Styron on the S.S. *United States* that the S.S. *United States* puts in its ads in all the magazines. I got to admire that," said Nelson out of the side of his mouth. "I always got to slink over."

"Nelson, you'd give a testimonial to the Miami Hilton if they put your picture in a magazine."

Algren looked hurt. He shook his head quietly as if to say, "You're going too far," but he ended with a carny grin. "I think I'll call Styron up the day this show goes on, tell him to look at it, and then pay him a visit for a month."

"After he sees the show, Styron'll put you up for a year."

Well, there we were. I couldn't help it. I liked Algren.

We started to talk about middleweight prizefighters. We talked of Henry Hank for a while, and of Reuben Carter who Nelson was certain could take Dick Tiger. I told him Tiger was the best fighter pound for pound in the world. "He was," said Algren, "but Fullmer took a lot out of him."

"Well, we'll see."

"Yes."

We stepped out of the studio together. Algren was going to get an hour of sleep before taking off to Aqueduct for the day. I had an impression he was wondering whether to ask me along. On the street, we hesitated. Then I stuck out my arm and we shook hands. Two middleweight artists had fought a draw in Baltimore.

BOITES AND BRUISERS: *Poems and Short Hairs*

Commuter Pool

Each time I think of some little thing
I can do to get ahead,
                    I feel as if
a foul fierce art from the nightmares
of constipation, the flaming waste of
stagnation
            (Chime! Chime! the Vowels!)
has forced its way
               up up into my brain
and played the lyre from Hades' heart.

So I say to myself (I am growing deaf,
my dear) I say to myself: Boy,
you are getting ready to trade
the possibilities of the future,
otherwise known as soul,
                  for the ego,
the beans and the booze
    Remember: that Guy died for us.

But oh those dreams and how they burn.
    oh those dreams and how they burn.

Heaven cannot have a bitch
so royal as the root of my sweet itch.

Bar Twists

I await her
  hot-breathed
  cigaretted
  garlicky
  version
  of all the lost days.

Cheer up
  whispers she
  (silently)
  hugging
  the other
  mugger.

Hurts me
  loathe chicks
  second wife
    did me in
    I cannot
    forswear
    to gaze
    said the rage.

  Other drunks spit.
  Creepy girls giggle.
  Pigs niggle
    at the root.

Prose

That's what
    it means
      to be
        in love
          you can't tell
            a dame
            to go
            fuck
            herself.

Sorrow said:
    nothing
    but salt
      in water
      to soothe
          my
          sore

181

Epitaph of a Rail

I used to drink
until six
   in the morning
so I could make
      dames
and now I drink
until six
   in the morning
watching other
      guys
   make dames.
   Eheu Fugaces.
Which means:
   Fuck aces!
   before the fleeting
   years go by

Every time
I stop
smoking
I feel
as if
I can't find
my teeth.

The alleviation of ague in the advertising age

Nothing tastes better than a good cold glass of Rheingold
    Nothing is better for taste than a good glass
        of cold Rheingold
        Be bold, my love
        Death is near
        Kiss my bier.

I'm such a turd
when she asked
   me for the
   abortion
I gave her
   one thousand
   and never said
      a word
      —why didn't I give
         her
            nine hundred and ninety-nine?

When you
   have
   fruition
you
   have
   frustration
   said
   the retired
      Dick

I always say
  what I think
  crooks usually do
  cops go through hoops
    and hell
    because
  they do not believe
    that is why
      they tie ribbons
        on crooks
      they're particularly
      fond of

Au fond,
  cops are like ladies
Au fondest fond
  cops are like
    ladies
      in a bad mood.

He
who
travels
alone
travels
least
said
the
police
pounding
the beat
in
pairs

There was a meet for the boys
The moolahs, the mozzers, the Maf, the Coast and the Nose
even the bonze and the dunes.
They were in to get acquaints for a new soft commodtz
and general affiliation.

How, said the Coaster to the Nostrand
do you think soft sell began?
Well, I'll tell you, said the Maf, we said to the dunes
Whaderya trying to shove that shit
      down people's troat for?
Slip it up their stroonz
      you asshole
Strike a match!

Said the dunes to the Maf,
Whaderya want to give me a hardon for?
you have hurt my feels
how much can the heart of my feels take
before the heart of some other Guinea's feels
      is forced to break?
Listen, said the dunes to the Maf—you're a dunze
Don't get hit!

So they had a ruining
They had the runs.
That was some thunder.
Those fartsaroons came close to eating all the prunes.

You
  can
    never
      imitate
      a creation
    said
  the
mimic.

BOITES

I love Bobby, Bobby's divine
  The Windsors came to
     see him
    and the Duke
     kept calling for
  Bye Bye Blackbird
over and over again.
It was a glorious night.
I borrowed mascara
  from the Duchess
before we were done
we were crying
   so hard
    even the Duke.
How were we to know
  that in five years
    give ten
  the West
    Old World
  would shiver from blight
  and I would turn
    to a Prince
    of the Congo
saying: embrace me
  darkest delight
for in your firmament
are stars.

Oh blackbird
  do not banish us
  banish not
    the lovers
    of Bobby

when he sang
Blackbird
bye-bye
for can it be
we heard
the chord
of the cannibal
sharpening his knife
on a blooded stone
and wept for you
as well as us.

Young winners
make weak old losers
said Bobby
removing his mask
to show
he was now
King
of our
Congo.

It's amazing
  how many
  ladies
  never crack
  a book
  it hurts
    the spine.

9 · OUR ARGUMENT SOMEWHAT CONTINUED

*Two interviews follow. They are in fact three, for the first piece
consists of two interviews done a season apart, but put together
here. This first piece, here titled "Petty Notes on Some Sex in America,"
was done for* Playboy, *for two* Playboy *panels with the formidable titles
"Sex and Censorship in Literature and the Arts," starring Maurice Girodias,
Barney Rosset, Otto Preminger, Norman Mailer, Ralph Ginzburg, Thurman
Arnold, and Albert Ellis, and "The Womanization of America," billing Dr.
Theodor Reik, Alexander King, Dr. Ashley Montague, Mort Sahl, Edward
Bernays, Dr. Ernest Dichter, Herbert Mayes, myself again. The panels, like*
Playboy, *are overprocessed. The editors formulated questions (in a style
you will be presented soon enough), gave them to the* Realist's *Reichs-
marschall Paul Krassner, who was obliged to interview me by reading Herr*
Playboy's *questions, and yr arthur's answers were then collated by the
editors into the panel—the panelists all separately interviewed, but with all
answers interlocked to give the impression the eight gents were in one
room at the same time all working for* Playboy. *The result is flatulent. For
most of the Symposium, nobody answers anybody else; no real reactions—
just replies at a tangent to pretend to satisfy the needs of a supposed col-
lective dialogue which was never collective, and one's answers were chopped
up, the questions were shifted, parts of the answers were dropped forever.
My necessity, here, then, was to reconstitute—if able—my individual inter-
views, and I've touched them up in order to try to find the original flavor,
the original cheerless flavor of answering Herr Krassner von der Realismus
while he asked me questions worked up by a Spectorsky committee. A pity,
for the answers are sufficiently sensible to reproduce here, although
singularly charmless. Wit is altogether absent. Solemnity pervades.*

    The other interview was done for Paris Review's *Writers at Work series
and the questions were gathered by the honorable Steven Marcus who
worked up a careful structure for his questions so that the interview built in
the interest of a reader as it progressed, and some rudiments of style were
present in my answer. It has been cut by two-thirds for its show here since
the early portions were autobiographical and have no bearing on the affairs
of this book; what remains is about the art of writing in general, thus it
touches on the plague.*

But note my emphasis. The first interview, the double panel interview, is sound, but dispiriting in tone, not I grant you so dispiriting as reading an article in Harper's *while sipping Alka-Seltzer, but still dialogue in which no living human can feel pride. The other, the* Paris Review *interview, although later fortified by specific questions from the editors (which broke the spell) and worked on stylistically by me at home (which broke the integrity), has nonetheless a unity of voice which came out of the critical and careful nature of a clear confrontation.*

There is everywhere now a passion to dislocate the mood of an event, to remove it from the site of its confrontation. Any reader of the original Playboy *panel must have felt uneasy at the center of his perceptions all the while he was reading, since the panel never had a physical existence. That leaves a trace of the void. Especially if one is not told. Similarly, a show on television at midnight, taped two hours before, induces a slipping at the base of one's perception of time. Style is root. The tension in the years of the plague is to cut the root and wait for style to expire or accelerate itself into the grandiloquent. If Camp is the flower of this plague, the first interview to follow falls into a form which has yet no name, some sturdy vegetable and weed of the plague, common as the intelligence of a newspaper column, liberal in tone but totalitarian as a lack of bell-bottom trousers at her highness' ball.*

PETTY NOTES ON SOME SEX IN AMERICA

PLAYBOY

In G. Legman's classic study of censorship, *Love and Death*, he says: "Murder is a crime. Describing murder is not. Sex is not a crime. Describing sex is. Why?"

MAILER

I don't know that I have the answer offhand, but I think one possibility is this: reading about murder very often *voids* the desire, whereas reading about sex often *increases* the desire. Now it's obvious that censors are not interested in increasing the amount of sexual desire in a country. There seems to be some relation between high sexuality and low productive level. Countries with the most sexuality have the lowest productive level. In countries like India, where poor people—not intellectuals—are absorbed in sex, productivity has stayed at a very low level for centuries. The same was true in China, and in a lesser sense, perhaps, in Russia before the revolution. At any rate, there does seem to be some relation between sexual repression and the increase of productivity. Censors often feel that they are guarding the *health* of the nation by repressing sexuality.

PLAYBOY

It used to be said, in the book-publishing business—and only partly in jest—that the banning of a book in Boston was a better sales stimulant than a dozen full-page ads. Yet there does exist a kind of tacit censorship, by an author who wants to stay out of trouble, and by his publisher, who may have the same motives, or who may hope for a book that it will be "pure" enough to be acceptable to a major book club, thus earning more money for himself and his author. Do you find this kind of voluntary or tacit censorship among book publishers?

MAILER

It's not so much a matter of censorship as embarrassment. Often publishers consider certain sexual writing in bad taste. They may often try, with the best intentions, to censor a book because they feel they have the author's interest in mind. They may know very well that certain important reviewers are going to be repelled by certain chapters or passages, and it's going to hurt the reviews they give the book.

As a practical matter, it's even true that there are many reviewers, especially for the smaller newspapers, who don't dare give a book a good review if the sexual material is too intense, too direct, too explicit, because, if they do, they're going to get into trouble with their newspapers. There will be readers writing in to the editor. Of course, it may not even be as direct as that. There may be just a general air of displeasure that the reviewer chose to approve of the book. The result is the sort of censorship that I call *motherly* censorship. The people who do the censoring consider it distasteful, but they're doing it for the child's—in this case, the author's—own good. For that reason, it's the most insidious kind of censorship, for people who are censoring you very often are your friends; they like you, they feel they're doing it for your good, and so it's harder to fight back. You're not able to say to yourself, "This censor is my enemy and I resist him and take my stand here." Instead, you have to argue with a close friend whom you've worked with for years, who may even have a certain practical wisdom in what he's saying. So it weakens the writer, vis-à-vis the publisher, and many of the more compromised, more reflective, more sensitive, more timorous parts of his nature are brought forth, and it's harder for him to fight back. Of course, my feeling is that a short gain is taken for a long loss. It's no good for a writer to retract anything he's written that's good.

I would argue with the censor on his own ground that there's no use trying to resist a wave of real interest and even perhaps of biological intensity by trying to suppress it. If there's going to be any censorship—and I'm not certain there should be—it ought to recognize that an intimate and serious evocation of sex is part of the very *marrow* of a nation's culture, and when the marrow is drained through brutal or stupid censorship, then the country beings to sicken. I won't say it *causes,* but it certainly *accelerates,* the sickness of the country.

PLAYBOY

J. Edgar Hoover has stated: "We know that in an overwhelmingly large number of cases, sex crime is associated with pornography. We know that sex criminals read it, are clearly influenced by it. I believe pornography is a major cause of sex violence. I believe that if we can eliminate the distribution of such items among impressionable children, we shall greatly reduce our frightening crime rate."

MAILER

There's a subterranean impetus toward pornography so powerful that half the business world is juiced by the sort of half sex that one finds in advertisements. You get enormously attractive girls selling cigarettes, which is a perversion of sex because an enormously attractive girl should be presented for what she is, and not as a handmaiden to a little box containing some paper, tobacco and cellophane.

I think this bad "art" that one gets in the mass media, on television, in the movies, does the nation far more harm than if one were to remove all controls from pornography and obscenity. Being half excited and half frustrated leads to violence. Whenever one is aroused sexually and doesn't find a consummation, the sex in one's veins turns literally to violence. It's no accident that most frigid people are sadistic.

I refuse to take pornography seriously as a danger to the country until the things that are really dangerous to the country—like the mass media—are subjected to a little scrutiny. When *they're* ready to clean *their* house, I'll say we writers will be ready to clean our house. Of course there are books that don't have a drop of pornography in them that are also evil. I think a reasonably good play on television that is truthful for the first two acts and becomes completely false in the third act is evil, because it arouses certain expectations in people, makes them start considering their lives, and just at the point when they're most open they're turned away with a lie. It's exactly like *coitus interruptus*. *Coitus interruptus* is evil.

PLAYBOY

One of the evils of pornography, according to James Jackson Kilpatrick in his book *The Smut Peddlers*, is that "when a youth accepts the idea of sex without love he is stained inside."

MAILER

The stimulus to pornography is that few people in the country really find love. Because they don't find it, the only way they can begin to get back on the track of finding it is to find some excitation. I think what happens over the years is that most people in America sink sooner or later into a profound depression about sex. They've failed at it so many times in so many ways. Pornography at least charges their batteries, and they go out again, and they search for it again, and again they fail. The argument, I think, comes down to this: that the half state of acceptance America has for pornography is probably intolerable. The tragedy of many people is that they don't find love not because their bodies are inadequate to love, but their minds are. Love is an enormously complex matter, and we have absolutely no preparation for it in this country.

NOTE:
By now, I think the point has been made. It is needless to go on with the interview as a pure interview. I will cut what remains and give a few worked-over parts. More often than not, the questions from Playboy *will also be deleted. Immediately, however, upon conclusion of the panel, a nose-gay of poems will follow. They are titled: Petty Poems on Some Sex in America.*

ON LADY CHATTERLEY

I read *Lady Chatterley's Lover* in college. The unabridged edition. In the Treasure Room at Widener. It changed my life. It was the first thing I'd ever read that gave me the idea sex could have beauty. I learned from Lawrence that the way to write about sex was not to strike poses, but be true to the logic of each moment. There's a subtle logic to love. I think one of the reasons people are absorbed in love is because it's one of the only ways in which they can find a logic to their lives. Looking back on it now, I think *Lady Chatterley's Lover* is not a very good book. It's probably one of the greatest of the bad books—it's much too simple—it tries to capture the essence of sex and yet has nothing to say about the violence which is part of sex. One doesn't arrive at love by getting into bed with a woman and getting better and better at it, and exploring more and more deeply. A man and woman can't *just* explore more and more deeply into one another. Any number of things keep happening—the world keeps impinging on sex. The lovers keep testing one another; lovers not only create but they also destroy one another; lovers change one another; lovers resist the change that each gives to the other. Lawrence, by avoiding these problems, wrote a book that was more mythical than novelistic and terribly sentimental. Yet, it's a book I would defend to the death. If it had entered the general literature at the time it was written, our sexual literature today would be better, more subtle, sensitive, profound. It was exactly because *Lady Chatterley's Lover* was kept in a state of suppression for many years that it took on a power it didn't really possess.

ON TROPIC OF CANCER

What is marvelous about *Tropic of Cancer* is that it is the exact opposite of Lawrence. *Tropic of Cancer* gets the beauty of sex another way, the way people who care a great deal about prize fighting can go to a club fight and enjoy all of it, the ugliness; the blood, the cigar smoke, the spit on the floor, the body odor; it's all part of something whose end is unforeseen. In *Lady Chatterley's Lover,* as I remember, there was not even a description of Mellors' cottage—you don't know what the bed's like —but when you read about sex in Miller, you know how the sheets scratch. For anyone who's interested in getting sexual pleasure from a book, *Tropic of Cancer* is more exciting than *Lady Chatterley's Lover.* When one reads Lawrence there's a certain wistfulness, one feels. Most people don't find sex that pure, that deep, that organic. They find it sort of partial and hot and ugly and fascinating and filled with all sorts of day-to-day details. I'd like to achieve something *between* Miller and Lawrence.

ON THE WOMANIZATION OF AMERICA

Before World War I, America was not a place engaged in world history, but an island *sheltered* from world history, a place where people could go and be free of the deteriorating effects of the crises of history. But when America became a world power and began to have ambitions to become the only world power, American men began to want something else: not to be successful in the old way of building large families, a business, moving into new country, into the frontier, creating something that was going to expand; but rather, living in a relatively stratified society now, they wanted to rise through these strata and acquire more and more power in a world no longer open and viable but on the contrary like an enormously subtle and complex machine. Well, when they desired this, they began to look for something different in women. I think the womanization of America comes not only because women are becoming more selfish, more greedy, less romantic, less warm, more lusty, and more filled with hate—but because the men have collaborated with them. There's been a change in the minds of most men about the function of marriage—it isn't that they're necessarily becoming weaker vis-à-vis their wives, it's that they've married women who will be less good for them in the home and more good for them in the world. The kind of woman who doesn't wash a dish is usually a beauty who'll spend 10 to 12 hours in bed and will take two hours to make up; she has' to have a nurse for the children, but she'll be a wow at a party and will aid the man in his career because when they both go to the party, everybody envies him, covets his woman, so forth. What he wants is a marvelous courtesan with social arts. A courtesan who can go out into the world with him.

ON CHIVALRY

Chivalry consists of opening a door for a woman; that means you've got to be alert, you can't retire for a moment into your own preoccupations. There you are: in position to open the door. The irony is that women who get the kind of man who's marvelous at these small attentions are always profoundly dissatisfied by his lack of depth. When they get a man with depth, they are miserable at his incapacity to take care of them in small ways.

MEN DOING THE HOUSEKEEPING

The fact that men are washing dishes doesn't necessarily mean we are in the final womanization of America; there's been, as I said, a shift in the social and biological function of the woman. She is now expected not to create a home so much as to be aide-de-camp or staff general to an ambitious opportunist. Part of the unspoken contract is that therefore she won't wash a dish. She won't wash it because she realizes that's not a necessary part of her present function. Her husband would love her to wash the dishes, but he knows damn well she won't, because the kind of women who can serve as courtesans and/or aide-de-camps don't wash dishes.

PLAYBOY

What do you think of this remark by Dr. Ernest Dichter, founder and president of the Institute for Motivational Research? "We recently did a study in one of the European countries on birth control. . . . There's a definite relationship between the social class and the use of birth-control techniques. I am talking primarily about the lower-income group. . . . Our statistical knowledge with the birth-control association has shown that the instruction reaches primarily the middle class and upper-middle class. The real problem is reaching the lower-income-group people, for they are the ones who have many children.

MAILER

Well, that's the trouble with motivational research. There's no attempt to consider the possibility that a woman might be right—biologically right, instinctively right—in *not* wanting to use a contraceptive. If you take ignorant women, they're not going to be able to express themselves at all. Their reasons for not wanting to use birth-control pills would be rather vague. Suppose unconsciously they feel a deep biological aversion to having sex without the possibility of conceiving. Maybe a woman obtains her deepest knowledge of herself and of the world by the way in which she conceives. You see, the fact that she *can* conceive alters the existential character of her sex. It makes it deeper. She's taking more of a risk. It's more dangerous, more responsible, it's graver. Because it's graver, it's deeper. Since it's deeper, it's better. The reason she may not want to use a contraceptive is because she senses somewhere within her—in dim fashion, no doubt—that there's something alien to the continuation of her, her species, and her family, if she uses a contraceptive. Yet she may also feel a great shame about all this, because, after all, here's this very impressive gentleman with the eyeglasses, taking down every word she says, and there's the attitude of her husband and all the people around her, and her children, about using contraceptives, and so she begins to feel that, well, maybe she's wrong, and confusion is the result. And this pitiful confusion is immediately processed into statistics, which are psychotic in their lack of attachment to the biological reality.

ON HOMOSEXUALITY

I think there may be more homosexuals today than there were 50 years ago. If so, the basic reason might have to do with a general loss of faith in the country, faith in the meaning of one's work, faith in the notion of oneself as a man. When a man can't find any dignity in his work, he loses virility. Masculinity is not something given to you, something you're born with, but something you gain. And you gain it by winning small battles with honor. Because there is very little honor left in American life, there is a certain built-in tendency to destroy masculinity in American men. The mass media, for instance—television first, movies second, magazines third, and newspapers running no poor fourth—tend to destroy virility slowly and steadily. They give people an unreal view of life. They give people a notion that American life is easier than it really is, less complex, more rewarding. The result is that Americans, as they emerge from adolescence into young manhood, are very much like green soldiers being sent into difficult terrain ignorant of the conditions. A lot of virility immediately gets massacred.

PLAYBOY

Does the future of American womanhood—and manhood—really bode ill, or can we hope for a gradual process of mutual adjustment which will place the sexes on a basis of equilibrium in which each is aware of—and respects and understands—that difference proverbially implied in the Frenchman's cry of *"Vive la différence!"*

MAILER

This country's entering into the most desperate, nightmarish time in its history. Unless everyone in America gets a great deal braver, everything is going to get worse—including the womanization of America.

NOTE: *Here are the poems promised upon conclusion of the panel. I think we may as well dedicate them to America's most dedicated publishing team, Chicago and* Playboy's *own Hef and Spec.*

PETTY POEMS ON SOME SEX IN AMERICA

Triple Pop Hair Short Art

The theory
    behind these
    short hairs
      is that
      every
      child
    is a poem
someone conceived
    in short space
for instance I am Dracula,
I will suck your blood
You are Hamlet
you will
    suck
    my dick
    O Shakespeare said Baroness Orczy
      you go in
    and out
      of beauty
    like the night.

I don't think
I can
accept
any more
compliments
cried the
maiden
determined
never to
let a
bugger
prosper.

Mr. Answer Man
  what is
    a weapon
      worse
        ten times
        worse
      than the
        Hydrogen
        Bomb?

Why a cunt
  which is
  ten times
    larger
  than the largest
      cock
      extant,
      Sandy.

Dégoutante,
  said Sandy,
  kissing nuns
  to hedge the bet.

A Universal Cure for Illness
don't go to bed
until you
fall
in
it

Mr. Answer Man
   what is
   a good
   lay?

Why, Sandy,
   a good lay
   is a miracle
   of the night
      for it means
      they were not
      altogether
      bad
      for each other.
They just didn't
   make it
   wowsy-boom
   like you
      and me.

Your idea
of sucking cock
quoth Romeo to Juliet
   is
   mistletoe
   Mother fucker!

Mother fucker?
Why, when I feel
   violence, Christmas dear,
I go down
   to look
      at
      ashes
said
      cocksucker

Never
contemplate
nothing
said
the saint.

THE ART OF FICTION: A Paris Review *Interview*

What writers have you learned the most from, technically?

MAILER

E. M. Forster, I suppose. I wouldn't say he is necessarily one of the novelists I admire most. But I have learned a lot from him. You remember in *The Longest Journey* somewhere about the fourth chapter, you turn the page and read, "Gerald was killed that day. He was beaten to death in a football game." It was quite extraordinary. Gerald had been very important through the beginning of the book. But now that he was suddenly and abruptly dead, everyone else's character began to shift. It taught me that personality was more fluid, more dramatic and startling, more inexact than I had thought. I was brought up on the idea that when you wrote a novel you tried to build a character who could be handled and walked around like a piece of sculpture. Suddenly character seemed related more closely to the paintings of the new realists. For instance I saw one recently which had a painted girl reclining on a painted bed, and there was a television set next to her in the canvas, a real one which you could turn on. Turning on the literal factual set changes the girl and the painting both. Well, Forster gives you something of that sensation in his novels. I suppose what I realized, after reading Forster, was that a novel written in the third person was now impossible for me for many years.

INTERVIEWER

Forster has never written a novel in the first person.

MAILER

I know he hasn't, but in some funny way Forster gave my notion of personality a sufficient shock that I could not manage to write in the third person. Forster, after all, had a developed view of the world. I did not. I think I must have felt at that time as if I would never be able to write in the third person until I developed a coherent view of life. I don't know that I've been able to altogether.

INTERVIEWER

Would you say something about style, prose style, in relation to the novel?

MAILER

A really good style comes only when a man has become as good as he can be. Style is character. A good style cannot come from a bad undisciplined character. Now a man may be evil, but I believe that people can be evil in their essential natures and still have good characters. Good in the sense of being well tuned. They can have characters which are flexible, supple, adaptable, principled in relation to their own good or their own evil—even an evil man can have principles; he can be true to his own evil, which is not always so easy, either. I think good style is a matter of rendering out of oneself all the cupidities, all the cripplings, all the velleities. And then I think one has to develop one's physical grace. Writers who are possessed of some physical grace may tend to write better than writers who are physically clumsy. It's my impression this is so.

INTERVIEWER

Have you ever written to merely improve your writing, practiced your writing as an athlete would work out?

MAILER

No. I don't think it's a proper activity. That's too much like doing a setting-up exercise; any workout which does not involve a certain minimum of danger or responsibility does not improve the body—it just wears it out.

INTERVIEWER

In writing your novels, has any particular formal problem given you trouble—let's say a problem of joining two parts of a narrative together, getting people from point A to point B?

MAILER

You mean like getting them out of a room? I think formal problems exist in inverse proportion to one's honesty. You get to the problem of getting someone out of the room when there's something false about the scene.

INTERVIEWER

Have you ever written about a situation of which you have had no personal experience or knowledge?

MAILER

I don't know. Let's see . . . *Barbary Shore,* for example, is the most imaginative of my novels. But I did live in a rooming house for a short period while I was writing *The Naked and the Dead.* I certainly didn't live in it the way my characters lived in it. I never met an F.B.I. agent, at least I had no sense of having met one at the time I was writing *Barbary Shore.* They didn't necessarily introduce themselves to me. I had never met an Old Bolshevik, either. But notice this! Writing about F.B.I. agents and Old Bolsheviks in *Barbary Shore,* the greatest single difficulty with the book was that my common sense thought it was impossible to have all these agents and impossible heroes congregating in a rooming house in Brooklyn Heights. Yet a couple of years later I was working in a studio on Fulton Street at the end of Brooklyn Heights, a studio I have had for some years. It was a fine old studio building and they're tearing it down now to make room for a twenty-story building which will look like a Kleenex box. At any rate, on the floor below me, worked one Colonel Rudolph Abel who was the most important spy for the Russians in this country for a period of about eight or ten years, and I am sure we used to be in the elevator together many times. I think he literally had the room beneath me. I have always been overcome with that. It made me decide there's no clear boundary between experience and imagination. Who knows what glimpses of reality we pick up unconsciously, telepathically.

INTERVIEWER

To what extent are your characters modeled on real people?

MAILER

I think half of them might have a point of departure from somebody real. Up to now I've not liked writing about people who are close to me, because they're too difficult to do. Their private reality obviously interferes with the reality one is trying to create. They become alive not as creatures in your imagination but as actors in your life. And so they seem real while you work but you're not working *their* reality into your book. For example it's not a good idea to try to put your wife into a novel.

Not your latest wife, anyway. In practice I prefer to draw a character from someone I hardly know.

INTERVIEWER

Can you describe how you turn a real person into a fictional one?

MAILER

I try to put the model in situations which have very little to do with his real situations in life. Very quickly the model disappears. His private reality can't hold up. For instance, I might take somebody who is a professional football player, a man let's say whom I know slightly, and make him a movie star. In a transposition of this sort, everything which relates particularly to the professional football player quickly disappears, and what is left, curiously, is what is *exportable* in his character. But this process while interesting in the early stages is not as exciting as the more creative act of allowing your characters to grow once they're separated from the model. It's when they become almost as complex as one's own personality that the fine excitement begins. Because then they are not really characters any longer—they're beings, which is a distinction I like to make. A character is someone you can grasp as a whole, you can have a clear idea of him, but a being is someone whose nature keeps shifting. Like a character of Forster's. In *The Deer Park* Lulu Meyers is a being rather than a character. If you study her closely you will see that she is a different person in every scene. Just a little different. I don't know whether initially I did this by accident or purposefully, but at a certain point I made the conscious decision *not* to try to straighten her out; she seemed right in her changeableness.

INTERVIEWER

Is Marion Faye a character or a—

MAILER

No, he's a being. Everybody in *The Deer Park* is a being except the minor characters like Herman Teppis.

INTERVIEWER

How did Marion Faye emerge?

MAILER

The book needed something which wasn't in the first draft, some sort of evil genius. One felt a dark pressure there in the inner horizon of the book. But even as I say this I know it's not true to the grain of my writing experience. I violate that experience by talking in these terms. I am not sure it's possible to describe the experience of novel writing authentically. It may be that it is not an experience.

INTERVIEWER

What is it, then?

MAILER

It may be more like a relation, if you will—a continuing relation between a man and his wife. You can't necessarily speak of that as an experience because it may consist of several experiences which are braided together; or it may consist of many experiences which are all more or less similar, or indeed it may consist of two kinds of experiences which are antagonistic to one another. Throughout all of this I've spoken of characters *emerging*. Quite often they don't emerge; they fail to emerge. And what one's left with is the dull compromise which derives from two kinds of experiences warring with one another within oneself. A character who should have been brilliant is dull. Or even if a character does prove to be first-rate, it's possible you should have done twice as much with him, three times as much.

INTERVIEWER

You speak of character as emerging, and I gather by that that you mean emerging from yourself and emerging from your idea?

MAILER

They are also emerging from the book. A book takes on its own life in the writing. It has its laws, it becomes a creature to you after a while. One feels a bit like a master who's got a fine animal. Very often I'll feel a certain shame for what I've done with a novel. I won't say it's the novel that's bad; I'll say it's I who was bad. Almost as if the novel did not really belong to me, as if it was something raised by me like a child. I know what's potentially beautiful in my novel, you see. Very often after I've done the novel I realize that that beauty which I recognize in it is not going to be recognized by the reader. I didn't succeed in bringing it out. It's very odd—it's as though I had let the novel down, owed it a duty which I didn't fulfill.

INTERVIEWER

Would you say that there was any secret or hidden pattern being worked out in your novels?

MAILER

I'd rather leave that to others. If I answer the question badly, nothing is accomplished. If I answer too well, it's going to discourage critics. I can imagine nothing more distressing to a critic than to have a writer see accurately into his own work. But I will say one thing, which is that I have some obsession with how God exists. Is He an essential god or an existential god; is He all-powerful or is He, too, an embattled existential creature who may succeed or fail in His vision? I think this theme may become more apparent as the novels go on.

INTERVIEWER

When did this obsession begin?

MAILER

I think it began to show itself while I was doing the last draft of *The Deer Park*. Then it continued to grow as a private theme during all the years I was smoking marijuana.

INTERVIEWER

You have spoken so often of the existential view. What reading, or individuals, brought you to this?

MAILER

The experience came first. One's condition on marijuana is always existential. One can feel the importance of each moment and how it is changing one. One feels one's being, one becomes aware of the enormous apparatus of nothingness—the hum of a hi-fi set, the emptiness of a point-less interruption, one becomes aware of the war between each of us, how the nothingness in each of us seeks to attack the being of others, how our being in turn is attacked by the nothingness in others. I'm not speaking now of violence or the active conflict between one being and another. That still belongs to drama. But the war between being and nothingness is the underlying illness of the twentieth century. Boredom slays more of existence than war.

INTERVIEWER

Then you didn't come to existentialism because it was a literary influence?

MAILER

No. I'd hardly read anything by Sartre at this time, and nothing by Heidegger. I've read a bit since, and have to admire their formidable powers, but I suspect they are no closer to the buried continent of existentialism than were medieval cartographers near to a useful map of the world. The new continent which shows on our psychic maps as intimations of eternity is still to be discovered.

INTERVIEWER

What do you feel about the other kinds of writing you have done and are doing? How do they stand in relation to your work as a novelist?

MAILER

The essays?

INTERVIEWER

Yes: journalism, essays.

MAILER

Well, you know, there was a time when I wanted very much to belong to the literary world. I wanted to be respected the way someone like Katherine Anne Porter used to be respected.

INTERVIEWER

How do you think she was respected?

MAILER

The way a cardinal is respected—weak people get to their knees when the cardinal goes by.

INTERVIEWER

As a master of the craft, do you mean?

MAILER

As a master of the craft, yes. Her name is invoked in an argument. "Well, Katherine Anne Porter would not do it *that* way." But by now I'm a bit cynical about craft. I think there's a natural mystique in the novel which is more important than craft. One is trying, after all, to capture reality, and that is extraordinarily and exceptionally difficult. I think craft is merely a series of waystations. I think of craft as being like a St. Bernard dog with that little bottle of brandy under his neck. Whenever you get into *real* trouble the thing that can save you as a novelist is to have enough craft to be able to keep warm long enough to be rescued. Of course this is exactly what keeps good novelists from becoming great novelists. Robert Penn Warren might have written a major novel if he hadn't had just that little extra bit of craft to get him out of all the trouble in *All the King's Men*. If Penn Warren hadn't known anything about Elizabethan literature, the true Elizabethan in him might have emerged. I mean, he might have written a fantastic novel. As it was, he knew enough about craft to . . .

INTERVIEWER

To use it as an escape hatch?

MAILER

Yes. And his plot degenerated into a slam-bang of exits and entrances, confrontations, tragedies, quick wits and woe. But he was really forcing an escape from the problem.

INTERVIEWER

Which was?

MAILER

Oh, the terror of confronting a reality which might open into more and more anxiety and so present a deeper and deeper view of the abyss. Craft protects one from facing those endless expanding realities of deterioration and responsibility.

INTERVIEWER

Deterioration in what sense?

MAILER

The terror, let's say, of being reborn as something much less noble or something much more ignoble. I think this sort of terror depresses us profoundly. Which may be why we throw up our enormous evasions— such as craft. Indeed, I think this adoration of craft, this specific respect for craft makes a church of literature for that vast number of writers who are somewhere on the spectrum between mediocrity and talent. But I think it's fatal for somebody who has a large ambition and a chance of becoming a great writer. I know for myself, if I am going to make this attempt, that the only way to do it is to keep in shape in a peculiar way.

INTERVIEWER

Can you explain what you mean by that?

MAILER

It's hard to talk about. Harry Greb, for example, was a fighter who used to keep in shape. He was completely a fighter, the way one might wish to be completely a writer. He always did the things which were necessary to him as a fighter. Now, some of these things were extremely irrational, that is, extremely irrational from a prize-fight manager's point of view. That is, before he had a fight he would go to a brothel, and he would have two prostitutes, not one, taking the two of them into the same bed. And this apparently left him feeling like a wild animal. Don't ask me why. Perhaps he picked the two meanest whores in the joint and so absorbed into his system all the small, nasty, concentrated evils which had accumulated from carloads of men. Greb was known as the dirtiest fighter of his time. He didn't have much of a punch but he could spoil other fighters and punish them, he knew more dirty tricks than anyone around. This was one of his training methods and he did it over and over again until he died at a relatively early age of a heart attack, on an operating table. I think he died before he was thirty-eight, or so. They operated on him, and bang, he went. Nothing could be done. But the point I make is that he stayed in training by the way he lived his life. The element which was paramount in it was to keep in shape. If he was drinking, you see, the point was to keep in shape *while* drinking. I'm being a touch imprecise about this . . .

INTERVIEWER

Well . . . what?

MAILER

He would not just drink to release his tension. Rather, what went on was that there was tension in him which was insupportable, so he had to drink. But reasoning as a professional he felt that if he had to drink, he might as well use that too. In the sense that the actor uses everything which happens to him, so Greb as a fighter used everything which happened to him. As he drank he would notice the way his body moved. One of the best reasons one drinks is to become aware of the way his mind and body move.

Well, how do you keep in shape?

Look, before we go on, I want to say a little more about craft. It is a grab bag of procedures, tricks, lore, formal gymnastics, symbolic super-structures, methodology in short. It's the compendium of what you've acquired from others. And since great writers communicate a vision of existence, one can't usually borrow their methods. The method is married to the vision. No, one acquires craft more from good writers and mediocre writers with a flair. Craft after all is what you can take out whole from their work. But keeping in shape is something else. For example, you can do journalism, and it can be terrible for your style. Or it can temper your style . . . in other words you can become a *better* writer by doing a lot of different kinds of writing. Or you can deteriorate. There's a book came out a few years ago which was a sociological study of some Princeton men—I forget the name of it. One of them said something which I thought was extraordinary. He said he wanted to perform the sexual act under every variety of condition, emotion, and mood available to him. I was struck with this not because I ever wanted necessarily to have that kind of sexual life, but because it seemed to me that was what I was trying to do with my writing. I try to go over my work in every conceivable mood. I edit on a spectrum which runs from the high clear manic impressions of a drunk which has made one electrically alert all the way down to the soberest reaches of depression where I can hardly bear my words. By the time I'm done with writing I care about I usually have worked on it through the full gamut of my consciousness. If you keep yourself in this peculiar kind of shape, the craft will take care of itself. Craft is very little finally. But if you're continually worrying about whether you're growing or deteriorating as a man, whether your integrity is turning soft or firming itself, why then it's in that slow war, that slow rear-guard battle you fight against diminishing talent that you stay in shape as a writer and have a consciousness. You develop a consciousness as you grow older which enables you to write about anything, in effect, and write about it well. That is, provided you keep your consciousness in shape and don't relax into the flabby styles of thought which surround one everywhere. The moment you borrow other writers' styles of thought, you need craft to shore up the walls. But if what you write is a reflection of your own consciousness, then even journalism can become interesting. One wouldn't want to spend one's life at it and I wouldn't want ever to be caught justifying journalism as a major activity (it's obviously less interesting than to write a novel), but it's better, I think, to see journalism as a venture of one's ability to keep in shape than to see it as an essential betrayal of the chalice of your literary art. Temples are for women.

INTERVIEWER

Temples are for women?

MAILER

Temples are for women.

INTERVIEWER

Well, Faulkner once said that nothing can injure a man's writing if he's a first-rate writer.

MAILER

Faulkner said more asinine things than any other major American writer. I can't remember a single interesting remark Faulkner ever made.

INTERVIEWER

He once called Henry James a "nice old lady."

MAILER

Faulkner had a mean small Southern streak in him, and most of his pronunciamentos reflect that meanness. He's a great writer, but he's not at all interesting in most of his passing remarks.

INTERVIEWER

Well, then, what can ruin a first-rate writer?

MAILER

Booze, pot, too much sex, too much failure in one's private life, too much attrition, too much recognition, too little recognition, frustration. Nearly everything in the scheme of things works to dull a first-rate talent. But the worst probably is cowardice—as one gets older, one becomes aware of one's cowardice, the desire to be bold which once was a joy gets heavy with caution and duty.

INTERVIEWER

What kind of an audience do you keep in mind when you write?

MAILER

I suppose it's that audience which has no tradition by which to measure their experience but the intensity and clarity of their inner lives. That's the audience I'd like to be good enough to write for.

INTERVIEWER

Do you feel under any obligation to them?

MAILER

Yes. I have a consciousness now which I think is of use to them. I've got to be able to get it out and do it well, to transmit it in such a way that their experience can rise to a higher level. It's exactly . . . I mean, one doesn't want one's children to make one's own mistakes. Let them make better mistakes, more exceptional mistakes.

INTERVIEWER

What projects do you have for the future?

MAILER

I've got a very long novel I want to do. And beyond that I haven't looked.

INTERVIEWER

You once said you wished to become consecutively more disruptive, more dangerous, and more powerful, and you felt this sentence was a description of your function as a novelist. I wonder if you still think that?

MAILER

I might take out "disruptive." It's an unhappy word to use. It implies a love of disruption for the sake of disruption. Actually, I have a fondness for order.

INTERVIEWER

Do you enjoy writing, or is such a term irrelevant to your experience?

MAILER

Oh no. No, no. You set me thinking of something Jean Malaquais once said. He always has a terrible time writing. He once complained with great anguish about the unspeakable difficulties he was having with a novel. And I asked him, "Why do you do it? You can do many other things well. Why do you bother with it?" I really meant this. Because he suffered when writing like no one I know. He looked up in surprise and said, "Oh, but this is the only way one can ever find the truth. The only time I know that something is true is at the moment I discover it in the act of writing." I think it's that. I think it's this moment of intellection, this moment of seizure when one knows it's true. One may not have written it well enough for others to know, but you're in love with the truth when you discover it at the point of a pencil. That in and by itself is one of the few rare pleasures in life.

INTERVIEWER

And to be writing—to be a writer?

MAILER

Well, at best you affect the consciousness of your time, and so indirectly you affect the history of the time which succeeds you. Of course, you need patience. It takes a long time for sentiments to collect into an action, and often they never do. Which is why I was once so ready to conceive of running for Mayor of New York. I wanted to make actions rather than effect sentiments. But I've come to the middle-aged conclusion that I'm probably better as a writer than a man of action. Too bad. Still it's no little matter to be a writer. There's that Godawful *Time* Magazine world out there, and one can make raids on it. There are palaces, and prisons to attack. One can even succeed now and again in blowing holes in the line of the world's communications. Sometimes I feel as if there's a vast guerrilla war going on for the mind of man, communist against communist, capitalist against capitalist, artist against artist. And the stakes are huge. Will we spoil the best secrets of life or will we help to free a new kind of man? It's intoxicating to think of that. There's something rich waiting if one of us is brave enough and good enough to get there.

10 · OUR ARGUMENT ALL BUT

DISCONTINUED

Two short stories follow. Because the first, called The Killer, *is fiction, no comment is called for (other than to satisfy our scheme by remarking that the confrontation is conceivably between a man and some advancing orders of emptiness). The second story is a correspondance and may stand by itself.*

THE KILLER: *A Story*

"Now," he said to me, "do you think you're going to bear up under the discipline of parole?"

"Yessir," I said.

He had white hair even though he was not more than fifty-two. His face was red. He had blue eyes. He was red, white, and blue. It was a fact I noticed before. They had this coloring. Maybe that was why they identified with the nation.

"In effect you're swearing that you won't take a drink for eight months."

"I know, sir, but I haven't had a drink inside for four years." Which was a lie. Three times I had come in with my cellmate on part of a bottle. The first time I was sick. The second time we had a fight, a quiet fight which I lost. He banged my head on the floor. Without noise. The third time we had sex. Democratic sex. We did each other.

"You understand that parole is not freedom."

"Yessir."

They asked these questions. They always asked the same questions, and they always got the same answers. It had nothing to do with what you said. It had nothing to do with how you shaved or how you combed your hair because you combed your hair the way everybody else did, and the day you went up to Board you shaved twice. Maybe, it had to do with how many shaving cuts you had, but I didn't have any. I had taken care, wow. Suppose it had to do with the way you moved. If two of the three men on the parole board liked the way you moved, you were all right, provided they didn't like the way you moved too much. Sex. No matter who I'm with, man or woman, always get a feeling off them. At least I used to. I always could tell if they were moving inside or moving away, and I could tell if anything was going on inside. If we ever touched, I could tell better. Once I was in a streetcar and a girl sat down next to me. She was a full barrel. A very fat girl. Pretty face. I don't like fat. Very fat people have no quick. They can always stop. They can stop from doing a lot of things.

This girl and me had a future however. Her hip touched. I could feel what I did to her. From side of my leg, through my pants, and her dress, through some kind of corset, cheap plastic corset, something bad, through that, through her panties, right into her, some current went out of me, and I could feel it in her, opening up future. She didn't do a thing, didn't move. Fixed.

Well, five minutes, before I got off at my stop. In those minutes I was occupied by a project with that girl where we projected five years. I knew what I could do to her. I say without exaggeration I could take her weight down from one hundred eighty to one-eighteen in a year and it would have been a pleasure because all that fat was stored-up sugar she was saving. For somebody. She was stingy, congealed like lard, but I had the current to melt that. I knew it would not be hard to pick her up. If I did, the rest would happen. I would spend a year with her. It is difficult to pick up a fat girl, but I would have used shock treatment. For example, I would have coughed, and dropped an oyster on her skirt. I think it is revolting to do something like that, but it would have worked with this fat girl because disgust would have woke her up. That's the kind of dirt sex is, in the mind of somebody fat and soft and clammy. Sex to them is spit and mucus. It would have given me the opportunity to wipe it off. I could trust my fingers to give a touch of something. The point to the entire operation (people watching in the streetcar, me standing with my handkerchief, apologizing) would be that my fingers would be doing two things at once, proper and respectful in the part of my hand everybody else could see, flame through the handkerchief on her lap. I would have begun right there. For the least I would get her name. At the end of the five minutes I turned to take a look at her, and under that fat face, in the pretty face which could be very attractive, I could see there was a dumb look in her eyes that nothing was going to improve. That stopped me. Putting in a year on a girl like that would be bad unless she was all for me at the end. Stupidity is for nothing, not even itself. I detest stupidity in women—it sets me off. So I got off the car. Didn't even look at the girl. After she gets married to somebody fat and stupid like herself she will hate any man who looks like me because of that five minutes. Her plastic corset must have had a drug-store smell after I got off the trolley car. Think of plastic trying to smell.

I tell this as an example. On the outside it used to be that I never sat down next to anybody that I didn't feel them even when we didn't touch and two or three times a week, or even a day, I would be close to the possibilities of somebody like the fat girl. I know about certain things. I know with all policemen, detectives, correction officers, turn-keys, hacks, parole-board officials, that sex is the problem with them. Smartest cellmate I had said one time like a philosopher, "Why, man, a judge will forgive any crime he is incapable of committing himself." My friend put it right. Sex is a bitch. With police. They can't keep their hands off. They do, but then it builds tension. For some it's bad. They can get ready to kill. That's why you comb your hair. Why you must look neat. You have to be clean. Above sex. Then a cop can like you. They ask you those questions knowing how you will answer. Often they know you are lying. For example they know that you will take a drink in the next six months. What is important is not that you are lying, but the kind of lie they hear in your voice. Are you afraid of them? Are you afraid they will see down into your lying throat? Then you are okay. They will pass you. If you are afraid of them, you're a good risk. But if you think they are stupid, faintest trace of such a thought in yourself, it comes through. Always one of them will be sensitive to condescension. It gets them ready to kill. A policeman never forgives you when you get him ready to kill. Obviously he can't do it, especially in a room performing official duty with a stenographer at the side. But the adrenalin goes through him. It is bad to take a flush of adrenalin for nothing. All that murder and nowhere to go. For example when you're standing up talking to a parole board it's important the way you stand, how tight your pants are. Good to be slim, trim, shipshape, built the way I am, provided you are modest. Do not project your groin forward or your hips back. It is best if your pants are not tight-fit. Younger juvenile delinquents actually make this sort of mistake. It is not that they are crazy so much as egotistical. They think older men will like them so much they will give them parole in order to look them up. A mistake. Once read in the newspapers about a Russian soldier who picked up a German baby and said, "It's beautiful," but then he got angry because he remembered the baby's father had been shooting his children, so he killed the baby. That's a cop. If you strut, even in good taste and subtle, they will start to get a glow where it is verboten, and they will like you, they will get a little rosy until they sense it goes nowhere, and wow the sex turns. Gets ready to kill you. If cops have an adrenalin wash for their trouble, you are remembered badly. It is much better to be slim, trim, shipshape, and a little peaked-looking, so they can see you as a thrifty son, which is the way they must have seen me because they gave parole that day, and I was out of there in a week. Out of prison. Out of the can. I think I would have died another year. Liver sickness or go berserk.

Now you may ask can police be so dumb as to let me go on an armed-robbery sentence, six years unserved out of ten. Well, they saw me as thrifty. I was careful that day with voice and posture. But how can police be so stupid as to think in categories like thrifty? That's easy, I can answer. Police are pent up, they're apes, they're bulls. Bulls think in categories.

2

Well, I've been feeling small for four years now. Prison is a bitch for people like me. It cuts your—I don't want to use doubtful language. It's a habit you build up inside. Some do use language that way. Some lifers. Spades. People who don't give a damn. They're playing prison as if it is their life, the only one they are going to have. But I am conservative in temperament. I comb my hair every morning, I comb it the same way. Minor matter you may say, but it isn't for me. I like to comb my hair when I feel like it. Animal of the woods. I have the suspicion—some would call it superstition—that combing my hair can spoil some good ideas. I would never say this to a hack but why is it not possible that some ideas live in your hair, the way the hair curls. I have very wavy hair when it is left to itself. Whenever I get a haircut, I have the feeling I'm losing possibilities I never got around to taking care of. Put it this way: when I comb my hair, it changes my mood. So naturally I prefer to comb it when I want to. In prison forget that. Comb your hair the same time same way every day. Look the same. If you're smart, keep your mood the same way. No ups. Nor downs. Don't be friendly. Don't be sullen. Don't offer company. Don't keep too quiet. If you stay safe, in the middle, and are the same thing every day you get a good report. The reason I get parole first time out, six years off a ten-year sentence is that I was a model prisoner which means just this: you are the same thing every day. Authorities like you if you are dependable. Be almost boring. I think what it may be about is that any man in authority finds his sleep important to him. People in authority can't stand the night. If you wear a uniform and you go to bed to sleep and a certain prisoner never bothers your dreams, you'll say a good word for him when it comes time to making out reports.

Of course you are not popular. Necessarily. My bunky shakes my hand when I get this good news, but I can see he is not happy in every way. So I complain about details. I am not to possess liquor at home, nor am I to frequent any bar even once, even at Christmas. Moreover, I am not to eat in any restaurant which serves liquor.

"What if you don't drink? But just eat there?"

"I'm not to go into any premises having a liquor license."

"A restaurant that don't serve liquor is a tearoom or a hash house."

"Crazy," I say. I don't like such expressions, but this is perfect to express my sentiments.

"Well, good luck."

It is possible we are thinking of the same things, which is the three times he got a bottle into the cell and we drank it together. The first time sick, second time we had a fight, third time sex. I remember I almost yelled in pain when my rocks got off, because they wouldn't stop. I was afraid I'd hurt myself. It had been so long. It seemed each time I took liquor something started in me that was different from my normal personality. By normal I mean normal in prison, no more. You wouldn't want a personality like that on the outside any more than you would want to smell like a laundry bag. But so far as inside personality went, I couldn't take liquor and keep the same. So if I started drinking on the secret when outside, I was in trouble. Because my style of personality would try to go back to what it was before, and too many eyes would be on me. My parole officer, people in the neighborhood. The parole board was getting me a job. They just about picked out the room where you lived. They would hear about it even if I didn't get into a rumble when I was drunk. If I kept a bottle in my room, I would have to hide it good. The parole officer has been known to come around and pay a friendly visit which is to say a sneak visit. Who could enjoy the idea of him sniffing the air in my room to see was there liquor on the breeze? If they caught me drinking in the eight months, back I would be sent to here. A gamble, this parole. But I was glad to take it, I needed out. Very much. Because there was a monotony in me. It had been coming in day after day. I didn't have the feeling of a current in me any more, of anything going. I had the feeling if I sat down next to a girl like the fat girl now, and our legs touched, she would move away cause there was a blank in me which would pass into her. Something repulsive. There was something bad in me, something very dull. It wasn't in my body, it wasn't even in my mind, it was somewhere. I'm not religious, but it was somewhere. I mean I didn't know if I could keep control or not. Still, I couldn't have done it the other way. Eight more months. I might have flipped. Talking back to a hack, a fight. I'd have lost good time. There is only one nightmare in prison. It's that you don't get out, that you never get out because each time you come close the tension has built up in you so that you have to let it break out, and then your bad time is increased. So it's like being on the wrong escalator.

"Take it slow, take it easy," said my bunky. "Eight months goes by if you get yourself some sun."

"Yeah, I'm going to sleep in the sun," I said. "I'm going to drink it."

"Get a good burn your first day out, ha-ha. Burn the prison crap out of your pores."

Maybe the sun would burn the dullness away. That's what I was thinking.

MINISTERS OF TASTE: *A Story*

A very short story in the form of two real letters written by Norman Mailer to Robert B. Silvers, editor of The New York Review of Books, *with copies directed to the associate editors, publisher, and several interested observers.*

February 22, 1965

Dear Bob,

Your letter, January 26, invites me to an "essay" of eighteen hundred words on the new Hubert Humphrey. In the last year you have also asked me to review biographies of Johnson (Jack) and George Patton. Since it is not easy to think of three books which could attract me less, I expect I must make my position clear. Forgive me for digging in old ground.

A year and a half ago, you asked me to review *The Group*. Said you had offered the novel to seven people—all seven were afraid to review it. You appealed to my manhood, my fierce eschatological sword. St. Mary's wrath (according to you) was limned with brimfire. Would I do it, you begged, as a most special favor to you. Perhaps, you suggested, I was the only man in New York who had the guts to do it. A shrewd appeal. I did it. Two months later my book (*The Presidential Papers*) came out. You had given the copy to Midge Decter for review. Her submitted piece was, in your opinion—I quote your label—"overinflated." That is to say, it was favorable. Changes were requested. The reviewer refused to make them. The review was not printed. No review of *The Presidential Papers* appeared in *The New York Review of Books*. Only a parody. By a mystery guest. Now, we have my new book, *An American Dream*. I hear you have picked Philip Rahv to review it, Philip Rahv whose detestation of my work has been thundering these last two years into the gravy stains of every literary table on the Eastern Seaboard.

In the name therefore of the sweet gracious Jesus, why expect me to do eight words on your subject? To the contrary, experience now suspects

that a state of cordial relations with *The Review* is congruent to a lack
of cordial relations with *The Review*, and marks you, Bob, on this note:
negotiations with your Editorship are, by open measure, inching, tedious,
and impoverished as spit. But cheer up, dear Silvers. The letter is for
publication, and so should enliven the literary history of your unbloodied
rag.

Yours in trust,

Norman Mailer

cc: Barbara Epstein   Samuel N. Antupit
     Elizabeth Hardwick   George Plimpton
     Eve Auchincloss   Jason Epstein
     Alexandra T. Emmet   Midge Decter
     A. Whitney Ellsworth   Malcolm Muggeridge
     Terry Ehrich

April 4, 1965

Dear Bob,

I have decided to use again our particular method of correspondence by
copy. All reports say you enjoy it.

Now, your last letter informs me the *Review* has no intention of pub-
lishing my previous letter because you feel the disclosures are inappropri-
ate. That your methods (which inspired my letter) may not be any more
appropriate seems not to have entered your grasp of the issue.

In any case I want to make one more effort to change your decision.
The alternative is, after all, disagreeable. I will be forced to publish the
letter somewhere else: that small communication which in your pages
might leaven the *Review*'s worthy academic yeastings will, printed in
another place, take on a literary history larger than its merits. Further-
more, it will be out of our hands. We will both look like fools. That is

disagreeable, but I have habits for playing the fool; it will bother me less, it is expected of me. Whereas—it bruises sensibility to point this out— most Americans don't know old Bob Silvers, they don't know what a marvelous and complicated fellow he is. They won't know his private reputation among his devoted friends is rich and various. No, you will be inserted most unfairly into literary history as the editor who wouldn't print an entertaining letter about himself and so gave the letter twenty times its natural publicity. That would be awful. I fear you must now face the unendurable, and make up your mind. Print or do not print my letter. Still, be of good cheer. It is these difficult decisions which make field marshals or tycoons of us all, kid.

Your devoted friend,

Norman Mailer

cc: Barbara Epstein   Samuel N. Antupit
     Elizabeth Hardwick   George Plimpton
     Eve Auchincloss   Jason Epstein
     Alexandra T. Emmet   Midge Decter
     A. Whitney Ellsworth   Malcolm Muggeridge
     Terry Ehrich

ESPRIT DE SOMMELIER

Waiter!

Yessir!

Are you
   Diner's Club?

No sir,
   we are not
   Upper Mediocrity

Well fuck
     you

Thank you sir
we are quite aristocracy

Which
aristocracy?

Quiet aristocracy, sir,

Oh, well thank you.
Say did you know
that cops are like
ladies in a
    bad mood?

Ha, ha.
   that is funny, sir
   so, that is very
   funny. You must
   bitter please join
   our Quit Aristocracy
     credit club.

· Mon dieu, Feinspan,
   it's you.

Yessir, will presumption
   never cease?

Ian Fleming Revisited

I had a spider once
and fed it neon tubes
until its web did gleam
like Las Vegas in the dawn
Roulette I used to call her
and the spider
drinking dew from grapefruit rind
to oil the knees
would smile and say:
every Roulette has her croupier.

11 · OUR ARGUMENT ADVERTISED
ONCE MORE

*Soon we enter the fourth part. We will be back in the arena
again. The smell of the Twentieth Century—that hint of the
odor of burning blood just beyond the horizon—will come into the air
again. Perhaps it is provided in these excerpts about architecture (which
are taken from pieces in* Architectural Forum *and* The New York Times
Magazine), *for the Argument in Part Four seeks to hunt for the sign of
the plague in the diseases of form, and nowhere is this disease so prominent
as in the assault of modern architecture upon the horizon and the sky.*

ARCHITECTURAL EXCERPTS:

a) *A Piece for* The New York Times

In Lyndon Johnson's book, *My Hope for America,* the fifth chapter is
titled "Toward the Great Society." It contains this paragraph:

> . . . *fifty years from now, . . . there will be four hundred million
> Americans, four-fifths of them in urban areas. In the remainder of this
> century, . . . we will have to build homes, highways, and facilities equal to
> all those built since this country was first settled. In the next forty years we
> must rebuild the entire urban United States.*

It is a staggering sentence. The city we inhabit at this moment is
already close to a total reconstruction of the world our parents knew in
their childhood. If there is no nuclear war, if we shift from cold war to
some kind of peace, and there is a worldwide rise in the standard of
living, then indeed we will build a huge new country. It is possible
that not one in a thousand of the buildings put up by 1899 will still be
standing in the year 2000.

But what will America look like? How will its architecture appear? Will it be the architecture of a Great Society, or continue to be the architecture of an empty promiscuous panorama where no one can distinguish between hospitals and housing projects, factories and colleges, concert halls, civic centers, and airport terminals? The mind recoils from the thought of an America rebuilt completely in the shape of those blank skyscrapers forty stories high, their walls dead as an empty television screen, their form as interesting as a box of cleansing tissue propped on end. They are buildings which reveal nothing so much as the deterioration in real value of the dollar bill. They are denuded of ornament (which costs money) their windows are not subtly recessed into the wall but are laid flush with the surface like a patch of collodion on the skin, there is no instant where a roof with a tower, a gable, a spire, a mansard, a ridge or even a mooring mast for a dirigible intrudes itself into the sky, reminding us that every previous culture of man attempted to engage the heavens.

No, our modern buildings go flat, flat at the top, flat as eternal monotony, flat as the last penny in a dollar. There is so much corruption in the building codes, overinflation in the value of land, featherbedding built into union rules, so much graft, so much waste, so much public relations, and so much emptiness inflated upon so much emptiness that no one tries to do more with the roof than leave it flat.

As one travels through the arbitrary new neighborhoods of the present, those high squat dormitories which imprison the rich as well as the poor, one is not surprised that the violence is greater than it used to be in the old slum, up are the statistics for juvenile delinquency and for dope addiction. To live in the old slum jungle left many half crippled, and others part savage, but it was at least an environment which asked for wit. In the prison vistas of urban renewal, the violence travels from without to within, there is no wit—one travels down a long empty corridor to reach one's door, long as the corridors in the public schools, long as the corridors in the hospitals at the end of the road; the landscape of modern man takes on a sense of endless empty communications.

Sterile as an operating table is the future vista of suburban spread, invigorating as a whiff of deodorant is the sight of new office buildings. Small elation sits upon us as we contemplate the future, for the picturesque will be uprooted with the ugly, our populations will double, and in a city like New York, the brownstone will be replaced by a cube sixteen stories high with a huge park for parking cars and a little grass. The city will go up a little and it will go out, it will spread. We will live with glass walls in a cold climate. The entire world will come to look like

Queens Boulevard. We will have been uprooted so many times that future man will come to bear the same relation to the past that a hydroponic plant bears to soil.

Yet some part of us is aware that to uproot the past too completely is a danger without measure. It must at the least produce a profound psychic discomfort. For we do not know how much our perception of the present and our estimate of the future depend upon our sense of what has gone before. To return to an old neighborhood and discover it has disappeared is a minor woe for some; it is close to a psychological catastrophe for others, an amputation where the lost nerves still feel pain. This century must appear at times like a great beast which has lost its tail, but who could argue that the amputation was not self-inflicted?

There seems at loose an impulse to uproot every vestige of the past, an urge so powerful one wonders if it is not with purpose, if it is not in the nature of twentieth-century man to uproot himself not only from his past, but from his planet. Perhaps we live on the edge of a great divide in history and so are divided ourselves between the desire for a gracious, intimate, detailed and highly particular landscape and an urge less articulate to voyage out on explorations not yet made. Perhaps the blank faceless abstract quality of our modern architecture is a reflection of the anxiety we feel before the void, a kind of visual static which emanates from the psyche of us all, as if we do not know which way to go.

If we are to spare the countryside, if we are to protect the style of the small town and of the exclusive suburb, keep the organic center of the metropolis and the old neighborhoods, maintain those few remaining streets where the tradition of the nineteenth century and the muse of the eighteenth century still linger on the mood in the summer cool of an evening, if we are to avoid a megalopolis five hundred miles long, a city without shape or exit, a nightmare of ranch houses, highways, suburbs and industrial sludge, if we are to save the dramatic edge of a city— that precise moment when we leave the outskirts and race into the country, the open country—if we are to have a keen acute sense of concentration and a breath of release, then there is only one solution: the cities must climb, they must not spread, they must build up, not by increments, but by leaps, up and up, up to the heavens.

We must be able to live in houses one hundred stories high, two hundred stories high, far above the height of buildings as we know them now. New cities with great towers must rise in the plain, cities higher than mountains, cities with room for 400,000,000 to live, or that part of 400,-000,000 who wish to live high in a landscape of peaks and spires, cliffs and precipices. For the others, for those who wish to live on the ground and with the ground, there will then be new room to live—the traditional small town will be able to survive, as will the old neighborhoods in the cities. But first a way must be found to build upward, to triple and triple again the height of all buildings as we know them now.

Picture, if you please, an open space where twenty acrobats stand, each locking hands with two different partners. Conceive then of ten acrobats standing on the shoulders of these twenty, and five upon the ten acrobats, and three more in turn above them, then two, then one. We have a pyramid of figures: six thousand to eight thousand pounds is supported upon a base of twenty pairs of shoes.

It enables one to think of structures more complex, of pyramids of steel which rise to become towers. Imagine a tower half a mile high and stressed to bear a vast load. Think of six or eight such towers and of bridges built between them, even as huge vines tie the branches of one high tree to another; think of groups of apartments built above these bridges (like the shops on the Ponte Vecchio in Florence) and apartments suspended beneath each bridge, and smaller bridges running from one complex of apartments to another, and of apartments suspended from cables, apartments kept in harmonious stress to one another by cables between them.

One can now begin to conceive of a city, or a separate part of a city, which is as high as it is wide, a city which bends ever so subtly in a high wind with the most delicate flexing of its near-to-numberless parts even as the smallest strut in a great bridge reflects the passing of an automobile with some fine-tuned quiver. In the subtlety of its swayings the vertical city might seem to be ready to live itself. It might be agreeable to live there.

The real question, however, has not yet been posed. It is whether a large fraction of the population would find it reasonable to live one hundred or two hundred stories in the air. There is the dread of heights. Would that tiny pit of suicide, planted like the small seed of murder in civilized man, flower prematurely into breakdown, terror and dread? Would it demand too much of a tenant to stare down each morning on a flight of 2,000 feet? Or would it prove a deliverance for some? Would the juvenile delinquent festering in the violence of his monotonous corridors diminish in his desire for brutality if he lived high in the air and found the intensity of his inexpressible vision matched by the intensity of the space through a fall?

That question returns us to the perspective of twentieth-century man. Caught between our desire to cling to the earth and to explore the stars, it is not impossible that a new life lived half a mile in the air, with streets in the clouds and chasms beyond each railing could prove nonetheless more intimate and more personal to us than the present congestions of the housing-project city. For that future man would be returned some individuality from his habitation. His apartment in the sky would be not so very different in its internal details from the apartments of his neighbors, no more than one apartment is varied from another in Washington Square Village. But his situation would now be different from any other. His windows would look out on a view of massive constructions and airy bridges, of huge vaults and fine intricacies. The complexity of our culture could be captured again by the imagination of the architect: our buildings could begin to look a little less like armored tanks and more like clipper ships. Would we also then feel the dignity of sailors on a four-master at sea? Living so high, thrust into space, might we be returned to that mixture of awe and elation, of dignity and self-respect and a hint of dread, that sense of zest which a man must have known working his way out along a yardarm in a stiff breeze at sea? Would the fatal monotony of mass culture dissolve a hint before the quiet swaying of a great and vertical city?

b) A *Statement for* Architectural Forum

The essence of totalitarianism is that it beheads. It beheads individuality, variety, dissent, extreme possibility, romantic faith; it blinds vision, deadens instinct; it obliterates the past. It makes factories look like college campuses or mental hospitals, where once factories had the specific beauty of revealing their huge and sometimes brutal function. It makes the new buildings on college campuses look like factories. It depresses the average American with the unconscious recognition that he is installed in a gelatin of totalitarian environment which is bound to deaden his most individual efforts. This new architecture, this totalitarian architecture, destroys the past. There is no trace of the forms which lived in the centuries before us, none of their arrogance, their privilege, their aspiration, their canniness, their creations, their vulgarities. We are left with less and less sense of the lives of men and women who came before us. So we are less able to judge the psychotic values of the present: overkill, fallout shelters, and adjurations . . . to drink a glass of milk each day. . . .

People who admire the new architecture find it of value because it obliterates the past. They are sufficiently totalitarian to wish to avoid the consequences of the past. Which of course is not to say that they see themselves as totalitarian. The totalitarian passion is an unconscious one. Which liberal, fighting for bigger housing and additional cubic feet of air space in elementary schools, does not see himself as a benefactor? Can he comprehend that the somewhat clammy pleasure he obtains from looking at the completion of the new school—that architectural horror!—is a reflection of a buried and ugly pleasure, a totalitarian glee that the Gothic knots and Romanesque oppressions which entered his psyche through the schoolhouses of his youth have now been excised? But those architectural wounds, those forms from his childhood, not only shamed him and scored him, but marked upon him as well a wound from culture itself— its buried message of the cruelty and horror which were rooted in the majesties of the past. Now the flat surfaces, blank ornamentation, and pastel colors of the new schoolhouses will maroon his children in an endless hallway of the present. A school is an *arena* to a child. Let it look like what it should be, mysterious, even gladiatorial, rather than look like a reception center for war brides. The totalitarian impulse not only washes away distinctions but looks for a style in buildings, in clothing, and in the ornamentations of tools, appliances, and daily objects which will diminish one's sense of function and reduce one's sense of reality by reducing such emotions as awe, dread, beauty, pity, terror, calm, horror, and harmony. By dislocating us from the most powerful emotions of reality, totalitarianism leaves us further isolated in the empty landscapes of psychosis, precisely that inner landscape of void and dread which we flee by turning to totalitarian styles of life. The totalitarian liberal looks for new schools and more desks; the real liberal looks for more difficult books to force upon the curriculum. A good school can survive in a converted cow barn.

Yes, the people who admire the new architecture are looking to eject into their environment and landscape the same deadness and monotony life has put into them. A vast deadness and a huge monotony, a nausea without spasm, has been part of the profit of American life in the last fifteen years—we will pay in the next fifteen as this living death is disgorged into the buildings our totalitarian managers will manage to erect for us.

Our commodities are swollen in price by false, needless and useless labor. Modern architecture is the child of this fact. It works with a currency which (measured in terms of the skilled and/or useful labor going into a building) is worth half the real value of nineteenth-century money. The mechanical advances in construction hardly begin to make up for the wastes of advertising, public relations, building union covenants, city grafts, land costs, and the anemia of a dollar diminished by armaments and taxes. In this context the formulas of modern architecture have triumphed, and her bastards—those new office skyscrapers—proliferate everywhere: one suspects the best reason is that modern architecture offers a pretext to a large real-estate operator to stick up a skyscraper at a fraction of the money it should cost, so helps him to conceal the criminal fact that we are being given a stricken building, a denuded, aseptic, unfinished work, stripped of ornament, origins, prejudices, not even a peaked roof or spire to engage the heavens.

It is too cheap to separate Mafia architects with their Mussolini Modern (concrete dormitories on junior-college campuses) from serious modern architects. No, I think Le Corbusier and Wright and all the particular giants of the Bauhaus are the true villains; the Mafia architects are their proper sons; modern architecture at its best is even more anomalous than at its worst, for it tends to excite the Faustian and empty appetites of the architect's ego rather than reveal an artist's vision of our collective desire for shelter which is pleasurable, substantial, intricate, intimate, delicate, detailed, foibled, rich in gargoyle, guignol, false closet, secret stair, witch's hearth, attic, grandeur, kitsch, a world of buildings as diverse as the need within the eye. Beware: the ultimate promise of modern architecture is collective sightlessness for the species.

There's
something
infantile
about
a
square
sighed
the good
air
wearing
widow's
weeds

SEMINARS

A short hair is the chromosome of a short story
said the sadist, an assistant protestant professor
of creative composition. His words danced
like genes in the gism of a hate filled lair.

It was the air before his face
down from the burning glass
of his spectacle lens
to the razor of his mouth

Kill talent by teaching it procedure
said the sphincter of his nostril.
Doctor Category, said the hair
within his nose, you stifle me now

But I will grow in your grave
like ivy without a root
entwining myself in the orbital
locket of your skull

For I, royal hair of the rebellion
am the last of a lover's nerve
the poet lover who created you
old gray-haired sadistic dad
I am father of your categories
    on the short hair.

Said the assistant protestant professor:
kill me, artist, curl your hair
into the bone of my grave
but I love your work

Forgive my passion for category
I must believe that God is a tidy man
besides I will go before you
there are machines to replace me

Univac and One-Hole-Trac
They will bring death to your nerve
deeper than I ever dreamed.
Upon one another we fell sobbing

Like men before the bitch of ice
on came her machine. Yes, it said,
the short hair used to be the
chromosome of the short shory

Now it is the fiber in fiberglass.
I gave one cry back clear back
to Coleridge on his lonely alp
for the horror of the albatross
        was its malignant wings

Death we have betrayed your sting
and licked the long dry tongue of intellection
        much too long

We will die from anemia of the soul
in some plenitude of electronics
        and her suburb

PART FOUR: ARENA

12 · OUR ARGUMENT FULLY RESUMED

The art of the absurd was the postwar art which gave pleasure. And it gave great pleasure. Audiences had begun to laugh at a sequence of non sequiturs which seemed to speak as links of a new logic. At very least the interruptions, the style, the quality of these interruptions seemed to have more meaning than the matter they interrupted. Where an art work had been measured once by the skill and daring, or consummate grace, or extraordinary insight with which a theme was developed and made lucid, now its measure was in the taste and tone of its interruptions. Because one dealt with silences, and the death of little moods, and offered hints of silent machines of the night, so the art of the absurd was anonymous in part as silences are anonymous, and scenes characteristic of one play were often characteristic of another. The fragment which follows happens to have been written by the pencil here at your service, but in fact as a fragment, as a lantern slide of the method of the absurd, it could have been written by any of a dozen writers.

Curtain up. A bedroom in the dark. Twin beds. A body in each. One is awake. The other snores. Loudly. Insinuatingly. With fury. A most abrasive snoring.

MAN: *Penelope! Pssst. Penelope! Stop snoring!*

WOMAN: (Snores louder)

MAN: *Pssst!*

WOMAN: (Snores louder still)

MAN: *Penelope!*

WOMAN: (Continues snoring)

245

MAN: (Gives vent to a burst of snoring in imitation of her. It is even louder, even more abrasive.)

PENELOPE: (Stops snoring suddenly)

(Now the moon shines brighter in the room. It becomes more and more brilliant, until the man gets out of bed and tries to cover the window with his pillow. Goes back to his bed. Pillow falls off the window sill. The moon shines brighter still. Penelope starts to snore again. The man takes a glass of water on the night table and throws it to the floor.)

PENELOPE: *Why did you do that?*

MAN: *I couldn't sleep.*

PENELOPE: *You're crazy.*

MAN: *You're crazy too. You snore like you're crazy.*

PENELOPE: *I don't snore. Attractive women don't snore. Not unless they're pregnant.*

MAN: *They pee on toothpaste. They tinkle.*

PENELOPE: *Tell the moon to go away.*

MAN: *She's a princess, you ass.*

PENELOPE: *I love Filipinos with purple hair.*

If the playlet has been at all successful, it is annoying to stop. But nothing has been violated in the art of the absurd by breaking here. The absurd is an art which is built not only on interruptions but annoyance. It is built profoundly upon annoyance. It assumes that annoyance, not love or passion or dedication or climax or interest or mood or mind or even matter, but annoyance, is the foundation of modern existence, and the progressively most common condition for everyone alive is interruption and annoyance, interruption and annoyance. One plans one's life—there is war to interrupt it; one plans to visit Heaven—who is certain nuclear bombs will not dispose also of Heaven? One plans to eat—one has to wait for the food to unfreeze; one calls a friend on quick impulse—the line is busy; start to contemplate —the refrigerator will begin to speak; look to pour a friend a drink—the telephone will ring; begin to watch a show—a commercial comes in. Contemplate a city vista—an ugly building will smash the view; start to make love—stop and look for the diaphragm, or—did you take your pill? did you take your pill?

Never make a bet on the length of this list—it is as long as your ability to cite the details of the day. Is a man reading a newspaper—the story is broken by the turn to another page. Is there coffee for breakfast? No cream. The wife has forgotten again. Rush to catch the subway? Wait for the change teller. In a hurry to take the elevator? The doors won't close—they are automatic and their timing is not yours.

Sunday supplement, humor with eggs? in fact, we are talking of the modern man's ability to swallow nausea. From infancy, the very style of the synapses of his nervous system is built not only on the sensuousness of the breast but on the click of the electric light switch. Born in a sterile room, the new baby does not die of puerperal fever, nor does his mother. Rather at eighteen months, he shows his first sign of genius—he turns on the television set by himself. Soon his consciousness is formed on collisions and interruptions, trips on highways with billboards, radio blasts, construction blasts, car horns, brakes, a train goes by tying the nineteenth century to the twentieth. That nineteenth century raised babies on frustration. The art which came out of that late nineteenth century of iron frustration was the early-twentieth-century art of self-expression with Joyce and Picasso to lead the list. The children who came after the Second World War grew up however not on frustration but interruption—so the arts of the mid-century are the arts of the absurd and deal with categories and hierarchies of discontinuity and the style of their breaks. Art is here on earth to uplift us, to encourage the religious and the nonreligious to feel a heavenly glow—so declared the caretakers of art for two thousand years. But now art is a heart pill—nitroglycerine—it binds shattered nerves together by shattering them all over again with style, with wit, each explosion a guide to building a new nervous system. Animals subjected to constant interruption go mad, but not humans, not yet. Art, the mother of us all, goes out to hustle fifty themes in an hour—take any magazine, take my favorite, Playboy. *Stories by leading world writers, and Playgirls with rose and cinnamon tits, marshmallow-ass, butter-ass,* Playboy *and the Pill, Pop art to help you digest those billboards on the highway and the tons of cartons of soup cans which stood like chasms overhead in infancy in supermarkets, comic strips, whap, whap, first art of the interruption, Tracy's face on a painting 6 feet high, high as he looks in the mind of a child—nose near the comic strip.*

What does each interruption signify, but shock, shock to expectancy, shock to nerve, shock to rhythm; at last—apathy. Then there is need for stimulus, a shock which stimulates rather than stops. Physiology now runs on two systems—the old one, sympathetic and parasympathetic, act and rest; now, with it, an electric overlay of a new system: depressant and stimulant, apathy and shock, depression and mania, flipped-out, back-on.

There is a piece coming next called: The First Day's Interview, which at-

tempts by way of a leisurely dialogue to discuss the nature of mood. We live, remember, in a time which interrupts the mood of everything alive, DDT in the trees, artificial arrival for the bull's sperm—mood is being squashed, sliced, smashed, exploded, wrenched, torn (untimely from his mother's womb the murderer Macbeth) and yet if it is mood—whatever mood may be—which suffers the impact of the shock of interruption, if something mysterious as mood is made flat or is deadened by the break in any deepening of concentration, if it is mood which bears the shock, so, too, is it broken mood which stirs a new wave. The oldest metaphor of mood is the sea, for the ocean collects all, it collects everything, and with each shock of its action upon the shore a new wave comes to carry away the interruption of the last. It is the gravitational field of the moon, we are told, which makes the waves, that same moon which calls to the insanity of all of us when she is full, for the moon is the mother of pain and loss (so says science—it is certified—it is certified metaphor) and when the wastes have been too great, and the shocks have deadened what was best, then the moon stirs waves of madness. And waves pass through the deadened and raise them, even as corks rise on the wave, and the wild riders of the wave accelerate, the motorcycles ride in the night. A people deadened by interruption go mad. The moon helps.

THE FIRST DAY'S INTERVIEW

INTERVIEWER

Will this work be called *The Psychology of the Orgy?*

MAILER

Perhaps.

INTERVIEWER

The orgy. That calls to mind some of your declarations about the orgasm.

MAILER

I dislike that word.

INTERVIEWER

You virtually made it a parlor game to talk about it.

MAILER

If I did, I'm sorry.

INTERVIEWER

You must have known what you were doing.

MAILER

That's why I'm sorry. I did it to attract attention to myself. Now I pay the price.

INTERVIEWER

You seem to think you can get away with anything if you tell the truth about yourself. The fact of the matter is that I for one would like to like you. I like your work. (*Pause*) As a matter of fact I have to admit I like it more today than I did when it came out.

MAILER

Yes.

INTERVIEWER

But I don't like your aggressiveness. Why can't you let the work speak for itself? Why all these . . .

MAILER

Stunts?

INTERVIEWER

Precisely. Why must you attract attention to yourself?

MAILER

I'm weary of that now.

INTERVIEWER

I should think so. The rules for literary conduct are the effective essence, after all, of the experience of a good many writers in the past. You break too many rules. I know that people critical of your ideas often advance the argument that you have insufficient respect for the culture of the past.

MAILER

I have to agree.

INTERVIEWER

All right. I must say you are very modest today. You asked me here as a literary referee to help you keep close to your subject. Whatever that will turn out to be! You said you wished to have an interview because it is easier than an essay.

MAILER

It is. You see, my mind wanders. It dissipates. I have no patience left for quiet exposition. In an essay you must obey formal concerns which I have not the enthusiasm to obey any longer. So I decide to say my piece in a minor form.

INTERVIEWER

Call you to order. You are hurting morale. Please say something agreeable about the form of the interview.

MAILER

It is natural for our time. We will talk about the kind of things one should discuss on television. We will be superficial but quick. We will not slip into the gulf of unreadable prose. We will be interesting.

INTERVIEWER

Mann once said, "Only the exhaustive is truly interesting."

MAILER

He was right. But one needs huge loins to be not merely exhaustive but artful as well. I can hope at best to do no more than pass lightly over treacherous philosophical ground. We will discuss in one or another of a hundred contexts the meanings of such resistant words as "dialectical" and "existential." As an immediate illustration of the method, I believe I'll point out that an interview is dialectical. Any dialogue between two people is a natural dialectic. Each creates the response of the other. So it is possible that the experience of acquainting oneself with my grab bag of ideas, notions, arguments, examples, and *lapses* (as they are illumined and dissipated by your responses) will provide the reader with a sense of the dialectic that will be better than any exposition of the word by me.

INTERVIEWER

What about existentialism? Is the form of the interview also suited for that?

MAILER

Do you have a comfortable idea of what the word means?

INTERVIEWER

I've read a smattering of Sartre. I have a dim familiarity with the work of Jaspers and Heidegger.

MAILER

And know a little more about Kierkegaard, Nietzsche and Dostoevski?

INTERVIEWER

Et cetera, et cetera. I admit it. I don't have a comfortable sense of the word. It makes me uneasy. I use it all the time myself. Sometimes with authority. I'll say, "Oh, yes, Mailer's trying to become a Marxian existentialist"—mind you, I don't really talk about you that much—and I get a laugh, I must say. You know I've noticed that one need only put large words together with authority in the voice and people will laugh. Let an actress playing a grande dame exclaim on a stage, "Oh yes, what fearful decoration. *Puerile Baroque*," and everyone will roar.

MAILER

Most large words remind people of feces.

INTERVIEWER

Why do you say that?

MAILER

I don't know. It seems right. I feel the truth of the thing first, and discover the explanations later.

INTERVIEWER

Very existential.

MAILER

All interviews are existential so far as they are not edited, and are descriptive of the mood of the conversation. Which is another argument for trying to express one's ideas in this form. It gives the reader a sense of the present. That's the first notion to grasp about existential philosophy. The underlying assumption is that nothing in one's metaphysical scheme is as important as one's sense of the present. The truth is found first in the Gestalt. Not in the abstractions of logic.

INTERVIEWER

I think I have a firm grasp of "Gestalt" as a word, but it would be helpful to those who read this interview.

MAILER

You define it.

INTERVIEWER

Well, Gestalt is context. It's *swarm*, if you know what I mean. It's the mood, the totality of an experience.

MAILER

Too vague.

INTERVIEWER

Napoleon lost the battle of Waterloo because he couldn't sit on his horse. The Gestalt would add that he had a venereal disease which made his saddle an instrument of torture.

MAILER

Well, I don't know. It's still too logical. Gestalt is as bad a word as existential. Let us say that as we're talking an insect crosses my field of vision. A brown worm the size of a maggot. I reach forward and crush it. Nausea turns a small spasm in my throat, but I go on talking. Can what I say be possibly the same as it would have been without the insect? No, is my answer. Given the severest discipline of mind, my words may be the same, my thought may not waver from its intention, but my voice will alter just perceptibly and as it does, my argument will affect your unconscious more or less agreeably, since the unconscious, unlike the mind, listens not to words, but to the voice.

INTERVIEWER

I'm going to be literal. Why will your voice change?

MAILER

Because I've just killed something, I have altered the Gestalt of the room, shifted the rhythms of life which are present. Gestalt, as I use it, is the harmony or discord of the life present in the context, which in this case is you, me, the furniture, the room and the insect.

INTERVIEWER

Why include the insect? Men are men and insects are insects.

MAILER

But men and insects are not separate if each can give emotion to the other. This, you see, would be one of the implicit logics in existentialism. Existence precedes essence. Emotion determines causality. For instance, I know nothing about Heidegger, but I get the impression from Barrett's book, *Irrational Man,* that Heidegger might argue mood has precedence over matter. I know I would argue that.

INTERVIEWER

Why?

MAILER

Too difficult to talk about yet.

INTERVIEWER

Let me be the judge.

MAILER

Mood is a harmony. The harmony of a Gestalt. The harmony of the life in the room, or the harmony one senses in a landscape. And harmony permits one to relax. As one relaxes, so new perception comes from the conduits of the unconscious, and one has added one's contribution to the mood, which is now subtly different but is still alive in the growing *tissue* of previous sensation, precisely that tissue which was the mood of the previous moment. When a mood is shattered, the life in the room contracts, and a new mood, discontinuous to the last, begins its existence.

INTERVIEWER

Most sensuous.

MAILER

Now I contract with annoyance. In a second or a minute, depending on your sensitivity, you will sense my annoyance and react in turn. A new mood will begin. It will be perhaps less interesting than the last.

INTERVIEWER

You are annoyed. Why did my expression "most sensuous" irritate you?

MAILER

Because it was obvious. And I was chasing a thought which was just at the end of my limited reach. One does not trap a butterfly by clapping one's hands.

INTERVIEWER

You are too delicate to live.

MAILER

I may be too delicate to think. (*Lights a cigarette*) All right. Since you bring me to a full stop, I may as well make a confession. My character is such that I must confess a small viciousness in order to prime a new thought. So I will admit I was irritated when you said, "Most sensuous," because quite contrary to breaking my mood, you accelerated it, which is another matter entirely. A sexual example came to mind immediately and it was a good one. It would have made my remarks about mood less tenuous.

INTERVIEWER

Then why didn't you give it instead of abusing me?

MAILER

My ambition interfered.

INTERVIEWER

Your ambition? Your mind is most elliptic.

MAILER

My ambition at the moment is to seduce all those readers who detest what they think are my ideas. They are the readers I wish to keep.

INTERVIEWER

I wonder why.

MAILER

Because obviously it is more exciting to capture a hostile reader than tickle a friendly one. And these hostile readers have a preconceived notion of my character which makes it most difficult to talk to them. They see me as oppressive, clumsy, brutal, and mired in the lowest expositions of sex. So my plan was to march lightly for the first few days and reconnoiter no sexual thicket.

INTERVIEWER

Charming. You'll never get power if you give away your maps before you've begun to move.

MAILER

I don't know if I want power any more. I think I would rather be clear in my mind. The compromises one has to make in acquiring power dull the brain irreparably.

INTERVIEWER

Since you are now too pure for power, would you then betray your ambition and give your sexual example.

MAILER

I think I've lost the mood.

INTERVIEWER

Ugh.

MAILER

You disapprove?

INTERVIEWER

The mark of a serious man is that he is capable of restoring his mood.

MAILER

I'm no longer as young as I want to be. An abrupt restoration of mood is as punishing to the body as starting an automobile in high gear. It's the sort of thing that brings on a cold.

INTERVIEWER

Do complaints also prime new thought?

MAILER

They enable me to recover old thoughts. I was speaking of mood as a harmony. You invoked the qualities of the sensuous. So I thought of sex. Of a particular kind of sex. Sensuous sex. The sex of . . . I do not like to use the word "mature." The sex, let us say, of those who have been with sex for more than a little time. They are not young. They do not have that mixture of lust and private fantasy which makes for onanistic heat, for dirty heat, the sex let us say of two adolescents who burst on one another with the excitement of smashing a taboo. No, there is that other sex which comes to people when they are older, a sex of mood. Each one feels the mood of the other, each moves more delicately, aware now that one is no longer altogether attractive, and so one is vastly more attentive to the small offerings and polite withdrawals of the gift.

INTERVIEWER

I don't want to interrupt.

MAILER

I'm glad you did. The description embarrasses me. It is too chaste. But the alternative is to speak prematurely of the parts of the body, the odors of the act. Let us put it this way. Sex-as-mood is a conversation with respect for nuance. Does one raise one's voice to make a point?—one may soften the next remark. Does one wait too long?—the whip of wit must intervene. The dialogue of such sex is tender, it is respectful—it respects the slow conversion of character into mood, it seeks for an artful loss of each separate identity in order to find and give life to the mood which passes from body to body.

INTERVIEWER

This is the only way sex-as-mood can exist?

MAILER

No. It is only one way. When I spoke of mood as a harmony of everything which lives in the Gestalt, I should have explained that not .all harmonies are peaceful. There are moods of apprehension, of unrest, excitement, of dread, horror, fear, pending cruelty, whatever one cares to name.

INTERVIEWER

What separates a mood of horror from a mood which is suddenly shattered and so creates horror?

MAILER

You are close to the difficulty. I don't know if one can explain it. But it may be worth the attempt. Conceive of a landscape which is mysterious. Let me be banal—a landscape which is suggestive of doom. A landscape fit for a nightmare, a dark field across which one must walk. The shadows of the moon are cruel. Now across the field a laugh is suddenly heard, a merry laugh. Does it break the mood?

INTERVIEWER

I should think so.

MAILER

Not necessarily. The laughter can give new intensity to the mood, offer ironic substance to its shape.

INTERVIEWER

You speak as if the mood is alive.

MAILER

In a sense mood may be alive.

INTERVIEWER

Like an organism?

MAILER

You anticipate me. I was about to say that a mood is a psychic organism. Like all living things it reacts to each new breath of the environment. It can grow, be wounded, weakened, changed, colored, fortified, it can adapt itself to many a change or shift in its circumstances. It can also be killed. As a psychic organism, it is obviously more delicate than any other kind of organism, and so it takes very little to kill a mood. But like any other organism, a mood is mysterious, and the most exceptional intrusions can give it life. In my conventional landscape of horror, it may take precisely the sound of a merry laugh to give individuality to the horror. The laughter may sustain the mood just as it was ready to languish, or equally, the laughter may wither the mood by revealing it to itself as absurd. As is true of all organisms, the possibilities are sometimes limitless.

INTERVIEWER

But what is the ground? What is the field, or the seat of the mood? To be literal, where is it located?

MAILER

We must avoid science fiction. If I start to speak of the air, or of psychic waves, or psychic fields of energy, we will both be lost in a terminology for which we have no aptitude and no qualifications. We are literary men, more or less. Let us keep the subject evocative. It may be possible that literature has more to offer on the nature of the universe than the cyclotron.

INTERVIEWER

The alternative is to leave the reader altogether confused. You cannot talk of psychic organisms without trying to describe some of their properties. Otherwise the suspicion arises that you invoke nothing more serious with your talk of psychic organisms than our old friend the poltergeist.

MAILER

(*Sighs*) The subject is ineffable. If I try to describe it, I will kill it. There are those who will know what I am talking about and those who won't. I can only hint at the possibility of a new direction or two, for those who know already what I am talking about.

INTERVIEWER

I thought you wanted to reach the readers who were hostile to you.

MAILER

The irony is that most of the people who are hostile to my work are precisely those people who have the deepest sense of what I am writing about.

INTERVIEWER

I think you must do better than this.

MAILER

Can we avoid that total worry of where a mood exists? Whether it exists in the separate bodies of the people and objects who make up the mood, or whether it races through the air between them, or envelops all in a cloud, or is all of these things at once. It is enough to say: it exists because I feel it. What it looks like I do not know, but how it feels I am not likely to forget.

INTERVIEWER

Is that really satisfactory as an explanation?

MAILER

Do you use the word "relationship" in your speech?

INTERVIEWER

Often. It is a modern word.

MAILER

Do we have a relationship?

INTERVIEWER

Of sorts.

MAILER

Can you think of a definite relationship you have with someone?

INTERVIEWER

My wife.

MAILER

What does it look like?

INTERVIEWER

What does it look like?

MAILER

The relationship.

INTERVIEWER

. . .

MAILER

Scored a point.

INTERVIEWER

Do you feel like quitting for the day?

MAILER

I've never had the sense to quit when I'm ahead.

INTERVIEWER

Nonetheless, one of my functions is to serve as an aerial editor who cuts so to speak on the fly. And I think we've done enough. What I ask for tomorrow is a presentation which will be a degree more formal.

MAILER

I promise nothing.

13 · A NOTE OF APOLOGY TO THE FIRST DAY'S INTERVIEW AS A WAY OF PREPARATION FOR WHAT FOLLOWS

The interview you just finished was an experiment. Written as a play to be read in private rather than seen by an audience, a play with two characters, an interviewer and myself, I know of nothing very much like it except perhaps for Gide's Corydon, *and the differences are obvious. In fact, this specific interview, written in 1960 and printed about a year later in* Paris Review, *was not only an experiment but is now an abridgment. I cut some of the early pages where the manner is directly cloying. Even so, the piece bears on the discussion and serves as a curtain-raiser to two vastly more ambitious dialogues called in the order of their appearance,* The Metaphysics of the Belly *and* The Political Economy of Time. (*These both appear further on in this book, the first following immediately.*) *Begun two years after* The First Day's Interview *was written, and done consecutively as two chapters of a projected book on Picasso, these later dialogues were kept in rough manuscript until* The Metaphysics of the Belly *was gotten ready for* The Presidential Papers. *I take the unusual step of reprinting it here because it is indispensable to understanding* The Political Economy of Time, *and it seemed an imposition on those readers who were most interested to send them away from this book into the pages of another book which might not be convenient to purchase or even be found in a store. On the other hand, desirous of giving value to every purchaser, the author has rewritten* The Political Economy of Time *most specially for this book. Such particulars uncovered, I would ask the reader to note how the interviewer and his subject get down to talking about the topics in* Cannibals and Christians *and—I whisper it—*An American Dream. *What job opportunities this will provide for the critics in fifty years. So we may hope, yes, reader? And as you read, note how you come closer to the mystery of what precisely is at the heart of this Argument, for at best we explore up a river no airplane may glimpse, nor even, for certain, the sun.*

THE METAPHYSICS OF THE BELLY

INTERVIEWER

I feel anxious today. I can't seem to get serious. A year ago we had an interview. "The First Day's Interview," you called it. You said at the time it was the beginning of a book. You were going to call it *The Psychology of the Orgy*. Then I don't hear from you again. Months go by. All these months. The piece gets printed. I become a bit of a figure. Suddenly you call me up. Let's go on with the interview, you say. I arrive tape recorder in hand. Now you say you want to do a book on Picasso. I'm confused. I don't know anything about Picasso.

MAILER

That's one reason you were chosen.

INTERVIEWER

I feel like the old lady in *Death in the Afternoon*. Tell me, what happened to *The Psychology of the Orgy*? That pricks the ears much more than Picasso. *Psychology of the Orgy*—it's not like you to throw away a good title.

MAILER

What I have to say about Picasso may not be so dull.

INTERVIEWER

I think he'll be the pretext for you to express yourself on a thousand subjects. I wonder if you have any real personal attachment to Picasso's work?

MAILER

Picasso is good for my eyesight.

INTERVIEWER

Look, I have a confession to make. Our last interview was a vast success in certain limited circles. Marvelous, people kept saying to me, the way you weren't afraid to talk back to Mailer. Oh, he's not so hard to talk to, I would tell them, he's really rather reasonable.

MAILER

So you have a vested interest in continuing to talk back to me.

INTERVIEWER

Let's say I was innocent in the first interview, and didn't realize I was being that effective. Now I look at you professionally. I can't afford to have you drop my standards by making facetious remarks that Picasso is good for your eyesight.

MAILER

I was telling the simple truth. My eyes have been bad lately. I read a book for an hour and suffer eyestrain the rest of the day. Eye specialists have done their best. So have all sorts of eyeglasses. Even Mr. Huxley was no use. I tried the exercises in *The Art of Seeing*. They only strained my eyes somewhat further. But looking at Picassos does not tire them. In fact I've started work for the day with severe eyestrain, having awakened from a sleep which has been more or less satisfactory for every part of my body but my eyes, and after a morning of studying twenty, fifty, or a hundred reproductions of Picassos, my eyes have felt a bit relaxed for the first time in months.

INTERVIEWER

Do you have any idea why this is so?

MAILER

The idea is too complex to be introduced so quickly. I would be obliged to compress it, and so seem facetious all over again.

INTERVIEWER

Give me a hint.

MAILER

We see with the mind as well as the eye. Since the eye leads through the retina back to the mind, we can say that we see objects with two halves of the mind, with a physiological apparatus, and with a part of the psyche. If these two halves of the mind are critically different, one is seeing in two ways at once. Strain develops.

INTERVIEWER

Sounds like schizophrenia.

MAILER

Nothing so royal. Look. If I read a line of prose, its immediate meaning is clear to my physical vision, to that part of my mind which is literal and therefore moves quickly. "Now is the time for all good men to come to the aid of the party" I read. "Perfectly clear" says the muscle of my eye, and moves on to the next sentence. But my conceptual faculty holds onto the sentence. It makes associations with the words. "Now" signifies the present, which is an enormous word to me. I write often of the enormous present, of psychopathy, of how mass man has no sense of past or future, just Now. So that word halts me conceptually. I cannot afford to ignore the way it is used in a sentence. And then there's "time," which is the most remarkable and mysterious of words. It's even more mysterious than "God." We can have an idea of God, most of us do sooner or later, but who has any concept of what time might be? And the construction "Now is the time," which makes a subject and noun of "Now," is particularly interesting if one believes, as I sometimes do, that the secrets of existence, or some of them anyway, are to be found in the constructions of language which have come down to us. "Now is the time" is an odd way of putting things, as if "Now" is palpable and "time" is some sort of appurtenance which is attached to one place or to another, to Before, or to Now. I won't go into discussing "good men" or "party" but they are obviously capable of stirring a number of unconscious thoughts and dim associations which must be ignored if I'm to keep on reading at a reasonable rate. The result is that one part of my mind works against the other. My eyes begin to feel like an automobile driven by a man who has one foot on the accelerator, and the other on the brake.

INTERVIEWER

Shouldn't this be true for all of us?

MAILER

No. Most people keep concepts firmly in category. "Now" is the flat quiet moment of the present, "time" is a few simple numbers one reads from a watch.

INTERVIEWER

But not in their unconscious, I presume.

MAILER

Their unconscious doesn't erupt into the conscious routine acts of their daily life, as does mine. They save all larger thoughts for sleep, which is the tidy way to do it.

INTERVIEWER

Whereas your ambition drove your unconscious out of the water, so so speak, and into the light.

MAILER

So to speak.

INTERVIEWER

One of the ground rules is not to mock each other's metaphors.

MAILER

Certain artists, those who see associations and connections everywhere, tend to live in a psychic medium which is heavier, more dense, than the average man's. It is harder for them to move because there is more conscious mind for them to move. Joyce is the first example. And he went blind. Which does no harm to my thesis. If the mind reacts too powerfully to the stimuli before it, then the eye must see less in order to keep one's inner pressure at a bearable level. One goes blind not from seeing too little but from the overladen possibilities of seeing too much.

INTERVIEWER

Almost as if there's a biological law.

MAILER

But I'm sure there is. Beauty, as the Greeks kept nagging, was harmony. Well, it has other qualities as well I hope, danger, ecstasy, promise, the transcendence of terror—all the emotions which give life to us in the West—but harmony, I fear, is what beauty is first. It means that separate parts function in a lively set of rhythms with one another. No organ is too fast or too slow vis-à-vis another organ. The pleasant relation inspires proportions in the outer forms which are healthy, harmonious, and beautiful.

INTERVIEWER

This is not insignificant, you know.

MAILER

I know.

INTERVIEWER

You're taking an important stand here.

MAILER

May it be the first of many.

INTERVIEWER

Hold on. You're saying that aesthetics is not abstract, that our concepts of beauty are not arbitrary but a function of nature.

MAILER

It's obviously more complicated than that. Upon occasion we can see beauty in disease, or beauty in the sinister, beauty even in the ugly. But that is because we have traveled a private road whose events have reinforced a few of our faculties. Compassion, for example, illumines the ugly, makes it beautiful. As we look upon an ugly face—provided it is *our* kind of ugly face—we see how it could have been beautiful, we see the loss implicit in it, we feel tender toward the disproportionate or even anomalous development of features in it. Their inversion of beauty stimulates some inner sense in us of a beauty which failed to be, at least until that moment when we conceived that this ugly sight could have been beautiful. So at that instant, looking at a plain face we can feel intimations of beauty. Beauty—so runs this argument— has its root in any being which is harmonious, imaginative, adaptable, brave, artful, daring, good for life, good for the continuation of life.

INTERVIEWER

Fantastic!

MAILER

Why?

INTERVIEWER

Do you realize the enormity of what you're saying? It turns a good many ideas on their head.

MAILER

That is the function of fashion: to turn modest ideas on their head.

INTERVIEWER

How about art for art's sake?

MAILER

Art for art's sake. My notion reinvigorates that notion, doesn't it?

INTERVIEWER

Yes, because aesthetes are not going into an ivory tower any longer, not by your logic. If they devote themselves to a search for beauty, they are engaged in a most valuable act—at least, according to you—to discover those secrets of life which give life.

MAILER

Well, I don't know. Only noble artists discover noble secrets and manage to give them back as art. Most of the artists who believe in art for art's sake are overelegant greedy sorts. The debate still continues, you see. One can argue which kind of life is harmonious and what is not. The leaves and vines Aubrey Beardsley adored so completely grew only in a hothouse, a conservatory, or a tropical garden. There was no toughness in such beauty.

INTERVIEWER

But if a great artist believed in art for art's sake . . .

MAILER

He would be closer to life, I think, than a great politician who believed in politics for politics' sake.

INTERVIEWER

I understand what you're saying about beauty, and I don't even know that I disagree with it, I mean I can see its relation to your sexual theories.

MAILER

Please don't anticipate the argument.

INTERVIEWER

But in any case I don't see how you can apply your yardstick to the present. Look at the particular aesthetic experiences which give beauty to people today. In music, John Cage's *One Minute and Thirty-Six Seconds of Silence* or whatever the title is; on the stage, *The Connection*, or Albee's work, or Tennessee Williams and his deep mahogany scatology; the novel, well leave it with William Burroughs whom you admire and his violent jangled shattering sense of obscenity; and then the Abstract Expressionists and their messes—talk of scatology. I still don't understand *their* painting —and the Surrealists, full of abortions, Picasso and his mistresses whom he chooses to make look like monstrosities. Well, I could fulminate, I could say, "Call me Square and give me Velasquez," but to tell the truth I do get a sense of beauty from all these artists, or at least a sense of very private excitement like meeting a woman at a dinner party and knowing you were meant to go off with each other if you each had enough courage. . . . Whereas Greek sculpture, natural function, that leaves me gasping up the Muse on a dead dead beach.

MAILER

It bores me as well. But it was the beginning of beauty. It stated the basic condition. Perhaps Greek sculpture is no longer so beautiful to us because it lacks the sense of danger with which we live.

INTERVIEWER

Modern art has that sense of danger?

MAILER

It has a sense of doom.

INTERVIEWER

Doom of what?

MAILER

The species. Take the artists you mentioned. Suppose the condition of our existence is now so plague-ridden that we have sunk beneath the level of scatology.

INTERVIEWER

I don't follow. You mean we've sunk so low that scatological thoughts give life?

MAILER

For a good many people they do.

INTERVIEWER

Life may not be so bad as that.

MAILER

There are horrors beneath the surface, cannibals in all of us, mad animals. And for a reason. It's as if we're stifling, as if the air we breathe is no longer air but some inert gas. (*Holds up a hand*) Look, I've gotten into serious matters much too soon. I think a discussion of beauty is premature, I think it would need all of this book to explain anything at all. Let me say just that the modern condition may be psychically so bleak, so overextended, so artificial, so plastic—plastic like styrene—that studies of loneliness, silence, corruption, scatology, abortion, monstrosity, decadence, orgy, and death can give life, can give a sentiment of beauty.

INTERVIEWER

You cannot desert the argument until you give some indication of how this is possible.

MAILER

May I use the word soul instead of psyche?

INTERVIEWER

If it encourages the expression of ideas, yes.

MAILER

Postulate a modern soul marooned in constipation, emptiness, boredom and a flat dull terror of death. A soul which takes antibiotics when ill, smokes filter cigarettes, drinks proteins, minerals, and vitamins in a liquid diet, takes seconal to go to sleep, benzedrine to awake, and tranquilizers for poise. It is a deadened existence, afraid precisely of violence, cannibalism, loneliness, insanity, libidinousness, hell, perversion, and mess, because these are the states which must in some way be passed through, digested, transcended, if one is to make one's way back to life.

INTERVIEWER

Why must they be passed through, transcended?

MAILER

Because the scatology is within and not without. The urge to eat another does not exist in some cannibal we watch in the jungle, but in the hinge of our own jaws. The love of death is not a mass phenomenon; it exists for each of us alone, our own private love of death. Just as our fear of death is also ours all alone. These states, these morbid states, as the old-fashioned psychologists used to say, can obtain relief only by coming to life in the psyche. But they can come to life only if they are ignited by an experience outside themselves. If I am secretly in love with death and terrified of it, then the effort to restrain and domesticate these emotions and impulses (which are no less than the cross-impulses of suicidal bravery and shame-ridden cowardice) exhaust so much of my will that my existence turns bleak. A dramatic encounter with death, an automobile accident from which I escape, a violent fight I win or lose decently, these all call forth my crossed impulses which love death and fear it. They give air to it. So these internal and deadly emotions are given life. In some cases, satisfied by the experience, they will subside a bit, give room to easier and more sensuous desires.

INTERVIEWER

Not always?

MAILER

Not always. Hemingway, it seems, was never able to tame his dirty ape.

INTERVIEWER

Dirty ape?

MAILER

It's a better word than id or antisocial impulse.

INTERVIEWER

I think it is.

MAILER

Once we may have had a fine clean brave upstanding ape inside ourselves. It's just gotten dirty over the years.

INTERVIEWER

Why couldn't Hemingway tame his ape?

MAILER

Because he may have had too wild a one inside him. The grandeur of one's work is a measure of how outrageous is the ape. People were always criticizing Hemingway for being self-destructive, obsessed with death, immersed too deeply in a cult of violence, perpetually trying his manhood, and so forth. Well, as I'll try to argue a little later, the first art work in an artist is the shaping of his own personality. An artist is usually such an incredible balance of opposites and incompatibles that the wonder is he can even remain alive. Hemingway was on the one hand a man of magnificent senses. There was a quick lithe animal in him. He was also shackled to a stunted ape, a cripple, a particularly wild dirty little dwarf within himself who wanted only to kill Hemingway. Life as a compromise was impossible. So long as Hemingway did not test himself, push himself beyond his own dares, flirt with, engage, and finally embrace death, in other words so long as he did not propitiate the dwarf, give the dwarf its chance to live and feel emotion, an emotion which could come to life only when one was close to death, Hemingway and the dwarf were doomed to dull and deaden one another in the dungeons of the psyche. Everyday life in such circumstances is a plague. The proper comment on Hemingway's style of life may be not that he dared death too much, but too little, that brave as he was, he was not brave enough, and the dwarf finally won. One does not judge Hemingway, but one can say that the sickness in him was not his love of violence but his inability to live as close to it as he had to. His proportions were tragic, he was all but doomed, it is possible he would have had to have been the bravest man who ever lived in order to propitiate his particular dwarf.

INTERVIEWER

But at any rate, if I follow you, encounters with danger were not self-destructive but healthy for Hemingway.

MAILER

He could feel good next day. His psyche was out of the dungeon. He could work. His insides were not tense and empty.

INTERVIEWER

Because—I'm trying to think in your way now—the death within him had met a death without, and so a temporary peace was found?

MAILER

Let's say he was going out to shoot a lion and felt marvelous. Well, there is a kind of mind which would say, "He's self-destructive. He feels good because he's going to kill himself." What I'm trying to argue is that he felt good because encountering death would give him more chance to live. From a very early age he must have felt his ordinary death within him (his routine sickbed death that is) as a kind of slow oncoming plague of washed-out memories and burned-up talents. So he was brave enough, as not many of us are, to go looking for death (since if he survived, his life would be better) but he was finally not brave enough to triumph at this kind of life. It was a desperate imbalance. What made him great as a writer was that he could ride it so long.

INTERVIEWER

Talk of death always makes me contemplate loneliness. You've stimulated me. I think I could guess now what you might say about John Cage and his silent musical compositions.

MAILER

What would I say?

INTERVIEWER

Well, roughly, that there is a frightening detachment in each of us, an inner silence, neither divine nor doomed, just lost in endless orbit. Nothing seems able to reach it. It is as if our souls are stricken. An arbitrary period of silence in a concert hall might encounter that anguish. There, could you have said it better?

MAILER

I would have tried to find one turn of wit.

INTERVIEWER

Well, I'm new at this.

MAILER

You're doing all right.

INTERVIEWER

I must say your ideas are not unathletic. I feel more or less vigorous now.

MAILER

Still, you were leading up to a point. And you seem to have lost it.

INTERVIEWER

Oh! Wait! What was I talking about?

MAILER

Many things. Were you leading up to the mess?

INTERVIEWER

Scatology. Of course. Death may be noble, and loneliness also, but how does a scatological art work raise the reader or the audience to catharsis? Why is such an aesthetic experience good for life?

MAILER

I don't want to discuss scatology now. It's too complex. It may be more complex than death. So I'm going to stay away from this now. I prefer to steal back to it from time to time.

INTERVIEWER

You have to give a hint, however.

MAILER

Why must I?

INTERVIEWER

I hoped I could avoid having to say this, but your name does not inspire the sort of confidence which keeps people waiting. You are not Lord Russell after all, or Wittgenstein, or Heidegger, or Sartre.

MAILER

Not yet.

INTERVIEWER

Perhaps not ever.

MAILER

No doubt never.

INTERVIEWER

A hint.

MAILER

Feces are seen as the most distasteful and despised condition of being. They are precisely that part of the alimentation in the universe which we have rejected, and, mind you, rejected not morally, not emotionally, not passionately—

INTERVIEWER

In the sense that vomit is passionate?

MAILER

In the sense that vomit is passionate. No, feces have been rejected viscerally. It is our being, our organism, which rejects them. They are a total statement of our nature. This cannot be used, says our nature, this is not to be absorbed but to be cast away, this is to be: not chosen. From deep within ourselves, our cells have chosen what can be used and what can not. Nothing is more despised than what we have chosen not to want.

INTERVIEWER

I've heard the Arabs feel so strongly about this that they institutionalize their hands. With their right hand they eat and wash their faces. With their left hand they wipe themselves. The left hand is never allowed to touch food.

MAILER

Yes.

INTERVIEWER

One hand for life, the other for death.

MAILER

You set up your opposites much too neatly. An attractive opposite, tersely worded, can bury more thought than it uncovers. One hand for life, the other for death.

INTERVIEWER

What does that bury?

MAILER

Why, it buries one's understanding that feces are not equivalent to death, and that all of us have a very bad conscience about shit, which is exactly why it is so obsessive to us.

INTERVIEWER

Would a healthy man have a bad conscience?

MAILER

No. But few of us qualify for the word. Our characters are usually not as rich as the food we eat.

INTERVIEWER

So we excrete not only what we despise but what is too good for us as well?

MAILER

Or too special. The act of elimination is excruciating to some part of the psyche. I expect it is the part which governs the digestive processes of the body. Because we eat, I imagine, not what our cells need, so much as what our habits demand.

INTERVIEWER

Suddenly, you're too abstract for me.

MAILER

I'm saying that a cell is like a little animal. It knows exactly what it wants to eat, what is good for it. But a cell is not a psychic structure. It may be a part of the machine which makes up a habit, it may work for a habit, but it has no powers of command. It cannot choose what it wants, it can only receive it.

INTERVIEWER

Please carry this further.

MAILER

A habit is a psychic structure. What it's composed of literally need not concern us, but since it is a construction of mind which sits in authority upon the body, we can think of it as a law which is intangible but more or less absolute in its effect upon citizens.

INTERVIEWER

Make this concrete. You're still too metaphorical.

MAILER

A man goes into a store to choose some food. His cells, a good many of them, let us say, need calves' liver that evening, but his habit is to please his dinner guests and liver seems insufficiently festive, so frogs' legs are ordered. Later that night, the cells make do with frogs' legs, but liver was their need.

INTERVIEWER

You're speaking of a decision; of a choice, not a habit.

MAILER

The habit is at several removes from the cells. The habit is to please one's guests. If liver is out of fashion, it will not please the guests. The habit which dominates the cells is that they must conform to fashion. What is significant here is that the part in a civilized man which makes the decision to choose his food has little to do with his need.

INTERVIEWER

You would argue that he can't feel his need as clearly as a savage would.

MAILER

Of course not. Habits usually are anti-sensuous structures. They are built up and they are maintained precisely by insulating our senses from most stimuli.

INTERVIEWER

I don't see how you have anchored this thesis. Your man wanted liver, he got frogs' legs, but what's there to keep him from making the best of it, from extracting the good juices out of the meat in old Froggie's thigh, and getting rid of the gristle? Where does bad conscience come in?

MAILER

You have the instinctive vice of American thought.

INTERVIEWER

You're just annoyed because I blew a hole in your thesis.

MAILER

But you didn't. You took my example, assumed it was all of the reality, and proceeded to draw a moral to your own satisfaction. But I gave you just a few of the facts, not all of them. Reality is always more complex than the example. That's why I hate to get into explanation too soon.

INTERVIEWER

Defend your thesis.

MAILER

My man ordered frogs' legs. But the urgency of his cells, their cry for liver, registered as a dull lust in his mind. So as he stared about the gourmet shop, he bought a little tin of foie gras.

INTERVIEWER

You didn't mention this before.

MAILER

An example is not a logical universe. I can do with an example whatever I wish, because its purpose is to explain, not to prove.

INTERVIEWER

I concede, but I still think it's unfair.

MAILER

He eats the foie gras with his drinks, eats it with relish. Ceremoniously it enters his stomach, which receives it in the way a High Church serves a rich wedding. But there is so little foie gras! And he cannot gorge. He must serve his guests first. Which involves other habits. Habit-life precedes cell-life in civilized man. Just a little foie gras and his cells need a lot of liver. Upon this cruel disproportion follows another—the frogs' legs. The part of the psyche which oversees digestion, let us call it The Eater, has to make a new decision, because its powers of digestion cannot do an equally good job on liver and frogs' legs both.

INTERVIEWER

Why not?

MAILER

Because the chemicals necessary for each would adulterate one another.

INTERVIEWER

Is there scientific proof of this?

MAILER

I'm sure there's not. I invoke a simpler principle. One can't do two good and difficult things at once and do them both very well. I can't write a book with my right hand and paint a picture with my left. At the same instant, I can't make love and sing high opera. Nor can I digest foie gras and frogs' legs equally well. One or the other must suffer.

INTERVIEWER

Your stomach may not work the way you do.

MAILER

It's bound to. There would be very few problems in life if our organs could perform two or more complex highly differentiated functions equally well at once.

INTERVIEWER

For the sake of the argument I concede again. I want to know where you're heading. I think I see it.

MAILER

If you do, take over yourself.

INTERVIEWER

Go one more step.

MAILER

The Eater chooses the frogs' legs. Reluctantly. He would prefer the foie gras, but there is simply not enough and the intestines would have too much work evacuating half-digested frog flesh—I exaggerate the imperfection of the process, of course. Therefore, the arts of digestion are applied to the frogs' legs. The best sweets in the foie gras, digested as formal second choice, are lost. The inner savory of their wealth is not reached.

INTERVIEWER

Why not?

MAILER

Because life in its need to protect itself tends to make what is best in itself most inaccessible.

INTERVIEWER

Whereas civilization tries to make the best in itself most available.

MAILER

Well, it would claim to.

INTERVIEWER

I think that's the first ideal of democracy. To make the best most available. What a logical impasse! In your terms democracy is then opposed to life.

MAILER

It endangers life in the name of a noble ideal.

INTERVIEWER

We'll never get to Picasso, thank God.

MAILER

We're getting there. Once we look at the pictures I won't want to stop in order to discuss these matters. But now I must ask you: I know where we are, but where *were* we?

INTERVIEWER

Yes. I know. The foie gras. The best of it was lost. The richest parts.

MAILER

The Eater took a middle course. What was useless, despicable, or un-interesting in the frogs' legs and in the foie gras was eliminated. But what was superior in the foie gras was also lost.

INTERVIEWER

So in despising his waste, the man is partially dishonest.

MAILER

Since his cells cannot inform him of the small tragedy they underwent last night, he has only an imperfect sense that there was something wrong with the foie gras. "It disagrees with me," he says, "I won't order it any more." Three days later he buys three cans, gorges on it at lunch, and then upbraids himself for lacking discipline and eating the things which are bad for him. Except for this sense of guilt at his poor character, it would have been a marvelous lunch.

INTERVIEWER

You're saying that civilization hurts the inner communication of mind to body and body to mind.

MAILER

Go further. Say the obsession of many of us for scatology is attached to the disrupted communication within us, within our bodies.

INTERVIEWER

I had the impression for just an instant that there's a theory of disease possible in this somewhere.

MAILER

There is the possibility of illness every time opposites do not meet or meet poorly, just as there is the air to gain life every time opposites meet each other nicely.

INTERVIEWER

Dilate a bit on this.

MAILER

They can be opposites within us—the part of my eye which sees physi-ologically as opposed to that part which views conceptually. But one can speak of opposites between man and nature, or man and man: the water I drink, the block of marble worked by the sculptor, the audience and the play, a mood and its occasion, the good rider and his good horse, the blocking back and the linebacker, the skier on the snow, the style of sex, a sail into the wind. I become conventionally rhapsodic; the point is that life seems to come out of the meeting of opposites. Communication is a poor word, because life does not come from communication but from meetings and confrontations, from opposites coming together.

INTERVIEWER

Communications has a technological connotation to me.

MAILER

It involves machines and electronic apparatus and services of distribution. It invariably implies the injection of information into a passive being. But one can use it in speaking of the body, one can say that a particular part of the body communicates poorly with another part because we are by now not only biological but mechanical. There are habits in all of us which function with the precision of a machine. And when certain functions in our body are unable to meet other functions at the necessary instant, one can speak of a failure of communication. One may even well suspect that the basis of chronic disease and the excessive virulence of much infectious disease, particularly the viruses, comes precisely from an inner field of communications which is poorly designed or badly abused. The message which did not get from Ghent to Aix is the metaphor for a drama which goes on constantly within us. My man who wanted liver and got frogs' legs would, if his stomach had been able to speak to him with the clear simple chords of an animal's belly, have escaped bad conscience and a touch of indigestion.

INTERVIEWER

But if bad communication is virtually the sole basis of disease—a fascinating concept, by the way—why do you equate it to scatology or at least make the connection there?

MAILER

Because feces are the material evidence of the processes of communication within us. Life comes from the meeting of opposites. Conceive of man as a tube, mouth at one end, anus at the other. In that sense man is like a worm, a pipe, a tunnel, a drill which bores through a bed of nutrition, disgorging it behind. We cannot see the air we exhale, not normally, not unless we have tobacco smoke with which to shape it, but we can study our urine and feces. In one way or another, most of us do. They are the expression of what we have done well and what we have done badly to that medium of food through which we passed. When we have communicated nicely within ourselves, the stool reflects a simple reasonable operation (cowflop is, for example, modest in its odor) but where we have failed, as with the foie gras, the odors and shapes are tortured, corrupt, rich, fascinating (that is attractive and repulsive at the same time) theatrical, even tragic. There are odors not alien to beauty in the dung. The sense of life they give has tragic beauty which tells us something rare and very good for us has been lost again, something fine is just beginning to rot. The history of the life we never see within us, its triumphs, tragedies, states of calm and states of inanition are returned to us in the color, the shape, the odor and the movement of our stool. For those qualities are the curious stricken record of our near past. We despise what we had once and now can possess no longer, especially if we fear having used it badly. Yet we cannot forsake it altogether. Obsessively we return to the study because hope for how to turn our life into more life is contained in that history.

INTERVIEWER

Eloquent. I must observe that it is rash for you to be too eloquent on this subject.

MAILER

I wished to avoid it earlier.

INTERVIEWER

True enough. But since we now find ourselves here, let me say I still don't understand, not really, the intense virulence of people's reactions to scatology.

MAILER

Perhaps the prophetic aspects create the rage.

INTERVIEWER

I don't follow you.

MAILER

The food you ate yesterday was too rich for you, says the odor in the water closet. Eat as improperly today and you will be ill. But this is much too simple. Say rather that the senses bring deep messages to the unconscious, quick deep messages. And they are measured carefully by the scale of past experience. A carpenter makes a hundred measurements a day. If you ask him to mark off five inches without a tape, he is bound to be able to do it within an eighth of an inch. So it is with our stool. Our senses know what it says to us. But so often the messages are intolerable. You are sickening slowly, remarks the wad, your life as you lead it now is hopeless. You must engage death, perversion, promiscuity, and the fear of hell before you will be better. Your health is to eat the body of your mate, your secret desire is to be trampled in an orgy. This is what the oracle of the unconscious may divine from the feces. No wonder shit is despised. Its message is too terrible.

INTERVIEWER

Isn't this a little too much to discover from the inner history of a meal?

MAILER

Food possesses character. We consume character when we eat.

INTERVIEWER

I'm not so certain. Food may be no more than food. How do we know is isn't?

MAILER

I don't. I guess. It seems more reasonable to me that food possess character than that it doesn't. One man leads a sedentary life, and another works hard, wouldn't the bicep of one be different in character from the other? Why, if we were to eat both biceps—

INTERVIEWER

You take the plunge into cannibalism?

MAILER

Only for the sake of the argument that one bicep would communicate qualities of strength, fortitude, and discipline, whereas the other would tend to make one lazy, slack, and unregenerate.

INTERVIEWER

But which is which?

MAILER

I assume the worker's bicep communicates fortitude and power.

INTERVIEWER

It might be just the reverse. The worker's arm might be disgusted, used
up. All that's left in his cells which can feed you is the desire to be lazy.
Whereas the lazy arm is bursting with unused energy.

MAILER

Three cheers for overtaking me. But will you now agree that food may
possess character?

INTERVIEWER

We don't know what character it possesses.

MAILER

I suspect our unconscious does.

INTERVIEWER

How convenient is this unconscious.

MAILER

The hand is plucked instinctively from the flame before the mind
realizes the finger is in the fire. Let's save time. Of course the unconscious
is close to the senses, it is the animal part of oneself. And it studies what
it eats, it knows the inner life of the body's organs, it hears what
has happened to the food, what qualities it possessed, what reactions
it aroused. Take steak, assume it provides strength for the muscles. Or
if not steak there must be obviously one or another particular food to
provide such strength. Whatever the food may be which offers strength,
we can be sure it is good for a man doing heavy work, and that it is
probably poor for a lady whose strength may depend upon the excellent
demands of her weakness. For an intellectual beginning a program of
conditioning exercises, steak may be just a little too full of strength, it may
fire his muscles into doing too much too soon. So The Eater might decide
to digest the steak cursorily, might decide to pass by the molecules con-
taining the kernel of the strength. The stool, bursting next day with the
most vital elements of the steak, might give back in its form and odor the
dispiriting news that The Eater in the intellectual had indeed decided he
was not yet strong enough for steak.

INTERVIEWER

But if The Eater knows this already and so makes a decision to eschew
the qualities of finest strength in the steak, why does the unconscious have

to discover it in the stool? I thought The Eater was part of the unconscious.

MAILER

Not all parts of the unconscious communicate perfectly well with one another. That is part of the theory of disease we postulated. There are ways for the unconscious to speak from one part of itself to another, but we are not always able to use them.

INTERVIEWER

Being receptive to the message of the bowels is one way?

MAILER

Children are always asking you to look at their stool, and are disappointed when we say, "That's nice, dear," and turn away.

INTERVIEWER

You're saying that our prevailing social habit is to lay a foundation in the child for a future failure of communication?

MAILER

In certain people this particular tension is sufficient to find not only the sight but the subject of feces quite sickening. It is for example particularly abhorrent to the English. Their intellectual categories offer no course in the archaeology of the Self. The French on the other hand know that *merde* has a purchase on fortune.

INTERVIEWER

I don't want to be grisly, but if old scata has so much to do with fortune and telling the future, why aren't there cults? Why isn't divination from the stool some small but worthy competitor to the horoscope or numerology?

MAILER

People who go to hear their fortune are not existentialists, but essentialists. Full of self-pity, they wish to believe that their fortune is already written, and to their advantage of course. They do not want to discover that they are still responsible for what they do with themselves. So what kind of interest could they have in any testament of the bowels which might speak of the history within themselves? Such study reveals character—informs them of their moral fortune.

INTERVIEWER

What is moral fortune? I never heard that expression before.

MAILER

If there is Heaven and if Hell exists, one's moral fortune indicates where one is likely to go. I suppose it is not unlikely that a man bound for Hell could sniff out the fact this was his destination. Such a man might detest all thought of shit.

INTERVIEWER

Herr Doktor, you've been talking about the bowels much too long, and it's getting on my nerves.

MAILER

The trouble is that I have to present one more large annoying idea before we can go on.

INTERVIEWER

Certain large ideas can be expressed briefly.

MAILER

You'll agree that a society is best judged by the way it treats the citizens, the slaves, the subjects, the masses who compose it.

INTERVIEWER

What do you want to say?

MAILER

That food be considered capable of possessing a soul.

INTERVIEWER

You mean that as we eat we are like a society acting upon its citizens, that food clanks from its cradle to the tomb as through us it moves, that noble souls in the food are not sufficiently appreciated by us and so die tragically, just as societies sometimes lose the gifts of some of their best men? Presenting this enormous metaphor merely to say that food has a soul! Why should it, why indeed should food have a soul?

MAILER

Because it is a being.

INTERVIEWER

A being. It's a good existential word, I know, but you've got to do something for it. What is a being? Please don't tell me a being is something which is alive.

MAILER

I won't. Especially since certain organisms which are alive cannot be called beings.

INTERVIEWER

Then a being is not all of life?

MAILER

A being is anything which lives and still has the potentiality to change, to change physically and to change morally. A person who has lost all capacity for fundamental change is no longer a being.

INTERVIEWER

Being is used then as synonymous to soul?

MAILER

Soul is eternal. At least that is the general agreement on its meaning. Soul is what continues to live after we are dead. It is possible, I should think, that if the soul does exist, that if there is such an entity, that if there is indeed a part of us which is eternal, or which can under certain conditions remain eternal, that the soul could well have the property of being able to migrate from body to body, from existence to existence, sometimes rising, sometimes falling, sometimes getting lost forever.

INTERVIEWER

Whereas being is corporeal, is there before the eyes?

MAILER

I think so. I would assume that when the soul enters a particular tangible existence, it weds itself to that existence. So long as the soul is part of a creature it is not free of it, not free to leave when it chooses, not unless sudden death is chosen. So long as the soul resides in a body or is trapped in a body or at war in a body or indeed even enamored of the body in which it finds itself, the soul must exist in a relation with that body which is not unlike marriage. The soul affects the body, the body is able to affect the soul, they grow together or apart, they are good for one another or they may be bad, they can be tragic for one another or merely cool and efficient, tolerating one another because they would be savage and wasteful if apart. A panoply of possibilities exists in every being, because a being is a creature which lives in the world, which has shape, color, form, which has life and a soul within it, a soul which will be changed by its existence in the world. Or at least that is how I would postulate a being.

INTERVIEWER

Being is the existence of soul in the world?

MAILER

Being is first the body we see before us. That body we see before us is that moment of the present for a soul, a soul which must inevitably be altered for better, for worse, or for better and worse by its presence in a body.

INTERVIEWER

And individual cells have souls, individual souls?

MAILER

I think they do. I think everything which lives had a soul at its birth, or it could not otherwise have been born.

INTERVIEWER

Fresh food has a soul?

MAILER

Yes, usually.

INTERVIEWER

But canned food. What about that?

MAILER

Less soul.

INTERVIEWER

It's dead.

MAILER

Not altogether. Let's say for the present it's in a kind of limbo. What characterizes food, I would speculate, is that the soul tries to cling to it as long as it can. A tin of sardines is still a being of sorts, a being of a lesser category. It may not be alive as an organism, but its flesh retains life, the cells have not rotted, the protein molecules are intact, if you will, and the oils and the carbohydrates still retain in their structure the character of the sardine.

INTERVIEWER

Let me recapitulate. Character in this case is the still-standing structure of the carbon molecule given the cells by the previous history within one little sardine of its soul at war with and/or loving its body?

MAILER

Let's say the soul left a taste. Some sardines taste better than others.

INTERVIEWER

It's one thing to have a taste. It's another to have a soul.

MAILER

Why does one sardine taste better than another?

INTERVIEWER

Because its meat is better.

MAILER

What does that mean?

INTERVIEWER

The meat is healthier, that's all.

MAILER

And health? What is that?

INTERVIEWER

A harmonious condition of body.

MAILER

How does that come about?

INTERVIEWER

In the case of the sardine?

MAILER

Yes.

INTERVIEWER

From being a better swimmer than the average sardine. Naturally good constitution inherited from its mother.

MAILER

Who was also a superior swimmer?

INTERVIEWER

Yes.

MAILER

Why was she so good?

INTERVIEWER

You're tireless.

MAILER

Humorless.

INTERVIEWER

You're going to insist the mother's soul was superior to the soul of other sardines and so left a superior taste?

MAILER

I think I will.

INTERVIEWER

Why this passion to put the soul into the sardine?

MAILER

Because the act of eating is always a small execution.

INTERVIEWER

And you find it less hideous if a soul is released, as a cell is devoured?

MAILER

If I believed a calf had one single chance to live, no more, I could not in good conscience eat it. I might eat it anyway but logic would say I should be a vegetarian.

INTERVIEWER

Whereas now, the soul of the calf passes into you, becomes a part of your being.

MAILER

Yes.

INTERVIEWER

I see now why Mexicans eat bull's balls.

MAILER

A delicacy.

INTERVIEWER

Why don't all men eat bull's balls? Why aren't they worth twice their weight in platinum?

MAILER

Because very few people are ready to receive them.

INTERVIEWER

You mean your soul has to be the equal of the souls you ingest?

MAILER

There has to be a meeting of opposites.

INTERVIEWER

A feminine man would enjoy bull's balls?

MAILER

Or a masculine man. You mustn't puzzle too hard at these celestial mechanics.

INTERVIEWER

Oh, I think they're first-rate, I just don't navigate among them too well as yet.

MAILER

Allow me then to signify the bull's balls as equal to virility. For the sake of my demonstration let it be that whoever eats them gains virility. The meeting of opposites takes place therefore between a male principle, the bull's balls, and something female in the soul of the man who eats.

INTERVIEWER

Or the woman.

MAILER

Or the woman. It doesn't matter, you see, whether you have a masculine man, a feminine man, a masculine woman, or a feminine woman. What characterizes all of them is that in partaking of the bull's balls each of them wishes to gain virility.

INTERVIEWER

To simplify it, let's speak just of men. Why, in the first place, wouldn't all men wish to gain virility?

MAILER

Virility implies more than the stamina of a stud. It offers power, strength, the ability to command, the desire to alter life. So its consequences in life are often to increase responsibility or danger. A virile man can be afraid of more virility. If he's driving his car too fast already, he may look for cream of chicken or malted milk. So with the feminine man. He may not want more virility because he has no habits for it. What's the use of commanding women he could not command before, if he does not know how to fight off other men, and is not ready to learn. What freezes the homosexual in his homosexuality is not fear of women so much as fear of the masculine world with which he must war if he wishes to keep the woman.

INTERVIEWER

What you're saying then might be put this way: in choosing bull's balls, the man whether strong or weak must be ready to offer up something feminine in himself. So as to leave himself less feminine afterward?

MAILER

Perfect.

INTERVIEWER

Which is to say that we cannot select effectively unless the action we choose exists in a real and close correspondence to the new proportions our soul desires for itself.

MAILER

Yes.

INTERVIEWER

If we wish to be more masculine we must first satisfy something feminine in ourselves.

MAILER

The reverse is also true. If we eat a bland food, a food we can dominate completely, that is to say a food whose character, whose—permit me—whose echo of the soul, is compliant, tender, passive to our seizure of it, we satisfy something masculine in ourselves. A man with ulcers is burning with the masculine need to dominate details in his life he simply cannot dominate. So in drinking milk, a bland food, a food more feminine than himself, he can discharge this backed-up masculinity. But of course he uses up masculinity in eating bland food, he alters his proportions.

INTERVIEWER

You imply he has no choice?

MAILER

Not if he's sick with an ulcer. Bull's balls and tequila would have him run amok or fall into a hospital bed.

INTERVIEWER

Since the proportion of masculinity and femininity in oneself would tend I think to remain more or less stable, what it comes down to is that people choose bull's balls only when they want to change.

MAILER

Yes. Only a few people want bull's balls at any one time. The existential gamble is too fine, it leads to greater seriousness, greater commitment in one's life, or to greater danger. One might think one wanted such change, but at the moment of digesting it, at the moment of choosing to open those reservoirs of enzymes, those ductless glands which are able to reach the finest molecules, The Eater might to his surprise feel panic, might be too cowardly to take on the consequences implicit in the essence of true bull's balls. So an imperfect cowardly digestion would take place. And its odor, the odor of fear, would be revealed next day in the stool, revealed to that part of the unconscious we may just as well begin to call The Critic. The Critic having a fine edge for form would also detect that the shape of the stool was slack.

INTERVIEWER

If The Eater accepted the challenge, the stool would be different?

MAILER

The smell of a decent death would be present, the soul in the balls of the bull would have entered the body of the man who ate it. That particular soul would have risen to a higher existence. So the stool would have an aroma of content. As indeed it often does. What is so particularly hideous in a really bad smell is that one breathes the odor of a partial death, a soul has been torn on a rack. Part of it was seized by The Eater, part was refused, and so is dying in the stool.

INTERVIEWER

Is it the fault of The Eater? What if the food is bad?

MAILER

Then the choice is more complex, as for fact it always is in life. For no food is altogether perfect, and if it is almost perfect, it is still bound to have a most particular character which may not correspond too closely to the specific need of The Eater. Sometimes good food cannot be digested well because the requirements of The Eater were too narrow. So the partial death of the food might smell bitter, it would know the bitterness of being rejected by a larger being which was too stingy. Or conversely it might be digested too greedily, too avariciously, by The Eater, and so suggest it was bruised. Such a death might smell of wine. The corruption of The Eater would be present within it.

INTERVIEWER

And bad food. What of bad food?

MAILER

Its death would almost always be partial I should think, and it would be drowned in bile, the body of The Eater would express his contempt at how bad the life had been, at how little the death had to offer. But if the best were extracted from the bad food, its odor might also prove decent or half decent. It might have died well.

INTERVIEWER

How could that be?

MAILER

Something good in the bad food might have taken a brave leap and met The Eater. So there might be some trace of dignity in the death of those souls. They might be complete, not partial. There might be the decent smell of a hay field. Grass and weeds are mediocre after all, but their death is complete when they're reaped, and if the weather is good they die well. There are arts to digesting bad food. The poor know them better than the rich. Most of the people on earth would get indigestion from good food.

INTERVIEWER

What about the man with ulcers?

MAILER

The greater part of milk becomes urine and urine is another discussion.

INTERVIEWER

No soul in it?

MAILER

Just spirit.

INTERVIEWER

To think I asked a simple question about a man with an ulcer who takes a glass of milk.

MAILER

I wish you hadn't.

INTERVIEWER

Do you feel ready to discuss the meaning of urine and its link to the Spirit?

MAILER

I don't. I fear I don't. It is a day's journey.

INTERVIEWER

Later perhaps.

MAILER

Later. We must discuss it later.

INTERVIEWER

Let's go back to where we were.

MAILER

(*Gloomily*) I distrust all talk of Soul and Spirit. I dislike styles which use such words.

INTERVIEWER

I want to know what happens with food which is the reverse of bull's balls, with food which is weaker than The Eater, calming, sedative, gentle, feminine, creamed chicken and so on.

MAILER

A brave man who wishes to become less brave is eating it?

INTERVIEWER

If you wish.

MAILER

At the critical moment, at the meeting of the opposites, he might give up his courage with grace, he might absorb the gentler qualities his being requested for that meal with good spirit and deep relaxation. His stool would have a happy smell. A gentle soul would have been received completely. But if, at the critical moment, The Eater rebelled, was horrified at the amount of manliness which must be devoted to the chicken, if The Eater felt shame at deserting danger and looking for calm, then indeed the chicken would be poorly used, the death of its souls would be most incomplete, and the odor would be sour. Gentleness refused turns sour. It curdles.

INTERVIEWER

You're saying that the secret emotions of one's being, the basic emotions, courage and cowardice, betray their presence in the odor.

MAILER

And greed as well, or cupidity, ambition, compassion, love, trust, tenderness, savagery. The way in which we take souls from the food is the mirror of the dirty ape inside. If most of us abhor shit, it is because most of us are a little hideous inside.

INTERVIEWER

Tyrants to the weak?

MAILER

Tyrants to the souls in the food who at that moment are more helpless than ourselves. Beyond a doubt.

INTERVIEWER

Of course there's always ptomaine.

MAILER

(*Ignoring this*) Ambitious people pass bad shit. Because they use people around them. They certainly use people who are under them. I once met a very wealthy man whose mistress could talk about nothing but food. She was obsessed with what everyone around her had had to eat that day. It's taken me until now to realize that she saw herself as food for the tycoon, his family, and friends. Everyone at her dinner table was a potential cannibal to her person. So she had to know what you ate the night before because that to her was a clue which showed whether you had designs on her precise flesh.

INTERVIEWER

You mean she saw herself as a certain kind of food?

MAILER

Rock hen, no doubt.

INTERVIEWER

You're beginning to enjoy yourself too much. I think it's time we closed for the day.

MAILER

What a long day.

INTERVIEWER

Would you round off our inquiry with a remark?

MAILER

A commercial remark?

INTERVIEWER

Let us say a capsule.

MAILER

Ambitious societies loathe scatalogical themes and are obsessed with them.

INTERVIEWER

Disappointing.

MAILER

Not at all. One could study the past with such a thesis as the tool. If indications in Mayan culture show much scatology, one can assume that civilization died from an excess of ambition which throttled the Being of too many.

INTERVIEWER

And if there is no trace of scatology?

MAILER

If by the internal logic of the findings, the art, the fecal or non-fecal forms of the pottery, the wall painting, the architecture, there seems little scatology, one may assume there was not enough ambition, that the culture was calm, well-regulated, and was probably destroyed by a catastrophe which left it too passive to find the power to rise again.

INTERVIEWER

You're enjoying yourself much too much. Tomorrow you must speak more of form.

MAILER

I will not enjoy myself much tomorrow.

INTERVIEWER

You know you never came back to Picasso and why he is good for your eyes.

MAILER

Now I fear we will never get back.

INTERVIEWER

Of course we will. Why not?

MAILER

Beyond form is soul, spirit, madness, eternity, and the void.

INTERVIEWER

I will try to sleep on that.

BREADLINES: *Poems and Short Hairs*

PHOSPHORESCENCE AND NOURRITURES

Caviar is marvelous we agreed
but if one eats too much of it
(and I do love the taste of the soul
in each little dead little egg)
one does have to entertain the thought
that perhaps knowing too much of the sea,
                           perhaps,

oh dear God no,
perhaps next life
I will be a fish.

fizz
fire
flash
foo
flesh
   went the bubbly.

Como no, señor
   said the sommelier
   I know some fine
     accommodations
     in the sea.

The ocean voyage always spoils the wine we agreed
it is the movement of the waves upon
the memory of a grape
Water lapping water is too sensual to the touch
wine delivers its love to the bottle
before the trip is out.
Ohhhh. Unhappy continent
livid America
the taste of wine, of foreign wine which crossed the sea
is like the taste of love the second time.
Poor wine said Lady Grape shedding a tear.

If Camembert is the King of cheeses
foul, corrupt, redolent of old uses, dirty royal feet
and wealth beneath the ground
then Brie is my Prince
said the young fresh air of morning to her appetite.
Still, said Camembert, monarchies produce architecture,
princes bastards
and morning speaking to her appetite is mud
to those who drink with Faust at night
Yes, adventurers gargle the sour blood of dukes
and eat me says Camembert
Power is nothing without the smell
of a royal crevice at your finger.
Oh, says Brie, nothing is so lovely
as the milk of morning on my mouth.
Do not let the world sodden us with its liver,
its poor colon and a smell of the hoarded past
Good architecture comes from young men
stealing the better half of form
from the royal round rump of some majestic lady
who smuggles jewels to the prince
and embezzles deeds from the king.

If poetry is the food of the soul
then some poems are like pot roast
lots of meat, pannikins of gravy and
a great deal of taste all very
much the same.
                    Other poems are fishy
tang, pepper, weed, and green like the
sea. I know a few which stick to the
fingers. Poetaster in patis-
serie. But my poems—
                    I want my poems
to be like bones. Bones make it possible
to stay in good form.
                    And there are
poems which taste of grass, air, earth,
rock salt and old lady granite in the
minerals (not to mention all
the dairy products, milky poems,
vegetables and gourds.)
                    But I want
my poems to be like bones and shine
silver in the sun.
                    For poems which
are like bones crackle in my teeth.
Look for the death within the death.

A Balance of Power

The prime minister said:
  everything
    which tastes good
  betrays me
  and everything
    which makes
      me warm
    tastes foul.

Fiddler's Fluck

FOR A SQUARE DANCE

On the meat of the rich
And the urge of the poor
The purge of the ore
And the grease of the bitch
A lady was burning
A whore was a-scorch
Gorge was the cheese
And ass the itch
Of Pussy and Pick-nose
And swish out the twitch
Deep hurted the liver
Raw buried the sauce
Hotshit the hurricane
Herded the gourd
Howligan, hooligan
Hurry up all
Tonight is the night
Of the Hip Hole Ball

Perfume and fart
Snatch squinch and squeeze
Ear-wax and dingle
Fuck tit and dong
Fling a hole on your point
And sweeten the joint
Tonight is the night
Of the Hip Howl Ball.

The bright in mind are often flatulent
They breathe the gas of the dead within them
searching like harpies for a whiff of the treasure
some dead departed failure chose to take away.

One cannot give a funeral service to the fart
and yet there are broken winds which walk the plank in pride.

14 · OUR ARGUMENT AT LAST PRESENTED

Now I will give you a set of equations. They are not mathemat-
ical, but metaphorical; and therefore full of science. I repeat:
they are equations in the form of metaphor; so they are full of science. It
is just that they are not scientific. For they are equations composed only of
words. I am thus trying to say my equations are a close description of
phenomena which cannot be measured by a scientist. Yet these observations
are clear enough to say that interruption is shock, and shock deadens mood,
but mood then stirs itself to rouse a wave. Why? Well, the sum of one's
experience might suggest that it is probably in the nature of mood to
restore itself by raising a wave. Of course, if the wave is too vigorous a
response to the shock, new waste may be left behind. But if the wave is
adequate to the impulse which begot it, the wave can clear the waste away.
So we come to the measure of the absurd, and its enigma: some art move-
ments serve to wash out the sludge of civilization, some leave us deeper in
the pit. The art of the absurd is here to purify us or to swamp us—we
do not know—suddenly, we are back at the GULF *sign. Only now we*
must recognize that we are confronted by no less than the invisible church
of modern science. No small matter. Science has built a wall across the
route of metaphor: poets whine before experts.

The difficulty is that none of us, scientists first, are equipped to measure
the achievements of science. That vast scientific work of the last
fifty years has come most undeniably out of the collective efforts of the
twentieth century scientist, but the achievement came also out of the
nineteenth century, the Enlightenment, and the Renaissance. Who may now
measure where the creativity was finest? The scientists of the last five cen-
turies were the builders of that foundation from which modern scientists
have created a modern science. Only these ancestors may have been more
extraordinary men. They were adventurers, rebels, courtiers, painters, diplo-
mats, churchmen. Our scientists are only experts; those of the last decade
are dull in person as experts, dull as Jonas Salk, they write jargon, their
minds are narrow before they are deep. Their knowledge of life is incar-
cerated.

The huge industrial developments and scientific advances of the twentieth
century—the automobile, antibiotics, radium, flight, the structure of the

atom, relativity, the quantum theory, psychoanalysis, the atom bomb, the exploration of space—may speak not so much for the genius of the twentieth century as for the genius of the centuries which preceded it. Modern science may prove to be the final poisoned fruit of the rich European tree, and plague may disclose itself as the most characteristic invention of our time. For science was founded originally on metaphor, would go our Argument, and the twentieth century has shipped metaphor to the ghetto of poets. Consider: science began with the poetic impulse to treat metaphor as equal to equation; the search began at that point where a poet looked for a means (which only later became experiment) to measure the accuracy of his metaphor. The natural assumption was that his discovery had been contained in the metaphor, since good metaphor could only originate in the deepest experience of a man; so science still remained attached to poetic vision, and scientific insight derived from culture—it was not the original desire of science to convert nature, rather to reveal it. Faust was still unborn when Aristotle undertook his pioneer observations.

There is a danger in metaphor, however; the danger which is present in poetry: contradictory meanings collect too easily about the core of meaning; unconnected meanings connect themselves. So, science sought a methodology through experiment which would be severe, precise, and able to measure the verity of the insight in the metaphor. Experiment was conceived to protect the scientific artist from ambiguity.

Experiment, however, proliferated; as the scientist ceased to be a great amateur and became expert, experiment ran amuck, and laboratory men of partial, determined, fanatic brilliance became the scientist's director rather than his assistant. The laboratory evicted the mind; the laboratory declared itself the womb of scientific knowledge; laboratory methodology grew as cumbersome as the labor codes of a theatrical union. Metaphor disappeared.

It was replaced by a rabidity of experiment, a fetishism of experiment. Mediocrity invaded science. Experiment became a faith, experiment replaced the metaphor as a means of inquiry, and technological development pushed far ahead of even the most creative intuition. Penicillin was discovered by accident, as a by-product of experiment—it did not come at the end of a poetic journey of the mind. No, it was an orphan and a bastard. And by similar mass methods were all the other antibiotics uncovered, by observing the bactericidal action of a million molds: those which gave the best laboratory evidence of success were marketed by drug companies. But the root of the success was not comprehended. There was no general theory to point to a particular mold for a specific disease. No metaphor. Metaphor had been replaced by gross assay.

Metaphor. The word has been used generously. Would an example be welcome? The Argument can try to provide it. A modern disease, for example, as it is comprehended in a laboratory, is explained to the laboratory technician, the student, and the layman, as a phenomenon made up of its own pimples, rash, swelling and development, but the disease is not ever presented as a creature—real or metaphorical—a creature which might have an existence separate from its description, even as you and I have an existence which is separate from the fact that we weigh so many pounds and stand so many inches tall. No, the symptom is stripped of its presence. Of course, psychoanalysis made an attempt to say that the root of one disease could be similar to the root of another whose symptoms were different; it was a way of hinting that the metaphor ought to return. Such an approach might have wished ultimately to demonstrate that a malfunction of the liver and an inflammation of the eyes were both connected to despair at one's position in society. But psychoanalysis was hungry, and dependent upon the sciences: like most welfare cases it was therefore not in a rush for poetry—rather it rushed to advertise the discovery of each new tranquilizer for each disorder in emotion. It was anxious to show itself respectable. So psychiatry became pharmacology.

Let us, however, try to travel in the other direction, let us look for an extreme metaphor of disease. Let us suppose that each specific ill of the body is not so much a dull evil to be disposed of by any chemical means whatever, but is, rather, a theatrical production presented by some company in oneself to some audience in oneself. To the degree then that our illness is painful, detailed, clear, and with as much edge as a sharply enunciated voice, the particular disease is a success; *the communion of the body (the statement sent from stage to audience) is deep, is resonant. The audience experiences catharsis—at the end of the drama, the body is tired but enriched. By the logic of our metaphor, that is a good disease. The illness has waged conflict, drama, and distress through the body, and has obliged the body to sit in attention upon it, but now the body knows more. Its experience has become more profound, its intimate knowledge of its own disharmony is more acute.*

By this reckoning, a disease is the last attempt (at a particular level of urgency) *to communicate from one part of the body to the other, a last attempt to tell us that if we do not realize the function before us is now grievously out of harmony, then we will certainly sicken further. On the other hand, if the disease which presents itself is not accepted, if one's suffering is not suffered, if there are no statements of our suffering enunciated through the caverns of the body, but if instead our disease is averted by antibiotic, or our pain is silenced by a sedative, then the attempted communication of the illness has failed. The disease having no other expression, sinks, of necessity, into a lower and less elegant condition, it retreats from a particular pain or conflict into a bog of disharmony. Where one organ or two might have borne the original stress, now ten organs share ubiquitous tension. A clear sense of symptom tends to disappear. Infection begins to be replaced by virus, a way of saying the new diseases are not classifiable—their symptoms reveal no characteristic form. One is close to the plague.*

If my metaphor is valid, then drugs to relieve pain, and antibiotics to kill infection, are invalid. They are in fact liquidators of possibility, for they deaden the possibility of any quick dramatic growth. A disease checked by an antibiotic has taught the body nothing—nothing to terminate ambiguity—for the body does not know how well it could have cured itself, or even precisely what it had to cure. Yet ambiguity is the seat of disease. Ambiguity demands double communication to achieve a single purpose. It demands we be ready for a particular course of action and yet be ready for its exact opposite. So it demands double readiness or double function for single use. Ambiguity is therefore waste. A man brought back from death by chemicals his own body did not manage to provide cannot know afterward if he should be alive. Small matter, you may argue; he is much alive, is he not? But he has lost biological dignity, he is crucially less alive in a part of his mind and his body. That is one reason metaphors are not encouraged near to science now, for one would then have to say that the patient is alive, but his soul has died a degree.

So the Argument would demand that there be metaphors to fit the vaults of modern experience. That is, in fact, the unendurable demand of the middle of this century, to restore the metaphor, and thereby displace the scientist from his center. Would you call for another example? Think of the elaborate architecture in the structure of a protein molecule. The scientist will describe the structure and list the properties of the molecule (and indeed it took technological achievements close to genius to reach that point) but the scientist will not look at the metaphorical meaning of the physical structure, its meaning as an architectural form. He will not ponder what biological or spiritual experience is suggested by the formal structure of the molecule, for metaphor is not to the present interest of science. It is instead the desire of science to be able to find the cause of cancer in some virus: a virus—you may count on it—which will be without metaphor. You see, that will then be equal to saying that the heart of the disease of all diseases is empty of meaning, that cancer is caused by a specific virus which has no character or quality, and is in fact void of philosophy and bereft of metaphysics. All those who are there to claim that disease and death are void of meaning are there to benefit from such a virus, for next they can move on to say that life is absurd. We are back once again at the enigma surrounding the art of the absurd. Except now we have hints of the meaning. For if the Argument would propose that a future to life depends on creating forms of an intensity which will capture the complexity of modern experience and dignify it, illumine—if you will—its danger, then the art of the absurd reveals the wound in its own heart and the schizophrenia of its impulse, for the art of the absurd wars with one hand against the monotonies of all totalitarian form in politics, medicine, architecture, and media communication, and with the other, trembles and is numb to any human passion and is savage toward discourse, for the danger is palpable and the discovery of new meaning may live in ambush at the center of a primitive fire.

Well, enough of such metaphor. Let us go off to explore the tributaries of form.

THE POLITICAL ECONOMY OF TIME

MAILER

We have had an agreeable dialogue until now. It has been super-
ficial in all too many places, and the reasonings have been limited finally
by my ability to reason, which is famously limited, but our subject mat-
ter proved rich. Feces, after all, are first cousin to gold. If we were obliged
to talk of death, there was at least a sense of blood. But today we're
off on emptier matters—out in the vacuums of metaphysics, and I have
slept poorly, and dreamed of barren landscapes, empty beach, and
stagnant pools on a winter day. There will be the taste of this in what
we talk of next.

INTERVIEWER

Your mind is dull, you say.

MAILER

It is overstimulated and next to empty. I've had too much coffee, and
excitation put upon depression seems to produce an excess of electric in
the nerve.

INTERVIEWER

You advance this metaphor as the secret of everything electric?

MAILER

I steal away from it.

INTERVIEWER

Good. Because we are here to talk about form; and electricity, I sus-
pect, has no form, only property.

MAILER

(*In gloom*) We are here to talk about form.

INTERVIEWER

Make then a formal beginning.

MAILER

Instead let me start by paying my respects to an irony. It is that some fundamental subjects are easy to discuss. The word "soul," for example, lends itself to speculation. But "form!" There's a treacherous word. It can mean the opposite of itself.

INTERVIEWER

To me, form is an easy word. I think I understand it.

MAILER

You do?

INTERVIEWER

Form always means the shape of something.

MAILER

(*Shows a fraction of interest*) The form of an umbrella is the shape of the umbrella?

INTERVIEWER

Absolutely. That's all there is to it. An umbrella has a form which is identical to its shape. (*Interviewer stops*) Actually, I must admit that, in fact, it has two shapes. Its shape when it is open, and its shape when it is closed.

MAILER

Then it has two forms?

INTERVIEWER

Yes.

MAILER

What about a tree?

INTERVIEWER

(*Takes his time*) A tree has a form which is its own form, its own particular form. But I see what you are driving at. It also has a form which is the form of all trees of its species.

MAILER

These two forms of the tree are different from the two forms of the umbrella? That is—we are speaking of different kinds of categories?

INTERVIEWER

I think we are.

MAILER

Consider this: what is the form of an amoeba?

INTERVIEWER

An amoeba has no form. It's shapeless.

MAILER

Modern coffee tables are cut into what is presumably a shape called amoeboid.

INTERVIEWER

(*His confidence is back*) The word means no more than that an object is presented in meaningless curves. It does not mean an amoeba has shape. Take the two forms of the tree. Can't I say that not only does the amoeba not have an individual shape, and so not have a particular form which is like the first form of the tree (that is to say, its form at a given moment) but that all amoebae taken as a class do not possess a general shape, a secondary group shape we might call amoeboid, a shape that would be like the second form of the tree.

MAILER

The fact remains: the amoeba may have a shape at any instant.

INTERVIEWER

(*Full of momentum*) Not if it changes constantly. If it keeps changing, the amoeba can have a shape only if you insist on picking a moment when you freeze time. Very much against time's own will, if I may speak that way. A microphotograph would give the amoeba a shape. But only arbitrarily. A concept like the differential of time, dt, in calculus might be able to give it a shape. But those are stage tricks. If the amoeba keeps changing, it cannot possess a particular shape.

MAILER

Suppose when examined closely, the amoeba moves for an instant, is still, then moves again? Can't we select each moment it is at rest and call that a particular shape?

INTERVIEWER

Suppose the amoeba is never completely at rest?

MAILER

Then there is no *particular* form. A *particular* form cannot be detected without a moment of rest. But that should not keep the amoeba from possessing an ideal form.

INTERVIEWER

An ideal form? You speak of the second kind of form? Like the second form of the tree? The form which is the form of all trees?

MAILER

Yes. A man, for example, might possess an ideal form. We could say his ideal form remains unchanged whether he is running, walking, or sleeping. That is because when we speak of his ideal form, we are speaking of a shape he can *probably* assume. (Of course he may have to go on a diet to demonstrate it.) But note that it is not his particular shape until he assumes it.

INTERVIEWER

I can agree with that.

MAILER

Now the amoeba may not possess such an abstract ideal form. I have no idea if it does. But whether it owns an ideal form or not seems to me on reflection not to the point. I wish you only to agree that the amoeba, hypothetically, may have a set of consecutive shapes as discernible as the successive frames of a movie film.

INTERVIEWER

We come back to the problem of rest. Why should I concede to you that the amoeba may have a consecutive set of particular shapes if you have not yet demonstrated that it can ever be discovered at rest? All of it—at rest—all at once.

MAILER

Perhaps I can never demonstrate it to you at rest. Perhaps you can demonstrate that it is *never* at rest. You cannot. Will you concede that the amoeba *may* have a set of consecutive shapes?

INTERVIEWER

It may. I still have the feeling it does not have a form. If it's not shapeless, the amoeba is next to shapeless. Because nothing in it seems to remain the same.

MAILER

You demand of form that it have not only shape but security. It must last?

INTERVIEWER

Yes. It must have a shape in time.

MAILER

So it seems we are talking about time as well. About shape and time. Can you then agree that when we speak of form, we are talking of more than shape?

INTERVIEWER

Maybe we are.

MAILER

Would you concede the likelihood that shape is not equal to form, but merely a first best clue to it?

INTERVIEWER

I may have to. But go on.

MAILER

That is, shape is a clue to form if you can see the shape.

INTERVIEWER

I knew I should concede nothing. What has a form you cannot see?

MAILER

Would you permit a symphony to have form?

INTERVIEWER

It must. I see what you're up to. Of course. The sounds we hear in a symphony vary each instant. Only when it's done do we remember the successive sounds as a shape. A shape composed of many sounds heard in a period of time. (*Stops*) I know you may think I am playing with the word, but I believe it is fair to speak of the shape of a piece of music. In my memory, it has not only permanence but a shape.

MAILER

Already you are talking of form in space, and form in time, of forms we see, forms we hear? You see why I did not wish to get impaled on the amoeba at rest?

INTERVIEWER

I see why exactly. And I still say permanence is the first feature of form.

MAILER

Let us say it is a feature of many forms which exist in space or in time. But can't we speak of forms which exist in other conditions?

INTERVIEWER

I should think form can only have a shape in space or time. What else is relevant here?

MAILER

Can taste have form?

INTERVIEWER

. . .

MAILER

Or smell? Or touch? Can they have form?

INTERVIEWER

I don't see how.

MAILER

Could you say the taste of wine is a form?

INTERVIEWER

You're leading me to some borderland of the concepts.

MAILER

To what?

INTERVIEWER

To forms which might exist in being. In Being! You bring in Being because you're an existentialist. Dammit all to hell.

MAILER

I'm thinking of a famous wine. Château Margaux '47. Each time one drinks, the taste comes upon the palate in clear acts. Sweet, cool, then earthy and sad, sweet and cool, earthy, sad. If one drinks too much, the sorrow turns to rust. Such wine has a shape in time. The permanence of its form resides in my memory.

INTERVIEWER

You are trying to connect form to Being. Perhaps you even succeed. To some slight degree. I distrust your motive. You wish to return to a discussion of the soul. So you are trying to smuggle form over into Being.

MAILER

In order to smuggle Being over to soul?

INTERVIEWER

That might be your route. I would remind you that we are far from done with the amoeba and the tree. I started this discussion by remarking that form was the shape of something. Since an amoeba had no consistent shape, it could have no form. You then pointed out that the amoeba's movement contained hypothetical instants of rest, and so one could speak of a possible succession of forms. But I still say the amoeba does not have a permanent shape in time. It is the opposite of a tree. Precisely because a tree has a shape to which you can return in your mind. An ideal shape which is related to an ideal form. There you are! Ideal form suggests permanence. Everything to do with form speaks of permanence.

MAILER

I now propose to demonstrate that ideal form is a treacherous hypothesis. Follow me. There is a kind of form which appears to have a durable shape in time as well as in space. This form you presume is there for the tree. Ideal form, you call it. But there is another kind of visual form which has no shape in any kind of time we can perceive. The amoeba, for example. This lack of shape is perceived as lack-of-shape because we are using man as the measure of time. Only because of that. If we dispense with ourselves as the measure, then I think I can show that the amoeba has a shape which is conceivably definite or indefinite, just as ideal or not ideal, as permanent or impermanent as the shape belonging to the tree.

INTERVIEWER

Let us see you make such a demonstration.

MAILER

To us, a tree changes slowly. Its shape in time alters imperceptibly. But if we take a movie of the tree, if we mount a camera on the wall of a garden during the first season the tree is planted and proceed for the next hundred years (which for simple calculation we may suppose to be the life of the tree) to click off no more than one single frame of film each separate week, we might end with fifty-two hundred frames of film for a century, which by all lightnings of calculation is less than four minutes of projection. In the finished movie our tree would pass through a year in two and a half seconds. Its trunk would sprout and climb toward the sky, its branches would open as fast as an umbrella, the change of color in its leaves from green to red to brown would be a flicker the eye could barely detect. The action of the tree would look spasmodic, convulsive, near to spastic. It might be even reminiscent of the shift of shape in the amoeba.

INTERVIEWER

Still, the tree moves out of a logic which suggests a kind of shape in time. One can see it rise, bud, leaf, lose its leaves, bud again, and go on through a hundred cycles of the years until its death.

MAILER

If the tree were situated in a windless space, one might see that. But assume a small breeze blows the branches one way this week, and the other the next. Then the movements of the tree would have no apparent purpose in our film. Tree limbs would thrash like cilia in a paramecium; the branches would not even possess an outline, but would seem to offer some indefinite nebulous transparent edge.

INTERVIEWER

That is because you film one frame a week. The tiny segments of time you record are unrelated to one another.

MAILER

Only in part are they unrelated. The filmed movement of the branches may be relatively arbitrary, but the film is obedient to the general growth of the trunk and the limbs.

INTERVIEWER

I insist you are being more arbitrary in the way you look at the tree than the way you look at the amoeba.

MAILER

It may be that every procedure we have for looking at anything not human is arbitrary. That is an inhuman remark. Still, I must ask you to conceive of a being on some distant star, some cosmic giant who lives in another rhythm or scale of time, in some relation to time altogether different from ours. A wink of his eyelash occupies a year for us; to him, it is just a wink (that is to say, his personal subjective impression of the duration of his wink is approximately equal to our impression of the duration of our wink). If we close our eye and open it, we have the sensation that a small but definite interval of time has elapsed, something like a second. The giant also feels as if no more than a second has passed, but he is large, his proportions are huge; in fact a year by our measure has passed. Think then of what he might see through some telescope worthy of his size when he studies a tree on earth. It must appear to him as fantastic, nervous, illogical, rapid and shapeless as an amoeba. More so. The life cycle of the tree might look perhaps like a doll or a ballerina who rises from a crouch, shivers, pirouettes and collapses in ninety seconds.

INTERVIEWER

You do not even beg the question, you violate it. What right have you to give this giant another scale of time than ours?

MAILER

I have no right. Neither of us has rights in a discussion of time. Nobody knows anything about time. Consider—what right have you to assume that time is equal anywhere? That its measure is a clock? My notion of time is as reasonable as yours. I use the giant; you use the clock. With the clock, certain kinds of time have to be measured in numbers so great that man is run off the stage and we speak of light-years. I think it is more agreeable to measure time by beings.

INTERVIEWER

What then measures time in each separate being? Soul?

MAILER

Soul.

INTERVIEWER

The amoeba has a soul?

MAILER

Yes.

INTERVIEWER

The tree?

MAILER

Yes.

INTERVIEWER

And their measure of time is proportionate to their relative size?

MAILER

One might say it is probably not unrelated. It seems reasonable to assume that a short interval for the tree might seem like a larger one for the amoeba.

INTERVIEWER

Man and the tree, however, are relatively near to each other in their measure of time?

MAILER

Not necessarily. The condition of Being is so different for each. The hundred years of life a tree can know might seem not nearly enough, a month perhaps to it.

INTERVIEWER

There is a clock in nature. We call it night and day The tree shares night and day, dark and light with each of us. So does the amoeba in the pond.

MAILER

They do, but they do not necessarily do it in the same way. What is a day for us may be no more than an inhalation of breath for the tree; as we sleep through the night so the tree exhales its breath, the way we might exhale breath as we blink our eyes.

INTERVIEWER

And the amoeba?

MAILER

A day might seem a century in the soul of an amoeba; the night an entombment worthy of Pharaohs. As we look through the microscope we see two tentacles reach out from the amoeba and encircle a morsel. Snap! The morsel is whipped toward the nucleus. Half a second by the clock, or five seconds, or three minutes required. But as we study the amoeba in the field of the microscope, our vision distorted by glass, reflected light, optical ache and biological concept, we may be not unlike my slumbering giant. He sees the tree through a telescope which spans heavens. What adventures and distortions in the air and light! The atmospheres of planets, the echo of meteors, and huge seas of radiation twist his comprehension of the tree. So do the concepts of his gigantic mind. His fingers exhaust our decade in the time it takes him to light a cigarette. His concepts involve actions which take centuries, millenniums, some dull eons. So he cannot conceive the sweet complexity of a day or month for us. Men or trees are a flicker in his lens. His concept of time, his feeling for time's duration, exists in him only by what is suitable to his measure—which is gargantuan, not human, so that he misses everything of human scale just as we are all but closed off from the gargantuan. Look! Man has a decent sense of the hours, the minutes, the days, the years, the seasons, the decades, the instants, the lifetimes, the moments and the centuries. For these he has built a clock. But for the light-years or the micromillionth of a second he has no clock. There, his sense of time is blind. Man's clock becomes absurd. Light-years or micromillionths of a second are categories of time outside the proportions of our life, or our situation in the universe. A being like you or me can comprehend any unit of time, whether arbitrary and measured like a minute or natural like a moment, if it is at least part of the length of our life, if it is pertinent to what I wish to call our *enlifement*—our subjective or biological conception of the size of time. We can only be sensitive to those proportions of time which are a measure of our life. Conversely, we can only have the confidence to understand the sense of time of beings like ourselves. For this reason, we can have reasonable hope of understanding such creations as man. But a being which exists in a radically different enlifement, a being like an amoeba, or like a tree, will have a different measure. *Snap!* go the tentacles of the amoeba. Just three seconds taken. But for the amoeba, those three seconds may have been a convocation of events as complex as the movements of a modern army—those three seconds could have been a year's campaign in the mud, and the particle of food as differentiated and as dangerous as an enemy force. Its form might have been exceptional if we had proper eyes and concepts, which is to say if we lived in the very amoeboid time necessary to glimpse what had been before the amoeba.

INTERVIEWER

Don't you exaggerate? May it be not just an amoeba? Nothing going on but a little wiggle to snap up some food?

MAILER

My cosmic giant might have been able to see the German armies surrounded at Stalingrad. Without his telescope, however, the battle could have looked to him no more impressive than one of those larger amoebae, half the size of the head of a pin, which one can sometimes see on the surface of a pollen in a quiet pond.

INTERVIEWER

Which is a way of saying all of us are insignificant.

MAILER

Maybe it is the giant who is insignificant; maybe it is *his* emotions which are dim. We may be weak in relation to the power of the giant, but he may be insignificant in his emotions, in his perception. His size could speak for the heroic, or could mean no more than that the giant lost all conception of a future and so chose to proliferate himself into an enormous but sluggish space. The giant might be no more interesting than a million miles of styrene.

INTERVIEWER

Space is the measure of power, you are saying, but time is the index of what is possible.

MAILER

That is possible.

INTERVIEWER

So the amoeba is more glorious than you or me.

MAILER

It may be; maybe it is not. Some amoebae are doubtless glorious, some odious. There may be at this instant wars amoebae are fighting which mean more to the future of our being than all rocket ships. We don't know. The amoeba's lack of size and its tremendous number may signify less than we know.

INTERVIEWER

Their number! There are millions of amoebae for each one of us. Or is it billions? They cannot be individual.

MAILER

What if they are some other kind of being altogether? What if all the amoebae in one freshwater pond constitute no more than one soul, one very special sort of soul, not really a soul if you will, but some element of Being, some spirit of the pond. Postulate more men on earth than ponds. If there is an exceptional creation to each pond—

INTERVIEWER

You cheat. You speak of every amoeba possessing a soul, now you speak of all the amoebae within a pond as one single soul. I think you want to bring the conversation around to some back alley, some purlieu of the soul, where no philosophical rigor can catch up to you.

MAILER

We've come to a point of such fearful complexity that I may as well confess that after our conversations of yesterday I have been up half the night trying to find a way to explain some notions to you. But then I began our conversation with complaints. Still, I wish you would understand that I have no desire to discuss the soul. On the contrary, that opens empty vistas, as if indeed you can use up your soul by talking about it. For one thing, the language is unendurable. You must employ words which have been used by the worst churchmen, wardens, editors, policemen, politicians, generals, statesmen and financiers of each century, just such words as God, soul, Devil, spirit, vision, eternal and universal. It may be possible to bring new connotations to these words, although I doubt it. But the alternative is, after all, worse; it is to make up your own words: call the soul psyche or being-in-itself; the will, ego; the conscience, super-ego; call God the Force of Life or the Being of Being; call the Devil Negation; call eternity a limitless parameter; translate the Vision into transcendental numina. There is nausea in such procedure. So I take the words as they are, talk of soul and spirit. I am, you see, obliged to go on because I can't leave our conversation unfinished here. That alternative is even meaner to contemplate. Yet, if I proceed, understand that I am filled with a sense of discomfort. The continuation will be, I expect, so intangible, changeable, and contradictory that the task of communicating it will be similar in difficulty to taking hold of a spider's web in order to pass on something intact. What compounds the nuisance is that this intellectual transaction will take us far from a discussion of form, out very far out, into some unexplored unfeasible regions. We will be talking after all about death, a subject intolerable to most, and are going to be taking the most witch-ridden aspect of it, for we will assume that death is not conventional death—death as the common end—but to the contrary, will talk of death as a continuation, a migration, a metamorphosis. That means we must now enter into speculation of an outrageous sort. And yet we must speculate, and in just such fashion, for if death is continuation—at least for some—then hints and portents are everywhere about us.

INTERVIEWER

So you now forsake all talk of form?

MAILER

I cannot explain form without talking of time. We are agreed upon that. But I think we should not talk about time unless we speculate about death.

INTERVIEWER

You've left me. Here you've left me.

MAILER

Death and time meet in critical fashion.

INTERVIEWER

Beware of banality.

MAILER

No, I am trying to say, and I don't know how to make it easy for you, that time is the continuation from life into death—it commands, if you will, both terminals of the tunnel—that is my supposition.

INTERVIEWER

It is a large one.

MAILER

I offer you something bigger. Soul and Time (if we may, for an instant, speak in the upper case) bear so profound a relation to one another, they are identical.

INTERVIEWER

The soul is equal to time?

MAILER

Nothing less.

INTERVIEWER

So you speak of the soul to explain form. You are neat today.

MAILER

Form, you said, is a shape in time. I try to suggest that the only measure of time—no, put it more directly—its only *container* is an enlifement, that mode or character or style by which time is perceived in each different kind of being. It is a way of saying that time does not have a universal existence, an overall existence like a blanket, nor is it even like a projectile carrying the universe in a cannonball; no, rather it is a set of separate creations similar to the points of pigment so close to light in the paintings of Seurat. Any general sense of time is then a fiction. A clock is a philosophical fiction among men, at best an accommodation between a hundred million or a million million separate creations, each embodying some separate continuation of (not a sense of time, but) time itself.

INTERVIEWER

Man is time?

MAILER

The soul of man is one kind of time.

INTERVIEWER

We are up the garden path by now.

MAILER

It is as far as I can go in this direction without devoting the next ten years to a study of physics, and physicists I have been assured get no new ideas after twenty. So let us slide over in our discussion from time to the more comfortable terrain of soul and death. Do you see already how more intimate they are?

INTERVIEWER

Classmates.

MAILER

. . .

INTERVIEWER

I recapitulate. It seems to me you suggest that an appreciation of form is related to a comprehension of death, not my idea of death—that final sound I hear echoing in old stone walls and over the wind of burial grounds—but, no, your more athletic presentation of the matter, death as sea change, voyages, metamorphoses. So we have to talk of the soul, that damn *ghost,* and I don't know bean-pie of what you have in mind. I suspect you will carry me into some sort of discussion clear on the other side of the divide.

MAILER

What is your sense of what I have tried to say?

INTERVIEWER

I recollect that you were sufficiently carried away to speak yesterday of souls in food. Among other items, we fixed on a tin of sardines, and spoke of the fortified soul of a superior sardine in the tin. I feel a little claustrophobic about that.

MAILER

I didn't extend the meaning of the word "soul" beyond its own elasticity, I hope.

INTERVIEWER

Beyond any reasonable comprehension of its meaning? I think you did. Look! Once a body is dead—what do you do then with the soul? Do you contemplate it? Do you eat it? Once you get specific, you're drowning in sardine oil.

MAILER

Take the soul in that sardine. Can we proceed to eat it literally, and go on to think of it philosophically as the same entity which was once in the sardine's body?

INTERVIEWER

That is my question.

MAILER

Yes, can we eat that precise soul-and-body equal to one sardine which we chose yesterday to call one being? I don't know if we can. The intellectual discomfort is too great.

INTERVIEWER

You agree?

MAILER

It is too hard to imagine a soul in a body and alive; then alive without a body, yet unchanged—no, I think we can conceive of it remaining the same only in the way a light beam remains in some manner constant after it has been banked off a mirror, reflected through a lens, and bent in water. Such a light beam is now going in another direction, and for all we know is altered seriously in character; it may possess, for example, electromagnetic properties which are different from its previous possessions, just so different as its new direction. Still, we can say we are probably studying the same light beam we were looking at before its physical adventures. Let us try then to follow the transition, let us speculate upon it. When the soul inhabits a body, it tries to exercise its intent within that body. Sometimes it satisfies itself, often it fails, but it carries some instinct which leads it toward something mysterious, something I will be so mistaken as to now call the Vision (of which more later may be said) but since the word is capitalized let me say that I do not want to beg the quality of its character, nor imply it is routinely religious. The Vision may be beatific, heroic, epic, contemplative, tragic, harmonious, or even Faustian; the Vision may shift in its direction; perhaps it is capable of a Satanic contract—we do not know—each of us would indeed postulate a different kind of Vision. For now, it is enough to say that by our definition the soul has an instinct which leads it toward that part of the Vision it can sense or comprehend, and the soul—goes our next hypothesis—is resisted in this attempt by all those forces in the world, whose desire is to frustrate every soul in this attempt.

INTERVIEWER

You speak again of the Devil?

MAILER

For the moment I wish to emphasize only this: the body to which the soul is wed, or bound in love with, or at war against—forgive these legalisms, but that marriage here called soul-to-body is complex beyond imagination—yes, that body at any rate which is ground for a soul, sooner or later dies, it ceases to function, it enters a state of decomposition. Let us consider that.

INTERVIEWER

What then happens to the soul?

MAILER

Well, I would postulate a new condition for it. So long as it was part of a body, it was free, free existentially, it could attempt to do what it wished to do, it could war against everything which resisted it; if it failed, there was failure, but the attempt was at least possible. The soul existed as a dynamic will. And the reason: it was part of a body which was able to change its environment. Yet once the body is dead, a soul is no longer free, or at least it is no longer free to alter its environment actively through the agency of a body. The body was its instrument; without such a tool, the soul enters a radically different state, for now it is passive and acted upon by environment.

INTERVIEWER

It is worn down, it is eroded. Like a material? Like a piece of driftwood?

MAILER

Yes.

INTERVIEWER

Can it be worn literally out of existence?

MAILER

I think it can be said that, other things being equal, it is worn down.

INTERVIEWER

But are you speaking of the soul as here having still a physical existence? It must if it is being worn down.

MAILER

It is idle how I speak of it. The soul may have some physical existence after the death of the body, or it may not—

INTERVIEWER

I'm sure everyone must talk in private like this.

MAILER

Jokes on your philosopher's vocabulary could be endless.

INTERVIEWER

Proceed. I will bridle my wit until it bleeds at the gums.

MAILER

Blood is the whiskey of the soul. The point I try to make is that the soul, whether physical or immaterial, is still a creature of properties and desires, forced into the anguish of a situation largely more passive than before, so that whatever in its new situation is not essential to it must be lost. Unfree of an opportunity to act, it is acted upon by all the forces of man, nature, good will, ill will and the wind, and is therefore (in an absence of dramatic events) reduced down to a state where it can be reduced no more. At that point it is the essence of itself.

INTERVIEWER

You are speaking perhaps of the Greek conception of the atom, of that particle which cannot be divided further.

MAILER

That suggests a materiality we do not have to consider here. Even disembodied, the soul may still have a physical existence, or again it may not—we won't be so fancy as to say. But whether it is material, astral, spectral, or most modestly psychic, one likelihood presents itself—that it must take up an abode in some already prepared form which is independent of itself.

INTERVIEWER

So that is when it becomes attached to a body again?

MAILER

Oh, no. No, no. When a soul is an essential part of a being, it is born with the body and grows with the body, perhaps it is even present at the conception of the body. But I talk here rather of the soul in its outlaw state, after the death of the body. This new form it appropriates serves as a shell—we may almost view directly the hermit crab and the empty shell of the snail. This new form is a house, you see, not a body; unlike a body it is not capable of adapting to the demands or desires of the soul, and therefore the soul, an outlaw from life, has taken to it only from a kind of desperation, for we are assuming the most existential of conditions for this disembodied state, we are picturing the soul in a time of voyages, and anguish, and loss, the diminution of its properties. For protection it chooses an abode.

INTERVIEWER

You postulate this state as true for everyone who dies.

MAILER

I don't begin to postulate. I offer you images, that is all.

INTERVIEWER

Your presentation is perhaps too general to speak of images.

MAILER

Very well. Let us be precise. Think of the driftings of one particular soul; let it be the disembodiment of a man drowned at sea. This outlaw soul—

INTERVIEWER

You mean, this nautical soul.

MAILER

Call it a Salt. This Salt—disembodied—moves mutely through the water from object to object, from a mussel shell to a barnacle to a drift of seaweed torn from its embedment on the rocks. Finally it chooses a piece of wood whose shape is halfway agreeable to it, a piece of wood whose form is not unlike a particular human face which was once part of the memory of that soul. Of course, there may be other souls attached to the wood already; perhaps a battle of subtle influences is about to ensue; but this is certainly too novelistic a situation to follow further at this point. Let us stay most impoverished. Let us stay lean and philosophical. Assume rather the wood is uninhabited except for our one particular soul which—notice this and bless it—proceeds by the salt of its conviction, by the crystallization of its previous experience, to mobilize its conception of a face into that wood, and so etches the driftwood closer to the Salt's idea of a face it can use. Hold still on this and I'll try to explain what I mean by "use." A week goes by, a month; the wood is illumined by the Salt, which is to say it is *carved* by the soul, for the wood now is able to defend itself against the washing of the water, that is, it is worn down unequally with what is now a particular determination to save a few special artful parts of its potential form. Thrown up on shore, half the size it was, the wood is now more like the face the soul had glimpsed. Treated by the sun, it rots with dry design. One of us goes strolling along the beach, falls upon it, brings the driftwood back, brushes it, takes it home, and stares at the find. The face, created in part by the soul of the dead sailor, haunts us a little, it shapes our motives, just a touch—that Salt has entered us, just a touch, psychically.

INTERVIEWER

Not physically?

MAILER

That is yet to come. That is another epic.

INTERVIEWER

Sketch it.

MAILER

We change. We tire of the face, we put the driftwood into the fire and burn it. A whiff of smoke comes into our nostrils, shocking, clear, aromatic. It has character in its odor. Surprised, we breathe deep, and the Salt has entered our lungs, is now attached to a cell in the blood, red as a root. From that blood cell it must make its way through a thousand adventures to the sperm. It must travel through the perils of enzymes, catalysts, glands and juices, attach itself to and disconnect itself from molecule after molecule until it reaches a form which offers life.

INTERVIEWER

Like the protein molecule DNA, for example, in the chromosomes of a sperm?

MAILER

Something like that. Never doubt it.

INTERVIEWER

If this is religion, it is not agreeable. What is there of eternal slumber, universal verities? This is hectic.

MAILER

Call it ceaseless suffering.

INTERVIEWER

It is not rest.

MAILER

Still, it is an existence. The Salt clinging to a piece of wood can have the pleasure of drifting on an ocean of long summer swells, it can be warmed by the sun, lit by the moon, and even feel a fraction divine as it works along, rapt in the labor of working a design upon the wood. That Salt could say: I, now, subtly, inevitably, insinuate myself into form, I reveal the shape of my Being—just like God.

INTERVIEWER

But why? Why just like God—if indeed He is there—why would God wish to reveal the shape of *His* Being?

MAILER

It is the most elegant way He can communicate Himself, for it avoids the danger of communicating Himself to those who hate Him most.

INTERVIEWER

Do I follow? Not much.

MAILER

The pious response would be: the devil hates nature. I expect I must agree. Now, *I* am solemn. But it is reasonable to assume that the devil hates nature so much he cannot bear to look at it. He must name what he sees before he sees it. Or instantly after. He must dominate nature because it does not belong to him. That is why he cannot bear to contemplate it. (*Pause*)

INTERVIEWER

But now you are suddenly silent and don't go on.

MAILER

I am afraid. This inquiry we are pursuing satisfies a definition just given of the Satanic.

INTERVIEWER

I assure you, you are far from communicating yourself to this believer.

MAILER

(*Cheerfully*) Then perhaps it is safe to proceed.

INTERVIEWER

Nonetheless, you now look worried again. In fact, you look damn worried. It's just come all over you.

MAILER

I've been feeling a contradiction in everything I said earlier. There's something makes me uneasy. I am worrying the possibility that a soul must have something in kind to work upon, something in the driftwood which I might be forced to call spirit, the spirit of the driftwood. But this proposes an indigestible complication, and the truth is that I am a little uneasy of your temper. (*Holds up boths hands to emphasize the measure*) Yes, I think we now say goodbye to all hope of arriving at anything elegant in our speculations. For at this instant, a hundred difficulties rush into the argument, and the first is the worst. I've just come to the grim conclusion that I must change the terms of our discussion, or to be less polite to myself, must now admit that I have to shift my terms around to include another mysterious element in these metamorphoses, an element I expect is far more mysterious than soul: spirit, yes spirit, spirit.

INTERVIEWER

What then!—you shift the terms—well, what then is spirit?

MAILER

That is what I am not sure of.

INTERVIEWER

Yet you choose to begin?

MAILER

I may become more certain as I talk. Often I do.

INTERVIEWER

Or contradict yourself further.

MAILER

Either.

INTERVIEWER

You are certainly an existentialist.

MAILER

I began to feel in trouble about the time we started to talk of the soul of the amoeba. Perhaps it does have one, but then, if you remember, I wasn't certain, I began to postulate the possibility that all the amoebae in the pond composed one exceptional soul. And that notion was unsatisfactory. I think what I was trying to say was that the soul of the pond was not a soul but a spirit. And now the idea becomes more clear because one can think more easily of some pullulating unhappy swarm of amoebae all making up the spirit of a slime on the pond, perhaps even a malignant and powerful slime which may be why you dislike amoebae so, and why, secretly, all the while I was promoting their virtues, I found them near to repulsive.

INTERVIEWER

That slime of amoebae on the pond—it is a spirit, you claim now? It is one kind of spirit?

MAILER

Yes.

INTERVIEWER

Tell me of others.

MAILER

I think it would be easier if you ask a few questions.

INTERVIEWER

Is the tree also a spirit?

MAILER

I have no idea. Maybe it is soul *and* spirit.

INTERVIEWER

Once again you've succeeded in whipping up our collective confusions.

MAILER

I feel new ideas emerging, but they make me uneasy. I remember I began to feel uneasy when I spoke of the amoeba as an army. An army after all is a spirit.

INTERVIEWER

An army is made up of men. Of a hundred thousand men, we may say. Which by your count is one hundred thousand souls. Do all of these souls—one hundred thousand—make one spirit?

MAILER

So far as they give themselves to an effort thrust on them by some larger spirit *or* soul, why yes, then that part of them which is obedient to the army obviously contributes to the *function* of the army. (*Happily*) The function is the center of the spirit. That may be a beginning. Suppose that souls possess a personal life and thus are unpredictable and full of turns, but a spirit is a function. It can only wax strong or weak.

INTERVIEWER

Realize what you've said. You are implicating us in the idea that the cells in our body are spirits and souls. But cells certainly seem to possess far more of one or another specific function than any suggestion of a personal life. They must be spirits.

MAILER

Perhaps they are.

INTERVIEWER

Then you do overthrow much of what you said earlier. And I have no idea of what bearing this has on form.

MAILER

My difficulty is that I do not necessarily have a message to unfold which was once carefully folded. Rather my problem may vary from severing a series of knots to excavating a tomb.

INTERVIEWER

There are too many ideas at once.

MAILER

Yes. Could it be that a cell is a spirit composed of many souls?

INTERVIEWER

A parenthesis: (From where do these souls arrive?)

MAILER

(From their travels.)

INTERVIEWER

And where in the cell are they to be found?

MAILER

In the nucleus if it will make you happy. In the chromosomes of the nucleus. In your DNA molecule. In particles too small for the electron microscope to discover. God knows. Their precise residence is not a part of this discussion.

INTERVIEWER

But the spirit of the cell rules over the souls within that cell. It makes them offer up allegiance to the government of the spirit?

MAILER

Yes. I will say yes.

INTERVIEWER

A man—a soul!—would, however, command the spirits of his cells?

MAILER

More or less. If he is in command of his cells. If a malignancy had not begun. But forgive me for these examples. They lead but to further confusion.

INTERVIEWER

Still, if one is to stake out the ground in a general way—anything to keep your metaphor afloat—I could go on to ask if people considered in social groups may be seen as collections of *whole souls*—engrave those words!— or if such associations are not too loose to be termed spirits.

MAILER

Some spirits are cohesive, some are not. A bag of beans is probably a spirit—a very weak one, of course.

INTERVIEWER

Groups of men form spirits then, some loose, some cohesive. Yes? In turn the collision of these spirits makes a nation?

MAILER

Yes.

INTERVIEWER

A nation which has a soul? A soul over all these spirits?

MAILER

Some nations seem to have a soul.

INTERVIEWER

Some seem to have a spirit. Soul. Spirit. You have opened a pair of categories which are hopeless. Some people have spirits, others have soul?

MAILER

Yes.

INTERVIEWER

Characterize the difference. Make at least some attempt. What is the difference to me if I am a soul or a spirit?

MAILER

A creature who is a spirit is hardly the same as a man who has spirit. Someone who has spirit is a soul, a fortunate soul, rather a powerful soul.

INTERVIEWER

Whereas, someone who *is* a spirit is selfless?

MAILER

Precisely. The sort of people we say are full of soul actually are spirits. Beautiful spirits perhaps.

INTERVIEWER

That helps a bit. Still you spoke earlier of a cell which might have a
soul *and* a spirit. There is a ladder of dominations you seem to be always
about to construct—spirit dominated by a soul who in turn is dominated by
a higher spirit which is then dominated by yet a higher soul. Just as
we are about to arrive, you confound the two together again. If we are
to avoid intolerable ambiguities, you must now try to speak in some decent
detail about the properties of soul and spirit, the more particular proper-
ties. You must try to separate them.

MAILER

Suppose I define soul by saying it is a sort of creature, doubtless invis-
ible, which has a purchase on eternity. It also has an individual life, a
personal life, which is contained in itself, and this personal life is carried
through its metamorphoses. It is the soul's character in the same way the
taste of the sardine is the sardine's character.

INTERVIEWER

Is this character immutable?

MAILER

Of course not. It can change as quickly as a taste can rot. But it is at
least continuous. Change in character is the continuing line of the soul.

INTERVIEWER

You speak of character. Is this the moral character of the soul?

MAILER

The Vision is moral. The soul, as we suggested, works its way toward
the Vision. But the soul is itself amoral.

INTERVIEWER

Oh, no! Just when I was beginning to understand.

MAILER

I've been too timid in this exposition. We are not dealing with logic
but metaphor. Metaphor exists to contain contradiction. I repeat: the
soul is amoral. Its purpose is not to be ethical, but to live. Its desire is to

live. So long as it is a healthy soul, its nourishment comes from growth and victory, from exploration, from conquest, from pomp and pageant and triumph, from glory. Is this sufficiently simple for you? It lives for stimulation, for pleasure. It abhors defeat. Its nature is to become more than it is.

INTERVIEWER

But you might just as well be talking of a Roman. Worse. The soul according to you has no impulse to civilize a thing.

MAILER

Civilization is a spirit. I propose to you that the soul is an animal carrying a burden of existence toward the Vision. Like an animal the soul is able to fight, to endure, to war, to kill, to flee, to become lean, wily, hard, a mink, a minx, a wild cat, puma, leopard or tiger. The soul can even descend within a body, and assume the secret sluggish wisdom of a clam, resist change with the force of a clam's valve.

INTERVIEWER

What sort of person would have a soul like a clam?

MAILER

A banker. A banker of the worst sort.

INTERVIEWER

A fair image. Can the soul have no gentle qualities?

MAILER

It can become brave like a lion, noble like a good ape, it can grow as distrustful as an owl, as graceful as a cat, or fierce as a lobster.

INTERVIEWER

Can it love? Can the soul feel love?

MAILER

(*Carried away*) Like a frump, like a poodle, like a fury. Passion comes from the soul. But the soul can only love what offers it growth. It loves most what offers it the happiest, richest growth. It detests sickness, dying, death.

INTERVIEWER

Yet by your definition Romeo and Juliet loved with their soul.

MAILER

Yes And died for it.

INTERVIEWER

Exactly. They died for love. I thought the soul detested death?

MAILER

It does. The only true and passionate lovers are those who love each other because they give life to one another.

INTERVIEWER

What kind of life?

MAILER

Whatever the particular soul needs most. If it needs violence, it will love the violent. There are souls which can be expressed—that is, *un-deadened*—only by violence.

INTERVIEWER

You make the soul sound like the unconscious.

MAILER

But of course it is the unconscious. What did you think it was?

INTERVIEWER

Very well, then. Can the soul be drawn to compassion, to justice, to order?

MAILER

To the degree that an animal can. Perhaps a little more.

INTERVIEWER

An animal has need of justice?

MAILER

An animal dies from injustice. The soul needs justice much as it needs air. But few souls can offer justice.

INTERVIEWER

Compassion?

MAILER

I expect it is even more rare than justice. Still the soul cannot do without the giving of compassion and the receiving of it.

INTERVIEWER

Doesn't the offering of compassion sometimes interfere with one's own growth? Since one must give rather than receive, so the soul is obliged to dispense a part of its wealth?

MAILER

In offering compassion, some souls feel an exquisite sense of beauty.

INTERVIEWER

The soul needs beauty?

MAILER

Like the body needs food.

INTERVIEWER

Why?

MAILER

Beauty is the blood and bone of the soul.

INTERVIEWER

I thought whisky was the blood of the soul.

MAILER

Let us say whisky is the blood and vinegar of the soul.

INTERVIEWER

All right. Now I have a picture. Of sorts. I still don't know why Romeo and Juliet died for love if the soul detests death, and I certainly don't know why if beauty is the blood and bone of the soul, you have so many fucking souls going around blasting up beauty and destroying it, but I think it would be better to wait. I do not want complications here.

MAILER

Oh, they are coming again.

INTERVIEWER

I'm convinced of it. Still I've got some grip at last on what you're talking about. For soul, at any rate. I understand it except for one thing. If it is eternal—

MAILER

Yes.

INTERVIEWER

—why then is it so active?

MAILER

One reason is the metamorphosis from one life to another.

INTERVIEWER

I know about that, I think. It is poor man's Yoga. The soul resides in a cow in one life, a squid in the next, a man—ugh, what a man coming from a cow and a squid—in the third, a cockroach in the fourth, a brave cockroach, to a tulip in the fifth, very self-complacent; it blooms into a blade of grass in the sixth.

MAILER

The migrations sometimes turn out more modest.

INTERVIEWER

Rich Episcopalian, Presbyterian, modest Methodist, Negro Baptist, Puerto Rican Catholic? This is very poor man's Yoga.

MAILER

I neglected to tell you that we are still far from Yoga. I think there is
a Western obsession in the soul, a continuing obsession, which is at the
source of its activity, its anxiety, its insomnia, its mania, its violence, its
despair.

INTERVIEWER

Yes, now you're going to take me by surprise. I feel it. What are you
about to claim as the continuing obsession of the soul?

MAILER

It wonders if it will continue to exist, or if it will perish.

INTERVIEWER

I thought you said the soul was eternal.

MAILER

It has a purchase on eternity. It can manage to live forever. But only
if it *manages* to do so. Only if it is not finally defeated.

INTERVIEWER

So a soul can be eternal or die?

MAILER

Yes. It can die.

INTERVIEWER

That is the reason everything is so important to it? Is that why it feels
such anxiety about its particular metamorphosis, or even the place where
as an outlaw soul it may choose to take up its abode, whether in the
mussel shell or the seaweed?

MAILER

Yes.

INTERVIEWER

That is why it is so fierce, and so animal when once in a body? That is
why even if it needs beauty it might wish still to destroy it?

MAILER

Yes.

INTERVIEWER

Good. Something grows clear to me. In the suffering of the soul you talked about, in its anguish that it might be diminishing or coming close to a final death, there was a glimpse of another anguish. For many people there must be no other choice than to destroy something of beauty, or watch something of value die within themselves. So I wonder—would you agree to an elementary formula: if there is a God and a Devil both, and God creates beauty, then the Devil must attempt to steal it.

MAILER

Yes. And often he succeeds.

INTERVIEWER

How?

MAILER

By communicating himself to every pore of beauty. By convincing beauty it must fear whatever is good. And in fact, it must. Those who are good often hate beauty; they have been betrayed by it too many times. They know the devil which has come to live in beauty, that devil whose pleasure is to defeat possibility, deaden hope, waste effort. Therefore they feel as if they are killing the Devil when they loot the gallery. You see, in their mind, beauty is synonymous to waste.

INTERVIEWER

Do I keep up with you?

MAILER

Our soul needs beauty for its growth. But beauty is ready forever to betray it. So all too often the soul while remaining very much alive, none-theless ceases to grow. It becomes timid. It is drawn to beauty, but beauty destroys its possibilities. A fearful tension is begun. It is in the soul's nature to grow, to seek growth. That is not only its pleasure but its duty. It knows—I'm afraid I quote myself—that if it does not grow, it must pay more for remaining the same. Yet each time beauty slays a possibility, some nerve is blunted. A death begins within which must finally be passed out, or the soul is stifled. So the soul turns to murder.

INTERVIEWER

Tragic.

MAILER

You bet. Left to itself the soul might always look for the kind of love which would offer the greatest possible growth. But, in life, nobody or almost nobody comes within a million human beings of whom he really needs. Spirits and shattered communications lie between the soul and a clear sense of its desire. Anyone who searches seriously for love comes to realize it is more difficult to find than the Holy Grail, or the way to Kafka's castle. So that is why Romeo and Juliet kill themselves, each separately, each by choice. They know they will not find such a love again in life. Therefore they are ready to search for one another across eternity. That offers more life to their soul than the bleak hope of recovery and new love. But for any situation which is not tragic, the soul detests death and abhors suicide.

INTERVIEWER

Why? Why not choose suicide often in order to hasten into the next stage?

MAILER

Because deep in the economy of Being, huge waste must be caused by any indiscriminate odyssey of souls, any incoherent metamorphoses.

INTERVIEWER

Eternity desires tidiness?

MAILER

Not as a passion, but as a use, as a most useful function.

INTERVIEWER

You make eternity sound like a neat old spinster.

MAILER

You think of eternity as some complacent cerulean vault which can afford tidiness or untidiness. But I use the word in the existential sense where eternity is not automatically eternal.

INTERVIEWER

Eternity means not eternal?

MAILER

Eternity means the will and the possibility to be eternal. Whether it can succeed is another matter. Eternity can perish. Tidiness and some reasonable law of order are as necessary therefore to its survival as lack of clutter on a sailing ship.

INTERVIEWER

We are outward bound?

MAILER

I do not feel we are coming home.

INTERVIEWER

Eternity is on a voyage?

MAILER

Life and eternity are on a voyage, yes.

INTERVIEWER

To go where?

MAILER

Out. Out to where whatever created us wishes us to be, out to where it was conceived we would move.

INTERVIEWER

And we have not gone as far as we were supposed to go?

MAILER

I think we have not gone near to far enough.

INTERVIEWER

All right. I can take a breath on that. (*Lights a cigarette*) I suppose I have to. I've got a picture of the soul. Yes, it's clear. But spirit. Oh, yes. I knew I had something to be depressed about. There's spirit. Even thinking about it, I know I'm nowhere near spirit—it feels like a wet paper bag over my head. Tell me, is a spirit as capable of dying as a soul?

MAILER

(*Long pause*) I would assume its existence is never alive, not finally alive in the way a soul is alive. In that sense spirit does not die, it cannot —it is never really alive. Rather it waxes strong or weak—like a function. But it does not die. It ebbs.

INTERVIEWER

But spirit is the medium, the solution if you will, into which soul submerges after each little death?

MAILER

It is the culture, the nutrient, it is the abode; not the body, but the abode; as the driftwood was an abode for the Salt.

INTERVIEWER

A soul passes then through spirit after it dies, after its little death, the one which makes it ready for its metamorphosis?

MAILER

I think it must. Perhaps it passes through many spirits.

INTERVIEWER

I'm going to be brutal. Forgive the lack of amenities, but spirit as I see it is a collection of souls without bodies, a collection station for what you call outlaw souls.

MAILER

Presumably the soul passes through spirit. It is not however sealed permanently in it. Not necessarily. It may merely be working for it. Often against its will. On the other hand, I think a spirit may contain any number of souls who have lost the power to find further metamorphoses, souls no longer eternal but rootless, alienated from existence, souls which can no longer grow within a body. So they pass permanently into spirit. They are the part of spirit which gives spirit a character, a discontent, a demonic fury. A hurricane might be such a spirit.

INTERVIEWER

Spirit is then some kind of psychic embodiment?

MAILER

I think it can be material as well. Spirit is not so clear an entity as
soul. Spirit tends to *not* delineate its existence. Think of the cluster of
one-celled animals in a Portuguese man-of-war. That is one kind of spirit.
But the example is too clear. There are spirits you cannot picture. Psychic
spirits. Like a habit.

INTERVIEWER

A habit is a spirit?

MAILER

A predictable spirit.

INTERVIEWER

What is a lively spirit?

MAILER

A gay little brook.

INTERVIEWER

All right, then. What is the largest spirit of which you can conceive?

MAILER

The heavens.

INTERVIEWER

I meant to ask for the largest spirit we might both be able to see.

MAILER

The ocean.

INTERVIEWER

Speak of a large spirit which has a shape.

MAILER

Of objects which have a shape, I would think of a mountain range or
a cave.

INTERVIEWER

And what is the smallest spirit?

MAILER

A virus, I suspect.

INTERVIEWER

But the very smallest you could still see?

MAILER

A mildew or a mold. A drop of oil.

INTERVIEWER

What would be the most miserable spirit?

MAILER

A common cold.

INTERVIEWER

And the most palpable?

MAILER

A mood.

INTERVIEWER

What would be the most dramatic?

MAILER

A revolutionary spirit.

INTERVIEWER

And the most material?

MAILER

A tin of sardines.

INTERVIEWER

So now we have findings (of all sorts!) and may draw propositions, if we can find needles in haystacks. A soul, as I see it—this strapping little bugger—comes to the end of his existence in one body, and therefore

enters a spirit for rest and necessary rehabilitation until the happy day
he succeeds in moving his soul over to an embryo just begun.

MAILER

Yes.

INTERVIEWER

Then spirit must be always in flux. Souls coming in, souls saying fare-
well.

MAILER

You may think of a girl's dormitory.

INTERVIEWER

A spirit has no form?

MAILER

No form. It is a purpose, not an embodiment.

INTERVIEWER

What about the tin of sardines?

MAILER

The form of that is the form of the tin can. It could be filled with wax
or honey or anchovies and look the same. Spirit is not apparent in the
form but in the presence. You would have to open the can to discover
the presence.

INTERVIEWER

Do I understand you? A mountain peak is a spirit, but it is also a form.

MAILER

It is a presence. One could cut a road through it, and the spirit would
alter, but not because its shape was changed, but because birds left a
hillside. It is a presence.

INTERVIEWER

You say a cold is a spirit, but it has a form. It has a shape in time, a
run of symptoms.

MAILER

The symptoms do not make up a shape—rather they are indications that something is shrinking out of time. A cold is a presence which speaks of a partial death of soul.

INTERVIEWER

A partial death of soul?

MAILER

A loss of some part of soul.

INTERVIEWER

Can soul be lost in part?

MAILER

As particularly as a limb can be amputated from a body. A soul can lose its best qualities, its courage, its compassion, its grace, or it can slough off its worst features, its cowardice, its terror, its avarice, its sloth. A soul is changed by inhabiting a body. At the time of its little death, it is better or it is worse than when it entered that body. Its form has altered.

INTERVIEWER

But when it enters a spirit it does not retain its form?

MAILER

At such a time, it has a potential form, but no body. It has a style, it has a character. Given the opportunity it will try to shape creation in its fashion. I refer you to the piece of driftwood.

INTERVIEWER

But, ultimately, the soul must find a body?

MAILER

It must be present in some way at a conception.

INTERVIEWER

Might it not have to wait for centuries?

MAILER

It would have to wait long, I would think. Unless it was an exceptional soul.

INTERVIEWER

And then?

MAILER

It might so illumine the spirit in which it found itself that the spirit would encourage an act of conception which the soul could join.

INTERVIEWER

For instance?

MAILER

A moonlit night on a lake. A swimmer drowns saving a child. His exceptional soul might then rise to the moon, be gilded when the moon is full, ride back on a beam and glide into a lover's act. He could be conceived in the first moment after he died.

INTERVIEWER

But what if the exceptional soul had the bad fortune to be trapped in a lesser spirit? The spirit of a common cold?

MAILER

Why he might relax the sufferer and stir their sex.

INTERVIEWER

But a more ordinary soul?

MAILER

Would have to wait a period in any spirit in which it found itself. There might be no occasion for a leap.

INTERVIEWER

The soul can find a new body only by a leap?

MAILER

One would think so.

INTERVIEWER

A literal or a metaphorical leap?

MAILER

Either.

INTERVIEWER

But if no leap suggests itself, one must wait. Isn't it grievous to wait in a spirit?

MAILER

I could not suggest.

INTERVIEWER

Do you know I still have no real sense of what a soul is—I think I know, and then I realize I can't quite distinguish it from a spirit, at least not when it is once in the soup.

MAILER

But we have not said nearly enough about spirit. There's the difficulty. I've just come to the conclusion a spirit must be led by a soul. By a soul which has lost eternity.

INTERVIEWER

I am fortified to hear that every spirit has a leader. Would you offer an example?

MAILER

Every house is a spirit. Except, perhaps, a new ranch house. So every house has a leader. A fine house might have a cricket under the stair. Of course the leader can just as easily be a poor creation, an owl, a termite, a cockroach, an earthworm in the cellar. There are corporation buildings with walls of glass and aisles of stainless steel whose leader is a bitter confirmed molecule of urine adhering to the drain in the executive's urinal.

INTERVIEWER

Such a leader cannot last very long.

MAILER

He could surprise you. Some molecules are crab-shaped and adhere to the porcelain for years. Of course all the urine going by does its best to dislodge it. But the moment such a leader succumbs he is replaced immediately by another molecule very much like himself.

INTERVIEWER

That is the spirit of the corporation?

MAILER

The spirit of the corporation extends over its buildings, factories, stocks, workers, commodities, salesmen, advertising agencies, and so on. I was speaking only of the main office.

INTERVIEWER

What of the spirit of the total corporation? Who is its leader?

MAILER

A mind without a body. A soul which died forever.

INTERVIEWER

Some major soul?

MAILER

A large soul but not a major soul. Not a dramatic soul—certainly not a dramatic soul.

INTERVIEWER

This is becoming agreeable, but I'm going to bring it up short. Because I don't think you realize that you're now saying a spirit can also be an organism.

MAILER

I think it is more like a field, or a mood. A presence. If it is an embodiment, a slice of meat for instance, it still has no body, not in the sense of a set of organs which function with one another.

INTERVIEWER

But a corporation has such organs.

MAILER

Yes, but the organs of a corporation are not materially connected.

INTERVIEWER

So a spirit can have shape or be shapeless, have organs or be bereft of them, can be seen or invisible, can have odor, color, taste, or no properties at all.

MAILER

Yes.

INTERVIEWER

Air? Is air a spirit?

MAILER

Air is filled with spirits and is itself a spirit.

INTERVIEWER

So spirits inhabit other spirits.

MAILER

Oh yes.

INTERVIEWER

And souls-in-bodies can inhabit spirits? Souls-in-bodies! I mean, people.

MAILER

Yes, people can be a part of many spirits. In a sense, all words are spirit.

INTERVIEWER

In precisely that sense, I shall soon become a part of the spirit of vertigo.

MAILER

Think of an ambitious advertising executive. He works for the main office of the corporation we just discussed. He is obedient to the spirit of the main office. To that molecule of urine. He goes to Mass on Sunday. He is a good Catholic. He belongs, he is a small part of the considerably more indefinable spirit of the Catholic Church. He is a sports fan. He roots for a major-league team, which is a sharply defined spirit, but since it is about to move to a new stadium in a different city, he will soon be less a part of its sharply defined spirit. At midnight he regularly watches a television host on a variety show.

INTERVIEWER

This television host is the leader of a spirit?

MAILER

He is the leader of a television audience. It is a wide spirit but not an incisive one.

INTERVIEWER

Then a spirit is a convocation?

MAILER

As we said earlier, yes.

INTERVIEWER

An assemblage?

MAILER

Yes.

INTERVIEWER

A collection?

MAILER

Yes, it is any of these.

INTERVIEWER

And yet, to return to this point, to return again to a point which is too simple or too mysterious for me, I wonder how a cell can be a spirit. It is an organism, not a convocation.

MAILER

But a cell is not free. The average cell is part of a larger organism.

INTERVIEWER

Let us say it is a part of the liver. The liver is an organ. Does the liver have a soul?

MAILER

It may or it may not. In most cases I expect it does.

INTERVIEWER

But the liver is not free of the body.

MAILER

It can have freedom within the body. It can choose to cooperate with the body, or merely to put up with the body. It can do its best to cure itself when it is ill, or it can fold upon itself like an invalid, and call to other portions of the body for aid.

INTERVIEWER

You speak of organs as if they were states or countries.

MAILER

They have character, like nations. They too can be spirits or souls. Or close to nothing at all.

INTERVIEWER

And it is freedom, the very limited freedom of the liver which allows it to be a soul?

MAILER

France may be free, but it is not free to detach itself from the earth and ascend to the moon. It is not unnatural to speak of the soul of an organ. It is merely a soul with a fixed position. Its freedom lies elsewhere.

INTERVIEWER

But there are organs which are spirits, you say.

MAILER

Yes, finally I will agree. There are organs which are spirits and organisms which are spirits. They are without freedom. They are obedient to an external will. By themselves they are not able to adapt to new conditions. So there is a limit to how much they can help the body.

INTERVIEWER

A while ago you seemed to indicate that a spirit was not alive, not alive as an organism. You spoke of houses, systems of plumbing, of air, hurricanes, common colds, the ocean. Now you speak of organisms and organs and call them spirits.

MAILER

Spirits are habits, not innovations; functions, not creations; waves, not forms; not so much the act as the context; never the event, but the institution. So there are even people whom one may call spirits. Some years ago there was a fashion to call them other-directed.

INTERVIEWER

By now, have you not violated every category altogether?

MAILER

Not if we hold to the primary distinction. A spirit, no matter how close it approaches resemblance to a soul, is still a being in which something vital has died.

INTERVIEWER

But how would you define what is vital?

MAILER

It is a grasp upon the present which enables you to alter it in surprising fashion.

INTERVIEWER

Is this another way of saying that a human being becomes a spirit if his soul has died?

MAILER

If the soul has died while right within the body, if it has died finally right there, has ceased to exist forever, ceased to exist in eternity, then the living body remaining in such a man has become a spirit.

INTERVIEWER

Such a man could not create life?

MAILER

He could create life, but still be a spirit.

INTERVIEWER

How is that? Don't you betray your last distinction?

MAILER

The soul may exist still within the body, but it has surrendered.

INTERVIEWER

Surrendered what?

MAILER

Its hope of eternity.

INTERVIEWER

How fearful a state that must be.

MAILER

I think we all have intimations of such a condition.

INTERVIEWER

Still—it must be very painful. Yet, you are not logically scrupulous, you pass by a distinction which is most crucial. I ask you: if a man can create children, how can you say that he has nonetheless surrendered his hope of eternity?

MAILER

His children could be somebody else's purchase on eternity. Perhaps our sperm does not contain our soul, but others with their own separate chain of metamorphoses. Remember the effort of the Salt to return to the blood and the root? It could have been a stranger's blood, a stranger's root.

INTERVIEWER

Too poetic. And too quick. You deprive us of the claim that there are families in which a soul may reappear in a man's descendants. Don't forget you spoke earlier about the tidiness of eternity.

MAILER

Yes, I am not here to say it is impossible. Probably we are talking of the unspoken impulse behind family vaults and plots.

INTERVIEWER

Yes, if eternity is well managed, that would account for the weakness some of my friends feel before titles, or speaking to families of unbroken line.

MAILER

Yes, that could explain their weakness.

INTERVIEWER

Think of the metamorphoses in such a family. Why, they could move in a direct line. The body, just expired, of the master of the house is taken from the master bedroom to the family crypt. Presto! He is back from the tomb and bawling in the nursery, an infant now forced to put up with all the ice of a British infancy. It is orderly. It accounts for the complacency, the solidity, and the strength of certain families. They know the Lord does not have to put Himself out for them, and bear with migrations which travel too far and exhaust too much of His time.

MAILER

Once this used to be true, I'm sure.

INTERVIEWER

You think death now refuses to be so accommodating?

MAILER

Perhaps. It is restless. Modern death gives a hint of horror—as if it goes in two directions at once. Sometimes I think God may have lost His way.

INTERVIEWER

How could He have lost His way?

MAILER

He could be too far behind. We could have been too slow. Too many of us might have died, too many surrendered. God no longer knows whether to reduce our migrations to the family plot, or encourage the most exceptional surrealist journey.

INTERVIEWER

Brilliant! If you are saying that surrealism speaks of the migration of souls.

MAILER

It speaks of metamorphoses. Frightening metamorphoses. Startling metamorphoses. Teacups come to look like heads, and bodies turn to wooden toys. I am saying that eternity does not offer the rest it once possessed.

INTERVIEWER

You are so unhappy about all this. You insist that death is now worse than it has been.

MAILER

It is restless. The thought of death is equal to dread for the modern soul. Talk of the possibilities within death gives cheer to no one any longer. Maybe we are told each night in our sleep (by the great spirit of sleep!) that death is not the end of anything, but is instead a continuation of the worst terrors of life. Perhaps that is why people wish to see death as the end, as a final conclusion. It may be too awful to contemplate the debt there is to be paid each time the body dies (whatever that debt may be) and how do you bear your anguish if the soul must sink to a lower existence? There is always the terror that you may finally betray the deepest value of your experience. Besides, the soul must bear the weight of continuing to exist. Much of existence is now war; it is a grim war for most.

INTERVIEWER

A war against whom? Against what?

MAILER

Against the desire of something, some spirit perhaps, that life should end.

INTERVIEWER

Life end? Why should it? Why should there be a spirit which wishes life to cease?

MAILER

Life may now be intolerable to some other conception of Being—I would not know what else to call it but a plague—which is different from ourselves, more powerful perhaps, some conception so antagonistic to the Vision by which we try to discover our life that its presence has invaded our world, perhaps even our universe. The intent of such a plague is to deaden the soul of all of us, invite it to surrender.

INTERVIEWER

Couldn't the Devil be this spirit?

MAILER

Perhaps he is. But who can know? Perhaps the plague wishes to destroy spirit. Perhaps the plague collaborates with spirit.

INTERVIEWER

Is this plague equal to the Devil?

MAILER

Again I have no idea. Perhaps it wishes to destroy the Devil along with everything else. Perhaps the Devil bears the same relation to the plague that Faust bears to Mephisto.

INTERVIEWER

But whichever it is, the plague wishes that life cease to exist?

MAILER

Yes.

INTERVIEWER

And time would then cease?

MAILER

Time by our scheme is Being in its becoming, so time would cease.

INTERVIEWER

This bears, I suppose, some relation to Nietzsche's dictum that God is dead.

MAILER

Other than a suggestion that God is mortal, it bears no relation.

INTERVIEWER

Well, that saves time. In fact, you believe that God can be either eternal, or perish?

MAILER

His nature is to be eternal if He succeeds in remaining eternal. If He is not destroyed.

INTERVIEWER

Yes. I follow that. When you speak of the surrender of souls, it is as if you make the totality of them synonymous to God.

MAILER

They are not synonymous. There is the Spirit and the Vision as well. You must account for the Spirit and the Vision.

INTERVIEWER

But souls are the essence of God? His *élan vital?* His flux?

MAILER

They are His present tense. His moral nature exists, you remember, not in the soul but in the Vision. Good. I will give you a scheme. It will make you happy. Vision is the mind of God; soul, His body; and Spirit is what He has left behind. Literally. It is His excrement.

INTERVIEWER

So bad as that?

MAILER

Not so bad. Moral nature resides after all in the Spirit as well as the Vision.

INTERVIEWER

In the Spirit? In God's excrement? In the Devil?

MAILER

Think of this Devil as the echo of history, the lore of the past, the mansions of philosophy, as the blunt weight of every problem which has been solved and every lie which has succeeded. Think of this Devil as the spirit of magic and the dead spirit of institutional life, as mass communication, and the passing of the guards. Everything rich, hideous, poor, proud, nauseating and marvelous goes into that excrement, but it is God's excrement—it is more so. So take Spirit and pose it upon the Vision of the future—between just these two leviathans, at their junction, is moral nature. Of course this moral nature, this junction, is being rotted by the plague.

INTERVIEWER

You balance a cliché like a barbell. What I do not comprehend is whether this new Spirit with its capital S, this new property of God, is the same vast malign spirit which seeks to obliterate Time, or if it is some other Spirit altogether, a visitor from out of somewhere. Or has the Spirit of God become diseased by the plague? I see you preparing to object—you are about to say that you cannot possibly know the answer, your admission that you do not know where to place the Devil in relation to plague is the answer, that my question is therefore insulting because repetitious, yet I would present to you that the essential presumption of the enterprise makes one almost disappointed you are not ready to answer. For consider: what you have stated up to here is so obviously a philosophy of hugely paranoid proportions that for your own sake and for a general inspiring of confidence one would hope you are ready to offer some hint of a few objective criteria, some warrant that your ideas are not merely a projection from the eye of your brain to the wall of your brain. Now, I know it's getting late, and this is a demand of proportions—I can see by your eye that you think it's getting very late—

MAILER

Objective criteria overwhelm us. Their signs are everywhere.

INTERVIEWER

You will tell me the invasion of this malign spirit presents itself in flying saucers?

MAILER

Of course not. No need for saucers. Though nothing has to cause surprise, for existence approaches a climax.

INTERVIEWER

What then are the objective criteria? Display them.

MAILER

They show themselves in every crack of every detail in our lives, in the processing of our food is one seat of the plague, and in the plastic commodities we handle, the odor of vaginal jelly, the dead character of public communication, the pollution of air, the collective assaults upon human nerve.

INTERVIEWER

Are these criteria? or merely temporary technological trials?—just a list of your familiar prejudices?

MAILER

Look to the forms. The forms of the modern world break down. That is where you find all objective criteria—in the art of the twentieth century, above all in the architecture, in the empty monotonous interchangeable statements of our modern buildings.

INTERVIEWER

Not that again! Not all this reduced to still one more of your endless diatribes about modern architecture.

MAILER

I'm talking not of architecture but of form. Form is the deepest clue we possess to the nature of time in any epoch, to the style of the time, to the mode by which reality is perceived in the time, to the way time moves in the consciousness of man, where it possesses grace, where it is hobbled, how strength addresses itself to weakness. Time is all but equal to creativity, for time is the potential to create as it resides in each of us. So form is the clue to the vitality or lethargy of time, and the most pervasive forms of the modern world speak now of an absence of invention, a pall upon good spirit, an erosion of memory. Only in the corners is there preoccupation with complexity of form, with those interruptions of time we comprehend in the absurd. Full of feverish creativity and feverish destruction are the forms in the corners and the edges—in the center is nothing but an aesthetic desert, those pillars of salt which rise out of the plains of urban renewal, out of the triumph of that totalitarian spirit whose impulse is to betray form, to abstract form, until the meanings in its creation are lost. The passion of totalitarianism is to conceal its own process; so its passion is to abstract form into monotony for monotonous forms are superior at concealing the sinister processes of their creation since it drains vitality to study them. That bleakness of form speaks of an apathy in the heart of time, and by implication—a terror, an exhaustion. No rest. (*Sways slightly*)

INTERVIEWER

Not, I fear, in this metamorphosis. (*Smiles*) Tell me, when did eternity possess the sort of rest of which you speak?

MAILER

Why, when the Greeks thrived, the Goths hunted, and the Renaissance came to Rome, the guillotine to France.

INTERVIEWER

You look fatigued. I will not ask you more. Do you wish to end here?

MAILER

Not at all. But *you* look in need of a drink. So I take pity on us both, and crack out a glass.

INTERVIEWER

We have not finished properly.

MAILER

No. We have not even begun to discuss the subject. There is so much of which to talk. I have not mentioned the positive properties of spirit, the fields of communication it lays open, that subtle intimate collaboration of soul and spirit in everything alive, the secrets of grace where soul and spirit commune. (*Bitterly*) No, as always, I have spent my time talking of disease. But then, there is no end to metaphysics, they say. (*Stands up*) This is the place we stop. I offer you one last question. You may ask anything.

INTERVIEWER

Soon they will be reading your book. This book. This is therefore the moment for us to end and book reviewers to begin. So I would ask you —what is form?

MAILER

Did I not explain?

INTERVIEWER

You certainly didn't.

MAILER

My God!

INTERVIEWER

Is it now too late?

MAILER

My God. I could have sworn I explained it a thousand times.

INTERVIEWER

You did, but then you didn't. You see, now I know that form, and shape, and space, and time, and even death, I suppose, each give off their own special taste to every little pickle in the pickle barrel, but no, I could not tell a soul in five easy words just what we mean by form.

MAILER

I must help you. Certainly I must. Here, have a drink. (*Passes ice and glasses*) Maybe we must go back to the driftwood again. (*Scratches his head*) Is that too long a way for you to go back?

INTERVIEWER

Now that I have a drink it is easy.

MAILER

Driftwood is a fine form. It expresses the essence of form.

INTERVIEWER

Why? Why the essence!

MAILER

Because it proclaims the value of what is kept. Form always makes one tacit statement—it says: I am a definite *form* of existence, I choose to have character and quality, I choose to be recognizable, I am—everything considered—the best that could be done under the circumstances, and so superior to a blob.

INTERVIEWER

Bravo!

MAILER

Yes, driftwood is a fine form. It tells us what in a piece of wood proved most dear to the wood, what resisted decomposition the longest, what—if we know how to read it—was saved by accident, what was etched by design. The form of driftwood is the record of a siege.

INTERVIEWER

But driftwood rots from the outside in—which suggests that its center is not so much essential as most protected?

MAILER

What is most valuable is usually most protected. When the center is not valuable, it rots, it rots first. Occasionally we see driftwood which has hollows in its heart or holes. Form in general—now I let you in on the secret—is the record of a war.

INTERVIEWER

Of a war? Damn you! Of a war?

MAILER

It is the record, as seen in a moment of rest; yes, it is the record of a war which has been taking place. Don't you see whatever is alive, or intent, or obsessed, must wage an active war: it creates the possibility for form in its environment by its every attempt to shape the environment. Wherever the environment resists, the result is a form. When the soul is mighty and the environment resists mightily, the form is exceptional or extraordinary. Sometimes it speaks of what is great or exquisite. Stone hoisted up ramps by men became the pyramids. Cut by crude iron tools and harder stone, shaped over years by sculptors who attacked the rock out of the stone of their own being, one had Chartres, Notre Dame. Today the stones are made from liquid cooked in vats and rolled into blocks or sheets. Fiberglas, polyethylene, bakelite, styrene, styronware. The environment has less resistance than a river of milk. And the houses and objects built from these liquids are the record of a strifeless war, a liquidation of possibilities. But forgive me for the diatribe.

INTERVIEWER

Then let me give the emphasis here. You say—finally, now, at the end of the day, you remark: form is the record of a war. Of a good war? of a bad war? Of a sharp engagement? or a very dull one? Do I understand you correctly? You are claiming that it is the character of the war which creates the particular style of the form?

MAILER

In all sense of duty I answer: form is the detailed record of an engagement—war reveals the balance of forces, discloses the style of the forces, it hints at the move from potential to the actual.

INTERVIEWER

But what of memory? Does form have no existence in memory?

MAILER

An extraordinary existence in memory. Precisely in memory. You could even claim that memory like history is nothing but the record of all the oppositions in one's life, of cruel oppositions, calm oppositions, ecstatic oppositions—war, peace, and love, hurrah. Memory is the mind's embodiment of form; therefore, memory, like the mind, is invariably more pure than the event. An event consists not only of forces which are opposed to one another but also of forces which have no relation to the event. Whereas memory has a tendency to retain only the oppositions and the context.

INTERVIEWER

Then can't you say that form is the record of a relationship?

MAILER

Now that I've emphasized its warlike properties, I can agree with you—form is the record of a relationship.

INTERVIEWER

It is that part of the past which is carried into the present? Like memory?

MAILER

It is what survives the relationship. Form is the physical equivalent of memory.

INTERVIEWER

Do you know? This is interesting.

MAILER

(*Gloomy again*) Yes, but it encourages me to go back to our more difficult notions.

INTERVIEWER

Soul? More soul? (*Throws up his hands*) That bloody fucking word. I've heard it too much today. Every time you use it, it leaves an empty space in me.

MAILER

I'm afraid it does. I think the British chose the word so that nobody with blood would ever wish to discuss the subject. They didn't reckon on us poor landless inquirers. Well, we're done. I'm glad it's rounded off.

INTERVIEWER

No, we're not done. You've brought up soul again. What is its direct relation to form? Tell me again.

MAILER

But as I've just explained, it's the father of form. What did you expect it was?

INTERVIEWER

I hoped it would not be the mother.

MAILER

Form is the record of every intent of a soul to express itself upon another soul or spirit, its desire to reveal the shape—which is to say the *mystery* of the time it contains in itself. And it is aided or resisted in achieving that shape by every spirit it encounters. You see we did not begin to discuss a thing. All the problem is still there before us. (*Yawns*) Now, I quit. No more questions.

INTERVIEWER

You have not touched on one huge difficulty. It is false form. For example, I may smile when I am full of hate. Or a girl with small breasts might wear an inflated brassiere, yet you could not tell her breasts are false.

MAILER

Oh, but you could tell—that is what is meant by a fine eye for form.

INTERVIEWER

You cannot always tell.

MAILER

You cannot tell by the shape. But by the mood you can tell, by the presence. That is why form is not shape-by-itself, but shape in the frame of the spirit which contains it.

INTERVIEWER

Oh, now you are perfectly clear.

MAILER

But I am. To myself at any rate. You have pushed me right into the truth. One can distinguish false form from real form by its air, by its presence—do you see? A real form always attracts a spirit which bears a close relation to the war the form was engaged in.

INTERVIEWER

Why? Why should a real form necessarily attract an harmonious spirit?

MAILER

The spirit is not necessarily harmonious so much as truthful. We can detect a real form because it is surrounded by what we perceive subjectively as aesthetic satisfaction, or a sense of elegance, or what we may think of as an air of truth. That air is the spirit which is attached to the real form, and if you ask why a spirit should seek out a form appropriate to it and then manage to muster an air of truth, I tell you it is because spirit can come to rest only in those forms which offer a close relation to the experience of the spirit. Of course, conversely, rest for the spirit offers a glimpse of reality to the soul.

INTERVIEWER

And what does this glimpse of reality for the soul appear to be like?

MAILER

Like the passing sense of grace the alcoholic and the drug addict know. (*Swallows his drink*) And now, friend, I have gotten my mental rocks nicely shifted, and have blown a few miniscule hemorrhages in the upper brain—how we thinkers suffer—and so I will not go on to pursue even one further complication. I am done. I swear to you I am done.

INTERVIEWER

Then can it be you are ready to listen?

MAILER

You have much to offer?

INTERVIEWER

(*Obviously excited by the opportunity*) I've been thinking of what you said at the beginning of the day, about depression and excitation.

MAILER

What did I say?

INTERVIEWER

I think you said excitation applied to a depression creates electricity. Did you have anything in mind?

MAILER

Not that I know of. Of course one always has something in mind.

INTERVIEWER

Well, you know it occurred to me that a magnetic field is like a depression. Everything is pointed in one way. I suppose a magnetic field is the most intense expression of a mood that you could find.

MAILER

Yes, perhaps it is.

INTERVIEWER

So, perhaps, what you meant to say was that while electricity is created by moving a wire across a magnetic field, in the deeper metaphorical sense it is also created by the purposeful interruption of a mood. Would you care to comment on that?

MAILER

No, I am weary. It is all yours.

INTERVIEWER

I'm beginning to enjoy the Science of Metaphor. I feel ready to explore electricity.

MAILER

Just remember it is a spirit, not a soul. In fact it may even be the spirit of interruption.

INTERVIEWER

I'm pleased to have read your essay on the absurd.

MAILER

Thank you. Cannibals are Christians. And forms which look alike are alike. In some mysterious way. Or at least they are alike until the souls which create them become the spirit of treachery. So says Picasso, I suspect. And in that spirit let me wish you a hearty good night!

15 · THE ARGUMENT ALL BUT CONCLUDED

The next piece is one of a series written for Commentary *as an existential exegesis on Buber's* Tales of the Hasidim. *Metaphor is used here to explain a miracle, so the piece while rabbinical is nonetheless indispensable. It may as well be remarked that science once saw itself as the intellectual effort to comprehend each separate miracle. About the time (a) miracles ceased or (b) those cognitive senses which could perceive miracle had withered—then too did metaphor disappear from science.*

RESPONSES AND REACTIONS—V

The Fear of God

Once Zusya prayed to God: "Lord, I love you so much, but I do not fear you enough! Lord, I love you so much, but I do not fear you enough! Let me stand in awe of you like your angels, who are penetrated by your awe-inspiring name." And God heard his prayer, and his name penetrated the hidden heart of Zusya as it does those of the angels. But Zusya crawled under the bed like a little dog, and animal fear shook him until he howled: "Lord, let me love you like Zusya again!" And God heard him this time also.

There is an existential logic in this story which leads to a root in the meaning of miracles. Zusya is ambitious, he is intellectually ambitious, he wishes to feel a fear of God because he is secretly confident he will be able to withstand that fear and so acquire more knowledge of the universe, more revelation of the secrets of God and Nature. The request is Faustian. Yet God in revealing Himself further to Zusya terrifies him profoundly. Why? Does He terrify Zusya because He is Jehovah, a God of wrath and rectitude, an essentialist's God? Or is the fear which comes over Zusya a part of the profound fear God feels Himself, a fear that His conception of Being (that noble conception of man as a creature of courage and compassion, art, tenderness, skill, stamina, and imagination, exactly the imagination to carry this conception of Being out into the dark emptiness of the universe, there to war against other more malignant conceptions of Being) yes, precisely this noble conception will not prevail, and instead a wasteful, slovenly, slothful, treacherous, cowardly, and monotonous conception of Being will become the future of man—such a fear must for God be insupportable. It is the heart of existential logic that God's ultimate victory over the Devil is no more uncertain than the Devil's victory over God—either may conquer man and so give Being a characteristic Good or Evil, or indeed each may exhaust the other, until Being ceases to exist or sinks through seas of entropy into a Being less various, less articulated, less organic, more like plastic than the Nature we know. What a fear is this fear in God that He may lose eventually to the Devil! What abysses of anxiety and pits of woe in such a contemplation! Zusya, asking to fear God more, is given instead a vision of God's fear. Like any other man, Zusya draws back in terror.

But is not one of the secrets of the miracle just here? The miracle is revealed to those who can bear to undergo the terror which accompanies it. If intimacy with God is not merely a communion of love but a sharing of the Divine terror, then the beauty of any miracle delivered by God is always accompanied by a fear proportionate to the beauty. Because a miracle is not merely a breach in the laws of nature, but a revelation of the nature of the God behind Nature. If one cannot undergo the fear, one does not deserve the revelation. So our taste for miracles has left us. Man in the Middle Ages lived with dread as a natural accompaniment to his day. His senses uninsulated by the daily use of daily drugs (nicotine, caffeine, aspirin, alcohol, so forth), his mind not guarded by a society which was antisupernatural, medieval man was therefore able to live with gods, devils, angels, and demons, with witches, warlocks, and spirits. Miracles, while terrifying, were nonetheless a mark of merit. One was honored to receive them. Whereas we reach quickly and in terror for the first chemical which will flatten an affect, deaden our senses, damp our madness, or forestall a miracle. Conversely, we also look to a drug to induce a hallucination—because any visitation produced by a drug is exempt from the terror of engaging the supernatural. For we know, even as the experience is upon us, that we are not privy to a vision beyond the lip of death, but merely are offered a derangement of the senses produced by chemicals. Our modern pleasure is that one is witnessing not a miracle but miracle-in-a-theater.

"And the Fire Abated"

The tale is told:

The rabbi of Kalev once spent the Sabbath in a nearby village as the guest of one of the Hasidim. When the hour to receive the Sabbath had come, someone suddenly screamed, and a servant rushed in and cried that the barn in which the grain was stored was on fire. The owner wanted to run out, but the rabbi took him by the hand. "Stay!" he said. "I am going to tell you a story." The Hasid stayed.

"When our master Rabbi Zusya was young," said the zaddik, "he stoked the stoves in the house of the Great Maggid, for this duty was always assigned to the youngest disciples. Once when he was saying the psalms with great fervor just before the coming of the Sabbath, he was startled by screams from within the house. Sparks had fallen from the stove which he had filled with wood, and since no one was in the living room, a fire had started.

" 'Zusya!' he was reproached. 'There's a fire!'

" 'No matter,' he replied. 'Is it not written: And the fire abated!' At that very same moment the fire abated."

The rabbi of Kalev fell silent. The Hasid, whom he still held by the hand, did not dare move. A moment passed and someone called in at the window that the fire in the barn had gone out.

Mood is the earth of the miracle, its garden, its terrain. The mood created by a fire is always in some part Satanic. One senses an avid implacable relentless impatience, a greed to consume, a determination to destroy the material before it, indeed a lunatic intensity within the fire to appropriate the Time which is embodied in the object which is burning. That is why a fire in a fireplace offers comfort. The fire in this case is smaller than ourselves; the material it consumes, the Time it accelerates, are subservient to the mood of calm and benevolence with which we study the fire. We have the ability at any moment to put it out. We are not confronting the force of the devil but rather devil-in-a-theater. In effect, we are dealing with a commonplace miracle. We invoke the supernatural power of fire, but we control it. To primitive man fire was of course always a miracle, a dangerous miracle. He did not know, he could not know—for he had not yet codified the resources of fire—that he would necessarily be able to control it in every contingency. So he approached fire with profound respect, and prayed to various spirits as he put out a fire in order that the demons in the flame be not offended. How natural for him to assume that the intensity of the fire came from the rabidity of the evil contained within the material. By this understanding, it is not insignificant that the grain of the Hasid catches on fire. The grain is his hoarded wealth, his greed, his covetousness. If his heart has been impure and his plans for what he will do with the money he obtains from the sale of the grain are unholy, then the grain—by this unspoken logic —becomes filled with everything which is evil in the Hasid's soul, and so begins to smolder, then bursts into flame. The Hasid is ready to run to the barn, the rabbi restrains him. When the Hasid pauses to listen to the speech of the rabbi, he is in effect ready to relinquish his wealth. So what has been evil in him expires, and what has been heat for the flame in the grain is now cooled. Thus might go the religious logic. The question is whether this logic is utterly without foundation in the real. For philosophically is it not as plausible to assume we have a spirit which is communicable to other people and to the very properties of our environment as it is to assume that spirit does not exist or is not communicable? And is it not equally or almost equally comfortable to assume that a fire may be extinguished by a dramatic shift in mood? Let the burden fall on the philosopher who would prove that the existence of a fire can never be affected by a mood.

16 · A NOTE OF MODEST CONCLUSION

Maybe, it is appropriate to conclude with a piece of prophetic fiction. Assume then that the errors in reasoning and/or judgment you have detected for yourself in these pages are equaled only by the numerous errors you failed to detect. That, scientist and friends, is bound to be the measure of the error in the next prophecy.

The story was written in 1962, therefore was written with the idea of a President not altogether different from John F. Kennedy. L.B.J., needless to say, is altogether different. Go back, if you would go forward in time.

The original prefatory note is also reprinted. It may help to elucidate the style.

THE LAST NIGHT: *A Story*

NOTE TO THE READER: *Obviously a movie must be based on a novel, a story, a play, or an original idea. I suppose it could even derive from a poem. "Let's do* The Wasteland," *said a character of mine named Collie Munshin. The novel may be as much as a thousand pages long, the play a hundred, the story ten, the original idea might be stated in a paragraph. Yet each in its turn must be converted into an art form (a low art form) called a treatment. The treatment usually runs anywhere from twenty to a hundred pages in length. It is a bed of Procrustes. Long stories have their limbs lopped off. Too brief tales are stretched. The idea is to present for the attention of a producer, a director, or a script reader, in readable but* modest *form, the line of story, the gallery of characters, the pith and gist of your tale.*

But one's duty is to do this without much attempt at style and no attempt at high style. The language must be functional, even cliché, and since one's writing prepares the ground for a movie script, too much introspection in the characters is not encouraged. "Joey was thinking for the first time that Alice was maybe in love with him" is barely acceptable. An actor on contract could probably manage to register that emotion in a closeup. Whereas,

> *. . . the little phrase, as soon as it struck his ear, had the power to liberate in him the room that was needed to contain it; the proportions of Swann's soul were altered; a margin was left for a form of enjoyment which corresponded no more than his love for Odette to any external object, and yet was not, like his enjoyment of that love, purely individual, but assumed for him an objective reality superior to that of other concrete things,*

would bake the clay of a producer's face a little closer to stone. A producer is interested in the meat and bone of a story. His question as he reads a treatment is whether he should go on to assign a writer to do a screenplay of this story with specific dialogue and most specific situations added, or whether he should ask for another treatment with new characters and plot, or whether indeed he should write off the loss and quit right now. So a treatment bears the same relation to a finished screenplay as the model for a wind tunnel does to the airplane. Since a treatment is functional, any excellence must be unobtrusive. In fact, a good director (George Stevens) once told me that good writing in a treatment was a form of cheating because it introduced emotional effects through language which he might not as a director be able to repeat on film.

So, thus modestly, I present here a treatment of a movie. It is based on an original idea. It is a short treatment. Only a few of the scenes are indicated. As an example of the art of the treatment, it is not characteristic, for it is written in somewhat formal prose, but it may have the virtue of suggesting a motion picture to your imagination.

Best wishes. See you in the morning after this last night.—N.M.

We're going to describe a movie which will take place twenty years from now, forty years from now, or is it one hundred years from now? One cannot locate the date to a certainty. The world has gone on just about the way we all expected it would go on. It has had large and dramatic confrontations by heads of state, cold wars galore, economic crises resolved and unresolved, good investment, bad investment, decent management and a witch's bag full of other complexities much too numerous ever to bring into a movie. The result has been a catastrophe which all of us have dreaded, all of us expected, and none of us has been able to forestall. The world in twenty or forty years—let us say it is thirty-six—has come to the point where without an atomic war, without even a hard or furious shooting war, it has given birth nonetheless to a fearful condition. The world has succeeded in poisoning itself. It is no longer fit to inhabit. The prevalent condition is fallout radiation, anomalous crops, monstrous babies who grow eyes in their navels and die screaming with hatred at the age of six weeks, plastics which emit cancerous fumes, buildings which collapse like camphor flakes, weather which is excruciatingly psychological because it is always too hot or too cold. Governments fall with the regularity of pendulums. The earth is doomed. The number of atom bombs detonated by the Americans, Russians, English, French, the Algerians, Africans, the Israelis and the Chinese, not to mention the Turks, Hindus and Yugoslavians, have so poisoned existence that even the apples on the trees turn malignant in the stomach. Life is being burned out by a bleak fire within, a plague upon the secrets of our existence which stultifies the air. People who govern the nations have come to a modest and simple conclusion. The mistakes of the past have condemned the future. There is no time left to discuss mankind's guilt. No one is innocent of the charge that all have blighted the rose. In fact, the last President to be elected in the United States has come to office precisely by making this the center of his plank: that no one is innocent. The political reactions have been exceptional. Earlier in the century the most fundamental political notion was that guilt could be laid always at the door of one nation and one nation only. Now a man had been elected to one of the two most powerful offices in the world on the premise that the profound illness of mankind was the fault of all, and this victory had prepared the world for cooperative action.

Shortly after the election of this last of the American Presidents, the cold war was finally ended. Russia and America were ready to collaborate, as were Algeria and France, China, England, Western Europe, India and Africa. The fact had finally been faced. Man had succeeded in so polluting the atmosphere that he was doomed to expire himself. Not one in fifty of the most responsible government scientists would now admit that there were more than twenty years left to life. It was calculated that three-quarters of the living population would be gone in five years from the various diseases of fallout. It was further calculated that of the one-quarter remaining women and men, another three-quarters would be dead in the two following years. What a perspective—three-quarters of the people dead in five years, another three-quarters lost in two, one in sixteen left after seven years to watch the slow extinction of the rest. In the face of this fact, led by a President who was exceptional, who was not only the last but perhaps the greatest of America's leaders, the people of the world had come together to stare into the grim alternatives of their fate. All men and women who continued to live on earth would expire. Five hundred thousand at least could survive if they were moved to Mars, perhaps even as many as one million people could be saved, together with various animals, vegetables, minerals and transportable plants. For the rocketeers had made fine advances. Their arts and sciences had developed enormously. They had managed to establish a company of astronauts on Mars. Nearly one thousand had perished earlier on the Moon, but on Mars over a hundred had managed to live; they had succeeded in building a camp out of native vegetation found on the surface. Dwellings had been fabricated from it and, in triumph, a vehicle constructed entirely from materials found on Mars had been sent back to earth, where men and women received it with extravagant hope.

No space here, or for that matter in the movie, to talk of the endless and difficult negotiations which had gone on. The movie could begin perhaps with the ratification of the most astounding piece of legislation ever to be passed in any country. In this case the piece of legislation had been passed by every nation in the world. It was a covenant which declared that every citizen in each nation was going to devote himself to sending a fleet of rocket ships to Mars. This effort would be herculean. It would demand that the heart of each nation's economy be turned over completely to building and equipping ships, selecting the people, training them, and having the moral fortitude to bid them goodbye. In a sense, this universal operation would be equivalent to the evacuation of Dunkirk but with one exception: three-quarters of the British Expeditionary Force was removed safely from the beach. In this case, the world could hope to send up to Mars no more than one million of its people, conceivably less.

It was calculated that the operation must be accomplished in eighteen months—the spread of plague dictated this haste, for half of the remaining members of mankind might be dead in this time and it was felt that to wait too long would be tantamount to populating the ships with human beings too sick, took weak, too plague-ridden to meet the rigors of life on Mars.

It was indeed a heroic piece of legislation, for the people on earth had had the vision to see that all of them were doomed, and so the majority had consented to accept a minority from within themselves to go out further across space and continue the species. Of course, those who were left would make some further effort to build new rocket ships and follow the wave of the first million pioneers, but the chances of this were unlikely. Not only would the resources of the world be used at an unprecedented rate to build a fleet of ten thousand rocket ships capable of carrying one hundred persons each out so far as Mars, but, in fact, as everyone knew, the earth would be stripped of its most exceptional people, its most brilliant technicians, artists, scientists, athletes and executives, plus their families. Those who were left could hardly hope to form a nucleus or a new cadre brilliant enough to repeat the effort. Besides, it was calculated that the ravages of the plague would already be extreme by the time the fleet departed. The heroism of this legislation resided therefore in the fact that man was capable of regarding his fate and determining to do something exceptional about it.

Now the President of the United States, as indicated earlier, was an unusual man. It was a situation right for a dictator, but he was perhaps not only the most brilliant but the most democratic of American Presidents. And one of the reasons the separate nations of the world had been able to agree on this legislation, and the Americans in particular had voted for it, was that the President had succeeded in engaging the imagination of the world's citizens with his project, much as Churchill had brought an incandescence to the morale of the English by the famous speech where he told them he could offer them nothing but blood, sweat, toil and tears. So this President had spared no detail in bringing the citizens of America face to face with the doom of their condition. There were still one hundred million people alive in America. Of that number, one hundred thousand would voyage to Mars. One person in a thousand then could hope to go. Yet there were no riots in the streets. The reason was curious but simple. The President had promised to stay behind and make every effort to train and rally new technicians for the construction of a second fleet. This decision to remain behind had come from many motives: he had recognized the political impossibility of leaving himself— there was moreover sufficient selflessness in the man to make such a course tasteless to him—and, what was also to the point, his wife, whom he loved, was now incurably sick. It had been agreed that the first of the criteria for selection to the fleet was good physical condition, or at least some reasonable suggestion of health, since everyone on earth was now ill in varying degree.

In the first six months after the worldwide ratification of what had already become known as the Legislation For A Fleet, an atmosphere of cooperation, indeed almost of Christian sanctity and good will, came over the earth. Never before in the memory of anyone living had so many people seemed in so good a mood. There was physical suffering everywhere—as has been mentioned, nearly everyone was ill, usually of distressing internal diseases—but the pain now possessed a certain logic, for at least one-half the working force of the world was engaged directly or indirectly in the construction of the Fleet or the preparations surrounding it. Those who were to travel to Mars had a profound sense of mission, of duty and humility. Those who knew they would be left behind felt for the first time in years a sensation of moral weightlessness which was recognized finally as the absence of guilt. Man was at peace with himself. He could even feel hope, because it was, after all, not known to a certainty that those who were left behind must inevitably perish. Some still believed in the possibility of new medical discoveries which could save them. Others devoted themselves to their President's vow that the construction of the second fleet would begin upon the departure of the first. And, with it all, there was in nearly everyone a sense of personal abnegation, of cooperation, of identification with the community.

It was part of the President's political wisdom that the people who were chosen for the American Fleet had also been selected geographically. Every town of ten thousand inhabitants had ten heroes to make the trip. Not a county of five thousand people scattered over ten thousand square miles of ranches was without its five men, women, and children, all ready. And, of course, for each person chosen there were another ten ready to back them up in case the first man turned ill, or the second, or the third. Behind these ten were one hundred, directly involved in the development, training and morale of each voyager and his ten substitutes. So participation in the flight reached into all the corners of the country, and rare was the family which had nothing to do with it. Historians, writing wistfully about the end of history, had come to the conclusion that man was never so close to finding his soul as in this period when it was generally agreed he was soon to lose his body.

Now, calculate what a blow it was to morality, to courage, and the heart of mankind when it was discovered that life on Mars was not supportable, that the company of a hundred who had been camping on its surface had begun to die, and that their disease was similar to the plague which had begun to visit everyone on earth, but was more virulent in its symptoms and more rapid in its results. The scientific news was overwhelming. Fallout and radiation had poisoned not only the earth but the entire solar system. There was no escape for man to any of the planets. The first solar voyagers to have journeyed so far away as Jupiter had sent back the same tragic news. Belts of radiation incalculably fierce in their intensity now surrounded all the planets.

The President was, of course, the first to receive this news and, in coordination with agreements already arrived at, communicated it to the Premier of the Soviet Union. The two men were already firm friends. They had succeeded, two and a half years before, in forming an alliance

to end the Cold War, and by thus acting in concert had encouraged the
world to pass the Legislation For A Fleet. Now the Premier informed the
President that he had heard the bad news himself: ten of the one hun-
dred men on Mars were, after all, Russians. The two leaders met im-
mediately in Paris for a conference which was brief and critical in its
effect. The President was for declaring the news immediately. He had
an intimation that to conceal such an apocalyptic fact might invite an
unnamable disaster. The Premier of Russia begged him to wait a week
at least before announcing this fact. His most cogent argument was that
the scientists were entitled to a week to explore the remote possibility of
some other solution.

"What other could there possibly be?" asked the President.

"How can I know?" answered the Premier. "Perhaps we shall find a way
to drive a tunnel into the center of the earth in order to burn all im-
purities out of ourselves."

The President was adamant. The tragic condition of the world today
was precisely the product, he declared, of ten thousand little abuses of
power, ten thousand moments in history when the leaders had decided
that the news they held was too unpleasant or too paralyzing for the
masses to bear. A new era in history, a heroic if tragic era, had begun
precisely because the political leaders of the world now invited the citizens
into their confidence. The President and the Premier were at an impasse.
The only possible compromise was to wait another twenty-four hours
and invite the leaders of Europe, Asia, South America and Africa to an
overnight conference which would determine the fate of the news.

The second conference affected the history of everything which was to
follow, because all the nations were determined to keep the new and dis-
astrous news a secret. The President's most trusted technical adviser,
Anderson Stevens, argued that the general despair would be too great
and would paralyze the best efforts of his own men to find another solu-
tion. The President and Stevens were old friends. They had come to
power together. It was Stevens who had been responsible for some of the
most critical scientific discoveries and advances in the rocketry of the
last ten years. The Legislation For A Fleet had come, to a great extent,
out of his work. He was known as the President's greatest single friend,
his most trusted adviser. If he now disagreed with the President at this
international conference, the President was obliged to listen to him.
Anderson Stevens argued that while the solar system was now poisoned
and uninhabitable, it might still be possible to travel to some other part
of our galaxy and transfer human life to a more hospitable star. For
several days, scientists discussed the possibilities. It was admitted that no

fuel or system of booster propulsion was sufficiently powerful to take a rocket ship beyond the solar system. Not even by connecting to booster rockets already in orbit. But then it was also argued that no supreme attempt had yet been made and if the best scientific minds on earth applied themselves to this problem the intellectual results were unforeseeable. In the meantime, absolute silence was to be observed. The program to construct the Martian Fleet was to continue as if nothing had happened. The President acceded to this majority decision of the other leaders, but informed them that he would hold the silence for no more than another week.

By the end of the week, Anderson Stevens returned with an exceptional suggestion: a tunnel ten miles long was to be constructed in all haste in Siberia or the American desert. Pitched at an angle, so that its entrance was on the surface and its base a mile below the earth, the tunnel would act like the muzzle of a rifle and fire the rocket as if it were a shell. Calculated properly, taking advantage of the earth's rotation about its own axis and the greater speed of its rotation about the sun, it was estimated that the rocket ship might then possess sufficient escape velocity to quit the gravitational pull of the sun and so move out to the stars. Since some of the rocket ships were already close to completion and could be adapted quickly to the new scheme, the decision was taken to fire a trial shot in three months, with a picked crew of international experts. If the ship succeeded in escaping the pull of the sun, its crew could then explore out to the nearest stars and send back the essential information necessary for the others who would follow.

Again the question of secrecy was debated. Now Stevens argued that it would be equally irresponsible to give people hope if none would later exist. So, suffering his deepest misgivings, the President consented to a period of silence for three months while the tunnel was completed. In this period, the character of his administration began to change. Hundreds and then thousands of men were keeping two great secrets: the impossibility of life on Mars, and the construction of the giant cannon which would fire an exploratory ship to the stars. So an atmosphere of secrecy and evasion began to circle about the capital, and the mood of the nation was affected. There were rumors everywhere; few of them were accurate. People whispered that the President was dying. Others stated that the Russians were no longer in cooperation with us, but engaged in a contest to see who could get first to Mars. It was said that the climate of Mars had driven the colonists mad, that the spaceships being built would not hold together because the parts were weakened by atomic radiation. It was even rumored—for the existence of the tunnel could not be hidden altogether—that the government was planning to construct an entire state beneath the surface of the earth, in which people could live free of radiation and fallout. For the first time in three or four years, the rates of the sociological diseases—crime, delinquency, divorce and addiction—began again to increase.

The day for the secret test arrived. The rocket was fired. It left the earth's atmosphere at a rate greater than any projectile had yet traveled, a rate so great that the first fear of the scientists was substantiated. The metal out of which the rocket was made, the finest, most heat-resistant alloy yet devised by metallurgists, was still insufficient to withstand the heat of its velocity. As it rose through the air, with the dignitaries of fifty countries gathered to watch its departure, it burst out of the earth, its metal skin glowing with the incandescence of a welding torch, traced a path of incredible velocity across the night sky, so fast that it looked like a bolt of lightning reversed, leaping lividly from the earth into the melancholy night, and burned itself out thirty miles up in the air, burned itself out as completely as a dead meteor. No metal existed which could withstand the heat of the excessive friction created by the extreme velocity necessary to blast a ship through the atmosphere and out beyond the gravitational attractions of the sun and its planets. On the other hand, a rocket ship which rose slowly through the earth's atmosphere and so did not overheat could not then generate enough power to overcome the pull of the sun. It seemed now conclusive that man was trapped within his solar system.

The President declared that the people must finally be informed, and in an historic address he did so inform them of the futility of going to Mars and of the impossibility of escape in any other way. There was nothing left for man, he declared, but to prepare himself for his end, to recognize that his soul might have a life beyond his death and so might communicate the best of himself to the stars. There was thus the opportunity to die well, in dignity, with grace, and the hope that the spirit might prove more miraculous and mighty than the wonders man had extracted from matter. It was a great speech. Commentators declared it was perhaps the greatest speech ever delivered by a political leader. It suffered from one irrevocable flaw: it had been delivered three months too late. The ultimate reaction was cynical. "If all that is left to us is our spirit," commented a German newspaper, "why then did the President deny us three useful months in which to begin to develop it?"

Like the leaden-green airless evening before an electrical storm, an atmosphere of depression, bitterness, wildness, violence and madness rose from the echoes of this speech. Productivity began to founder. People refused to work. Teachers taught in classrooms which were empty and left the schools themselves. Windows began to be broken everywhere, a most minor activity, but it took on accelerated proportions, as if many found a huge satisfaction in throwing rocks through windows much as though they would proclaim that this was what the city would look like when they were gone. Funerals began to take on a bizarre attraction. Since ten to twenty times as many people were dying each day as had died even five years before, funeral processions took up much of the traffic, and many of the people who were idle enjoyed marching through the streets in front of and behind the limousines. The effect was sometimes medieval, for impromptu carnivals began to set themselves up on the road to the cemetery. There were speeches in Congress to impeach the President and, as might conventionally be expected, some of the particular advisers who had counseled him to keep silence were now most forward in their condemnation of his act.

The President himself seemed to be going through an exceptional experience. That speech in which he had suggested to mankind that its best hope was to cultivate its spirit before it died seemed to have had the most profound effect upon him. His appearance had begun to alter: his hair was subtly longer, his face more gaunt, his eyes feverish. He had always been unorthodox as a President, but now his clothing was often rumpled and he would appear unexpectedly to address meetings or to say a few words on television. His resemblance to Lincoln, which had in the beginning been slight, now became more pronounced. The wits were quick to suggest that he spent hours each day with a makeup expert. In the midst of this, the President's wife died, and in great pain. They had been close for twenty years. Over the last month, he had encouraged her not to take any drugs to dull the pain. The pain was meaningful, he informed her. The choice might be one of suffering now in the present or later in eternity. In anguish she expired. On her deathbed she seared him with a cruel confession. It was that no matter how she had loved him for twenty years, she had always felt there was a part of him never to be trusted, a part which was implacable, inhuman and ruthless. "You would destroy the world for a principle," she told him as she died. "There is something diabolical about you."

On the return from her funeral, people came out to stand silently in tribute. It was the first spontaneous sign of respect paid to him in some months, and riding alone in the rear of an open limousine, he wept. Yet, before the ride was over, someone in the crowd threw a stone through the windshield. In his mind, as he rode, was the face of his wife, saying to him some months before, "I tell you, people cannot bear suffering.

I know that I cannot. You will force me to destroy a part of your heart if you do not let me have the drugs."

That night the chief of America's Intelligence Service came to see the President. The Russians were engaged in a curious act. They were building a tunnel in Siberia, a tunnel even larger than the American one, and at an impossible angle; it went almost directly into the earth and then took a jog at right angles to itself. The President put through a call to Moscow to speak to the Premier. The Premier told the President that he had already made preparations to see him. There was a matter of the most extreme importance to be discussed: the Russians had found a way to get a rocket ship out of the solar system.

So, the two men met in London in a secret conference. Alone in a room, the Premier explained the new project and his peculiar position. Slowly, insidiously, he had been losing control in his country, just as the President had become progressively more powerless in America. Against the Premier's wishes, some atomic and rocket scientists had come together on a fearsome scheme which the Army was now supporting. It had been calculated that if an ordinary rocket ship, of the sort which belonged to the Martian Fleet, were fired out from the earth, it would be possible to blast it into the furthest reaches of our own galaxy, provided—and this was most important—a planet were exploded at the proper moment. It would be like the impetus a breaking wave could give to a surfboard rider. With proper timing the force released by blowing up the planet would more than counteract the gravitational pull of the sun. Moreover, the rocket ship could be a great distance away from the planet at the moment it was exploded, and so the metal of its skin would not have to undergo any excessive heat.

"But which planet could we use?" asked the President.

The two men looked at one another. The communication passed silently from one's mind to the other. It was obvious. With the techniques available to them there was only one planet: the earth.

That was what the Russian tunnel was for. A tunnel going deep into the earth, loaded with fissionable material, and exploded by a radio wave sent out from a rocket ship already one million miles away. The detonation of the earth would hurl the rocket ship like a pebble across a chasm of space.

"Well," says the President, after a long pause, "it may be possible for the Fleet to take a trip after all."

"No," the Premier assured him, "not the Fleet." For the earth would be detonated by an atomic chain reaction which would spew radioactive material across one hundred million miles of the heavens. The alloy vuranel was the only alloy which could protect a rocket ship against the electronic hurricane which would follow the explosion. There was on earth enough vuranel to create a satisfactory shield for only one ship. "Not a million men, women, and children, but a hundred, a hundred people and a few animals will take the trip to a star."

"Who will go?" asks the President.

"Some of your people," answers the Premier, "some of mine. You and me."

"I won't go," says the President.

"Of course you will," says the Premier. "Because if you don't go, I don't go, and we've been through too much already. You see, my dear friend, you're the only equal I have on earth. It would be much too depressing to move through those idiotic stars without you."

But the President is overcome by the proportions of the adventure. "You mean we will blow up the entire world in order that a hundred people have some small chance—one chance in five, one chance in ten, one chance in a hundred, or less—to reach some star and live upon it. The odds are too brutal. The cost is incalculable."

"We lose nothing but a few years," says the Premier. "We'll all be dead anyway."

"No," says the President, "it's not the same. We don't know what we destroy. It may be that after life ceases on the earth, life will generate itself again, if only we leave the earth alone. To destroy it is monstrous. We may destroy the spirit of something far larger than ourselves."

The Premier taps him on the shoulder. "Look, my friend, do you believe that God is found in a cockroach? I don't. God is found inside you, and inside me. When all of us are gone, God is also gone."

"I don't know if I believe that," answers the President.

Well, the Premier tells him, religious discussion has always fascinated him, but politics are more pressing. The question is whether they are at liberty to discuss this matter on its moral merits alone. The tunnel in Siberia had been built without his permission. It might interest the President to know that a tunnel equally secret is being constructed near the site of the old Arizona tunnel. There were Russian technicians working on that, just as American technicians had been working in Siberia. The sad political fact is that the technicians had acquired enormous political force, and if it were a question of a showdown tomorrow, it is quite likely they could seize power in the Soviet Union and in America as well.

"You, sir," says the Premier, "have been searching your soul for the last year in order to discover reasons for still governing. I have been studying Machiavelli because I have found, to my amusement, that when all else is gone, when life is gone, when the promise of future life is gone, and the meaning of power, then what remains for one is the game. I want the game to go on. I do not want to lose power in my country. I do not want you to lose it in yours. I want, if necessary, to take the game clear up into the stars. You deserve to be on that rocket ship, and I deserve to be on it. It is possible we have given as much as anyone alive to brooding over the problems of mankind in these last few years. It is your right and my right to look for a continuation of the species. Perhaps it is even our duty."

"No," says the President. "They're holding a gun to our heads. One cannot speak of the pleasures of the game or of honor or of duty when there is no choice."

He will not consent to destroying the earth unless the people of earth choose that course, with a full knowledge of the consequences. What is he going to do, asks the Premier. He is going to tell the world, says the President. There must be a general worldwide election to determine the decision.

"Your own people will arrest you first," says the Premier. He then discloses that the concept of exploding the earth to boost the power of the rocket had been Anderson Stevens' idea.

The President picks up the phone and makes a call to his press chief. He tells him to prepare the television networks for an address he will deliver that night. The press chief asks him the subject. The President tells him he will discuss it upon his return. The press chief says that the network cannot be cleared unless the President informs him now of the subject. It will be a religious address, says the President.

"The networks may not give us the time," says the press chief. "Frankly, sir, they are not certain which audiences share your spiritual fire."

The President hangs up. "You are right," he tells the Premier. "They will not let me make the speech. I have to make it here in London. Will you stand beside me?"

"No, my friend," says the Russian, "I will not. They will put you in jail for making that speech, and you will have need of me on the outside to liberate your skin."

The President makes the address in London to the citizens of the world. He explains the alternatives, outlines his doubts, discusses the fact that there are technicians ready to seize power, determined to commit themselves to the terrestrial explosion. No one but the people of the earth, by democratic procedure, have the right to make this decision, he declares, and recommends that as a first step the people march on the tunnel sites and hold them. He concludes his address by saying he is flying immediately back to Washington and will be there within two hours.

The message has been delivered on the network devoted to international television. It reaches a modest percentage of all listeners in the world. But in America, from the President's point of view the program took place at an unfortunate time, for it was the early hours of the morning. When he lands in Washington at dawn, he is met by his Cabinet and a platoon of M.P.'s, who arrest him. Television in America is devoted that morning to the announcement that the President has had a psychotic breakdown and is at present under observation by psychiatrists.

For a week, the atmosphere is unendurable. A small percentage of the people in America have listened to the President's speech. Many more have heard him in other countries. Political tensions are acute, and increase when the Premier of the Soviet Union announces in reply to a question from a reporter that in his opinion the President of the United States is perfectly sane. Committees of citizens form everywhere to demand an open investigation of the charges against the President. It becomes a rallying cry that the President be shown to the public. A condition close to civil war exists in America.

At this point, the President is paid a visit by Anderson Stevens, the scientist in charge of the rocket program, the man who has lately done more than any other to lead the Cabinet against the President. Now they have a conversation behind the barred windows of the hospital room where the President is imprisoned. Anderson Stevens tells the President that the first tunnel which had been built for the star shot was, from his point of view, a ruse. He had never expected that rocket ship, which was fired like a bullet, to escape from the earth's atmosphere without burning to a cinder. All of his experience had told him it would be destroyed. But he had advanced the program for that shot because he wished to test something else—the tunnel. It had been essential to discover how deeply one could dig into the crust of the earth before the heat became insupportable for an atomic bomb. In effect, the tunnel had been dug as a test to determine the feasibility of detonating the earth. And so that shot which had burned up a rocket ship had been, from Stevens' point of view, a success, because he had learned that the tunnel could be dug deep enough to enable a superior hydrogen bomb to set off a chain reaction in the fiery core of the earth. The fact that one hundred rocketeers and astronauts, men who had been his friends for decades, had died in an experiment he had known to be all but hopeless was an indication of how serious he was about the earth bomb shot. The President must not think for a moment that Stevens would hesitate to keep him in captivity, man the ship himself, and blow up the earth.

Why, then, asks the President, does Stevens bother to speak to him? Because, answers Stevens, he wants the President to command the ship. Why? Because in some way the fate of the ship might be affected by the emotions of everybody on earth at the moment the earth was exploded. This sounded like madness to some of his scientific colleagues, but to him it was feasible that if life had a spirit and all life ceased to exist at the same moment, then that spirit, at the instant of death, might have a force of liberation or deterrence which could be felt as a physical force across the heavens.

"You mean," says the President, "that even in the ruthless circuits of your heart there is terror, a moral terror, at the consequence of your act. And it is me you wish to bear the moral consequence of that act, and not you."

"You are the only man great enough, sir," says Anderson Stevens, bowing his head.

"But I think the act is wrong," says the President.

"I know it is right," says Stevens. "I spent a thousand days and a thousand nights living with the terror that I might be wrong, and still I believe I am right. There is something in me which knows that two things are true—that we have destroyed this earth not only because we were not worthy of it, but because it may have been too cruel for us. I tell you, we do not know. Man may have been mismated with earth. In some fantastic way, perhaps we voyaged here some millions of years ago and fell into a stupidity equal to the apes. That I don't know. But I do know, if I know anything at all, because my mind imprisoned in each and every one of my cells tells me so, that we must go on, that we as men are different from the earth, we are visitors upon it. We cannot suffer ourselves to sit here and be extinguished, not when the beauty which first gave speech to our tongues commands us to go out and find another world, another earth, where we may strive, where we may win, where we may find the right to live again. For that dream I would kill everyone on earth. I would kill my children. In fact I must, for they will not accompany me on the trip. And you," he says to the President, "you must accompany us. You must help to make this trip. For we as men may finally achieve greatness if we survive this, the most profound of our perils."

"I do not trust myself," says the President. "I do not know if my motive is good. Too many men go to their death with a hatred deep beyond words, wishing with their last breath that they could find the power to destroy God. I do not know—I may be one of those men."

"You have no choice," says Anderson Stevens. "There are people trying to liberate you now. I shall be here to shoot you myself before they succeed. Unless you agree to command the ship."

"Why should I agree?" says the President. "Shoot me now."

"No," says Stevens, "you will agree, because I will make one critical concession to you. I do it not from choice, but from desperation. My dreams tell me we are doomed unless you command us. So I will let you give the people their one last opportunity. I will let you speak to them. I will put my power behind you, so that they may vote."

"No," says the President, "not yet. Because if such an election were lost, if the people said, 'Let us stay here and die together, and leave the earth to mend itself, without the sound of human speech or our machines,' then you would betray me. I know it. You would betray everyone. Some night, in some desert, a rocket ship would be fired up into the sky, and twenty hours later, deep in some secret tunnel, all of us would be awakened by the last explosion of them all. No. I will wait for the people to free me first. Of necessity, my first act then will be to imprison you."

After this interview between Stevens and the President, the ruling coalition of Cabinet officers and technicians refused, of course, to let the people see the President. The response was a virtually spontaneous trek of Americans by airplane, helicopter, automobile, by animal, by motorcycle, and on foot, toward the tunnel site the President had named. The Army was quickly deployed to prevent them, but the soldiers refused to protect the approaches to the tunnel. They also asked for the right to see the President. The Cabinet capitulated. The President was presented on television. He announced that the only justification for the star ship was a worldwide general election.

The most brilliant, anguished, closely debated election in the history of the world now took place. For two months, argument licked like flame at the problem. In a last crucial speech the night before the election, the President declared that it was the words of a man now in prison, Anderson Stevens, which convinced him how he would vote. For he, the President, had indeed come to believe that man rising out of the fiery grave of earth, out of the loss of his past, his history, and his roots, might finally achieve the greatness and the goodness expected of him precisely because he had survived this, the last and the most excruciating of his trials. "If even a few of us manage to live, our seed will be changed forever by the self-sacrifice and nobility, the courage and the loss engraved on our memory of that earth-doomed man who was our ancestor and who offered us life. Man may become human at last." The President concluded his speech by announcing that if the people considered him deserving of the honor, he would be the first to enter the ship, he would take upon himself the act of pressing that button which would blow up the earth.

The answer to this speech was a solemn vote taken in favor of destroying the world, and giving the spaceship its opportunity to reach the stars.

The beginning of the last sequence in the movie might show the President and the Premier saying goodbye. The Premier has discovered he is now hopelessly ill, and so will stay behind.

The Premier smiles as he says goodbye. "You see, I am really too fat for a brand-new game. It is you fanatics who always take the longest trips."

One hundred men and women file into the ship behind the President. The rocket is fired and rises slowly, monumentally. Soon it is out of sight. In the navigation tower within the rocket the President stares back at earth. It is seen on a color television screen, magnified enormously. The hours go by and the time is approaching for the explosion. The radio which will send out the wave of detonation is warmed up. Over it the President speaks to the people who are left behind on earth. All work has of course ceased, and people waiting through the last few hours collect, many of them, in public places, listening to the President's voice on loudspeakers. Others hear it in radios in their rooms, or sprawled on the grass in city parks. People listen in cars on country crossroads, at the beach, watching the surf break. Quietly, a few still buy tickets for their children on the pony rides. One or two old scholars sit by themselves at desks in the public library, reading books. Some drink in bars. Others sit quietly on the edge of pavements, their feet in the street. One man takes his shoes off. The mood is not too different from the mood of a big city late at night when the weather is warm. There is the same air of expectation, of quiet, brooding concentration.

"Pray for us," says the President to them, speaking into his microphone on that rocket ship one million miles away. "Pray for us. Pray that our purpose is good and not evil. Pray that we are true and not false. Pray that it is part of our mission to bring the life we know to other stars." And in his ears he hears the voice of his wife, saying through her pain, "You will end by destroying everything."

"Forgive me, all of you," says the President. "May I be an honest man and not first deluded physician to the Devil." Then he presses the button.

The earth detonates into the dark spaces. A flame leaps across the solar system. A scream of anguish, jubilation, desperation, terror, ecstasy, vaults across the heavens. The tortured heart of the earth has finally found its voice. We have a glimpse of the spaceship, a silver minnow of light, streaming into the oceans of mystery, and the darkness beyond.

In the Jardin Exotique of Eze

In the Jardin Exotique of Eze
the cactus come up from the sea
like an anemone wooing a spider
or a pygmy with a blowgun dart.
Silently they smell the breeze,
       invertebrate,
their memory as long as the tripe of the Mediterranée.
Was it once or never? that a God from deep waters
             dreaming of the moon
fell in love with a gleam from the midnight sky
who, intoxicated with herself
and the rapture of the depths,
like a daughter most fortunate in family,
beautiful, spoiled, innocent of alarm,
wandered down an alley
dark as the pitch of blackest frustration
and there was trapped by the sound of need
in the murmur of an ape.
So did that God of dark waters woo a moon beam
and from their love leave a seed
on the spume of the wrack
which washes a desert shore.
Cactus,
mad psychotic bulb of light and dark
       spy of the deep sea
       intimate of the moon
your form inspires nausea
for love which dares too much
and has no soil but sand
flowers spines of lunar hatred
shapes tubers on the leaf
and gives no wine but visions from peyote
of ether and her gardens
which burn in gloom
of poison, bliss, the death of suns
and phosphorescent nights.

399

About the Author

Norman Mailer is the author of four novels: THE NAKED AND THE DEAD (1948), BARBARY SHORE (1951), THE DEER PARK (1955), and AN AMERICAN DREAM (1965). In addition, he has published three arrangements of shorter pieces, ADVERTISEMENTS FOR MYSELF (1959), THE PRESIDENTIAL PAPERS (1963), and CANNIBALS AND CHRISTIANS (1966), as well as DEATHS FOR THE LADIES (AND OTHER DISASTERS) (1962), a collection of poems and short prose.